KU-606-470

Conservation Biology

Conservation biology is a flourishing field, but there is still enormous potential for making further use of the science that underpins it. This series aims to present internationally significant contributions from leading researchers in particularly active areas of conservation biology. It focuses on topics where basic theory is strong and where there are pressing problems for practical conservation. The series includes both single-authored and edited volumes and adopts a direct and accessible style targeted at interested undergraduates, postgraduates, researchers and university teachers. Books and chapters should be rounded, authoritative accounts of particular areas with the emphasis on review rather than original data papers. The series is the result of a collaboration between the Zoological Society of London and Cambridge University Press. The series editors are Professor Morris Gosling, Professor of Animal Behaviour at the University of Newcastle upon Tyne, Professor John Gittleman, Professor of Biology at the University of Virginia, Charlottesville, Dr Rosie Woodroffe of the University of California, Davis and Dr Guy Cowlishaw of the Institute of Zoology, Zoological Society of London. The series ethos is that there are unexploited areas of basic science that can help define conservation biology and bring a radical new agenda to the solution of pressing conservation problems.

Published Titles

1. *Conservation in a Changing World*, edited by Georgina Mace, Andrew Balmford and Joshua Ginsberg 0 521 63270 6 (hardcover), 0 521 63445 8 (paperback)
2. *Behaviour and Conservation*, edited by Morris Gosling and William Sutherland 0 521 66230 3 (hardcover), 0 521 66539 6 (paperback)
3. *Priorities for the Conservation of Mammalian Diversity*, edited by Abigail Entwistle and Nigel Dunstone 0 521 77279 6 (hardcover), 0 521 77536 1 (paperback)
4. *Genetics, Demography and Viability of Fragmented Populations*, edited by Andrew G. Young and Geoffrey M. Clarke 0 521 782074 (hardcover), 0 521 794218 (paperback)
5. *Carnivore Conservation*, edited by John L. Gittleman, Stephan M. Funk, David Macdonald and Robert K. Wayne, 0 521 66232 X (hardcover), 0 521 66537 X (paperback)
6. *Conservation of Exploited Species*, edited by John D. Reynolds, Georgina M. Mace, Kent H. Redford, and John G. Robinson, 0 521 78216 3 (hardcover), 0 521 78733 5 (paperback)
7. *Conserving Bird Biodiversity*, edited by Ken Norris and Deborah J. Pain, 0 521 78340 2 (hardcover), 0 521 78949 4 (paperback)

Accession no.
01121446

WITHDRAWN

LIBRARY

Tel: 01244 375444   Ext: 3301

This book is to be returned on or before the
last date stamped below. Overdue charges
will be incurred by the late return of books.

UNIVERSITY COLLEGE
CHESTER

10 MAY 2008

CANCELLED

b
19.01.04

Reproductive Science and Integrated Conservation

Edited by

WILLIAM V. HOLT

Institute of Zoology, London

AMANDA R. PICKARD

Institute of Zoology, London

JOHN C. RODGER

*Co-operative Research Centre for Conservation
& Management of Marsupials*

DAVID E. WILDT

Smithsonian National Zoological Park

i557786

LIBRARY

ACC. No.
01121446

DEPT
OWL

CLASS No.
573·6 HOL

UNIVERSITY
COLLEGE CHESTER

Smithsonian
National Zoological Park

CAMBRIDGE
UNIVERSITY PRESS

PUBLISHED BY THE PRESS SYNDICATE OF THE UNIVERSITY OF CAMBRIDGE
The Pitt Building, Trumpington Street, Cambridge, United Kingdom

CAMBRIDGE UNIVERSITY PRESS
The Edinburgh Building, Cambridge CB2 2RU, UK
40 West 20th Street, New York, NY 10011-4211, USA
477 Williamstown Road, Port Melbourne, VIC 3207, Australia
Ruiz de Alarcón 13, 28014 Madrid, Spain
Dock House, The Waterfront, Cape Town 8001, South Africa

http://www.cambridge.org

© The Zoological Society of London 2003

This book is in copyright. Subject to statutory exception
and to the provisions of relevant collective licensing agreements,
no reproduction of any part may take place without
the written permission of Cambridge University Press.

First published 2003

Printed in the United Kingdom at the University Press, Cambridge

Typeface FF Scala 9.75/13 pt.   *System* LATEX 2$_\varepsilon$ [TB]

A catalogue record for this book is available from the British Library

Library of Congress Cataloguing in Publication data

Reproductive science and integrated conservation / edited by William V. Holt ... [et al.].
    p.   cm. – (Conservation biology ; 8)
Includes bibliographical references.
ISBN 0 521 81215 1 (hb) – ISBN 0 521 01110 8 (pbk.)
1. Conservation biology.   2. Reproduction.   I. Holt, W. V.   II. Conservation biology series
(Cambridge, England) ; 8.
QH75 .R458 2003   573.6 – dc21   2002067375

ISBN 0 521 81215 1 hardback
ISBN 0 521 01110 8 paperback

The publisher has used its best endeavours to ensure that the URLs for
external websites referred to in this book are correct and active at the
time of going to press. However, the publisher has no responsibility for the
websites and can make no guarantee that a site will remain live or that the
content is or will remain appropriate.

Contents

Contributors

TERESA ABAIGAR
Estacion Experimental de Zonas
Aridas, General Segura, 1, Almeria
4001, Spain.

HELEN S. BAILLIE
Section of Reproductive and
Developmental Medicine, University of
Sheffield, Jessop Wing, Central Sheffield
University Hospitals Trust, Tree Root
Walk, Sheffield S10 2SF, U.K.

JUAN MANUEL BLANCO
Centro de Estudios de Rapaces Ibericas,
Toledo, Spain. Poultry Production and
Product Safety Research Unit, Fayetteville,
AZ 72701, U.S.A.

JANINE L. BROWN
Conservation & Research Centre, National
Zoological Park, Smithsonian Institution,
Front Royal, VA 22630 and Washington,
DC 20008, U.S.A.

JENNIFER BUFF
Conservation & Research Centre, National
Zoological Park, Smithsonian Institution,
Front Royal, VA 22630 and Washington,
DC 20008, U.S.A.

TIM COULSON
Department of Zoology, University of
Cambridge, Downing Street, Cambridge
CB2 3EJ, U.K.

PHIL COWAN
Landcare Research and Marsupial CRC,
Private Bag 11052, Palmerston North, New
Zealand.

JOHN K. CRITSER
Department of Veterinary Pathobiology,
College of Veterinary Medicine, University
of Missouri-Columbia, 201 Connaway
Hall, Columbia, MO 65211-5120, U.S.A.

PAUL CURTIS
Department of Natural Resources, Room
114, Fernow Hall, Cornell University,
Ithaca, NY 14853-3001, U.S.A.

ALAN DIXSON
Center for Reproduction of Endangered
Species, Zoological Society of San Diego,
PO Box 120551, San Diego, CA 92112-0551,
U.S.A.

ANN M. DONOGHUE
Poultry Production and Product Safety
Research Unit, Fayetteville, AZ 72701,
U.S.A.

SUSIE ELLIS
Conservation International, 1919 M Street,
Suite 600, Washington, DC 20036, U.S.A.

TERRY FLETCHER
Co-operative Research Centre for
Conservation and Management of
Marsupials, Perth Zoo, 20 Labouchere
Road, South Perth, Western Australia 6151,
Australia.

GEORGE F. GEE
Patuxent Wildlife Research Center, Laurel,
MD 20708, U.S.A.

FRANK GÖRITZ
Department of Reproduction
Management, Institute for Zoo Biology and
Wildlife Research, Berlin, Germany.

HEATHER HALL
Zoological Society of London, Regent's
Park, London NW1 4RY, U.K.

NANCY HARVEY
Center for Reproduction of Endangered
Species, Zoological Society of San Diego,
PO Box 120551, San Diego, CA 92112-0551,
U.S.A.

PHILIP HEDRICK
Department of Biology, Arizona State
University, Tempe, AZ 85287, U.S.A.

ROBERT HERMES
Department of Reproduction
Management, Institute for Zoo Biology and
Wildlife Research, Berlin, Germany.

LYN A. HINDS
Pest Animal Control Cooperative Research
Centre, CSIRO Sustainable Ecosystems,
GPO Box 284, Canberra, ACT 2601,
Australia.

THOMAS B. HILDEBRANDT
Department of Reproduction
Management, Institute for Zoo Biology and
Wildlife Research, Berlin, Germany.

BILL HOLT
Institute of Zoology, Zoological Society of
London, Regent's Park, London NW1 4RY,
U.K.

JOGAYLE HOWARD
Conservation & Research Center, National
Zoological Park, Smithsonian Institution,
Front Royal, VA 22630 and Washington,
DC 20008, U.S.A.

ELODIE HUDSON
Renewable Resources Assessment Group,
T.H. Huxley School of Environment, Earth
Sciences and Engineering, Royal School of
Mines, Imperial College London, Prince
Consort Road, London SW7 2BP, U.K.

DONALD JANSSEN
Zoological Society of San Diego, San Diego,
CA 92112, U.S.A.

YVONNE K. KIRBY
Poultry Production and Product Safety
Research Unit, Fayetteville, AZ 72701,
U.S.A.

ROBERT C. LACY
The University of Chicago, Committee on
Evolutionary Biology, 1101 East 57th Street,

Chicago, IL 60637 and Department of
Conservation Biology, Chicago Zoological
Society, Brookfield, IL 60513, U.S.A.

VALENTINE A. LANCE
Center for Reproduction of Endangered
Species, Zoological Society of San Diego,
PO Box 120551, San Diego CA 92112,
U.S.A.

NAIDA M. LOSKUTOFF
Center for Conservation and Research,
Henry Doorly Zoo, 3701 South 10th Street,
Omaha, NB 68107, U.S.A.

SUSAN W. MARGULIS
Department of Conservation Biology,
Chicago Zoological Society, Brookfield,
IL 60513, U.S.A.

PAUL E. MARINARI
National Black-Footed Ferret Conservation
Center, U.S. Fish & Wildlife Service,
Laramie, WY 82070, U.S.A.

KAREN E. MATE
Cooperative Research Centre for
Conservation and Management of
Marsupials, Department of Biological
Sciences, Macquarie University, NSW
2109, Australia.

TOM G. MCEVOY
Scottish Agricultural College, Animal
Biology Division, Craibstone Estate,
Bucksburn, Aberdeen AB21 9YA,
U.K.

STEVEN L. MONFORT
Conservation & Research Center, National
Zoological Park, Smithsonian Institution,
Front Royal, VA 22630 and Washington,
DC 20008, U.S.A.

HARRY D. M. MOORE
Section of Reproductive and
Developmental Medicine, University of
Sheffield, Jessop Wing, Central Sheffield
University Hospitals Trust, Tree Root
Walk, Sheffield S10 2SF, U.K.

KEITH MORRIS
CALM Science Division, Department of
Conservation and Land Management,

PO Box 51, Wanneroo, Western Australia 6050, Australia.

AMY R. OBRINGER
Center for Research of Endangered Wildlife, Cincinnati Zoo & Botanical Garden, 3400 Vine Street, Cincinnati, OH 45220 *and* Biology Department, University of Saint Francis, 2701 Spring Street, Fort Wayne, IN 46808, U.S.A.

ALLAN A. PACEY
Section of Reproductive and Developmental Medicine, University of Sheffield, Jessop Wing, Central Sheffield University Hospitals Trust, Tree Root Walk, Sheffield S10 2SF, U.K.

MARILYN PATTON
Center for Reproduction of Endangered Species, Zoological Society of San Diego, PO Box 120551, San Diego, CA 92112-0551, U.S.A.

ROGER PECH
CSIRO Sustainable Ecosystems, GPO Box 284, Canberra, ACT 2601, Australia.

AMANDA R. PICKARD
Institute of Zoology, Zoological Society of London, Regent's Park, London NW1 4RY, U.K.

RANDALL S. PRATHER
Department of Animal Science, University of Missouri, Columbia, MO 65211, U.S.A.

GORDON MCGREGOR REID
North of England Zoological Society, Zoological Gardens, Chester, CH2 1LH, U.K.

L. K. RILEY
Research Animal Diagnostic & Investigative Laboratory, Department of Pathobiology, University of Missouri, Columbia, MO 65211, U.S.A.

JOHN J. ROBINSON
Scottish Agricultural College, Animal Biology Division, Craibstone Estate, Bucksburn, Aberdeen, AB21 9YA, U.K.

JOHN C. RODGER
Cooperative Research Centre for Conservation & Management of Marsupials, School of Biological & Chemical Sciences, University of Newcastle, Callaghan, NSW 2308, Australia.

TERRI L. ROTH
Center for Research of Endangered Wildlife, Cincinnati Zoo & Botanical Garden, 3400 Vine Street, Cincinnati, OH 45220, U.S.A.

KAREN KOENINGER RYAN
The University of Chicago, Committee on Evolutionary Biology, 1101 East 57th Street, Chicago, IL 60637, U.S.A.

JOANNA SETCHELL
School of Life Sciences, University of Surrey, Roehampton, West Hill, London SW15 35N, U.K.

RICHARD STONE
European News Editor, *Science*.

ANDREA C. TAYLOR
School of Biological Sciences, PO Box 18, Monash University, Victoria 3800, Australia.

PETER D. TEMPLE-SMITH
Department of Conservation and Research, Zoological Parks and Gardens Board *and* Department of Zoology, The University of Melbourne, Parkville, Victoria 3052, Australia.

PAUL F. WATSON
Department of Veterinary Basic Sciences, Royal Veterinary College, Royal College Street, London NW1 0TU, U.K.

DAVID E. WILDT
Conservation & Research Center, National Zoological Park, Smithsonian Institution, Front Royal, VA 22630 *and* Washington, DC 20008, U.S.A.

Grateful thanks go to North of England Zoological Society, for contributing to the cost of producing this book.

CHESTER

Foreword

RICHARD STONE

European News Editor, *Science*
(Author of *Mammoth: The Resurrection of an Ice Age Giant* (2001), Perseus
Publishing.)

By playing a role in the near-annihilation of a species, Theodore Roosevelt,
the president of the United States at the turn of the twentieth century, un-
wittingly laid the groundwork for the most dramatic triumph yet in the use
of artificial insemination (AI) to rescue a species from extinction.

In the early 1900s, waves of immigrants from Europe settled in the
American Midwest. As humans transformed the land, they declared war
on a perceived pest: the prairie dog. That might have seemed an affront to
Roosevelt, an ardent conservationist who was once quoted as saying, 'When
I hear of the destruction of a species, I feel as if all the works of some great
writer had perished.' Apparently, however, Roosevelt didn't think much of
the literary aspirations of prairie dogs. Delighted at the booming agricultural productivity in the country's heartland, his administration donated
poison and other weapons to the farmers. By World War I, only two prairie
dogs were left for every hundred alive when Roosevelt had assumed the
presidency in 1901.

An innocent victim of the eradication campaign was the black-footed
ferret, which preyed on the prairie dogs. By 1979, there were no more of
these weasel-like raiders to be found. The species rose from the dead two
years later, when 130 black-footed ferrets were discovered in a quiet corner
of a Wyoming ranch. Calamity struck in 1985, when canine distemper and
sylvatic plague wiped out all but 18 individuals. Scientists trapped the survivors and whisked them to a breeding facility for a last-ditch attempt to save
the species. Through dogged research on the animal's reproductive biology,
researchers over the last decade have learned how to get black-footed ferrets
to mate successfully, as Howard and her co-authors explain in this volume.

Using artificial insemination, Howard's team has brought the species out of the extinction red zone. Today, instead of poor reproduction, the most pressing threat to the black-footed ferret's re-establishment in the wild is a shortage of 'spare' prairie dog communities to be sacrificed for the sake of the predator's survival.

This story offers three crucial lessons. The first is that no species can be managed in isolation. Last century, the black-footed ferret was 'collateral damage' in the war on prairie dogs. Today, species management demands an enlightened ecosystem-wide approach, including balancing the population dynamics of predators and prey. That balancing act can be particularly daunting when attempting to reintroduce a species into a degraded habitat. But scientists have shown that it can be done, and not only with a single species. In Western Australia, three mammals – the woylie, the tammar wallaby, and the quenda – are being reintroduced successfully into the wild, thanks to a remarkable fox and cat control programme that Fletcher and Morris outline in this volume.

Returning to our black-footed ferret friends, the second lesson they give us is to expect frustration when trying to get a little-known animal to breed in captivity. As David Wildt and his colleagues point out in this volume, only 14 species – including humans, cattle and other domesticated livestock, and lab animals such as mice and cats – have received nearly all the attention of reproductive biologists. 'We have scarcely begun to investigate the most fundamental reproductive science in virtually all vertebrate species on Earth', they write. The problem is that this trove of knowledge about the reproductive predilections of any of these 14 familiar species rarely, if ever, corresponds to the predilections of wild animals. To cite a well-known Wildt epigram, a cheetah is not a cow. AI instruction manuals must be written species by species.

The third lesson is more heartening: 'high-tech' approaches to getting a species to procreate can work. Only a handful of radical thinkers would argue that AI and other techniques are a substitute for setting aside habitat and leaving wild animals to reproduce according to their own rhythms. But in instances where a species is imperilled because its habitat is severely fragmented or destroyed, AI and other eleventh-hour heroics not only have a place in conservation biology, but also may be vital to sustaining enough genetic diversity to keep a species afloat. As a population dwindles, so does its gene pool. As Thomas J. Foose put it eloquently in *Riders of the Last Ark*, 'The problem is that gene pools are being converted into gene puddles as the populations of species are reduced and fragmented. Gene puddles are vulnerable to evaporation.'

Because this evaporation is occurring all around us, the need is more urgent than ever to stockpile sperm, eggs, and other tissues of threatened or endangered species. While efforts to establish genetic resource banks (GRBs) have been under way for more than half a century, only recently have these projects started being coordinated to standardise their protocols. And too few GRBs are linked with managed breeding programmes. Such alliances would put cryopreserved gametes to the best use to '...prevent the decline of small populations of rare and threatened species by extending the population size, and allowing founders and ancestors to continue contributing to the gene pool,' as Holt and his colleagues note in this volume.

Although currently playing a limited role in species preservation, GRBs will assume greater importance as the technology of nuclear transfer, or cloning, matures. But as Critser and his colleagues warn in this volume, the potential success of cloning hinges on the depth of knowledge of a target species' reproductive biology. To make matters even more complicated, if a cloned embryo is implanted in a surrogate mother of a closely related species, the surrogate too must not be a reproductive black box to maintain any hope of success. Still, for a species down to its last few individuals – beyond the point of no return for natural mating or assisted breeding – cloning may offer the *only* hope of salvation. Clones resurrected from GRB samples could restore valuable genes to a population, replenishing genetic diversity. The dream of using cloning to bring back an extinct species like the woolly mammoth, meanwhile, will (and should) remain a fantasy until the technology matures such that several mammoth individuals – a breeding population – might be resurrected and introduced into suitable habitat.

Some experts argue that media attention on the possibility of using cloning to preserve endangered species is premature, feeding '...a myth that we are on the edge of using this sophisticated technology on a grand scale,' as Loskutoff notes in this volume. If so, wildlife biologists should speak up loudly and clearly to ensure that the public is getting a consistent message. Perhaps that message would emphasise that there is absolutely no substitute for conserving habitat and allowing animals to live in peace in the wild. But the message – geared both to the public and to funding agencies – might also emphasize that some imperilled species need not vanish from the Earth if resources are devoted to building a knowledge base in wildlife reproductive biology that will nurture high-tech approaches to conservation.

PART I

Introduction

Toward more effective reproductive science for conservation

DAVID E. WILDT, SUSIE ELLIS, DONALD JANSSEN
AND JENNIFER BUFF

INTRODUCTION

Reproduction is the foundation on which a species survives, thrives or, failing this, becomes extinct. Therefore, the study of reproduction is fundamental to conserving species, populations and, indirectly, the vitality of entire ecosystems. Historically, reproductive biology research has been directed at easy-to-study domesticated livestock, laboratory animals and humans. The general approach has been one of scholarly, systematic studies that emphasised understanding mechanisms, sometimes seemingly arcane information that had (or did not have) practical application (e.g. making livestock more reproductively efficient or combating human infertility).

Reproductive biologists involved with wildlife also conduct scholarly research, often in a challenging environment. These explorers are hampered by limited resources and the practical difficulties of accessing rare, intractable and sometimes dangerous study specimens. Nonetheless, there has been progress in the study of the reproductive biology of wildlife, including endangered species. Perhaps the most important lesson learned during the past quarter-century has been that species vary remarkably – and wondrously – in precisely how they reproduce. The mechanisms that regulate reproductive success in the cow are quite different from those that control reproduction in the elephant, dolphin, snake, shark, parrot or frog. This reproductive machinery varies significantly even within families, species positioned in the same branches of the evolutionary tree (Wildt et al., 1992, 1995). Therefore, for example, mechanisms controlling reproduction in the cheetah are likely to be different from those of a lion or snow leopard.

Understanding these species-specific strategies has become a top priority. The resulting discoveries provide intellectual capital that has practical value for monitoring, enhancing or controlling reproduction.

There is a perception problem about reproductive biology – the discipline is poorly understood by colleagues in the wildlife community. Reproduction is not even listed under 'topics of interest' in major journals devoted to biodiversity conservation (see, for example, publication guidelines for the journals *Conservation Biology* and *Animal Conservation*). One reason for such benign disregard is that reproductive scientists are often seen as enamoured with using 'high-tech' assisted breeding methods (artificial insemination, *in vitro* fertilisation, embryo transfer and even cloning). Conservation biologists traditionally have eschewed techno-fixes, fearing that reproductive technologies could divert funds from protecting habitat while giving a false sense of security that species on the brink of extinction could be easily resurrected (Wildt & Wemmer, 1999). We have presented alternative arguments in other venues showing how assisted breeding has contributed to species conservation, including *in situ* (Howard *et al.*, Chapter 16; Wildt *et al.*, 1997; Wildt & Wemmer, 1999).

The point remains – there is a need to change the way that reproductive biology is perceived so that the discipline provides more mainstream contributions to conserving threatened species. A commonsense first step is redefining 'reproductive biology' under the umbrella 'reproductive sciences'. This more inclusive and accurate descriptor embraces any and all skills required to address priorities for understanding, monitoring, enhancing or controlling reproduction. Historically, reproductive biologists have been sub-disciplinarians within animal behaviour, physiology and endocrinology. But ecologists, population biologists, geneticists, nutritionists, veterinarians and animal scientists have long studied reproductive patterns, performance and fitness. It is logical to develop a way of thinking that merges related disciplines to understand more clearly the factors that regulate reproductive success, a cornerstone of species management.

However, semantic change is a small step compared to the need to leap into larger and more coordinated research efforts for all threatened wildlife species. The general aim of this chapter is to discuss how the reproductive sciences can play a more valued role in conservation. We begin by introducing and advocating integrative research, cooperative multidisciplinary studies that can more efficiently address wildlife management problems. Our second objective is to provide evidence on the woeful amount of reproductive research accorded virtually all wildlife species on earth. The chapter concludes by exploring how the essence of the discipline, sex, is a provocative subject that gives rise to public curiosity. This inherent interest is not being exploited, and we cite our experience in using reproductive science stories to inspire and educate children, the next generation of conservationists.

REPRODUCTIVE SCIENCES IN AN INTEGRATIVE APPROACH

Uni-disciplinary to multidisciplinary

Scientists are highly trained specialists, many being experts in a defined sub-field (e.g. dominance behaviour, sperm function, ovarian–endocrine relationships) who focus on a single species (Figure 1.1*a*). This approach is the hallmark of academic research, inevitably resulting in fundamental knowledge. However, this 'uni-disciplinary' strategy applied to wildlife can have minimal practical impact on conservation. This is because conservation can be likened to a complex jigsaw puzzle where the puzzle pieces are issues, stakeholders or scientific disciplines themselves (Figure 1.2). It is unlikely that any single discipline (e.g. reproductive physiology, genetics, nutrition) could be the sole key to solving a particular conservation puzzle. However, assembling additional pieces (more disciplines to generate more knowledge) substantially increases the chances of solving the puzzle. Thus, a more 'conservation-effective' model can be represented by the scientist with specific tools and skills focused on a given species, but now in parallel and partnership with others (Figure 1.1*b*). These partners represent diverse stakeholders in the life sciences, as well as sociologists, economists, demographers and wildlife/habitat managers themselves. Multidisciplinary partnerships will be key to more efficient problem solving in conservation.

An integrative case study, the giant panda

The giant panda, a carnivore that eats bamboo, has been the object of fascination for centuries. An early descendant from the line leading to more modern ursids, the giant panda once thrived in nature. However, due to habitat erosion, there are now fewer than 1200 wild giant pandas restricted to the mountainous bamboo forests of the Sichuan, Gansu and Shaanxi provinces of China. The wild population also is compromised by its scattered demography among 32 fragmented reserves with no corridors to allow genetic exchange. The national protection programme is under-funded, and there are enormous needs for community development, education, reserve

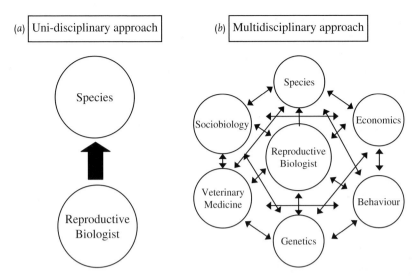

Figure 1.1 The 'uni-disciplinary' (a) versus the 'multidisciplinary' (b) model of conducting wildlife research for conservation.

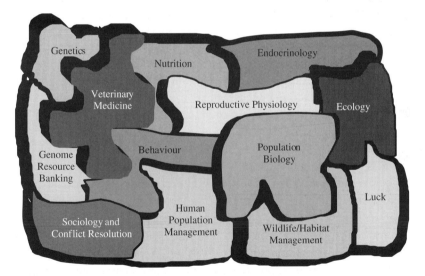

Figure 1.2 Conservation as a jigsaw puzzle where there are many 'pieces' including scientific disciplines, management, social processes and luck.

infrastructure (roads and buildings) and skilled staff to monitor habitat and prevent poaching.

The unstable status of wild giant pandas has provoked special interest in the *ex situ* management programme within China. Giant pandas in captivity provide some assurance that there is a hedge against potential extinction. This population also is a valuable source of new biological information from research and for educating the public about the precarious status of wild counterparts.

There are two independent *ex situ* panda populations within China, one under the authority of the State Forestry Administration (SFA, also responsible for pandas living in nature) and the other managed by the Chinese Association of Zoological Gardens (CAZG, under the Chinese Ministry of Construction or MoC). Because SFA and MoC have been placed in the position of competing for funding from the central government, communication and cooperation have been minimal. Nonetheless, both agencies have had serious concerns about the viability of the *ex situ* giant panda population. Substantial governmental funding has been allocated to zoos and breeding centres to develop a self-sustaining population that would eliminate the need ever to remove more pandas from nature. However, until recently, successful reproduction in giant pandas *ex situ* has been inconsistent.

In 1996, the CAZG requested advice from the Conservation Breeding Specialist Group (CBSG), a non-governmental organisation operating under the IUCN–World Conservation Union's Species Survival Commission. CBSG is renowned for its ability to assist in developing recovery plans for endangered species: as a neutral facilitator, it catalyses change, builds communication and encourages partnerships. Its effectiveness is amplified by a network of more than 800 members world-wide who volunteer expertise to assist in projects. As the result of the CAZG invitation, CBSG facilitated an *Ex Situ* Management Planning Workshop for Giant Pandas in Chengdu in 1996 attended by more than 50 Chinese specialists. CBSG's advisory team comprised five Western scientists. Working together, participants created a plan for managing the *ex situ* population (Zheng *et al.*, 1997). Action-based recommendations emerged during the week that would begin to address the observations of poor reproduction and health problems in all age classes. The most significant recommendation was for a Biomedical Survey of the extant population. The reasoning was simple: developing a self-sustaining population would require maximising the use of the healthy, reproductively fit individuals, which then could be intensively managed to retain existing genetic diversity. This could only be achieved if the health and reproductive status of the existing population was first known.

Biomedical Survey of giant pandas

CBSG was invited to organise and implement the Survey. This facilitated stakeholder buy-in and cooperation because, under the authority of the IUCN-World Conservation Union, CBSG was seen as neutral with no agenda other than to ensure excellent science. The Survey was conducted during the pre-breeding/breeding season (February/March) in 1998, 1999 and 2000 (Zhang *et al.*, 2000). Over this interval, the CBSG–USA team consisted of 20 specialists from seven institutions who represented the disciplines of veterinary medicine, reproductive physiology, endocrinology, animal behaviour, genetics, nutrition and pathology. This group was complemented by more than 50 Chinese counterpart specialists from MoC and SFA organisations. There was strong political support from the Chinese government, and the USA zoo community provided funding with equipment donations from corporations.

The overall objective was to thoroughly examine as many pandas as possible in order to identify the factors that limited reproductive success. Remediation then would allow the population to become self-sustaining. Teams worked together to collect and interpret data. Sixty-one animals were anaesthetised and subjected to an intensive medical examination that included multiple procedures for massive data collection (Table 1.1). Each animal was categorised according to the teams' consensus on its value to the future of the *ex situ* population. Seventy-eight per cent of the population appeared healthy and reproductively sound whereas 22% were compromised, some severely (Figure 1.3).

Limits to giant panda reproduction

Six factors were identified as limiting reproductive success: (1) behavioural incompatibility between males and females introduced for mating (primarily expressed by excessive male aggression); (2) many individuals with unknown paternity (following the common practice of natural mating with a single breeder male combined with simultaneous artificial insemination with sperm from a non-breeding, under-represented male); (3) genetic over-representation by certain individuals (reflected by a few individuals always producing offspring, causing disproportionately high distribution of 'common' genes); (4) suboptimal nutrition (a consequence of the feeding of a high protein, palatable concentrate that reduced bamboo and, thus, fibre intake; (5) stunted growth syndrome (whereby 9.8% of individuals were abnormally small in stature and experienced multiple medical complications), and (6) testicular hypoplasia or atrophy (as indicated by a unilateral small

Table 1.1 *Technical procedures applied to giant pandas (n = 61) in the Biomedical Survey.*

Histories (breeding/behaviour/pedigree)
Anaesthesia/monitoring
Physical examination (including ultrasound)
Body morphometrics
Blood sampling/analysis
Tissue sampling
Transponder/tattoo
Urine analysis
Parasite check
Diet evaluation
Semen evaluation
Laparoscopy

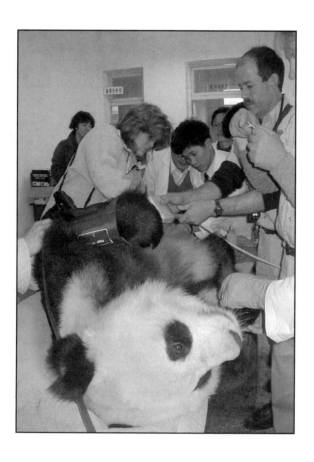

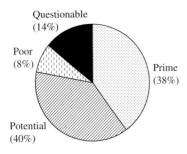

Prime or potential breeders, 78%
Little or no chance of reproduction, 22%

Figure 1.3 Giant pandas ($n = 61$) were objectively categorised as prime breeders, potential breeders (healthy, but prepubertal), questionable breeding prospects and poor breeding prospects.

testis). Isolated medical conditions were also identified, ranging from simple vaginal/cervical infections to untreatable squamous cell carcinoma.

Our multidisciplinary approach was key to revealing that no one variable was impeding reproductive fitness in giant pandas. Rather, failures appeared to be the culmination of multiple, linked factors (e.g. poor nutrition leading to compromised health that directly, or indirectly, decreased reproduction or offspring survivorship). Without the disciplinary collaboration, some causes and interactions would have gone undiscovered. In some cases, remediation was simple. Reproductive tract infections were treated with antibiotics that allowed some previously non-reproductive females to produce offspring. Others, such as modifying diet and sorting out paternities, were more complex and detailed systematic studies are in progress. Regardless, the point is that the Survey has provided the blueprint for continued action.

Another dividend of the project was the opportunity to conduct more basic research. For example, a by-product of male fertility evaluations was 'surplus' semen available for investigating the sensitivity of panda sperm to cooling and cryopreservation. New semen handling protocols emerged that have been useful for improving artificial insemination. One practical benefit was the production of a surviving cub from a wild-born, underrepresented male with a lethal squamous cell carcinoma. Up to this time, such an individual would have died, its genes unrepresented in future generations. Artificial insemination will continue to be important for genetic management, including circumventing sexual incompatibility problems as well as moving genetic material among breeding centres and from *in situ* to *ex situ*.

Other project benefits

Close partnerships that developed in the intensive working milieu (over anaesthetised animals) inspired trust between Chinese and American scientists. Chinese colleagues became comfortable with proposing the need for training courses. A veterinary workshop was held in Chengdu in 1999 that involved the training of 49 veterinarians from 27 Chinese institutions in veterinary diagnostics, anaesthesia, pathology and nutrition. Trainers included Western and Chinese specialists who had participated in the Biomedical Survey. Similar requests for capacity building have emanated from a CBSG facilitated workshop in 1999 on Conservation Assessment and Research Techniques conducted at the invitation of SFA (Yan *et al.*, 2000). The focus here was on the status of giant pandas in nature and research methods that could enhance the accurate monitoring of wild pandas while eventually linking *ex situ* and *in situ* populations. Again training emerged as a priority, especially in (1) remote sensing and geographical information systems (to assess habitat quality), (2) radiotelemetry (to track panda movements in nature) and (3) non-invasive DNA assessment (to identify individuals via molecular assessments of DNA extracted from faecal samples).

This project that began with a simple request from Chinese colleagues for information exchange has resulted in a remarkable cascade of (1) new biological data, (2) enhanced management practices and (3) capacity building. The project also illustrates the value of integrative, multidisciplinary research. Whether this is an 'ideal' model, to be touted for the future, is debatable. The charismatic giant panda is of inordinate interest so its high profile eased the way for the required approvals and funding. It may be more difficult to stimulate enthusiasm and to secure grants for less exciting species that may be as rare or even more ecologically important than the giant panda. Finally, there was widespread interest in participation by many USA specialists, thereby allowing the best scientists as well as those most likely to be team players to be selected. Not all multidisciplinary projects would have the luxury of unlimited numbers of eager scientists.

However, there were other project traits that should be considered in formulating similar studies in the future. Clearly, organising multiple institutions under a neutral entity like CBSG avoided the perception that any one organisation was empire building. Shunning a missionary mentality ('we are here to help') and focusing on developing personal relationships and knowledge-sharing inspired trust which was essential to working across diverse cultures. Resulting confidence and friendships facilitated later invitations to coordinate the training workshops. Enthusiasm for capacity building was enhanced by having the most skilled Chinese counterparts serving as co-trainers. Finally, it was critical that every priority emanated from the range country scientists and managers. The most significant contribution of the Western partners was sharing expertise and transferring tools to these local people who, ultimately, are responsible for preserving the biodiversity of their country.

THE NEED TO STUDY MORE SPECIES

Although the giant panda is a useful model for 'how to advance knowledge' in an integrative fashion, an equally important question is, 'how many species need this kind of attention?'

Most attention on too few species

Wildlife species harbour a wealth of new information on the mysteries of self-perpetuation and survival itself. There are more than 40 000 vertebrate species on Earth (Mittermeier *et al.*, 1997). Data in Figure 1.4*a* represent a highly conservative estimate of the actual number of extant species. How many of these 40 000 species have been studied?

From a reproductive biology perspective, most research to date has focused on common species. For mammals, there is a core group of 14 species, including the human, domestic livestock (cattle, horse, sheep, pig, goat) and various laboratory animals (dog, cat, rabbit, hamster, gerbil, guinea pig, rat, mouse), that have received virtually all of the attention. Billions of research dollars and thousands of scholarly papers have been devoted to this special group that represents only 0.3% of all known mammalian species (Figure 1.4*b*). How much comparable effort has been directed toward wildlife?

To objectively address this question, we examined the literature, specifically 10 well-known scientific journals. Half of these (*Journal of Reproduction and Fertility*; *Biology of Reproduction*; *Reproduction, Fertility and Development*; *Molecular Reproduction and Development* and *Theriogenology*) are exclusively

(a) Extant vertebrate species   (b) Studied vs. unstudied mammalian species

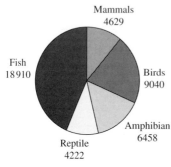 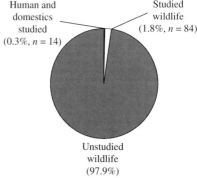

Figure 1.4 (a) Estimated numbers of species of mammals, birds, amphibians, reptiles and fish (adopted from Mittermeier *et al.*, 1997). (b) Among wild mammals, only 84 species (1.8%) have been well studied in terms of reproduction (on the basis of three or more citations in the described journals over the last decade; see text for more detail).

devoted to reproduction, and could be considered leading journals for the discipline. The others (*Journal of Mammalogy; Zoo Biology; Journal of Zoology (London); Journal of Experimental Zoology* and *General and Comparative Endocrinology*) also are prestigious and, often devote papers to non-reproduction topics, but also assign space to reproductive biology issues. Every citation in each table of contents of each issue of each journal was examined (from January 1990 to May 2000) for the name of a species (mammal, bird, reptile, amphibian or fish), which then was recorded in a database. When the title failed to reflect the species studied, that paper was excluded. Species were categorised as domestic or wild, and all non-human primates (even those studied as 'laboratory animals') were considered wild.

Contributions of leading journals to wildlife

Far fewer than 17% of all papers in the five leading reproductive biology journals were devoted to wildlife species (Table 1.2). Journals published in the USA (*Biology of Reproduction; Molecular Reproduction and Development* and *Theriogenology*) were especially negligent. For example, if laboratory non-human primates were excluded, fewer than 6% of *Biology of Reproduction*'s papers addressed other than common species (Table 1.2). When data were averaged across the publications, then we concluded that more than 90% of all space in these leading reproduction journals was allocated to already well studied species.

Table 1.2 *Proportion of published papers devoted to wildlife (mammal, bird, reptile, amphibian, fish) by leading reproductive biology journals (January 1990–May 2000)*

	Number of wildlife papers/total number of papers	Number of wildlife papers (excluding non-human primates)/ total number of papers
Journal of Reproduction and Fertility	292/1754 (16.6%)	261/1723 (15.1%)
Reproduction, Fertility and Development	81/615 (13.2%)	78/615 (12.7%)
Biology of Reproduction	291/3088 (9.4%)	176/2973 (5.9%)
Molecular Reproduction and Development	60/946 (6.3%)	41/927 (4.4%)
Theriogenology	68/1995 (3.4%)	64/1991 (3.2%)

Wildlife is being ignored, which may reflect extreme naïveté on the part of most reproductive biologists, a lack of interest or, perhaps, simply too few resources for such studies.

Numbers of species studied

The database was analysed for the number of species studied during the more than 10 years of publications in the 10 journals. By far, most of the publications were mammal-based in which 256 individual species were identified. When mammal species number was plotted against the number of publications per species, 51.9% (133 species) was represented by only a single publication (Figure 1.5). More than 75% of the 256 species ($n = 192$) was represented by three or fewer publications. Further, of the wild species studied rather extensively (10 or more citations), most were relatively common, ranging from macaques to marsupial mice (Table 1.3). Only three species (Asian elephant, African elephant, cheetah) were found on the IUCN Red List of Threatened Species (IUCN, 2000).

Finally, we arbitrarily defined a 'well studied' species as one with three or more citations in the database. Using this generous criterion, only 84 mammalian species (1.8% of all known mammals) were 'well studied' in reproductive biology. When this number was added to commonly studied species (i.e. human, livestock and laboratory animals, $n = 14$), it was concluded that 97.9% of all mammalian species have gone unstudied (Figure 1.4*b*).

Table 1.3 *The most common wildlife species studied in the*
reproductive sciences (number of citations in parentheses)

Macaque, rhesus (87)	Macaque, cynomologus (12)
Wallaby, tammar (47)	Shrew, musk (12)
Deer, red (36)	Elephant, Asian (12)[a]
Baboon (33)	Hyaena, spotted (12)
Possum, brushtail (24)	Elephant, African (11)[a]
Possum (19)	Deer, fallow (11)
Mink (16)	Cheetah (10)[b]
Dunnart (14)	Marsupial mouse (10)
Macaque, bonnet (13)	

[a] Endangered or [b] Vulnerable, according to the IUCN Red List.

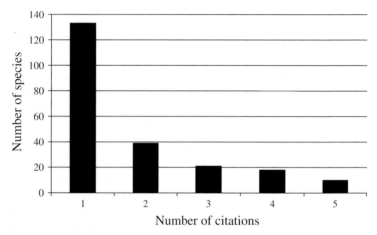

Figure 1.5 Of the 256 species identified in a literature survey of wildlife
reproductive biology studies (see text for details), 133 species were represented by
only a single citation with 192 species (75%) represented by three or fewer
references.

Because of even less effort for other vertebrate groups, the proportions of
unstudied birds, reptiles, amphibians and fish certainly would exceed 99%.
Clearly, we have scarcely begun to investigate the most fundamental reproductive science in virtually all vertebrate species on Earth.

CAPACITY BUILDING FOR THE NEXT GENERATION

Conducting integrative research on more species will require more resources of all kinds.

Public interest in reproduction

It is rare to encounter anyone who is not interested in the sexual anatomy, proclivities or challenges of controlling reproduction in wild animal species. People have an inherent interest in procreation and sex. Therefore, the reproductive sciences have a distinctive edge over other scientific disciplines in attracting attention. Yet reproductive scientists have done little to take advantage of this natural curiosity for raising funds or for education. We have begun to address the power of reproductive science for inspiring and educating children, the next generation of conservationists.

Scientists as role models

Scientists are bound to the creed of using the scientific method to increase general knowledge. But there also is a responsibility to advocate the value of what we do and to train and arouse interest in our profession. This is critical in the conservation community where there are too few resources, including scientists with abilities to generate and interpret data and apply knowledge to species and habitat preservation. But building science capacity includes more than mentoring graduate students and postdoctoral fellows or conducting training workshops in developing countries. There is a need to motivate children at a young age to consider careers in science.

In the early 1990s, we initiated an experiment in Washington DC schools, 'Scientists-in-the-Classroom'. The concept was simple – we speculated that contemporary stories about 'real' research presented by scientists in classrooms could inspire children. One project emphasised our studies of the genetically depauperate cheetah and its susceptibility to poor reproduction and disease epidemics (O'Brien *et al.*, 1985). The target was African American and Hispanic children 8–10 years of age being taught in inner city environments. To document children's perceptions before a researcher's visit to the classroom, teachers provided students with coloured pens and requested a drawing of a typical scientist. Figure 1.6 is emblematic of a child's view from virtually all of the schools tested. Scientists were classically represented as males (Caucasian, aged, bald and wearing glasses and white laboratory coats). These stereotypical traits certainly were uncharacteristic of how these children would ever perceive themselves as adults.

Children then met and talked with scientists, most of whom had travelled to exciting places abroad where they had studied amazing creatures. When asked again to draw a picture of a scientist, the drawings changed remarkably. Depictions became colourful with smiling faces, and the children

Figure 1.6 A 10-year-old African American's view of a scientist before (left) and after (right) meeting one.

most often drew themselves (including minorities and females) as a scientist (Figure 1.6). The message was clear – our research can have sway as functional stories that can change children's attitudes about the value of, and their own potential role in, science.

Beyond Science-in-the-Classroom

The Washington DC experiment suggested that scientists should consider doing more than classical research studies and training. To ensure (1) a sound future for the profession and (2) that there is a subsequent generation passionate about science as a career, contemporary scientists have an obligation to assist in promoting science to children. The timing is appropriate. School systems internationally are undergoing radical reforms (Hungerford, 1998). Parents and community leaders are requiring schools to document students' learning capabilities through the development of 'standards' and by testing for skills and knowledge. Many educators are seeking innovative, hands-on ways to motivate students while still meeting these new standards. In turn, scientists have unique abilities to bring staid textbook lessons to life. Required science (as well mathematics and social studies) principles can benefit from exciting research stories that involve real-world situations.

The Washington DC experiment encouraged us to develop new outreach programmes at the National Zoological Park's Conservation & Research Center (CRC) in northern Virginia. The plan was not simply to visit classrooms to give slide presentations, but to develop programmes compatible with community needs that met Virginia's Standards of Learning. A workshop that included scientists, local teachers and administrators formulated a mission and a strategy. The CRC Education Office served as the link to integrate the scientists and teachers.

One in-school programme, the 'Scoop-on-Poop', emanated from CRC's endocrinology laboratory that measures hormones non-invasively (urine/faeces) from wildlife species. Virginia students 12 years of age are required to learn data plotting and interpretation (standards for mathematics) as well as life systems (e.g. digestion, respiration, blood circulation, reproduction) (standards for science). The 'Scoop-on-Poop' programme evolved to provide real-life examples of raw data collected by scientists. Children plot the data and (working with lesson plans developed by teachers, CRC educators and scientists) interpret the information to make management decisions. One example is the housing together of a dominant cheetah with a subordinate female. The former is hormonally cyclic, and the latter is not. Students create graphs to realise eventually that dominance can suppress reproduction, and triggering reproduction in the subordinate will require the two cheetahs to be separated. Reproductive research with the endangered black-footed ferret (Howard *et al.*, Chapter 16) is another outreach example. Here the educators address the implications of population bottlenecks on genetic and reproductive fitness. An 'ambassador' black-footed ferret is brought to the classroom to illustrate a species that once was believed to be extinct. These popular programmes combine the need of educators to be creative in the teaching of static subjects while using reproductive science and wild animals to capture a child's attention.

Scientists also benefit by the 'feel-good' experience of sharing with the community and, most importantly, making science less mysterious. Using authentic data helps to eradicate the myth that most science is so arcane and complex that it is incomprehensible to the general public. Teachers and students are fully capable of understanding research strategies and data if presented in an appropriate fashion, and with passion. Objective evaluations have consistently revealed that these programmes change the way children perceive the value of science.

Multiplier effect through teacher training

The prominence of CRC's outreach efforts and the demand for assistance soon surpassed our educators' ability to provide service – some programmes are scheduled up to a year in advance. This pragmatic challenge then becomes linked to another observation, that is that educators are trained to 'teach' science, but not 'do' science. Teachers, as well as local, district and state administrators, have consistently indicated that a top priority is for teacher training. Interestingly, teachers articulate a personal need to spend time in laboratories and in the field to learn data collection, interpretation and species/habitat management. Teachers have a strong desire to learn, to adapt what scientists do for their own classrooms and to be inspired themselves to develop new creative approaches for educating their students.

We have realised that a more efficient plan is to allocate scarce CRC resources to more teachers and to fewer students. The outcome eventually will be a 'multiplier effect', training teachers to use our research methods that, in turn, will be taught to many more students than could be accommodated by CRC staff. We also recognise that this teacher interest is analogous to what many scientists routinely experience from advanced undergraduate students, people with an intense desire to learn, to be rejuvenated and perhaps to find new ways to impact the lives of others. Many teachers are expressing interest in internships in the laboratory.

Teacher training curricula have been developed at CRC and workshops conducted that are similar in form and function to training opportunities offered to conservation professionals from around the world. The success of these budding programmes is based on our scientists who teach the courses while our Education Office organises and facilitates the initiatives. The scientists are not trained educators. But learning theory, pedagogy and methodology are not the focus. Rather, the teachers prefer to learn about scientific content, including real-life examples, actions and conservation science protocols. Thus, scientists provide hands-on training of data collection, interpretation and use. Together the scientists, the teachers and the Education Office develop lesson plans that make the final link to the students. The importance and credibility of this programme is reflected in the Department of Education's recommendation that these resources be made available throughout the State of Virginia.

It is noteworthy that most scientists, especially biologists, were inspired to pursue science by some profound event during childhood – a discovery while walking in the woods, a National Geographic article, a motivated teacher or a one-on-one contact with an animal at the zoo. It is our obligation as scientists to consider how we can help create that magical, life-changing 'event' for a child who may not only understand the importance of science but who may even choose it as a career. The intrinsic allure of reproductive sciences in conservation biology is a potent tool for making this goal a reality.

CONCLUSION

The ability to reproduce is quintessential to species survival, thus making the reproductive sciences vital to conserving species and, indirectly, the survival of ecosystems. But the public, academia and even the wildlife community itself poorly understand the definition or the purpose of this general field. Historically comprised of behaviourists, reproductive physiologists and endocrinologists, the reproductive sciences now should include any area of study that contributes to the maintenance or re-creation of a reproductively fit population (e.g. genetics, population biology, veterinary medicine, nutrition, animal husbandry). It also is clear that the high-tech components of the reproductive sciences are not a 'quick-fix' for enhanced reproduction (in the case of endangered species) or fertility control (in the case of over-abundant populations). Rather, the primary role of the reproductive sciences is to characterise the remarkable differences in mechanisms regulating reproductive success among species (even within the same family) through rigorous and scholarly study. Data then are useful for management decision-making and more effective control of reproduction though natural and 'assisted' means. We also have illustrated the power of integrating reproductive findings with those from other disciplines (especially in the life sciences) to tackle problems more holistically. More such studies are required, including for the thousands of species (especially non-mammals) that have received virtually no research attention. Finally, we have shown that the reproductive sciences can attract the attention of non-scientists. Although appealing to the general public and decision-makers, perhaps the greatest potential is using these scientific studies to expand a legacy beyond simply more scientific publications. In particular, stories emanating from the sciences can be inspiring and useful for training teachers and developing school curricula to educate children, the next generation of conservationists.

ACKNOWLEDGEMENTS
The giant panda programme is conducted with a vast array of partners, including: Arlene Kumamoto, Mabel Lam, Eric Miller, Lyndsay Phillips, Mark Edwards, JoGayle Howard, Rebecca Spindler, Richard Montali, Xie Zhong,

Zhang Anju, Zhang Hemin, He Guangxin, Li Guanghan, Yu Jianqu, Zhang Zhihe and Ulysses Seal. Cooperating organisations include the Beijing Zoo, Chengdu Zoo, Chengdu Base for China Panda Breeding, China Research and Conservation Center for the Giant Panda, Chongqing Zoo, National Zoological Park, Zoological Society of San Diego, Zoo Atlanta, St Louis Zoo, Columbus Zoo, Memphis Zoo, the University of California-Davis, British Airways and the AZA Giant Panda Conservation Foundation. The authors also are indebted to Jennifer Bianco for creating the database on reproductive studies of wildlife, and to William McShea and Steven Monfort for their contributions to developing student/teacher outreach programmes.

REFERENCES

Hungerford, H. R. (1998). The myths of environmental education revisited. In *Essential Readings in Environmental Education*. Stipes Press, Champaign, IL.

International Union for the Conservation of Nature (IUCN) (2000). *Red List of Threatened Species*. IUCN Press, Gland, Switzerland.

Mittermeier, R. A., Robles Gil, P. & Mittermeier, C. A. (1997). *Megadiversity: Earth's Biologically Wealthiest Nations*. Conservation International and CEMEX, Washington, DC.

O'Brien, S. J., Roelke, M. E., Marker, L., Newman, A., Winkler, C. W., Meltzer, D., Colly, L., Everman, J., Bush, M. & Wildt, D. E. (1985). Genetic basis for species vulnerability in the cheetah. *Science* 227, 1428-1434.

Wildt, D. E. & Wemmer, C. (1999). Sex and wildlife: the role of reproductive science in conservation. *Biodiversity Conservation* 8, 965-976.

Wildt, D. E., Donoghue, A. M., Johnston, L. A., Schmidt, P. M. & Howard, J. G. (1992). Species and genetic effects on the utility of biotechnology for conservation. In *Biotechnology and the Conservation of Genetic Diversity* (Eds. H. D. M. Moore, W. V. Holt & G. M. Mace), pp. 45-61. Clarendon Press, Oxford.

Wildt, D. E., Pukazhenthi, B., Brown, J., Monfort, S., Howard, J. G. & Roth, T. L. (1995). Spermatology for understanding, managing and conserving rare species. *Reproduction, Fertility and Development* 7, 811-824.

Wildt, D. E., Rall, W. F., Critser, J. K., Monfort, S. L. & Seal, U. S. (1997). Genome resource banks: living collections for biodiversity conservation. *BioScience* 47, 689-698.

Yan, X., Deng, X., Zhang, H., Lam, M., Ellis, S., Wildt, D. E., Miller, P. & Seal, U. S. (2000). *Giant Panda Conservation Assessment and Research Techniques Workshop Report*. Conservation Breeding Specialist Group, IUCN-World Conservation Union, Species Survival Commission. Apple Valley, MN.

Zhang, A., Zhang, H., Zhang, J., Zhou, X., Janssen, D., Wildt, D. E. & Ellis, S. (2000). *1998-2000 CBSG Biomedical Survey of Giant Pandas in Captivity in China: Summary*. Conservation Breeding Specialist Group, IUCN-World Conservation Union, Species Survival Commission. Apple Valley, MN.

Zheng, S., Zhao, Q., Xie, Z., Wildt, D. E. & Seal, U. S. (1997). *Report of the Giant Panda Captive Management Planning Workshop*. Conservation Breeding Specialist Group, IUCN-World Conservation Union, Species Survival Commission. Apple Valley, MN.

PART II

Reproduction and population viability

> There are more things in heaven and earth, Horatio, than are dreamt of in your philosophy.
>
> *(Hamlet: Shakespeare)*

Successful biologists, whether they like it or not, must have a wide spectrum of knowledge to make sense of their own scientific specialities, including the meaning of their own data. How would a pharmacologist or a microbiologist fare without a background in biochemistry or cell function? Could an endocrinologist manage without having at least a rudimentary understanding of animal behaviour and physiology? The history of biology demonstrates that before the microscopic complexity of even the smallest life forms was revealed by pioneers such as Boyle, Malpighi and Leeuwenhoek, scientists more often than not simply made wrong conclusions. The spontaneous generation of worms in putrefying meat, and the 'discovery' of a circulatory system for sap in plants are classic examples.

Many scientists today persist in turning away or, worse yet, deprecating subjects they find dull and difficult. We, the editors of this book, have become particularly aware of this problem in the conservation biology world. We argue that all of the life science disciplines are important in conservation science because it is the *interconnectedness* of data *and* resulting concepts that solves some of the most urgent issues in species preservation and management today. It seem silly and self-defeating that some in the conservation field are so narrowly focused on their species, habitat or disciplinary interest that they fail to appreciate important advances in other fields, even when these have a direct impact on their own research questions. Reproduction in particular (so critical to species fitness and survival) is as vulnerable to genetic and environmental influences as a sapling in the wind.

Thus, the overall purpose of this section is to illustrate the value of looking beyond one's specialist field to examine the interrelatedness of what some would normally believe to be independent fields. On the contrary, behaviour, nutrition and genetics all have important modulating effects on reproduction, and consequently on the long-term survival of species. For example, the influence of behaviour as a modulator of reproduction is intriguing, in part, because all species develop characteristic behavioural strategies during the course of evolution. Yet, conditions can dictate behavioural norms – inappropriate management conditons *ex situ* (in zoos) or *in situ* (from disturbed habitats) can alter natural behaviours, easily disrupting successful breeding. Important synergies arise when research into the behaviour of animals in natural environments is applied to captive breeding programmes and reintroductions – the California condor is described as an example. But reproductive failure caused by sexual incompatibility between males and females is all too common within the highly managed world of captive breeding, where the overarching goals are to avoid the loss of genetic diversity in small populations. We are only beginning to understand how to sustain *in situ* behaviours in an unnatural *ex situ* environment.

The genetic goals of small population management, namely to avoid inbreeding, are well known. The consequences of incestuous matings can be devastating, but paradoxically the eventual real-life impacts are not always the same across, or even within, species. An analysis of inbreeding examples illustrates the variety in results, between the sexes, between closely related species and even between replicate, experimentally produced inbred populations. Applying this knowledge to both *ex situ* and *in situ* conservation strategies will help refine and customise our approaches to genetic management. How do these effects influence reproductive fitness? Some novel experimental insights into this question are presented, demonstrating that not only does inbreeding affect reproductive efficiency in the current generation, but also the survival and fitness of offspring at all stages of life. We wonder if managers in charge of captive breeding programmes realise that inbreeding gives rise to such subtleties, and whether genetic management strategies should be varied to suit different circumstances. For example, one specialised approach might be to concentrate upon maximising the diversity of Major Histocompatibility Complex genes within a population; this and other possibilities are reviewed. This analysis is useful because it shows that concentrating on this single aspect of inbreeding, while justified on theoretical grounds, actually can cause loss of important genetic diversity in other loci, and can therefore be counterproductive.

But behaviour and genes can be of secondary importance under a mantle of poor nutrition. Animals must eat to stay alive but also to reproduce. Moreover, it is now well known that how an animal is fed today not only affects its fitness, but the developmental/reproductive abilities of the next generation. In the analysis of nutrition and reproduction two very important observations stand out. One is that, although miniscule, the nutritional requirements for an embryo are specific in both time and nature. Inadequate nutritional support for this early life form is likely to have ramifications during the later life of the offspring. These effects are currently a hot topic in the epidemiology of human disease, where poor maternal nutrition is thought to be a determinant of future hypertension, stroke and diabetes. Another observation, well known to farmers, is that over-feeding can negatively influence reproductive rates through accelerated steroid metabolism in the liver. Anyone wandering through a zoo has seen fat animals, the consequences of too few exercise opportunities (again, the need for behavioural studies of enrichment) combined with over-zealous zookeepers feeding too much food. Normally, wild animals work hard in nature to meet energy and reproductive needs. Experiments showing that reproductive output in sheep is depressed by over-feeding are directly relevant to the mathematical models derived in the final chapter of this section. In these studies, birth rate and survival are identified as important factors determining the viability of populations, a finding derived from detailed observations linking population dynamics with environmental conditions over prolonged time periods. This neatly underscores the complexity of reproductive and environmental interactions, and cautions against naïve conservation strategies based on the production of offspring. While this may have immediate short-term benefits, the ultimate results are likely to be unsustainable.

2

Behaviour and reproduction

ALAN DIXSON, NANCY HARVEY,
MARILYN PATTON & JOANNA SETCHELL

INTRODUCTION AND OBJECTIVES

A distinguished student of human sexuality, John Money (1991), has commented that 'Reproduction is more respectable than sex. Reproductive biologists and sexologists seldom attend the same meetings or publish together in the same journals.' To some extent this bias against studies of behaviour, and especially studies of sexual behaviour, has also affected research on animal reproduction. However, the tide has begun to turn over the past two decades, and there are several reasons for this. Gamete biologists have begun to collaborate with behavioural scientists in order to explore the role played by 'sperm competition' and 'cryptic female choice' in the evolution of sexual behaviour and mating systems (Eberhard, 1985, 1996; Birkhead & Møller, 1992, 1998; Dixson, 1998). Stronger links have also been forged between behavioural biology and endocrinology; the emerging field of socioendocrinology seeks to understand relationships 'between social environment, hormones and behaviour, because they modulate the reproductive success of individuals' (Bercovitch & Ziegler, 1990). Finally, behavioural ecologists have taken a renewed interest in exploring the mating systems and mating tactics of a wide range of animals, especially because modern genetic techniques have made it possible to determine paternity and to measure the reproductive success of individuals in free-ranging populations (Davies, 1991; Martin et al., 1992; Birkhead & Møller, 1992).

Multiple relationships between behaviour and reproduction are illustrated in a schematic fashion in Figure 2.1. From before birth until reproductive senescence, physiological and behavioural events are intertwined in a complex fashion which determines whether an individual will succeed, or fail, in its attempts to reproduce and pass on its genes to future generations.

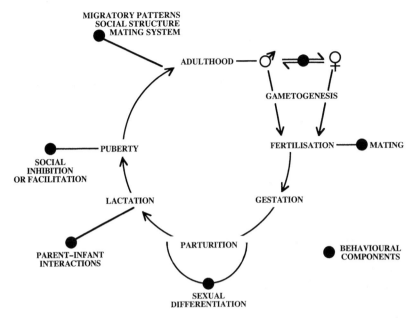

Figure 2.1 Relationships between behaviour and reproductive events during the lifetime of an individual.

Knowledge of behavioural biology therefore plays an integral role in efforts to conserve endangered species. Information on the social organisation, mating system, life history and seasonal patterns of reproduction of each species is required if we are to decide how populations can best be managed in the wild or how to implement captive breeding and reintroduction programmes.

This brief review will concentrate upon studies of captive populations of three endangered vertebrate species that have markedly different mating systems: the mandrill (*Mandrillus sphinx*), the Southern white rhinoceros (*Ceratotherium simum simum*) and the California condor (*Gymnogyps californianus*). In each case research on captive populations of these species has improved our understanding of their reproductive biology and has important implications for conservation of the animals in their natural habitats.

STATE OF THE ART

1. The mandrill (*Mandrillus sphinx*): what is its mating system?

The mandrill remains an enigmatic species for primatologists. Despite the impressive number of field studies conducted on primates, very little is

known about the mandrill in the wild, or about the closely related drill
(*M. leucophaeus*). Mandrills occur in Gabon, Congo, Rio Muni and in
Cameroon, to the south of the Sanaga River. The drill is found to the north
of the Sanaga, in Cameroon and Nigeria, and on the island of Bioko (Grubb,
1973). Both species are inhabitants of lowland rainforests, and both are
threatened by deforestation and hunting. These are the largest monkeys in
the world; an adult male mandrill weighs over 30 kilograms and is spectacu-
larly adorned with red and blue 'sexual skin' on the face, rump and genitalia.
In the wild, mandrill group sizes range from 15 to over 1000 individuals
(Hoshino *et al.*, 1984; Rogers *et al.*, 1996; Setchell, 1999). Because mandrill
groups are so difficult to locate and follow in the rainforests, most studies
have focused upon the mandrill's diet and feeding ecology (e.g. Sabater-Pi,
1972; Lahm, 1986; Harrison, 1988). The social organisation of the mandrill
is poorly understood but it has been reported that large groups fragment
into smaller units, each containing one fully adult male per 20–50 members. These reports, coupled with the marked sexual dimorphism of this
species and the male's striking secondary sexual adornments, have led to
the assumption that social groups of mandrills are composed of numerous
'one-male units' and that the mating system is polygynous (e.g. Jouventin,
1975; Stammbach, 1987; Barton, 2000). Are mandrills polygynous and do
they form one-male units ('harems') in the same way, for example, as the
hamadryas baboon (Kummer, 1968) or the gelada (Dunbar & Dunbar,
1975)? Male mandrills are huge and brightly coloured, as are male hamadryas baboons and geladas, so have these traits evolved as a result of similar
sexual selection pressures in all three species?

   Studies of semi-free-ranging mandrill groups in Gabon have greatly expanded our knowledge of the behaviour and reproductive biology of this
species. In 1983, 14 mandrills (8 females and 6 males) were released into
a naturally rainforested enclosure (6 hectares) situated in a valley at the
International Medical Research Centre, Franceville, Gabon. By 1991 the
group contained more than 50 mandrills, all the descendants of the founding individuals. Studies conducted between 1989 and 1992 focused on social organisation and sexual behaviour. In 1996, 24 mandrills were moved
to a second rainforested enclosure (3.5 ha) leaving 36 animals in the original
group. Between 1996 and 1998 observations on both groups continued, in
order to examine the physical and behavioural development of male mandrills, especially from puberty to adulthood. Because the mandrills were
captured annually for a veterinary check, it was also possible to obtain somatic measurements, as well as blood samples for DNA fingerprinting and
endocrine studies.

The picture that emerges from these studies is of a species that lives in 'female-bonded' social groups with a multimale–multifemale social organisation. A number of matrilines form the core of the social group; female relatives and their young offspring are frequently observed travelling together, foraging, grooming and associating during periods of rest and at sleeping sites. Females are philopatric, whereas male offspring emigrate from the natal group at 7–8 years of age. The enclosures were large enough to reveal this emigration process, as well as to quantify dominance relationships between adult males which remain in the social group, and those which lead a peripheral or 'solitary' existence. Intermale competition is intense in the mandrill, and alpha males have the brightest red sexual skin colouration. High rank is also associated with elevated plasma testosterone, larger relative testes size, and a more 'stocky' appearance due to fatting of the rump and flanks. By contrast, 'non-fatted' males exhibit muting of the secondary sexual adornments, lower testosterone levels and smaller relative testes size (Wickings & Dixson, 1992). In reality, 'fatted' and 'non-fatted' adult male mandrills are not completely distinct morphotypes; a continuous spectrum of possibilities exists between these two extremes (Setchell, 1999). Suppression of secondary sexual adornments is associated with lower rank, and/or a more peripheral/solitary social strategy in adult males. Removal of more dominant males from the enclosure resulted in pronounced changes in sexual skin reddening, elevations in plasma testosterone, increased testicular volume and higher group-association scores in a non-fatted male (Setchell & Dixson, 2002).

Although high-ranking males have the greatest mating success, and reproductive success as determined by paternity analyses (Dixson *et al.*, 1993), there are no 'one-male units' or 'harems' in semi-free-ranging mandrill groups. The mating system is multimale–multifemale under these conditions and females mate with a number of males. High-ranking males mate-guard *individual females* when they develop sexual skin swellings, during the annual mating season. This occurs during the driest period of the year, from June to October in Gabon. Most males are sexually active, however, and peripheral or solitary males may mate opportunistically with females. Females also present sexually to a variety of potential partners, although higher-ranking males do receive more of these sexual solicitations (Figure 2.2). This pattern of mating activity is quite unlike that which occurs in polygynous primate species, such as gorillas or hamadryas baboons, where the leader male of a one-male unit accounts for most, if not all, observed copulations (Harcourt *et al.*, 1980; Kummer, 1990). Because most female mandrills develop maximal sexual swellings and conceive during July and

FEMALES' PRESENTATIONS

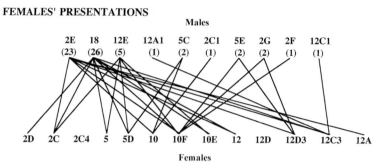

MALES' MOUNTS

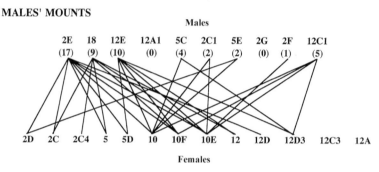

Figure 2.2 Webs of sexual relationships in a mandrill group. (Data are for the years 1996–98.) Males and females have code numbers and appear in order of social rank (the highest-ranking individual is on the left). Total sexual presentations received, and mounts by each male are given in parentheses, beneath his code number.

August, and because there are often several females fully tumescent at one time, even the alpha male is unable to mate-guard multiple partners during the peri-ovulatory period of their cycles (Dixson, 1998; Setchell, 1999). Under these circumstances, mate-guarding is a dynamic process; the male abandons one female as soon as her sexual skin swelling enters the 'breakdown' phase of detumescence and transfers his attentions to another partner (Figure 2.3). In baboons, ovulation is most likely to occur during the last few days of maximum sexual skin swelling (Wildt *et al.*, 1977); the same may be true in the mandrill, and this could account for the intense mate-guarding episodes which occur at this time.

Given the large social group sizes of mandrills, the dense nature of their rainforested habitat and the inability of males to mate-guard multiple females during conception periods, it seems highly unlikely that this species forms one-male units. Females are not passive in sexual contexts, and female

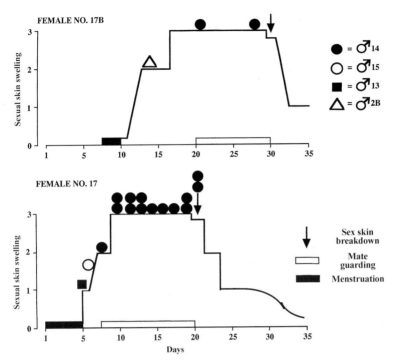

Figure 2.3 Mate guarding and copulation in mandrills. Data on sexual skin swelling are shown for two females (o = sex skin flat; 3 = fully tumescent). Data were collected in 1990, when Male 14 was the alpha male in the group. He accounts for all mate-guarding behaviour (open bars) and most copulations (dark circles) with both females. Three other males mate opportunistically, but at low frequencies and not when females are maximally swollen and likely to ovulate.

'mate-choice' doubtless occurs in mandrills. We have often seen females solicit copulations from certain males, while avoiding being mate-guarded by others. As the female is less than half the size of an adult male, she can, for example, take to the trees and more easily avoid her much larger partner than during terrestrial mate-guarding episodes. Kudo (1987) suggested that mandrills have a multimale–multifemale social structure, basing his arguments mainly upon studies of vocal communication in free-ranging groups. It seems likely that the mating system is also of a multimale–multifemale type in this species. Primates which have multimale–multifemale mating systems are characterised by possession of large testes in relation to adult male body weight (Harcourt et al., 1981). Sperm competition has favoured the evolution of large relative testes sizes in such cases, because females mate with multiple partners. Males which can sustain higher sperm counts in their ejaculates are more likely to sire offspring under these conditions. It is of interest, therefore, that male mandrills have large testes in relation to their body weight. Relative testes size in mandrills is comparable to that of many baboons and macaques, for example, and is much greater than occurs in polygynous primates such as the gelada or gorilla (Dixson, 1998).

Field studies of mandrills, such as those now in progress at the Lopé Reserve in Gabon may reveal, in time, the true nature of the social system and mating system. A working hypothesis is that this species has a multimale–multifemale system, and that the fragmentation of large groups may be for reasons of feeding ecology rather than representing 'one-male units' in the reproductive sense. Division of large social groups into smaller units probably occurs on a matrilineal basis, rather than because males have any direct control of female groupings. The 'solitary' males encountered in the wild may be maturing emigrants or fully adult individuals which spend varying periods separate from social groups. It is quite possible that such males are sexually active and contribute to the gene pool, however, since they may haunt the fringes of social groups, or actively immigrate into such groups during the annual mating season. The intense intermale competition and occurrence of social suppression of secondary sexual traits which occurs in semi-free-ranging mandrills, probably also occurs in the wild. Just as suppression of development of the 'cheek flanges' and other features occurs in subordinate male orang-utans in the wild, as well as in captivity (Kingsley, 1988; Maggioncalda *et al.*, 1999), we expect to find evidence of a spectrum of 'fatted' and 'non-fatted' males in free-ranging mandrill populations.

2. The white rhinoceros (*Ceratotherium simum*): is socioendocrinology important for reproduction?

The Southern white rhinoceros (*C. s. simum*) has returned from the brink of extinction, as a result of effective conservation of the population at Umfolozi and translocation of animals to other protected areas in southern Africa. More than 10,000 Southern white rhinoceros are thought to exist in the wild, whereas the closely related Northern subspecies (*C. s. cottoni*) survives only as a remnant population in the Garamba National Park, in the former Republic of Zaire (Emslie & Brooks, 1999).

Knowledge of the reproductive physiology of rhinoceros species is still very limited. As far as the white rhinoceros is concerned, there have been conflicting reports concerning the duration and endocrine characteristics of the ovarian cycle. All studies have involved the captive population of the white rhinoceros, however, and many females fail to reproduce in captivity.

Schwarzenberger *et al.* (1998) measured faecal pregnane excretion in 16 female southern white rhinoceros. Two females exhibited regular cycles of 10 weeks' duration, but most had cycles which varied in length from 4 to 10 weeks, or showed either limited luteal activity or none. Although Schwarzenberger and his colleagues suggest that longer (10-week) cycles are the norm for white rhinoceros, other studies support the view that shorter cycles may be more typical for this species (Hindle *et al.*, 1992; Radcliffe *et al.*, 1997; Patton *et al.*, 1999). The studies of Patton *et al.* included eight female rhinoceros at the Zoological Society of San Diego (Wild Animal Park) as well as five females housed in other collections. Measurements of faecal progesterone metabolites (allopregnane being the principal progesterone metabolite in the faeces of white rhinoceros) revealed two 'types' of oestrous cycles. Type I cycles averaged one month in duration (mean $\pm$ SEM $= 35.4 \pm 2.2$ days; $n = 10$). These appeared to be the most usual and normal type of cycle, by contrast to longer (Type II) cycles of approximately 2 months' duration (mean $= 65.9 \pm 2.4$ days; $n = 7$). Examples of both types of cycle are shown in Figure 2.4a, which also includes the faecal pregnane profile during pregnancy (Figure 2.4b). Pregnancy was detectable by 90 days after mating, as revealed by sustained elevations in faecal pregnane levels.

Unfortunately, no measurements of oestrogens or gonadotrophins are available for these females. However, nadirs in progesterone excretion coincided with mating resulting in conception, and this provides some indication of the likely timing of ovulation. The majority of cycles studied (59%) ranged from 29 to 44 days in length. Longer cycles involving extended luteal phases may have been related to a variety of factors including early embryonic loss or uterine pathology (Radcliffe *et al.*, 1997; Patton *et al.*, 1999). In addition, some females failed to show any luteal activity, as reflected by 'flat' profiles of faecal pregnane (Figure 2.4c). Interestingly, it was noted that social factors (removal or reintroduction of particular males) were correlated with loss (or resumption) of ovarian cyclicity, although these observations were anecdotal and have not been the subject of an experimental study.

Nutritional factors, as well as social stimuli, might affect reproduction of the white rhinoceros under natural conditions. In Zululand, South Africa, Owen-Smith (1975, 1988) recorded that although no restricted mating season occurs in this species, yet 'oestrus is apparently stimulated by a flush of green grass following a dry period'. The sexes are normally spatially separate; dominant males live in territories of approximately 2 km² in area whereas cows occupy larger ranges (10–12 km²) which may encompass the territories of six or seven males. Approximately one-third of adult males are non-territorial; they co-exist with territorial bulls, but do not show the

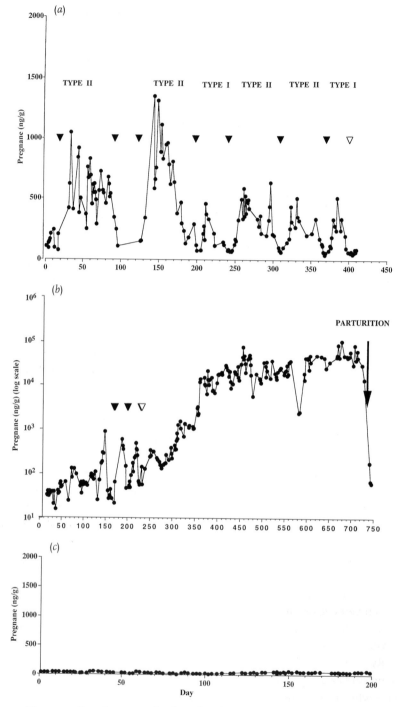

Figure 2.4 Faecal pregnane levels in female Southern white rhinoceros
(a) during Type I and Type II ovarian cycles, (b) during pregnancy and (c) when
no luteal activity was measurable. ▽, mounts; ▼, copulations.

ritualised urine-spraying and dung-scattering behaviours typical of territorial males.

Owen-Smith's observations indicate that female white rhinoceros come into oestrus at 30-day intervals, similar to the 'Type I' cycle lengths recorded in captivity. Dominant bulls associate with cows which enter their territories, and they attempt to mate-guard females which are entering oestrus. Initially, the male grazes nearby; but if such an attachment persists it is indicative that the cow is coming into oestrus. If this is the case, then the bull may attempt to block the female's departure from his territory, he may herd her away from the territory boundary or actively chase her. A dominant bull will repeatedly approach a female, uttering a distinctive 'hic-throbbing' vocalisation and sniffing her urine. Such approaches may extend over 15–20 hours before copulation occurs; copulations last for 20–30 minutes and courtships finish 2–5 days after mating is complete. Subordinate bulls do not usually court females or form consortships.

The possibility that the courtship behaviour, or mere proximity of dominant bulls (or their olfactory signals), might affect hypothalamic–pituitary–gonadal activity in female white rhinoceros has not been studied and deserves attention. It is possible that social factors, as well as nutritional status, influence the onset of oestrus in this species. In captivity, it has repeatedly been observed that the greatest breeding successes occur in those collections where white rhinoceros are kept in large groups and/or in large enclosures (Rawlins, 1979; Lindemann, 1982; Killmar, 1997). Lindemann's analyses of captive breeding successes indicate that it is the presence of two or more males which improves breeding performance by females, rather than provision of a large enclosure *per se*. However, since interactions between bulls, as well as between the sexes during the courtship phase, often involve aggression, it is clearly advantageous if the animals have sufficient space to accommodate such behaviour. At present we have no information about the endocrine profiles of dominant and subordinate bulls. Measurement of faecal steroids, in captivity and under natural conditions, might reveal interesting socioendocrinological effects in bulls. Likewise, it may be that female cycles are influenced by exposure to males of varying social rank. The reproductive success of dominant and subordinate bulls has not been measured; however, since it is possible to extract DNA from rhino dung (O. Ryder, personal communication) it should be possible to conduct DNA typing studies of paternity in free-ranging populations. The mating system of the white rhinoceros may allow some degree of 'mate choice' by females as they move through the territories of dominant bulls and encounter their dung piles and urine marks. These olfactory cues may also be of importance for captive animals, so that mate choice could also impact ovarian function under these conditions. All of these questions are open to inquiry by applying techniques developed for study of captive white rhinoceros to animals which can be followed individually, by use of radiotracking techniques, in their natural environment.

3. The California condor (*Gymnogyps californianus*): are captive pairs compatible?

Since the mid-1980s, when the last California condors were removed from the wild, captive breeding programmes at the San Diego Wild Animal Park, Los Angeles Zoo and World Center for Birds of Prey in Idaho, have succeeded in rescuing this species from extinction. From a founding population of 27 captive birds, there are now more than 180 condors, and over 50 have been returned to their natural habitat. California condors are sexually monomorphic, monogamous birds, which normally produce a single egg every two years. A replacement egg may be laid if the first egg is lost early in the season (January/February). Offspring are dependent upon their parents for at least one year, and reproductive maturity occurs at approximately 6 years of age (Koford, 1953; Snyder & Hamber, 1985).

Captive birds have been paired to maximise outbreeding, an important goal because deleterious genes may affect reproduction in such a small founding population (e.g. chondrodystrophy syndrome in condors; Ralls *et al.*, 2000). 'Mate choice' by the birds themselves has not, therefore, been a factor in the captive breeding programme. In most instances eggs have been removed in order to stimulate production of a second or third egg by the captive birds. Eggs thus removed have been artificially incubated and chicks have been hand-reared. However, since 1994 captive breeding facilities have attempted to allow condor pairs to retain their second or third egg of the season. Thus it has been possible to obtain quantitative data on incubation and chick rearing for comparison with the very limited information on parental behaviour in wild condors (Snyder & Snyder, 2000).

Eight breeding pairs are housed at the Zoological Society of San Diego, and videotaped records of parental behaviour are available for these birds throughout the incubation period and for the first 50 days post-hatching. From 1994 to 1999 the pairs had incubated their own eggs ($n = 9$), the eggs of Andean condors ($n = 4$) or dummy eggs ($n = 3$) which were supplied in order to provide them with additional experience. The incubation period for the eight viable California condor eggs was 55–60 days (mean $\pm$ SEM $= 57.5 \pm 0.55$ days). On average, both sexes spent the same percentage of time

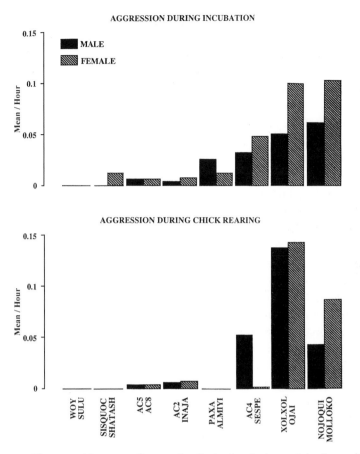

Figure 2.5 Mean rate of aggression during incubation and the first 30 days following hatch for eight pairs of captive California condors.

incubating the egg (males 44.4%; females 43.5%) and they manipulated it at similar frequencies (males 0.87/hour; females 0.91/hour). A significantly greater proportion of male ($- 17.71 \pm 6.43$ SEM) than female ($- 4.86 \pm 1.01$ SEM) nest-box entries occurred when the nest box was already occupied ($z - 2.24$, $P < 0.03$). Females had a higher rate of aggression ($- 0.036 \pm 0.016$ SEM) than the males ($- 0.022 \pm 0.025$ SEM) when in joint occupied nest boxes ($z = -1.69$, $P < 0.10$). Aggression included head-posture threats, displacing the partner, lunging, chasing and striking with wing, foot or beak. These events typically occurred as one bird attempted to re-place its partner in incubating the egg. Four of the eight pairs had higher combined rates of aggressive behaviour in the nest box, indicating that they were less compatible as mates than the remaining four pairs.

During incubation, none of the real eggs was damaged or destroyed by the pairs during agonistic interactions in the nest box. The same cannot be said during the chick-rearing phase. From 1991 to 2001, 20 chicks (13 California condor and 7 Andean condor chicks) were left with the eight pairs for rearing. While all the behavioural data have yet to be completely analysed, records show that all four of the pairs not characterised by aggression in the nest-box were successful in rearing all of their chicks ($n = 8$). However, the less compatible pairs identified during the incubation phase failed to rear 33.3% (4/12) of their chicks successfully (Figure 2.5).

The indications from these data are that despite lack of active choice, some of the captive pairs are sufficiently compatible to successfully incubate and rear their own offspring. However, the aggressiveness that occurs between partners as they change place to incubate or brood is a cause for concern. Such behaviour was noted in the wild condors (Snyder & Snyder, 2000) but at that time so few condors were left that patterns of mate choice were constrained and probably not normal. The behavioural analyses on captive birds presented here are far from complete. We wish to analyse the dynamics and outcome of male and female displays, which may have some significance during 'dominance' interactions, that may be related to agonistic interactions in the nest box. The *relationships* between members of a pair are more likely to be revealed by such analyses than by examining frequencies of individual display or aggressive behaviour.

SUMMARY AND CONCLUSIONS

The three species considered here represent variations on the theme of how to manage declining populations. In the case of the mandrill, a viable population of this magnificent primate still exists, especially in the north of Gabon. There is no room for complacency, however, as threats from logging and the bushmeat trade are on the increase. The drill (*M. leucophaeus*) has already been greatly affected by these problems in Cameroon and Nigeria; it is probably the most endangered primate species in Africa. Because so little is known about the social organisation and reproduction of mandrills and drills, the information summarised here on semi-free-ranging mandrill groups is of some interest. For far too long, mandrills and drills have been characterised in the published literature as polygynous primates in which large social groups are made up of one-male units. In reality the social organisation of the mandrill is likely to be multimale–multifemale, and the same is true of its mating system. Lone males occur, and they are likely to interact with social groups, especially during the annual mating season. Fragmentation of mandrill groups may occur for reasons of feeding ecology; large groups represent a huge biomass, and it may be difficult for the animals to find sufficient food throughout the year. Another possibility is that fragmentation of mandrill, or drill, groups may occur because of hunting pressures and deforestation. On Mt Kupe in Cameroon, for example, drill groups are smaller and more labile than they were 10 years ago; many monkeys have been taken by hunters throughout this period (C. Wild, personal communication).

Because mandrills and drills are semi-terrestrial and can move large distances through the rainforest, it has so far proved impossible to follow them and study their behaviour in any detail. Radiotracking studies may succeed in resolving this problem, and the information derived from studies of captive groups will be valuable in interpreting what occurs under natural conditions. In designing conservation programmes for both these species, data on population biology, social organisation and reproduction will be crucial. A useful start has been made in gathering some of this information.

The example of the white rhinoceros has been cited here because this species came very close to extinction. Protection of the animals, and their habitat, in the Umfolozi–Hluhluwe reserves has allowed their numbers to increase, and animals have been translocated to other reserves, as well as being placed in zoological gardens. Studies of captive rhinoceros have facilitated the development of non-invasive techniques to monitor their reproductive endocrinology. These techniques can now be applied to free-ranging white rhinoceros (as for the black rhinoceros; Garnier *et al.*, 1998), and they hold the promise of new insights concerning the mating systems of these fascinating animals. Important questions concern the socioendocrinology of the white rhinoceros, possible differences between dominant and subordinate bulls and effects of social stimuli upon ovarian function in females. Rhinoceros dung is a source not only of sex steroids, but also of DNA. Genetic studies may allow us to identify individuals in the wild and to measure their biological relatedness and reproductive success.

At the far end of the spectrum for declining populations is the California condor; only resorting to removal of the last individuals from the wild saved this species from extinction, and a reintroduction programme is still in its early stages. Reintroduction of the California condor to the wild is a difficult process. There are environmental challenges, such as lead and other pollutants. There are also behavioural problems. Some condors are inclined to approach human settlements and to be less fearful of human beings than normal. Of course, it is very difficult to define 'normal' behaviour for a species which could not be adequately studied in the wild before its population had been drastically reduced (Snyder & Snyder, 2000). In these circumstances we do not know, for example, whether hand-rearing techniques for captive condor chicks affect their later behaviour as adults. It is good news that in 2002 several pairs of released condors have succeeded in hatching eggs and caring for their chicks. Behavioural studies have a vital role to play in management of the captive and reintroduced populations of California condors. A huge, and costly, effort will be required over the next two decades to restore the California condor to the wild.

ACKNOWLEDGEMENTS

Our thanks to The International Medical Research Center (CIRMF) and to Dr Jean Wickings for the opportunity to study mandrills, to Randy Reiches (Curator of Mammals, San Diego Wild Animal Park) and keeper staff for assistance with research on white rhinoceros, and to Mike Mace (Curator of Birds), Cindy Woodward, Kristen McCaffrey, Don Sterner and keeper staff for data collection on California condors at the Wild Animal Park Condor Facility.

REFERENCES

Barton, R. A. (2000). Socioecology of baboons: the interaction of male and female strategies. In *Primate Males: Causes and Consequences of Variation in Group Composition* (Ed. P. M. Kappeler), pp. 97–107. Cambridge University Press, Cambridge.

Bercovitch, F. B. & Ziegler, T. E. (Eds.) (1990). *Socioendocrinology of Primate Reproduction*. Wiley-Liss, New York.

Birkhead, T. R. & Møller, A. P. (1992). *Sperm Competition in Birds*. Academic Press, London.

Birkhead, T. R. & Møller, A. P. (Eds) (1998). *Sperm Competition and Sexual Selection*. Academic Press, London.

Davies, N. B. (1991). Mating systems. In *Behavioural Ecology: an Evolutionary Approach* (Eds. J. R. Krebs & N. B. Davies), pp. 263–294. Blackwell Scientific Publications, Oxford.

Dixson, A. F. (1998). *Primate Sexuality: Comparative Studies of the Prosimians, Monkeys, Apes, and Human Beings*. Oxford University Press, Oxford.

Dixson, A. F., Bossi, T. & Wickings, E. J. (1993). Male dominance and genetically determined reproductive success in the mandrill (*Mandrillus sphinx*). *Primates* **34**, 525–532.

Dunbar, R. I. M. & Dunbar, E. P. (1975). *Social Dynamics of Gelada Baboons*. Karger, Basel, Switzerland.

Eberhard, W. G. (1985). *Sexual Selection and Animal Genitalia*. Harvard University Press, Cambridge, MA.

Eberhard, W. G. (1996). *Female Control: Sexual Selection by Cryptic Female Choice.* Princeton University Press, Princeton, NJ.

Emslie, R. & Brooks, M. (1999). *African rhino. Status survey and conservation action plan. IUCN/SSC African Rhino Specialist Group.* IUCN, Gland, Switzerland.

Garnier, J. N., Green, D. I., Pickard, A. R., Shaw, H. J. & Holt, W. V. (1998). Non-invasive diagnosis of pregnancy in wild black rhinoceros (*Diceros bicornis minor*) by faecal steroid analysis. *Reproduction, Fertility and Development* 10, 451-458.

Gartlan, J. S. (1970). Preliminary notes on the ecology and behaviour of the drill (*Mandrillus leucophaeus*), Ritgen 1824. In *Old World Monkeys: Evolution, Systematics and Behavior* (Eds. J. R. Napier & P. H. Napier), pp. 445-480. Academic Press, New York.

Grubb, P. (1973). Distribution, divergence and speciation of the drill and mandrill. *Folia Primatologica* 20, 161-177.

Harcourt, A. H., Fossey, D., Stewart, K. & Watts, D. P. (1980). Reproduction in wild gorillas and some comparisons with chimpanzees. *Journal of Reproduction and Fertility*, Suppl. 28, 59-70.

Harcourt, A. H., Harvey, P. H., Larson, S. G. & Short, R. V. (1981). Testis weight, body weight and breeding system in primates. *Nature* 293, 55-57.

Harrison, M. J. S. (1988). The mandrill in Gabon's rainforest: ecology, distribution and status. *Oryx* 22, 218-228.

Hindle, J. E., Mostl, E. & Hodges, J. K. (1992). Measure of urinary oestrogens and 20α-dihydroprogesterone during the ovarian cycle of black (*Diceros bicornis*) and white (*Ceratotherium simum*) rhinoceros. *Journal of Reproduction and Fertility* 94, 237-249.

Hoshino, J., Mori, A., Kudo, H. & Kawai, M. (1984). Preliminary report on the grouping of mandrills (*Mandrillus leucophaeus*) in Cameroon. *Primates* 25, 295-307.

Jouventin, P. (1975). Observations sur la socio-écologie du mandrill. *Terre et Vie* 29, 493-532.

Killmar, L. E. (1997). Captive rhinoceros reproduction at the Zoological Society of San Diego: a conservation success story. *Der Zoologische Garten* 67, 53-60.

Kingsley S. K. (1988). Physiological development of male orang-utans and gorillas. In *Orang-utan Biology* (Ed. J. H. Schwartz), pp. 123-131. Oxford University Press, New York.

Koford, C. B. (1953). *The California Condor.* National Audubon Society Research Report 4, 1-154.

Kudo, H. (1987). The study of vocal communication of wild mandrills in Cameroon in relation to their social structure. *Primates* 28, 289-308.

Kummer, H. (1968). Social organization of hamadryas baboons: a field study. *Bibliotheca Primatologia* 6, 1-189. Karger, Basel.

Kummer, H. (1990). The social system of hamadryas baboons and its presumable evolution. In *Baboons: Behavior and Ecology, Use and Care* (Eds. M. T. de Mello, A. Whitten & R. W. Byrne), pp. 43-60, Brasilia, Brazil.

Lahm, S. A. (1986). Diet and habitat preference of *Mandrillus sphinx* in Gabon: implications of foraging strategy. *American Journal of Primatology* 11, 9-26.

Lindemann, H. (1982). African rhinoceros in captivity. MSc thesis, University of Copenhagen, Denmark.

Maggioncalda, A. N., Sapolsky, R. M. & Czekala, N. M. (1999). Reproductive hormone profiles in captive male orangutans: implications for understanding developmental arrest. *American Journal of Physical Anthropology* **109**, 19-32.

Martin, R. D., Dixson, A. F. & Wickings, E. J. (Eds.) (1992). *Paternity in Primates: Genetic Tests and Theories.* Karger, Basel.

Money, J. (1991). The development of sexuality and eroticism in human kind. In *Heterotypical Behaviour in Man and Animals* (Eds. M. Haug, P. F. Brain & C. Aron), pp. 127-166. Chapman & Hall, London.

Owen-Smith, R. N. (1975). The social ethology of the white rhinoceros, *Ceratotherium simum* (Burchell 1817). *Zeitschrift für Tierpsychologie* **38**, 337-384.

Owen-Smith, R. N. (1988). *Megaherbivores: the Influence of Very Large Body Size.* Cambridge University Press, Cambridge.

Patton, M. L., Swaisgood, R. R., Czekala, N. M., White, A. M., Fetter, G. A., Montagne, J. P., Reiches, R. G. & Lance, V. A. (1999). Reproductive cycle length and pregnancy in the southern white rhinoceros (*Ceratotherium simum simum*) as determined by fecal pregnane analysis and observation of mating behavior. *Zoo Biology* **18**, 111-127.

Radcliffe, R. W., Czekala, N. M. & Osofsky, S. A. (1997). Combined serial ultrasonography and fecal progesterone analysis for reproductive evaluation of the female white rhinoceros (*Ceratotherium simum simum*): preliminary results. *Zoo Biology* **16**, 445-456.

Ralls, K., Ballou, J. D., Rideout, B. A. & Frankham, R. (2000). Genetic management of chondrodystrophy in California condors (*Gymnogyps californianus*). *Animal Conservation* **3**, 145-153.

Rawlins, C. G. C. (1979). The breeding of white rhinos in captivity: a comparative study. *Der Zoologische Garten* **49**, 1-7.

Rogers, M. E., Abernathy, K. A., Fontaine, B., Wickings, E. J., White, L. J. T. & Tutin, C. E. G. (1996). Ten days in the life of a mandrill horde in the Lopé Reserve, Gabon. *American Journal of Primatology* **40**, 297-313.

Sabater-Pi, J. (1972). Contribution to the ecology of *Mandrillus sphinx*, Linnaeus 1758, of Rio Muni (Republic of Equatorial Guinea). *Folia Primatologica* **17**, 304-391.

Schwarzenberger, F., Walzer, C., Tomasova., K., Vahala, J., Meister, J., Goodrowe, K. L., Zima, J., Straub, G. & Lynch, M. (1998). Fecal progesterone metabolite analysis for non-invasive monitoring of reproductive function in the white rhinoceros (*Ceratotherium simum*). *Animal Reproduction Science* **53**, 173-190.

Setchell, J. M. (1999). Socio-sexual development in the male mandrill (*Mandrillus sphinx*). PhD dissertation, University of Cambridge.

Setchell, J. M. & Dixson, A. F. (2002). Changes in the secondary sexual adornments of male mandrills (*Mandrillus sphinx*) are associated with gain and loss of alpha status. *Hormones and Behavior* **39**, 177-184.

Snyder, N. F. R. & Hamber, J. A. (1985). Replacement-clutching and annual nesting of California condors. *Condor* **87**, 374-378.

Snyder, N. & Snyder, H. (2000). *The California Condor: a Saga of Natural History and Conservation.* Academic Press, London.

Stammbach, E. (1987). Desert, forest and montane baboons: multilevel societies. In *Primate Societies* (Eds. B. Smuts, D. Cheney, R. Seyfarth, R. Wrangham & T. Struhsaker), pp. 112-120. University of Chicago Press, Chicago.

Wickings, E. J. & Dixson, A. F. (1992). Testicular function, secondary sexual development and social status in male mandrills (*Mandrillus sphinx*). *Physiology and Behavior* **52**, 909-916.

Wildt, D. E., Doyle, U., Stone, S. C. & Harrison, R. M. (1977). Correlation of perineal swelling with serum ovarian hormone levels, vaginal cytology and ovarian follicular development during the baboon reproductive cycle. *Primates* **18**, 261-270.

3

Nutrition and its interaction with reproductive processes

TOM G. McEVOY & JOHN J. ROBINSON

INTRODUCTION AND OBJECTIVES

Reproductive capabilities of mammals, birds and reptiles are influenced by nutrient provision at crucial stages of their life cycles. Nutrition of an individual inevitably depends also on that of its mother, irrespective of whether young are derived from egg-laying (birds, reptiles and prototherian mammals) or other (eutherian and marsupial) species. The maternal contribution is already pre-packaged as vitellus (yolk) at the time of oviposition in egg-laying species, and remains the sole nutrient source until post-hatch feeding commences. In contrast, most mammals rely on real-time maternally-derived nutrients throughout pregnancy and lactation.

Relative to maternal size, total nutrient requirements for production of mammalian offspring up to weaning are highly variable and exhibit enormous interspecies differences in relative distribution between pregnancy and lactation. An example is the kangaroo's trivial investment in pregnancy compared with the guinea pig's significant burden. Even within species, most notably those that produce litters, nutritional and genetic effects on numbers of ova shed and embryos surviving lead to major differences in maternal reproductive effort. It is against this background that we seek to identify feeding strategies which could enhance reproductive performance in endangered species. Central to this goal is greater understanding of specific nutrient roles in stimulating the expression of metabolic pathways that ensure reproductive success. In some cases the response to nutrition is immediate, operating directly upon target organs such as the ovary; in others full expression of nutritional effects is indirect and may not be manifest for months. Indeed, for both farmed and feral species, rarely if ever do available food supplies meet exact requirements for body maintenance and reproduction. Instead, periods of depletion and repletion of maternal tissues alternate, and this phenomenon of cyclical changes in body composition during reproduction, often imposed by the animal's environment, probably plays a central and necessary role in facilitating success. In terms of feeding strategies for improving the reproductive performance of endangered species, it is also notable that, while nutrient requirements of early embryos are quantitatively minute, these are both qualitatively and temporally specific. Consequently, dietary deficiencies of specific nutrients disrupt reproduction, particularly when the overall feeding level does not allow maternal catabolism to release the deficient nutrient.

We need also to consider the contribution of nutrition to reproduction among egg-laying birds and reptiles. Unlike placental mammals, these species must pre-package the nutrients required for all developmental processes from very early embryonic cell division to emergence of free-living offspring. Once hatched, most young reptilians fend for themselves from the outset whereas most of their avian counterparts rely on parental care, including provision of a diet that allows continued development up to and beyond fledgling stages. Food availability at this stage of their lives undoubtedly contributes to the numbers and well-being of birds surviving to juvenile and adult stages. However, the current review will focus on the relevance of egg-mediated nutrient supply to reproductive success, with emphasis on yolk-derived lipids in contrasting captive and wild conditions.

Regardless of species, one risk of reproductive disruption is that posed by parental ingestion and subsequent translocation of food-borne toxic substances to body tissues and/or egg constituents. Likewise, dietary deficiencies can be detrimental to offspring survival, with micronutrients such as cobalt among those needed for optimal survival and thrift of herbivorous mammalian neonates. In the wild, dietary deficiencies may be encountered on a seasonal basis whereas, for animals in captivity, micronutrient availability is likely to be dictated by feed storage conditions.

The preceding overview underlines the fact that nutrition of any species, whether free-living or in captivity, is a key determinant of its health and reproductive fitness and, ultimately, survival or extinction. Successful species have adopted numerous strategies to ensure their existence to date. Hereafter, however, many species will depend – ominously, perhaps – on the intervention of *Homo sapiens*. To help ensure that such intervention is not just well-meaning but also well-informed, this chapter examines the role of nutrition at various stages of the reproductive process in representative species and considers how, in the future, some crucial aspects of nutrient provision for reproductive fitness can be assured.

STATE OF THE ART

Foetal nutrition and subsequent reproductive performance

Analysis of reproductive performance records of hill sheep under a range of nutritional regimens led Gunn et al. (1995) to conclude that either foetal or early life undernutrition reduced adult reproductive performance, implying from their data that impaired reproductive performance was mediated through reduced embryo survival. Evidence that this effect may be programmed *in utero* comes from two follow-up studies by Borwick et al. (1997). In the first of these, restricting energy intake to half-maintenance for the first 47 days of gestation delayed the normal process of oogonial degradation in the foetal ovary. The second study confirmed this delay but went further by demonstrating that continuation of maternal undernutrition for another two weeks postponed the arrest of ovarian meiotic activity. Using the same treatment comparison (half-maintenance vs. maintenance, M), Rae et al. (2000) found higher numbers of germ cells at the preleptotene stage of meiosis in foetuses from ewes given the 0.5 M compared with the 1.0 M diet, again confirming delays in germ cell maturation and meiotic arrest. Further evidence of direct effects of maternal nutrition on the foetal ovary was provided by Da Silva et al. (2000). They found that nutritionally-mediated placental and foetal growth restriction reduced primordial and total follicle numbers in foetal ovaries at day 104 of gestation, and that this preceded any alterations in gonadotrophic gene expression in the foetal pituitary gland. In a study of water voles (*Arvicola terrestris*), not only ovarian but also adrenal function was compromised in prepubertal and adult female progeny of mothers that suffered food deprivation in early pregnancy (Yakovleva et al., 1997). All of these results thus provide new insights into the important contribution of foetal nutrition to long-term reproductive competence.

An example of nutrient limitation during foetal life that more generally affects functional competence and viability is 'swayback' in newborn lambs, arising from copper deficiency during pregnancy, a condition also found in feral species (Penrith et al., 1996). Another observation, also perhaps of relevance to endangered species, is reduced vigour of lambs, manifest as delayed standing and suckling, resulting from subclinical cobalt deficiency during early pregnancy (Fisher & MacPherson, 1991). The sequel is reduced passive immunity in those that survive, making them more vulnerable to disease.

Energy balance, stress and ovulation

Body energy balance and environmental signals interact to activate the gonadotrophin releasing hormone (GnRH) pulse generator in the brain and induce ovulation (reviewed by Adam & Robinson, 1994). However, the mechanisms linking the pulse generator to energy balance remain unclear, even under controlled experimental conditions (Foster & Nagatani, 1999; Adam, 2000). In the case of small rodents, circadian feeding patterns can result in large fluctuations in body energy balance during a 24-hour period. Here, hour-to-hour activity of the GnRH pulse generator reflects feeding patterns, inducing animals to resort to a 'gambling, opportunistic reproductive strategy' (Bronson, 1998) by ovulating when in positive energy balance. This approach may only succeed if, following mating, the environment quickly becomes more benign thereby reducing daily energy expenditure (field metabolic rate; Speakman, 1997) and/or the habitat provides greater quantities of food, harvested with minimal energy cost.

In large mammals in natural habitats circannual rather than circadian fluctuations in energy balance predominate in determining whether or not to ovulate. Furthermore, where there is potential for more than a single ovulation, for example in domestic sheep, actual ovulations are positively correlated with accumulative energy balance as measured by body condition score (Doney et al., 1982). Within this overall relationship there are long- and short-term modifications. The long-term ones coincide with ovulatory ovarian follicles leaving the primordial pool (c. 6 months before ovulation in ewes) whereas short-term modifications result from improved energy balance for as little as 6 days before ovulation (see Robinson et al., 1999b).

Among feral species, there is evidence that reproductive response to nutritional adversity or other stresses can be influenced by genotype, an example being the agouti locus which influences coat colour. Agouti protein may act directly on reproductive tissues and is known to antagonise melanocyte-stimulating hormone (Lu et al., 1994), which influences sexual behaviour and suckling. Following exposure to stresses such as food deprivation or relocation, reproductive responses of some rodents including deer mice (*Peromyscus maniculatus*) and water voles (*Arvicola terrestris*) apparently are influenced by the agouti locus (Hayssen, 1998; Bazhan et al., 1999). Reproduction in larger mammals also may be affected. For example,

LIBRARY, DIVISION

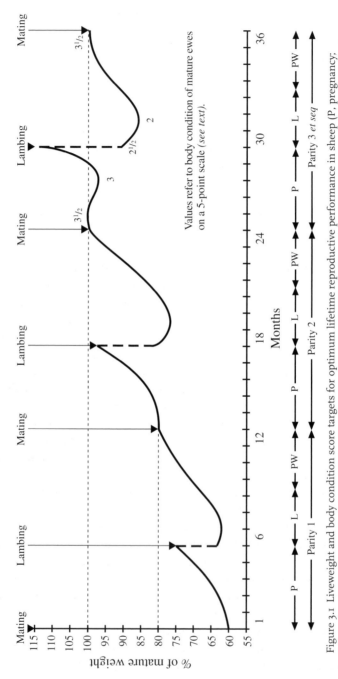

Figure 3.1 Liveweight and body condition score targets for optimum lifetime reproductive performance in sheep (P, pregnancy; L, lactation; PW, post-weaning). For additional information see text and bibliography references, Russel *et al.* (1969) and Meat and Livestock Commission (1983).

presence of a dominant mutation of the agouti locus (A^{wh}) in Icelandic sheep can suppress reproductive activity, resulting in fewer out-of-season lambings (Dýrmundsson & Adalsteinsson, 1980). Consequently, as noted by Hayssen (1998), the agouti locus may be involved in mediating effects of external cues on reproductive function.

Target body weights and condition scores

Identification of nutritional regimens for optimal reproductive performance in domestic animals took a major step forward with the introduction of the concept of species-specific targets for body weight at first mating and for weight gains during the first and subsequent pregnancies. These targets are now well defined for farmed species; as an example, and for the purpose of discussing their relevance to reproduction, stylised weight change curves for sheep, augmented with body condition scores, are presented in Figure 3.1.

The first important feature is target weight at first mating, which is set at 60% of estimated mature body weight. In many instances puberty occurs below the '60%' threshold, and mating has to be delayed. The second important feature in Figure 3.1 is the target weight at second mating of 80% of estimated mature weight, dictated by an upper limit to weight gain during primiparity, a point well illustrated by Wallace et al. (1999), using an adolescent ewe model. This experimental model demonstrates the adverse effects of rapid post-conception body growth (250–300 g/day) in the young animal on placental and foetal growth. Birth weights of singleton lambs are c. 3 kg compared with c. 5 kg for those from adolescent dams growing at 80 to 100 g/day, and thereby adhering to the target in Figure 3.1. Excessive partitioning of nutrients to the growing maternal body at the expense of the conceptus also leads to high neonatal mortality, causal factors being reduced neonatal vigour and, despite the excessive flow of nutrients to the maternal body, inadequate colostrum production.

Other important features of Figure 3.1 are the obligatory loss of body weight (mostly lipid) during lactation and the aim, in practical production systems, that ewes reach mature weight at the beginning of their third pregnancy. At this point, body condition (fat reserves) on a five-point scale (Russel et al., 1969) should be 3 to 3.5 for optimum ovulation and ovum quality. This also ensures ample body energy reserves to augment dietary inadequacies in late pregnancy and early lactation. In the month following mating the optimum feeding strategy for embryo survival is to avoid nutritional extremes (hence, maintenance of body weight and condition in Figure 3.1) while using a continuous cafeteria rather than stuff–starve eating pattern. The gradual move into negative energy balance during the second and third months of pregnancy reflects dwindling natural food supplies, but it also stimulates placental growth and, where adequate supplementary feed is given during late pregnancy, it results in increased neonatal size and vigour (Robinson *et al.*, 2000).

Alterations in sheep production systems that cause ewes to stray from the patterns of weight change and body condition illustrated in Figure 3.1 violate the underlying physiology of reproductive processes, with adverse effects on both dam and offspring; herein may lie a lesson for nutrition of species in captivity where rapid growth and over-feeding can compromise reproduction (Leus & MacDonald, 1997). Indeed, for carnivorous animals, strategies not aimed solely at reproductive advantage but with the potential to confer some benefits include more frequent feeding – thereby avoiding the stuff–starve scenario– and dietary regimens which reflect adaptation of species to seasonal patterns of food supply (Allen *et al.*, 1996; Young, 1997). For example, Bondrup-Nielsen & Foley (1994) concluded from their study of meadow voles (*Microtus pennsylvanicus*) that a period of postnatal food deprivation improved reproductive success relative to that achieved by counterparts reared on *ad libitum* diets.

Nutrient provision and reproductive success in egg-laying and other species

In ovipositing species, pre-hatch neural, organ and limb development relies on a finite reserve of nutrients initially residing in the egg vitellus and gradually absorbed by the growing embryo. The suitability of this pre-packaged nutrient store is a crucial determinant of hatchability of eggs from creatures as diverse as the alligator, ostrich and tortoise. While development may be modulated by environmental factors, notably incubation temperatures which determine gender in some species, the extent of nutrient provision and protection inevitably influences survival. Lipids constitute a major source of nutrients, and the fact that these will be stored for a significant period prior to uptake by the growing embryo means that antioxidant reserves must also be sufficient to safeguard the integrity of polyunsaturated fatty acids (PUFAs), especially those which are both vital and vulnerable, notably docosahexaenoic acid (DHA; 22:6n-3). DHA uptake and translocation to specific regions of the growing embryo, including the brain and retina, are features of development not only in egg-laying species but also in viviparous reptiles and mammals (Leskanich & Noble, 1999; Thompson *et al.*, 1999). Some felids are peculiarly dependent on dietary sources of

Table 3.1 *Polyunsaturated fatty acid parameters for wild (W) and captive (C) alligators (egg lipid or plasma lipid) and avians (egg phospholipid)*

	AA[a] (% w/w)		DHA[a] (% w/w)		n-6/n-3[b]		
Species	W	C	W	C	W	C	Reference
Alligator[c]	11.5	7.8***	8.1	3.9***	0.9	1.8	Noble *et al.* (1993)
Alligator[d]	4.7	3.4*	5.2	1.6*	0.9	2.2	Lance *et al.* (2001)
Kestrel	15.2	18.6**	5.5	3.7***	3.6	8.3	Surai *et al.* (2001)
Ostrich	4.4	6.4***	3.5	2.7***	2.9	5.1	Noble *et al.* (1996)
Partridge	5.6	7.3**	5.9	1.6***	2.8	14.2	Surai *et al.* (2001)
Pheasant	3.2	3.3	3.7	4.2*	1.6	4.7	Speake *et al.* (1999)

[a] AA: arachidonic acid, 20:4n-6; DHA: docosahexaenoic acid, 22:6n-3; data = mean values.
[b] Data in italics were calculated from mean n-6 and n-3 fatty acid values in the original publications; n-6/n-3 data were not tested statistically.
[c] Data refer to total lipid (n-6/n-3) or phosphoglyceride (AA, DHA) in eggs incubated at 33 °C, at which temperature male offspring develop.
[d] Data refer to fatty acids in plasma lipid collected from breeding and non-breeding females.
* $P < 0.05$; ** $P < 0.01$; *** $P < 0.001$.

essential fatty acids such as arachidonic acid (AA; 20:4n-6) and DHA because they lack the Δ-6 desaturase enzyme required for their synthesis from linoleic and α-linolenic acid, respectively. As obligate carnivores, felids overcome this limitation in the wild by eating freshly killed flesh. However, if diets are inappropriate in captivity, animals such as the cheetah (*Acinonyx jubatas*) may be compromised by limitations in Δ-6 desaturase activity (Bauer, 1997) and consequent inadequacies of essential fatty acids required for reproduction. Among egg-laying species, there is evidence that fatty acid reserves are suboptimal in captivity (see Table 3.1), generally reflecting a decreased abundance of n-3 fatty acids and an associated increase in the n-6/n-3 PUFA ratio, although the extent to which these account for frequently observed reductions in egg hatchability and offspring survival is unknown.

Herbivores and carnivores rely on plants and prey, respectively, in their natural habitat, or alternative sources when in captivity, to provide adequate n-6 and n-3 fatty acids, a number of which impinge directly on reproductive function. Arachidonic acid (20:4n-6) is involved in luteolytic mechanisms which ensure cyclical activity of non-pregnant females in ruminant and other species. Many PUFAs are crucial to functional competence of both mammalian and avian spermatozoa which, for example, rely on DHA for tail flexibility (Surai, 1999). In contrast to spermatozoa, mammalian oocytes and embryos may be susceptible to high PUFA concentrations (McEvoy *et al.*, 2000). Within egg-laying species, the vitellus must be buffered against oxidative degradation and, as PUFAs are incorporated into developing embryos, lipid-rich tissues and membranes also need antioxidants, supplies of which could depend on maternal diet (Lance *et al.*, 1983; Speake *et al.*, 1999). Even when dietary antioxidants are comparable, there can be considerable differences between species in respect of the antioxidant status of their eggs, precluding generalised extrapolation of dietary recommendations for one species to others. For example, Surai *et al.* (1998) found that chickens translocated dietary antioxidants to their eggs more effectively than turkeys, ducks or geese with the result that lipid-soluble α-tocopherol was 4- to 5-fold more abundant and carotenoid enrichment was nearly 2-fold greater in chicken egg yolk, with differences carried through to hatchling stages.

Feed toxins and reproductive repercussions

The extreme environments wherein many endangered species exist can expose them to toxins that occur either naturally or as a result of pollution. Plant toxins that compromise reproduction in domesticated species (reviewed by McEvoy *et al.*, 2001) are likely to have similar effects if ingested by wild herbivores, one example being ponderosa pine needle-induced abortions among both cattle and bison in North America (Short *et al.*, 1992). In addition, toxins not usually encountered by domesticated animals may be relevant to species in harsher environments. Susceptibility to plant toxins may, as in parts of Australia, depend on whether the animals concerned belong to native or introduced species; indeed, greater tolerance among the former can confer a comparative advantage that ensures their survival in habitats where would-be predators such as foxes or feral cats succumb. While co-evolution can offset the threat to wildlife populations from plant toxins, this is not the case with chemical poisons (Basson, 1987). Despite evidence that some species, for example herring gulls, can adapt parental behaviour to partially counteract adverse effects of poisoning on their young (Burger & Gochfeld, 1996), wildlife species generally are vulnerable to chemical pollutants. For various reasons, however, definitive cause-and-effect data on reproductive impairment are lacking (Hose & Guillette, 1995). Nevertheless, in species such as the endangered Florida panther (*Felis concolor coryi*), there is evidence that pre- and/or postnatal exposure to pollutants such as mercury and polychlorinated biphenyls contribute to demasculinisation of males, as evidenced by oestradiol concentrations similar to those in females (Facemire et al., 1995). Male reproduction can also be impaired by disruption of spermatogenesis, a case in point being the association of copper with sperm abnormalities in impala (*Aepyceros melampus*) (Ackerman et al., 1999).

Among captive species, an additional threat lies in the fact that their feeds are often stored prior to use and consequently can be contaminated by fungal or other organisms. While free-living species are by no means implicitly safe from effects of aflatoxins or other contaminants (Couvillion et al., 1991), it is recognised that special care must be taken to correctly monitor contaminant levels in feeds intended for wildlife (Thompson & Henke, 2000) as well as domestic species, especially in tropical climates (Kunavongkrit & Heard, 2000). Wildlife caretakers ought also to heed the plea by Smith & Akinbamijo (2000), albeit set in the context of domesticated species in tropical countries, to avoid reproductive impairment due to either toxic or deficiency effects of inappropriate dietary micronutrient provision. As discussed earlier in the context of avoidance of lipid degradation in feeds, diets also should include adequate antioxidant levels. Such provision could have the added benefit of combatting potentially damaging effects of some heavy metals. For example, the presence of cytoprotective α-tocopherol has been shown to reduce the toxic consequences of mammalian embryo exposure to low concentrations of cadmium *in vitro* (Warren et al., 2000).

PRIORITIES FOR THE FUTURE

Feed for fitness and recognise role of body reserves

Physiological processes of fat accretion and later loss are often entirely natural adaptations to accommodate inevitable but anticipated mismatches between nutrient supply and demand. Species such as the Arctic reindeer utilise maternal reserves during late pregnancy and early lactation to sustain foetal growth and milk production, while the grey seal relies entirely on body reserves in early lactation when she remains ashore to protect her pup. Cyclical changes in body composition also underpin the phenomenon whereby beneficial effects on placental growth and therefore size can accrue from mild undernutrition during mid-pregnancy (Robinson et al., 2000). If this advantageous adaptation to naturally declining food supplies also regulates reproduction in endangered species, well-intentioned policies of feeding for fatness rather than fitness could undermine captive breeding programmes.

Beware of overfeeding – consider growth targets

Among farm animals, pigs and sheep exhibit an inverse relationship between feed intake in early pregnancy and circulating progesterone concentrations with, in both species, associated reductions in embryo survival (Robinson *et al.*, 1999a). This may be relevant to other species for, as pointed out by Leus & McDonald (1997), endangered wild pigs kept in zoos invariably become obese with accompanying failure to reproduce. Such directly detrimental effects of overfeeding on embryo viability, together with the evidence that sequential growth targets optimise reproduction in farm animals (Figure 3.1, and related discussion), suggest that moderate feeding regimens (which assist endocrine actions and manage rather than maximise juvenile and young adult growth) could enhance lifetime reproductive performance in some endangered species.

Evaluate dietary adequacy in egg-laying species

Among egg-laying species, future tests of dietary adequacy for females that fail to generate offspring, especially where successful breeding is vital to species survival, should include investigation of the lipid, antioxidant and micronutrient status of their eggs or embryos. This would help identify dietary shortcomings with corrective changes then being monitored until adequate provision and protection of necessary nutrients are achieved. A possible blueprint is to echo investigations that have helped elucidate the contribution of vitamin E to viability of avian and mammalian spermatozoa and, in the context of offspring health, postnatal immune status (Surai, 1999).

Keep diets safe and use suitable feeding regimens

Finally, it is imperative that diets provided to endangered species should be free of harmful contaminants such as heavy metals, endocrine disrupting compounds and mycotoxins. They should be offered fresh, if possible, and in good condition. Future studies will need to determine which feeding patterns (stuff–starve, *ad libitum*, or others) are unsuitable for particular species so that revised regimens enhance rather than hinder reproduction.

CONCLUSION

Nutrient provision to endangered species, especially those whose survival depends on successful breeding of captive populations, must be recognised as a crucial determinant of their reproductive competence. Many species evolved to fit climates and habitats that generate cyclical or random patterns of plenty, adequacy and scarcity. Successful survival was therefore a consequence of careful entrainment of reproductive effort with food availability, via environmental cues such as photoperiod and temperature change. When species norms for reproduction depend on external cues, or have evolved to anticipate and cope with scarcity rather than abundance, it is hardly surprising that relocation to unfamiliar habitats and/or dramatic changes in feed provision can compromise their reproductive efforts and outcomes. Depending on the manner of reproduction in a particular species, diet and/or maternal body tissues and/or egg-yolk reserves play key roles in ensuring the birth of viable and vigorous neonates, capable of surviving to adulthood and, in their turn, generating healthy and reproductively competent offspring.

ACKNOWLEDGEMENTS

Original research from our laboratory presented in this review was funded by the Scottish Executive Environment and Rural Affairs Department and by the UK Department for Environment, Food and Rural Affairs. The authors are grateful to Professor Valentine Lance, Dr Brian Speake and Professor John Speakman for helpful comments and assistance.

REFERENCES

Ackerman, D. J., Reinecke, A. J., Els, H. J., Grobler, D. G. & Reinecke, S. A. (1999). Sperm abnormalities associated with high copper levels in impala (*Aepyceros melampus*) in the Kruger National Park, South Africa. *Ecotoxicology & Environmental Safety* **43**, 261-266.

Adam, C. L. (2000). Nutritional and photoperiodic regulation of appetite and reproduction in seasonal domestic mammals. *Reproduction in Domestic Animals* Suppl. **6**, 1-8.

Adam, C. L. & Robinson, J. J. (1994). The role of nutrition and photoperiod in the timing of puberty. *Proceedings of the Nutrition Society* **53**, 89-102.

Allen, M. E., Oftedal, O. T. & Baer, D. J. (1996). The feeding and nutrition of carnivores. In *Wild Mammals in Captivity* (Eds. D. G. Kleiman, M. E. Allen, K. V. Thompson, S. Lumpkin & H. Harris), pp. 139-147. University of Chicago Press, Chicago.

Basson, P. A. (1987). Poisoning of wildlife in southern Africa. *Journal of the South African Veterinary Association* **58**, 219-228.

Bauer, J. E. (1997). Fatty acid metabolism in domestic cats (*Felis cattus*) and cheetahs (*Acinonyx jubatas*). *Proceedings of the Nutrition Society* **56**, 1013-1024.

Bazhan, N. M., Yakovleva, T. V. & Makarova, E. N. (1999). Agouti locus may influence reproduction under food deprivation in the water vole (*Arvicola terrestris*). *Journal of Experimental Zoology* **283**, 573-579.

Bondrup-Nielsen, S. & Foley, P. M. (1994). Long-term effects of malnutrition on reproduction: a laboratory study with meadow voles, *Microtus pennsylvanicus*, and red-backed voles, *Clethrionomys gapperi*. *Canadian Journal of Zoology* 72, 232-238.

Borwick, S. C., Rhind, S. M., McMillan, S. R. & Racey, P. A. (1997). Effect of undernutrition of ewes from the time of mating on fetal ovarian development in mid-gestation. *Reproduction, Fertility and Development* 9, 711-715.

Bronson, F. H. (1998). Energy balance and ovulation: small cages versus natural habitats. *Reproduction, Fertility and Development* 10, 127-137.

Burger, J. & Gochfeld, M. (1996). Lead and behavioral development: parental compensation for behaviorally impaired chicks. *Pharmacology, Biochemistry & Behavior* 55, 339-349.

Couvillion, C. E., Jackson, J. R., Ingram, R. P., Bennett, L. W. & McCoy, C. P. (1991). Potential natural exposure of Mississippi sandhill cranes to aflatoxin B1. *Journal of Wildlife Diseases* 27, 650-656.

Da Silva, P., Aitken, R. P., Rhind, S. M. & Wallace, J. M. (2000). The effect of nutritionally-mediated placental growth restriction on fetal pituitary gonadotrophin gene expression and gonadal morphology at Day 104 of gestation. *Journal of Reproduction and Fertility, Abstract Series* 25, 94.

Doney, J. M., Gunn, R. G. & Horak, F. (1982). Reproduction. In *Sheep and Goat Production* (Ed. I. E. Coop), pp. 57-80. Elsevier Scientific, Amsterdam.

Dýrmundsson, Ó. R. & Adalsteinsson, S. (1980). Coat-color gene suppresses sexual activity in Icelandic sheep. *Journal of Heredity* 71, 363-364.

Facemire, C. F., Gross, T. S. & Guillette, L. J. Jr. (1995). Reproductive impairment in the Florida panther: nature or nurture? *Environmental Health Perspectives* 103 (Suppl. 4), 79-86.

Fisher, C. E. J. & MacPherson, A. (1991). Effect of cobalt deficiency in the pregnant ewe on reproductive performance and lamb viability. *Research in Veterinary Science* 50, 319-327.

Foster, D. L. & Nagatani, S. (1999). Physiological perspectives on leptin as a regulator of reproduction: role in timing puberty. *Biology of Reproduction* 60, 205-215.

Gunn, R. G., Sim, D. A. & Hunter, E. A. (1995). Effects of nutrition *in utero* and in early life on the subsequent lifetime reproductive performance of Scottish Blackface ewes in two management systems. *Animal Science* 60, 223-230.

Hayssen, V. (1998). Effect of transatlantic transport on reproduction of agouti and nonagouti deer mice, *Peromyscus maniculatus*. *Laboratory Animals* 32, 55-64.

Hose, J. E. & Guillette, L. J. (1995). Defining the role of pollutants in the disruption of reproduction in wildlife. *Environmental Health Perspectives* 103 (Suppl. 4), 87-91.

Kunavongkrit, A. & Heard, T. W. (2000). Pig reproduction in South East Asia. *Animal Reproduction Science* 60-61, 527-533.

Lance, V., Joanen, T. & McNease, L. (1983). Selenium, vitamin E, and trace elements in the plasma of wild and farm-reared alligators during the reproductive cycle. *Canadian Journal of Zoology* 61, 1744-1751.

Lance, V. A., Morici, L. A., Elsey, R. M., Lund, E. D. & Place, A. R. (2001). Hyper-lipidemia and reproductive failure in captive-reared alligators: vitamin E, plasma lipids, fatty acids, and steroid hormones. *Comparative Biochemistry and Physiology B* 128, 285-294.

Leskanich, C. O. & Noble, R. C. (1999). The comparative roles of polyunsaturated fatty acids in pig neonatal development. *British Journal of Nutrition* 81, 87-106.

Leus, K. & MacDonald, A. A. (1997). From babirusa (*Babyrousa babyrussa*) to domestic pig: the nutrition of swine. *Proceedings of the Nutrition Society* **56**, 1001-1012.

Lu, D. S., Willard, D., Patel, I. R., Kadwell, S., Overton, L., Kost, T., Luther, M., Chen, W. B., Woychik, R. P., Wilkison, W. O. & Cone, R. D. (1994). Agouti protein is an antagonist of the melanocyte-stimulating hormone receptor. *Nature* **371**, 799-802.

McEvoy, T. G., Coull, G. D., Broadbent, P. J., Hutchinson, J. S. M. & Speake, B. K. (2000). Fatty acid composition of lipids in immature cattle, pig and sheep oocytes with intact zona pellucida. *Journal of Reproduction and Fertility* **118**, 163-170.

McEvoy, T. G., Robinson, J. J., Ashworth, C. J., Rooke, J. A. & Sinclair, K. D. (2001). Feed and forage toxicants affecting embryo survival and fetal development. *Theriogenology* **55**, 113-129.

Meat and Livestock Commission. (1983). *Feeding the Ewe. Sheep Improvement Services*, 78 pp. Meat and Livestock Commission, Bletchley, UK.

Noble, R. C., McCartney, R. & Ferguson, M. W. J. (1993). Lipid and fatty acid compositional differences between eggs of wild and captive-breeding alligators (*Alligator mississippiensis*): an association with reduced hatchability? *Journal of Zoology (London)* **230**, 639-649.

Noble, R. C., Speake, B. K., McCartney, R., Foggin, C. M. & Deeming, D.C. (1996). Yolk lipids and their fatty acids in the wild and captive ostrich (*Struthio camelus*). *Comparative Biochemistry and Physiology B* **113**, 753-756.

Penrith, M. L., Tustin, R. C., Thornton, D. J. & Burdett, P. D. (1996). Swayback in a blesbok (*Damaliscus dorcas phillipsi*) and a black wildebeest (*Connochaetes gnou*). *Journal of the South African Veterinary Association*, **67**, 93-96.

Rae, M. T., Brooks, A. N., Kyle, C. E., Fowler, P. A., Miller, D. W., Lea, R. G. & Rhind, S. M. (2000). Effects of maternal undernutrition during early pregnancy on fetal sheep gonad development. In *Early Regulation of Mammalian Development*, p. 41. British Society of Animal Science International Symposium, Aberdeen, UK.

Robinson, J. J., McEvoy, T. G. & Sinclair, K. D. (1999a). Nutritional effects on foetal growth. *Animal Science* **68**, 315-331.

Robinson, J. J., McEvoy, T. G. & Sinclair, K. D. (2000). Maternal nutrition and foetal growth. *Reproduction in Domestic Animals* Suppl. **6**, 14-19.

Robinson, J. J., Sinclair, K. D., Randel, R. D. & Sykes, A. R. (1999b). Nutritional management of the female ruminant: mechanistic approaches and predictive models. In *Nutritional Ecology of Herbivores* (Eds. H.-J. G. Jung & G. C. Fahey, Jr), pp. 550-608. American Society of Animal Science, Savoy, IL.

Russel, A. J. F., Doney, J. M. & Gunn, G. B. (1969). Subjective assessment of body fat in live sheep. *Journal of Agricultural Science, Cambridge* **72**, 451-454.

Short, R. E., James, L. F., Panter, K. E., Staigmiller, R. B., Bellows, R. A., Malcolm, J. & Ford, S. P. (1992). Effects of feeding ponderosa pine needles during pregnancy: comparative studies with bison, cattle, goats and sheep. *Journal of Animal Science* **70**, 3498-3504.

Smith, O. B. & Akinbamijo, O. O. (2000). Micronutrients and reproduction in farm animals. *Animal Reproduction Science* **60-61**, 549-560.

Speake, B. K., Surai, P. F., Noble, R. C., Beer, J. V. & Wood, N. A. R. (1999). Differences in egg lipid and antioxidant composition between wild and captive pheasants and geese. *Comparative Biochemistry and Physiology B* **124**, 101-107.

Speakman, J. (1997). Factors influencing the daily energy expenditure of small mammals. *Proceedings of the Nutrition Society* **56**, 1119-1136.

Surai, P. F. (1999). Vitamin E in avian reproduction. *Poultry and Avian Biology Reviews* **10**, 1-60.

Surai, P. F., Ionov, I. A., Kuchmistova, E. F., Noble, R. C. & Speake, B. K. (1998). The relationship between the levels of α-tocopherol and carotenoids in the maternal feed, yolk and neonatal tissues: comparison between the chicken, turkey, duck and goose. *Journal of the Science of Food and Agriculture* **76**, 593-598.

Surai, P. F., Speake, B. K., Bortolotti, G. B. & Negro, J. J. (2001). Captivity diets alter egg yolk lipids of a bird of prey, the American kestrel, and of a galliforme, the red-legged partridge. *Physiological and Biochemical Zoology* **74**, 153-160.

Thompson, C. & Henke, S. E. (2000). Effect of climate and type of storage container on aflatoxin production in corn and its associated risks to wildlife species. *Journal of Wildlife Diseases* **36**, 172-179.

Thompson, M. B., Speake, B. K., Stewart, J. R., Russell, K. J., McCartney, R. J. & Surai, P. F. (1999). Placental nutrition in the viviparous lizard *Niveoscincus metallicus*: the influence of placental type. *Journal of Experimental Biology* **202**, 2985-2992.

Wallace, J. M., Bourke, D. A. & Aitken, R. P. (1999). Nutrition and foetal growth: paradoxical effects in overnourished adolescent sheep. In *Reproduction in Domestic Ruminants IV* (Eds. W. W. Thatcher, E. K. Inskeep, G. D. Niswender & C. Doberska). *Journal of Reproduction and Fertility* Suppl. **54**, 385-399.

Warren, S., Patel, S. & Kapron, C. M. (2000). The effect of vitamin E exposure on cadmium toxicity in mouse embryo cells *in vitro*. *Toxicology* **142**, 119-126.

Yakovleva, T. V., Bazhan, N. M. & Makarova, E. N. (1997). Effects of food deprivation in early pregnancy on the development of ovaries and adrenals in female progeny of the water vole (*Arvicola terrestris*). *Comparative Biochemistry and Physiology C* **116**, 103-109.

Young, R. J. (1997). The importance of food presentation for animal welfare and conservation. *Proceedings of the Nutrition Society* **56**, 1095-1104.

（4）

Environmental chemicals and the threat to male fertility in mammals: evidence and perspective

HELEN S. BAILLIE, ALLAN A. PACEY & HARRY D. M. MOORE

INTRODUCTION

Since the middle of the last century there has been a tremendous growth in the number and range of chemicals used for manufacturing processes. It has been estimated that 95% of all man-made compounds have been produced in the last 50 years. Inevitably, some of these chemicals pollute the environment. This may be caused by deliberate release, such as products to manage agriculture (e.g. herbicides, fungicides and pesticides); incidental release, such as waste products of industrial processes (e.g. sulphur dioxide and acid rain, dioxins, detergents and heavy metals); accidental chemical spills (e.g. oil tanker disasters, sewerage outflows); or the pervasive and continuous pollution of substances merely because of lack of proper controls and care. This environmental pollution, and the effects it might have on nature, has been recognised for many years and was highlighted by well-known scientists and ecologists (Carson, 1962). The stability and persistence of many man-made chemicals in the environment with their eventual distribution throughout the food chain is of very real concern and, although the apocalyptic forecasts of the destruction of nature from chemical pollution might now appear excessive, there have been enough examples of the effects of environmental chemicals on reducing animal populations for the need to be vigilant. Some classic examples of the effects of environmental chemicals on reproduction in vertebrates serve to illustrate this point. From 1950 to the 1970s, the organochlorine DDT (1,1,1-trichloro-2, 2-bis (*p*-chlorophenyl) ethane) was used profligately as a general pesticide. The active metabolite, DDE (1,1-dichloro-2-bis p-chlorophenyl-ethylene), caused birds of some species to produce eggs with thin shells. This then

led to a major decline in the numbers of several raptor species, most notably the peregrine falcon in North America and Europe. Polychlorinated
biphenyls (PCBs) were used in capacitors and transformers and in many
hydraulic fluids and are now widespread water contaminants that persist in
the food chain. In the Baltic, and other partially enclosed marine habitats,
PCBs are found in significant concentrations in herring and their predators,
seals. Only 27% of adult female ring seals in Baltic waters are pregnant at
any one time, compared to 75% elsewhere, owing to early foetal death (Chiu
et al., 2000). A final example is the effect of acid rain brought about by the
generation of sulphur dioxide in industrialised countries. Lowered pH of
freshwater systems can severely inhibit the reproductive capacity of many
species of fish (Beamish, 1976). Damage to the integument and branchial
epithelium of fry before and after hatching affects growth and can be fatal.

Here we outline briefly some of the evidence that exposure to environmental chemicals may compromise male reproductive health in mammals,
including man.

BRIEF HISTORICAL PERSPECTIVE

While there is a growing number of examples of the direct effects of
pollutants on reproduction in invertebrate and vertebrate species, with some
notable exceptions there is very little direct evidence that environmental
chemicals have a significant effect on fertility in most mammalian species.
Aquatic mammals (cetaceans, otters) are at risk because they may ingest
or absorb reproductive toxins directly from contaminated water, and occupational exposure by humans of a range of specific compounds may reduce fertility (Holloway & Moore, 1988). The latter is particularly well documented for male fertility and a good example is dibromochloropropane
(DBCP). In the late 1970s it was recognised that men working in a fac-
tory producing this fungicide/pesticide appeared to father fewer children
than might be expected for employees in comparable industrial plants. Subsequent studies revealed a strong link between occupational exposure to
DBCP, the occurrence of azoo- and oligozoospermia and a reduction in fertility (Whorton *et al.*, 1979). Following this landmark investigation, the quest
to identify further occupational and environmental exposures that could affect male fertility began in earnest. By 1983 occupational exposure to carbon
disulphide, ethylene dibromide and toluene diamine had also been identified as hazardous (Wyrobek *et al.*, 1983; Moore, 1986). More recently it has
been shown that exposure to a range of organic compounds, such as solvents (e.g. acetone, tetrachloroethylene, ethylene glycol ethers) and aromatic

hydrocarbons (e.g. styrene), carries with it a significant risk of a decrease in semen quality (Tas *et al.*, 1996; Cherry *et al.*, 2001). In addition, occupational and environmental exposure to lead and cadmium is also known to have detrimental effects on male fertility, with high blood and semen concentrations of these and other heavy metals related to compromised semen quality (Chia *et al.*, 1992).

ENDOCRINE DISRUPTING CHEMICALS

While all the chemicals outlined above are male reproductive toxicants and can have a significant effect on the reproductive capacity of individuals, whether human or other mammals (as shown from tests in laboratory rodents), the exposure of the population in general is limited. Much more serious has been the realisation in the last decade that a range of chemicals that are widespread and persistent in the environment have the potential of a more profound effect on the fecundity of animal populations – the so-called endocrine disrupting chemicals (EDCs; Colburn *et al.*, 1993). Such compounds affect the endocrine system, and therefore reproductive capacity (and immune responses) is particularly at risk. Not only do these chemicals include well known toxicants such as organochlorine pesticides (e.g. DDT) and PCBs but also alkylphenolic compounds used in detergent formulations for many manufacturing processes; coating compounds (for food tins) such as Bisphenol A; and phyto-oestrogens, such as foodstuffs with relatively weak oestrogenic-like properties but widely consumed. Specific synthetic pharmaceutical drugs (e.g. oral contraceptive pill, anabolic steroids) may also enter the environment. These can be excreted as highly bioactive stable compounds which are not readily degraded, or as inactivated metabolites which may be reactivated by microorganisms to bioactive pollutants (Cooper & Kavlock, 1997; Bolt *et al.*, 2001).

A major concern is that mammals, particularly males, might be especially at risk from EDCs. Sexual determination and differentiation in mammals occurs at a very early stage of foetal development and is exquisitely sensitive to endocrine disruption. Placental mammals have evolved a variety of mechanisms (e.g. sex hormone binding globulin, specific reductase and aromatase enzymes) to sequester or alter hormones and thereby reduce the biopotency of the naturally high concentration of maternal hormones during pregnancy which might otherwise compromise foetal development (Sharpe & Skakkebæk, 1993). But many man-made EDCs are resistant to degradation and the usual detoxification pathways in the liver, and fail to bind to specific serum proteins. By evading these processes, EDCs have the potential to interfere with key hormone receptor and signalling pathways of male gonadal and urogenital development (e.g. formation of testis, genital tract differentiation, descent of the testes, development of external genitalia). Although EDCs are often classified as environmental oestrogens, steroid receptors are usually promiscuous with respect to ligand binding, and as a result specific EDCs might have oestrogenic, progestagenic and androgenic activity. Moreover, EDCs can act synergistically. Exposure to any one compound may not be significant while exposure to a combination of chemicals (as is usually the case with environmental contamination) might present a real hazard. This is a major problem when trying to assess the risk to fertility.

The effect of oestrogens on male development can be illustrated by their action on development in marsupials such as opossums. In these mammals, sexual differentiation is postponed until after birth, possibly as an evolutionary strategy to avoid maternal hormone during this sensitive stage of development. Exposure of neonates to picogram quantities of oestrogen, or delaying birth by one day, leads to significant inhibition of testis development and, in more extreme cases, to total disruption of male development with instead the formation of a female phenotype (Baker *et al.*, 1990; Moore & Thurstan, 1990). In humans, an infamous example is the synthetic oestrogenic hormone diethylstilbestrol (DES), which was used to treat millions of pregnant women between 1945 and 1970 against abortion and pregnancy complications and, paradoxically, also to terminate pregnancy. DES resulted in sons having a high incidence of cryptorchidism (non-descent of testis), hypospadias (abnormal development of penis) and decreased sperm counts: all indicators of maldevelopment of the reproductive tract and testis (McLachlan & Dixon, 1977). EDCs could also affect males at puberty (initiation of spermatogenesis, secondary sexual characteristics) and in adulthood (continuation of spermatogenesis).

Thus, there is a reasonably strong theoretical case that exposure to EDCs, particularly during early foetal life, can potentially lead to alterations in the function of the testis and reproductive tract and subsequent reproductive capacity. But direct evidence to support this hypothesis is largely lacking and is at best equivocal (Cooper & Kavlock, 1997). This dearth of evidence has not diminished public and scientific concern about these chemicals and their effects in mammals. The debate has been fuelled in recent years primarily by reports that the reproductive health (related to semen quality, testicular cancer, urogenital abnormalities) of men from industrialised countries has declined in the last 50 years, and that pollutants in the sea, rivers and lakes can increase the proportion of animals with reproductive abnormalities (Carlsen *et al.*, 1992; Vos *et al.*, 2000). In the lay press, at least, the presumption has been that these topics are linked; however, a strong causal relationship between exposure to many EDCs and effects on male (or female) fertility in mammals has not been established. A difficulty is that exposure assessments are often absent, and the long latency period between potential exposure and fecundity masks any associations. Mechanistic studies do support the contention that exposure to relatively low levels of reproductive toxicants in laboratory rodents affects reproductive capacity (Gray, 1998), but it remains unclear whether most land mammals (at least) are exposed to such chemicals in the wild.

TRENDS IN THE REPRODUCTIVE HEALTH OF MEN

One of the most crucial areas of study, in parallel with the assessment of occupational and environmental exposure to reproductive toxins, is that of determining whether or not semen quality is actually declining. While this measure has the potential to provide vital information regarding the modes of action of such substances, attempts to assess the decline or otherwise of semen quality over recent years have produced varying results. The report that sparked an abundance of papers in reply was that by Carlsen and co-workers (1992), who presented a meta-analysis of 61 publications on semen quality in men. These investigators concluded that mean sperm concentration world-wide had decreased from 113×10^6/ml in 1940 to 66×10^6/ml in 1990, and that ejaculate volume had decreased from 3.40 ml to 2.75 ml during the same period. After re-analysis and examination of the data, this study was criticised on the statistics used and the fact that it did not allow for geographical differences in semen quality (Bahadur *et al.*, 1996). Differences among laboratories in methodology and the inherent variability in sperm concentration were also noted (Olsen *et al.*, 1995). Nevertheless, after further analysis of the data, taking into account the variety of counting methods used, and controlling for factors such as abstinence period, Swan & Elkin (1999) supported the original conclusions of Carlsen and co-workers. In the meantime, additional data from laboratories around the world have equally supported and refuted the claim of a decline in semen quality.

All the studies examining the apparent fall in human sperm counts in recent years have been retrospective. Many involve pooling and/or comparing data from different laboratories and sometimes different countries, a major consideration when semen quality is thought to differ between geographical locations (Fisch & Goluboff, 1996). Sample populations often consist of a specific group of men (e.g. potential sperm donors), thereby possibly introducing considerable bias into the results, and data are often collected by several operators who might vary their methods. All of these factors may go some way to explaining why there remains so much controversy surrounding this issue. Perhaps the only way to determine conclusively the decline, or otherwise, of semen quality, is to perform prospective studies that control for all of these variables and are repeated at regular intervals of time (e.g. every 5–10 years).

Other aspects of reproductive health such as congenital malformations of the male reproductive organs (e.g. hypospadias and cryptorchidism, androgen-dependent phenomena that are related to prenatal influences) also appear to have become more prevalent (Paulozzi *et al.*, 1997). However, problems associated with subject recruitment, diagnosis and registration of abnormalities (Dolk, 1998) and geographical differences in the incidence of these conditions, mean that they are not necessarily reliable indicators. Notwithstanding these difficulties, *one of the most significant findings in male reproductive health is that there has been a marked increase (up to 5-fold) in the age-standardised incidence of testicular cancer* within the UK (dos Santos Silva *et al.*, 1999), northern Europe (Adami *et al.*, 1994) and the USA (Zheng *et al.*, 1996), all of which have reliable cancer registers. Since the incidence of testicular cancer is known to be related to abnormal semen characteristics (Møller & Skakkebæk, 1999), this suggests a shared aetiology between the two conditions. Thus, claims of a decrease in semen quality in various countries around the world fit the apparent trend of an overall decline in male reproductive health, which might be related to environmental chemicals.

A problem with these data is that many confounding factors influence the epidemiological analysis. Lifestyle factors such as smoking, alcohol consumption and clothing type, as well as occupation, are all known to have the potential to adversely affect semen characteristics (Sharpe, 2000). To address these points a number of prospective studies are now in progress around the world. Our own group is involved in a study called the Chemicals and Pregnancy study, CHAPS-UK. The main aim of this multi-centre investigation is to assess the effects of occupational and environmental exposure on male fertility within the UK. In addition, the effect of lifestyle factors (e.g. alcohol intake, smoking), occupational physical factors (e.g. heat, vibration) and maternal factors (e.g. mother's diet during pregnancy, breast-feeding) will be assessed in relation to semen parameters. Further objectives are to determine whether or not there are any regional differences within the UK with respect to semen quality, and to create a database of semen profiles for UK men to be used as baseline data for future studies. The subsequent statistical analyses will determine whether factors such as occupation, exposure to specific chemicals, concentrations of substances in blood, urine and seminal plasma, smoking, alcohol intake, etc. differ between cases and referents. This database of baseline data will establish a reference for future studies to monitor semen quality within the UK over a number of years (Baillie & Clyma, for CHAPS-UK, 2000).

MAMMALS OTHER THAN MAN

While studies in laboratory rodents indicate clearly that exposure to environmental chemicals including EDCs may affect male fertility (Holloway *et al.*, 1990a,b; Sharpe, 2001), there is only anecdotal evidence with very small sample sizes that fertility of male wild mammals (other than cetaceans) might be affected. There have been reports of cryptorchidism in the Florida panther, the development of a small baculum in young male otters and genital abnormalities in polar bears (Chiu *et al.*, 2000; Vos *et al.*, 2000). But an association of these congenital abnormalities with exposure to environmental chemicals has not been made. It is of interest that all the above mammals are likely to be susceptible to contaminated food chains with bioaccumulation of EDCs. Recent findings indicate high persistent levels of such chemicals in several marine mammals.

PRIORITIES FOR THE FUTURE

Hundreds of new substances are introduced into industry and the environment every year, making the assessment of specific chemicals as potential inhibitors of male development and fertility increasingly difficult. In most cases, a causal relationship between exposure to environmental chemicals and any decline in the fecundity of mammal populations has not been established directly. However, current concerns about declining male reproductive health in man and in other mammals should not be discounted. More information is urgently needed regarding the risks to mammals of exposure to known, and as yet unknown, reproductive toxins.

ACKNOWLEDGEMENT
CHAPS-UK is funded jointly by UK governmental departments and agencies (Department of Health, Department of Environment, Health & Safety Executive) and the European Chemical Industry Council (CEFIC).

REFERENCES

Adami, H. O., Bergstrom, R., Mohner, M., Zatonski, W., Storm, H., Ekbom, A., Tretli, S., Teppo, L., Ziegler, H., Rahu, M., Gurevicius, R. & Stengrevics, A. (1994). Testicular cancer in nine Northern European countries. *International Journal of Cancer* **59**, 33-38.

Bahadur, G., Ling, K. L. E. & Katz, M. (1996). Statistical modelling reveals demography and time are the main contributing factors in global sperm count changes between 1938 and 1996. *Human Reproduction* **11**, 2635-2639.

Baillie, H. S. & Clyma, J-A. (2000). Chemicals and Pregnancy Study (CHAPS-UK) *Journal of Reproduction and Fertility, Abstract Series* **25**, 61.

Baker, P. J., Moore, H. D. M., Penfold, L. M. & Mittwoch, U. (1990). Gonadal sexual differentiation in the neonatal marsupial, *Monodelphis domestica*. *Development* **109**, 699-704.

Beamish, R. J. (1976). Acidification of lakes in Canada by acid precipitation and the resulting effects on fishes. *Water, Air and Soil Pollution* **6**, 501-514.

Bolt, H. M., Janning, P., Michna, H. & Degen, G. H. (2001). Comparative assessment of endocrine modulators with oestrogenic activity: definition of a hygiene-based margin of safety (HBMOS) for xeno-oestrogens against the background of European developments. *Archives of Toxicology* **74**, 649-662.

Carlsen, E., Giwercman, A., Keiding, N. & Skakkebæk, N. E. (1992). Evidence for decreasing quality of semen during the past 50 years. *British Medical Journal* **305**, 609-613.

Carson, R. (1962). *Silent Spring*. Houghton Mifflin Company, Boston.

Cherry, N., Labreche, F., Collins, J. & Tulandi, T. (2001). Occupational exposure to solvents and male infertility. *Occupational and Environmental Medicine* **58**, 635-640.

Chia, S. E., Ong, C. N., Lee. S. T. & Tsakok, F. H. (1992). Blood concentrations of lead, mercury, zinc and copper, and human semen parameters. *Archives of Andrology* **29**, 177-183.

Chiu, A., Chiu, N., Beaubier, N. T., Beaubier, J., Nalesnik, R., Singh, D., Hill, W. R., Lau, C. & Riebow, J. (2000). Effect and mechanisms of PCB ecotoxicity in food chains: algae, fish, seal, polar bear. *Journal of Environmental Science & Health* **18**, 127-152.

Colburn, T., Vom Saal, F. S. & Soto, A. M. (1993). Developmental effects of endocrine-disrupting chemicals in wildlife and humans. *Environmental Health Perspectives* **101**, 378-384.

Cooper, R. L. & Kavlock, R. J. (1997). Endocrine disruptors and reproductive development: a weight of evidence overview. *Journal of Endocrinology* **152**, 159-166.

Dolk, H. (1998). Rise in prevalence of hypospadias. *Lancet* **351**, 770.

dos Santos Silva, I., Swerdlow, A. J., Stiller, C. A. & Reid A. (1999). Incidence of testicular germ-cell malignancies in England and Wales: trends in children compared with adults. *International Journal of Cancer* **83**, 630-634.

Fisch, H. & Goluboff, E. T. (1996). Geographic variations in sperm counts: a potential cause of bias in studies of semen quality. *Fertility and Sterility* **65**, 1044-1046.

Gray, L. E. (1998). Xenoendocrine disrupters: laboratory studies on male reproductive effects. *Toxicology Letters* **102**, 331-335.

Holloway, A. J. & Moore H. D. M. (1988). Assessment of the effects of chemicals on gamete production in captive and wild animals. *Symposia of the Zoological Society of London* **60**, 29-37.

Holloway, A. J., Moore, H. D. M. & Foster, P. M. D. (1990a). The use of *in vitro* fertilization to detect reductions in the fertility of male rats exposed to 1,3-dinitro benzene. *Fundamental & Applied Toxicology* **14**, 113-122.

Holloway, A. J., Moore, H. D. M. & Foster, P. M. D. (1990b). The use of *in vitro* fertilization to detect reductions in the fertility of spermatozoa from males exposed to ethylene glycol monomethyl ether. *Journal of Reproductive Toxicology* **4**, 21-28.

McLachlan, J. A. & Dixon, R. L. (1977). Toxicologic comparisons of experimental and clinical exposure to diethylstilbestrol during gestation. In *Advances in Sex Steroid Hormone Research* **3**, 309-336.

Møller, H. & Skakkebæk, N. E. (1999). Risk of testicular cancer in subfertile men: case-control study. *British Medical Journal* **318**, 559-562.

Moore, H. D. M. (1986). Male reproductive tract. Target organ toxicity. In *Target Organ Toxicity* (Ed. G. Cohen), pp. 81-96. CRC Press, Florida.

Moore, H. D. M. & Thurstan, S. M. (1990). Sexual differentiation in the grey short-tailed opossum, *Monodelphis domestica*, and the effect of oestradiol benzoate on testis development. *Journal of Zoology (London)* **221**, 639-658.

Olsen, G. W., Bodner, K. M., Ramlow, J. M., Ross, C. E. & Lipshultz, L. I. (1995). Have sperm counts been reduced 50 percent in 50 years? A statistical model revisited. *Fertility and Sterility* **63**, 887-893.

Paulozzi, L. J., Erickson, J. D. & Jackson, R. J. (1997). Hypospadias trends in two US surveillance systems. *Pediatrics* **100**, 831-834.

Sharpe, R. M. (2000). Lifestyle and environmental contribution to male infertility. *British Medical Bulletin* **56**, 630-642.

Sharpe, R. M. (2001). Hormones and testis development and the possible adverse effects of environmental chemicals. *Toxicology Letters* **120**, 221-232.

Sharpe, R. M. & Skakkebæk, N. E. (1993). Are oestrogens involved in falling sperm counts and disorders of the male reproductive tract? *Lancet* **341**, 1392-1395.

Swan, S. H. & Elkin, E. P. (1999). Declining semen quality: can the past inform the present? *Bioessays* **21**, 614-621.

Tas, S., Lauwerys, R. & Lison, D. (1996). Occupational hazards for the male reproductive system. *Critical Reviews of Toxicology* **26**, 261-307.

Vos, J. G., Dybing, E., Greim, H. A., Ladefoged, O., Lambre, C., Tarazona, J. V., Brandt, I. & Vethaak, A. D. (2000). Health effects of endocrine-disrupting chemicals on wildlife, with special reference to the European situation. *Critical Reviews of Toxicology* **30**, 71-133.

Whorton, M. D., Milby, T. H., Krauss, R. M. & Stubbs, H. A. (1979). Testicular function in DBCP-exposed pesticide workers. *Journal of Occupational Medicine* **21**, 161-166.

Wyrobek, A. J., Gordon, L. A., Burkhart, J. G., Francis, M. W., Kapp, R. W., Jr, Letz, G., Malling, H. V., Topham, J. C. & Whorton, M. D. (1983). An evaluation of human sperm as indicators of chemically induced alterations of spermatogenic function. *Mutation Research* **115**, 73–148.

Zheng, T., Holford, T. R., Ma, Z., Ward, B. A., Flannery, J. & Boyle, P. (1996). Continuing increase in incidence of germ-cell testicular cancer in young adults: experience from Connecticut, USA. *International Journal of Cancer* **65**, 723–729.

5

Assessing the consequences of inbreeding for population fitness: past challenges and future prospects

ANDREA C. TAYLOR

INTRODUCTION AND OBJECTIVES

The worrying prospect that genetic deterioration may threaten the viability of wildlife populations was first brought to the attention of the conservation community by Frankel & Soulé (1981). The issue has since been hotly debated and widely researched. It is reasonable to assume that wildlife may suffer inbreeding and associated inbreeding depression resulting from continuing erosion of natural habitats and increasing reliance on captive breeding. Indeed all evidence points to this being the case (Ralls *et al.*, 1988; Crnokrak & Roff, 1999). In any case there exists a series of simple relationships providing a clear expectation that population viability may be threatened by inbreeding and loss of genetic variation. It is worth briefly reviewing those here.

Since genetic variability is the raw material for evolutionary adaptation, it follows that genetically invariant populations cannot adapt to environmental change, and are thus not 'buffered' against it (see Ryan *et al.*, Chapter 6). A corollary of this is that any trait that evolves must have genetic variation, and is consequently open to the effects of loss of genetic variation.

Demographic bottlenecks reduce genetic variability in a manner described by a series of theoretical relationships (Falconer & Mackay, 1996). In general, prolonged small population size is expected to cause a decline in allelic diversity and, to a lesser extent, heterozygosity. Conversely, if a population recovers quickly from a bottleneck then loss of genetic variation, especially heterozygosity, may be minimal. These expectations are fully borne out by experimental results and empirical data from wildlife (see Montgomery et al., 2000a).

Inbreeding (and consequent increased homozygosity) is inevitable in small populations. Even if mating with close relatives is generally avoided, after only a small number of generations the number of relatives exceeds the number of founders contributing to the population's gene pool. Consequently the genomes of all possible mating pairs will share many alleles identical by descent, and offspring will thus be highly homozygous. Again, these theoretical predictions are borne out by experimental results.

Inbreeding reveals recessive deleterious traits. Large outbreeding populations carry a genetic load of (mostly) deleterious alleles that are generally recessive, such that the traits they encode are only expressed at appreciable levels as a result of increased homozygosity (Falconer & Mackay, 1996). Small, inbred populations are therefore expected to express their genetic load as inbreeding depression. Inbred individuals have a relatively high probability of expressing a recessive deleterious trait and suffering reduced fitness as a consequence.

Individual fitness consequences of inbreeding depression may be reflected in demographics. Populations with a large proportion of individuals displaying reduced fitness will suffer reduced values for parameters such as birth and survival rates. This may be sufficient to decrease the population's growth rate, even resulting in population decline.

Populations with reduced growth rates are more extinction-prone. Small and declining populations are at increased risk of extinction due to stochastic environmental or demographic processes, each of which will interact with genetic processes.

The preceding list would appear to contain little to attract argument from biologists in any discipline, yet its logical implication, that inbreeding should be considered a risk to the viability of naturally outbreeding species, is not universally accepted (e.g. Elgar & Clode, 2000). At least some of this may relate to the common misconception that ecological and demographic factors operate independently of genetic ones. Thus, the onus has been placed on conservation geneticists to demonstrate directly that genetic factors have contributed to the extinction of wild populations. This requirement has now been met for both plants and animals (notably by Newman & Pilson (1997) and Saccheri et al. (1998)). There may still be voices of dissent, but these could surely only question that *all* populations will be at risk not that any will.

The study of population viability, as with all complex phenomena, has comprised a plethora of approaches, each constituting a piece of a jigsaw that has been slowly building over the last two decades. Much has been learned about the mechanisms and pathways by which inbreeding may impact population viability. The resulting wealth of information must now be applied to maximum benefit in conservation management. Ideally we would develop predictive guidelines for identification of taxa or populations most at risk of inbreeding depression. This information could then be used to enhance conservation management by aiding in the determination of taxon-specific minimum viable population sizes, and consequent approaches to management for that species. For example, it may be pertinent to allocate more of the limited conservation resources to species at greater risk of inbreeding depression. Perhaps more importantly, there is more than enough evidence for scientists to present a united stance to governments and communities: the great majority of populations forced *to inbreed will suffer deleterious and insidious genetic–demographic consequences and increased extinction risk.* The purpose of this chapter is to (1) review our understanding of inbreeding depression and evidence of its potential for threatening population viability (persistence over the short to medium term), (2) assess whether it is possible to identify unifying characteristics of taxa susceptible to inbreeding depression and (3) discuss recent technological and analytical advances that may be of use in future identification of populations at risk. The chapter focuses largely on animals, reflecting the overall content of the volume.

STATE OF THE ART

Inbreeding depression in wild species

Despite its low power of detection in captive endangered species (Kalinowski & Hedrick, 1999), inbreeding depression has been documented for a large proportion of captive wildlife populations (Ralls *et al.*, 1988; Ballou, 1997), and is being increasingly reported in wild populations. Crnokrak & Roff (1999) found that all 35 wild species for which appropriate data were available showed evidence of fitness reduction for inbred versus outbred individuals. For 83% of them this difference was statistically significant for at least one measured trait (see also Coltman *et al.*, 1998, 1999; Coulson *et al.*, 1998, 1999; Westemeier *et al.*, 1998; Marshall & Spalton, 2000; Slate *et al.*, 2000). The effect of inbreeding on fecundity of wild house mice is striking: inbred males show 57% less offspring production than their outbred counterparts (Meagher *et al.*, 2000). Additional wild populations of diverse species exhibit the correlated traits of small size, low genetic diversity and low reproductive capacity suggesting that they too may be suffering inbreeding depression (e.g. Eldridge *et al.*, 1999). This account is by no means an exhaustive review of inbreeding depression in wild species.

Essentially all well-studied, naturally outbreeding species that have undergone inbreeding exhibit inbreeding depression. In fact, Lacy (1997) concluded that there were no statistically defensible cases where inbreeding depression had not been detected in inbred mammal populations. Two factors may contribute to failure to demonstrate inbreeding depression for some species that may be expected to have reached critical inbreeding levels. The first, overwhelmingly evident from experimental inbreeding studies, is that manifestation of inbreeding depression is subject to large variation from a variety of sources. This has major implications for accurate identification of populations suffering from inbreeding depression, if approaches to its measurement do not adequately account for its variable expression. The second is the potential influence of prior bouts of inbreeding in the history of a population, during which time deleterious alleles may have been removed in a process referred to as 'purging'. I now deal with each of these issues in turn.

Variability in inbreeding depression and implications for its detection in wildlife populations – experimental results

While we expect to see inbreeding depression in wildlife populations, we do not expect it to be manifested in the same way as in agricultural species (Falconer & Mackay, 1996). Wildlife species are not typically subjected to long periods of intense artificial breeding selection. Our current state of knowledge yields no simple relationships predicting exactly how individuals and populations will respond to inbreeding. Experimental approaches have thus been vital for characterising wildlife responses to inbreeding. The more important findings are now described.

1. Extensive variation among experimental lines exists in response to inbreeding
Replicated inbred lineages created under identical protocols differ extensively in their response to inbreeding (*Tribolium* beetles: Pray *et al.*, 1994; *Peromyscus* mice: Lacy *et al.*, 1996), including extinction probability (e.g. *Drosophila*: Bijlsma *et al.*, 2000). In fact, variation among replicate lineages can be greater than that among lineages produced from different populations (Lacy *et al.*, 1996). This problem stems from the inevitable stochasticity of sampling different genomes from source populations, and means that extant populations of inbred species might represent the 'replicates' that have survived inbreeding.

2. Inbreeding depression is environment-dependent

The effects of inbreeding in experimental populations are differentially expressed according to the environmental conditions under which they are assayed, and are generally more severe under stressful conditions (Pray et al., 1994; Dahlgaard & Hoffmann, 2000). Experiments involving the release of inbred and outbred adult mice into the wild have demonstrated disproportionately high mortality of inbred individuals (e.g. Jiménez et al., 1994) and, more recently, reduced reproductive output for inbred males due to male–male competition (Meagher et al., 2000). Furthermore, the impact of environmental stress on experimental Drosophila populations increases significantly with inbreeding (Bijlsma et al., 2000), as is also observed in a wild population of Soay sheep with respect to parasite susceptibility (Coltman et al., 1999).

3. Inbreeding depression affects fitness traits and life history stages differentially

A variety of traits in experimentally inbred Peromyscus mice populations exhibit striking differences in inbreeding effects (Margulis, 1998; see also Ryan et al., Chapter 6). Furthermore, fitness reduction for inbred versus outbred house mice under wild conditions is greater at later life stages (Meagher et al., 2000). These and other studies suggest that examination of only one life-history stage, and especially early life ones (which are convenient to measure), will tend to underestimate or fail to detect the occurrence of inbreeding depression.

4. Inbreeding depression affects the sexes differentially

Loss of fitness attributable to inbreeding in some species appears to be more severe for one sex than the other, but the direction of differences may be difficult to predict as it probably relates to sex-specific environmental interactions and requirements. It is apparently male-biased in house mice owing to the reduced competitive ability of inbred male mice under wild conditions (Meagher et al., 2000), but may be female-biased in wild song sparrows (Keller, 1998). Males and females of three closely related gazelle species also exhibit differentially reduced fitness due to captivity-induced inbreeding (Alados & Escós, 1991; Gomendio et al., 2000), as occurs in red deer calves in the wild (Coulson et al., 1999). In the gazelle example, semen quality is significantly negatively correlated with individual inbreeding, but only in the most highly inbred of the three species (Gazella cuvieri) (Gomendio et al., 2000). Conversely, the influence of individual inbreeding coefficient on female lifetime reproductive success is least in G. cuvieri (Alados & Escós, 1991).

5. Inbreeding differentially affects closely related taxa

Substantial differences in response to experimental inbreeding by several closely related *Peromyscus* mouse subspecies are interpreted in part as having different genetic causes (Lacy & Ballou, 1998). The differential response of closely related species (see also the gazelle example described in 4, above) suggests that taxonomic trends in the genetic basis of inbreeding depression may be difficult to identify.

These experimental results have major implications for the detection of inbreeding depression in wild species. Its environmentally dependent nature means that it may be detected only if populations are translocated or otherwise subjected to marked environmental changes. In particular, inbred captive populations that appear 'healthy' may manifest inbreeding depression upon release into the wild. Fitness traits differ substantially in the degree to which they express inbreeding depression, and accurate assessment of the absolute effect of inbreeding on individual fitness can only be achieved by examining lifetime reproductive success. This is obviously problematic for most wild populations, in that it requires long-term studies of individually marked organisms, as well as accurate methods of determining their reproductive success and inbred status. Only two studies have thus far achieved this (island song sparrows: Keller, 1998; red deer: Slate *et al.*, 2000). Notably, in the red deer example, different components of fitness were negatively or positively associated with inbreeding and interaction with the environment, further accentuating the importance of assaying lifetime reproductive success (Coulson *et al.*, 1998, 1999). Finally, the unpredictable direction of sex biases in severity of inbreeding depression means that both sexes need to be monitored for effects of inbreeding.

Purging and the genetic basis of inbreeding depression

An important factor determining the occurrence of inbreeding depression may be whether populations have previously experienced bouts of inbreeding rendering them immune to future inbreeding depression, since natural selection during these periods may 'purge' their genetic load of detrimental and lethal alleles (Charlesworth & Charlesworth, 1987). It is important to note that protection from inbreeding depression via purging may only be effective in the environment under which purging occurred, as was observed when experimentally inbred and purged *Drosophila* populations were subjected to different environmental stresses (Bijlsma *et al.*, 1999).

The effectiveness of purging will depend on the nature of the genetic basis of the inbreeding depression. Two genetic mechanisms have been proposed to explain inbreeding depression: (1) partial dominance, where the elevated homozygosity resulting from inbreeding leads to increased expression of deleterious recessive traits, and (2) overdominance (hetero-zygote advantage), where individuals homozygous for a large proportion of their genome are relatively less fit than highly heterozygous individuals. Experimental data from *Drosophila* and plants implicate partial dominance as the predominant cause of inbreeding depression, although overdominance may be important for certain traits (Charlesworth & Charlesworth, 1999). However, the relative contributions of the two mechanisms are far from predictable, due to potentially large variance in selection and dominance coefficients. A variety of other factors such as epistasis, linkage disequilibrium, mutation and the number of loci contributing to genetic loads will also contribute to purging efficiency, but have not been subject to intense study.

If the predominant genetic mechanism underlying most inbreeding depression is indeed dominance (Charlesworth & Charlesworth, 1999), we might expect ancestral inbreeding to reduce susceptibility to inbreeding depression. Ballou (1997) looked for such evidence in a meta-analysis of 25 captive mammal populations. In only one of 17 species exhibiting inbreeding depression (the Sumatran tiger) was inbreeding depression significantly lower in inbred individuals with inbred ancestors, than in those without. In no species did purging eliminate a statistically significant inbreeding depression for any component, but it consistently had a minor effect across a wide variety of taxa. One possible explanation for the lack of a very strong effect is that overdominance contributes to the observed inbreeding effects. A similar conclusion was reached in an analysis of purging in plant populations (Byers & Waller, 1999): only one of even the most thorough studies reported evidence of purging. Thus there is evidence for purging in both plants and animals, but the effect appears to be very small and not likely to mean the difference between survival and extinction for populations (Ballou 1997; Byers & Waller, 1999).

Inbreeding effects on population viability

Inbreeding depression may reasonably be expected under some circumstances to limit population recovery following a decline (see Ryan *et al.*, Chapter 6). This applies whether the demographic disturbance resulting in the decline is independent of inbreeding, or is promoted or exacerbated by it. Computer models demonstrate that if recovery is slow, populations may be forced to persist at sizes at which they are at substantially increased risk of stochastic extinction (Gilpin & Soulé, 1986; Mills & Smouse, 1994; Tanaka, 2000). A variety of theoretical and experimental studies and a major empirical study of wild populations (Saccheri *et al.*, 1998) have now confirmed that such expectations are realistic, as summarised below.

Computer simulations confirm that the extinction probability of populations can increase upon inbreeding, particularly when the growth rate of the population is low (Mills & Smouse, 1994). In fact, the severity of inbreeding depression required to increase extinction risk is positively correlated with growth rate, i.e. populations with very low growth rates are affected even by only mild inbreeding depression (Mills & Smouse, 1994). Perturbations in sex ratio exacerbate inbreeding accumulation and hence extinction (Mills & Smouse, 1994). Inbreeding depression and environmental stochasticity act synergistically to cause extinction, even if neither alone is sufficient to do so (Tanaka, 2000). Population viability analyses of threatened species, performed with and without inbreeding depression, indicate strong effects of inbreeding depression on extinction risk (R. Frankham *et al.*, unpublished data). This is the case even when the incorporated cost of inbreeding is that reported by Ralls *et al.* (1988) for captive populations, rather than the sevenfold higher impact expected in the wild (Crnokrak & Roff, 1999).

Experimental results confirm that extinction probability increases with inbreeding (Frankham, 1995a; Newman & Pilson, 1997; Bijlsma *et al.*, 2000). The relationship apparently exhibits a threshold effect, with extinction risk increasing substantially from low to intermediate inbreeding levels (Frankham, 1995a). Importantly, the impact of environmental stress also becomes much greater at higher inbreeding levels in *Drosophila* (Bijlsma *et al.*, 2000). The latter effect was observed when populations had recovered in number many generations after bottlenecking, suggesting that a history of bottlenecks may leave populations more extinction-prone.

Rate of inbreeding will affect the efficiency with which natural selection can remove alleles responsible for inbreeding depression. Accordingly, slower inbreeding is less deleterious than faster inbreeding in *Drosophila* (e.g. Bijlsma *et al.*, 2000) and at least one *Peromyscus* mouse subspecies (Lacy & Ballou, 1998). However, population viability itself is apparently independent of rate of inbreeding: there was no significant difference in extinction probability of experimental *Drosophila* populations having reached similar levels of inbreeding at different rates (Frankham, 1995a). The mode of inbreeding, i.e. whether it results from prolonged small population size or a history of short-term bottlenecks, may also determine its effects on fitness. Each of these two scenarios had quite different fitness effects on experimental housefly (*Musca domestica*) populations: under benign conditions, long-term small populations declined in fitness monotonically over generational time, while bottlenecked populations initially rebounded in fitness. However, the two treatments resulted in the same low level of fitness under stressful environmental conditions, with fitness having reduced proportionately more in the bottlenecked lines (Reed & Bryant, 2000). Overall, available evidence suggests that the viability of populations that have reached similar levels of inbreeding is similar, whether they were bottlenecked or were small for a long time, and whether they inbred slowly or quickly (Frankham, 1995b).

Finally, a convincing example of extinction of natural populations due to inbreeding depression was reported by Saccheri *et al.* (1998), who showed that heterozygosity is the most significant factor in the viability of Glanville fritillary butterfly populations. The other side of the coin is that, because inbreeding threatens population viability, it should be possible to 'rescue' inbred populations genetically by reintroducing genetic variation. Restored reproductive fitness and population growth in small, inbred wild populations following introduction of genetically diverse individuals has been described for desert topminnow fish, greater prairie chickens and adders (Vrijenhoek, 1994; Westemeier *et al.*, 1998; Madsen *et al.*, 1999).

Can we predict population/taxon susceptibility to inbreeding depression?

The weight of evidence suggests that normally outbreeding species will eventually fall victim to inbreeding depression under appropriate conditions. Thus, the default assumption must be that an unstudied naturally outbreeding species will show inbreeding depression, and every effort should be made to manage species such that critical inbreeding levels are not reached. However, there may still be some value in identifying wild or captive populations that may be at more imminent risk of inbreeding depression. The severity of inbreeding depression is expected to be a function of its underlying genetic mechanism, along with the mating system and population history (Ballou, 1997). The latter two factors will determine the effective size of wild populations and therefore the amount of genetic load they maintain before undergoing inbreeding.

Modelling suggests that, under a dominance model, populations most susceptible to extinction via inbreeding depression are long-term large, randomly mating ones with no history of severe size bottlenecks and a low intrinsic rate of increase, that are rapidly decreased in size by an environmental factor (Tanaka, 2000). In this case, selection will work too slowly to reduce the large genetic load carried by the pre-crash population. The population's inherent low recovery rate may keep it small for several generations, during which the inbreeding coefficient will inevitably increase, with consequent unmasking of deleterious recessive traits as inbreeding depression. This model may provide the basis of a predictive framework for inbreeding susceptibility. Unfortunately an understanding of the genetics of inbreeding depression, accurate characterisation of natural mating system parameters (particularly variance in male reproductive success) and detailed knowledge of the population history are probably only available for a very small number of species. This dearth of data will severely hamper attempts to predict the susceptibility of populations to inbreeding depression. Genetic estimates of effective size may be available for wild populations prior to decline or introduction to captivity, since they do not rely on demographic information. However, testing predictions using current data sets may prove complicated, given expected difficulties in accurate identification of inbreeding depression.

There have been attempts to identify relationships between susceptibility to inbreeding depression in captivity, and effective population size and/or mating systems. For example, there were early suggestions that mammalian carnivores naturally have small effective population sizes, and therefore may suffer no, or only minimal, inbreeding depression (Chepko-Sade et al., 1987; Ralls et al., 1988). However, inbreeding depression has since been confirmed or strongly inferred for small, inbred carnivore populations: wild and captive grey wolves (Laikre & Ryman, 1991; Peterson et al., 1998) and captive brown bears (Laikre et al., 1996). A similar suggestion was made for koalas, on the basis that they have historically low population sizes, and that aspects of their mating system might lead to frequent father–daughter matings in the wild (Worthington-Wilmer et al., 1993). However, signs are now emerging that koalas may indeed exhibit inbreeding depression in captivity (Sherwin et al., 2000) and in the wild (Montgomery et al., 2000b).

At least for animals, there is little evidence at this stage that particular life-history characteristics of species will determine their susceptibility to inbreeding depression, and there is a similar lack of evidence for differences at higher classification levels. Mammalian orders show no significant differences in susceptibility to inbreeding depression in captivity (Ralls et al., 1988), nor do homeotherms and poikilotherms in the wild (Crnokrak & Roff, 1999).

PRIORITIES FOR THE FUTURE

Meta-analyses provide a very powerful approach to identifying universal patterns and trends in data sets (e.g. Ballou, 1997; Byers & Waller, 1999), and could be applied to developing predictive frameworks regarding inbreeding susceptibility. However, their effectiveness relies on the adequacy of data sets. Future work should aim to provide more accurate assessments of inbreeding depression in a large sample of species with known mating system and population history.

More effective documentation of inbreeding depression will require:

(i) Measurement of the most appropriate fitness trait: lifetime reproductive success. This information is required for both sexes. While female reproductive success may be relatively obvious through observations of maternal care, assessment of male reproductive success can be highly error-prone if based on behavioural observations alone (Pemberton *et al.*, 1992). Modern molecular and analytical techniques, in particular likelihood analysis based on microsatellite genotypes, offer much promise for improving estimates of both paternity and maternity (Marshall *et al.*, 1998).

(ii) Identification of pedigree relationships. Individual inbreeding coefficients are generally estimated from pedigree data, but these are available for only a proportion of captive populations and virtually no wild ones. Methods cited above for improved parentage assignment will enhance our ability to reconstruct pedigrees, thus allowing fitness comparisons among individuals with varying inbreeding coefficients in the same population (Pemberton *et al.*, 1999).

(iii) Identification of long-term inbreeding in particular family lineages. Even when they are available, pedigrees may not be sufficiently deep to allow detection of long-term inbreeding in particular family lineages. Similarly, heterozygosity is a useful indicator only of recent inbreeding. Thus, if inbreeding depression is due to longer-term inbreeding it may not be detected with either of these estimators, perhaps contributing to some negative results in the literature. Analytical methods recently devised for use with microsatellite data offer an exciting new approach to estimating cumulative inbreeding in particular lineages. Gene genealogical information is contained in microsatellite allele lengths, with alleles more different in size being more distantly related. A recently derived parameter, mean d^2, can be calculated from the microsatellite allele sizes at multiple loci in a given individual. This captures some gene genealogical signal, providing an indication of that individual's degree of ancestral outbreeding or cumulative inbreeding (Coulson *et al.*, 1998).

While individual fitness should ideally be measured as lifetime reproductive success, this will always be difficult in long-lived species and may preclude their study in this way. Given that estimates of population viability are the ultimate goal, a valuable alternative approach may be to focus on documenting inbreeding depression in particular life-history traits known to be important for population persistence, perhaps providing a much needed link between inbreeding depression and population viability. Species-specific approaches are likely to be most fruitful. For example, modelling of cheetah populations indicates that their viability is most dependent on adult survival rates, rather than juvenile survival, which is often the focus of discussions about cheetah endangerment (Crooks *et al.*, 1998).

CONCLUSION

Many approaches have been applied to measuring and characterising inbreeding depression, including modelling, laboratory experiments, meta-analysis and studies of wild populations. The accumulated evidence suggests that inbreeding depression may be a virtually universal response to inbreeding in naturally outbreeding species, and that it can threaten the viability of populations. However, the degree of variability in the magnitude of inbreeding depression is such that it is relatively unpredictable even under the controlled conditions possible in experimental studies. Partial dominance is considered to be the major cause of inbreeding depression, but it is probably not the exclusive one, with some indication of variability among traits. Little has emerged to suggest that a predictive framework may soon be available that could be of use in wildlife conservation management. Future work might focus on inbreeding depression for the total life cycle, and upon large-scale meta-analyses where taxa with different life histories are compared.

There are two approaches to managing inbreeding depression: minimisation of inbreeding and outcrossing to reverse its effects. The former adds to the need to redouble efforts to halt population decline and habitat loss. Unfortunately it is inevitable that species will continue to become extinct in the wild, and many may persist only in captive collections. The reproductive technologies discussed in this book will thus play an increasingly important role in genetic management of captive 'meta-populations', particularly via the development of methods of sperm collection, storage, transport and artificial insemination.

REFERENCES

Alados, C. L. & Escós, J. (1991). Phenotypic and genetic characteristics affecting lifetime reproductive success in female Cuvier's, dama and dorcas gazelles (*Gazella cuvieri, G. dama* and *G. dorcas*). *Journal of Zoology (London)* **223**, 307–321.

Ballou, J. D. (1997). Ancestral inbreeding only minimally affects inbreeding depression in mammalian populations. *Journal of Heredity* **88**, 169-178.

Bijlsma, R., Bundgaard, J. & Boerema, A. C. (2000). Does inbreeding affect the extinction risk of small populations? Predictions from *Drosophila*. *Journal of Evolutionary Biology* **13**, 502-514.

Bijlsma, R., Bundgaard, J. & Van Putten, W. F. (1999). Environmental dependence of inbreeding depression and purging in *Drosophila melanogaster*. *Journal of Evolutionary Biology* **12**, 1125-1137.

Byers, D. L. & Waller, D. M. (1999). Do plant populations purge their genetic load? Effects of population size and mating history on inbreeding depression. *Annual Review of Ecology and Systematics* **30**, 479-513.

Charlesworth, D. & Charlesworth, B. (1987). Inbreeding depression and its evolutionary consequences. *Annual Review of Ecology and Systematics* **18**, 237-268.

Charlesworth, D. & Charlesworth, B. (1999). The genetic basis of inbreeding depression. *Genetical Research, Cambridge* **74**, 329-340.

Chepko-Sade, B. D., Shields, W. M., Berger, J., Halpin, Z. T., Jones, W. T., Rogers, L. L., Rood, J. P. & Smith, A. T. (1987). The effects of dispersal and social structure on effective population size. In *Mammalian Dispersal Patterns: The Effects of Social Structure on Population Genetics* (Eds. B. D. Chepko-Sade & Z. T. Halpin), pp. 287-321. University of Chicago Press, Chicago.

Coltman, D. W., Bowen, W. D. & Wright, J. M. (1998). Birth weight and neonatal survival of harbour seal pups are positively correlated with genetic variation measured by microsatellites. *Proceedings of the Royal Society of London B* **265**, 803-809.

Coltman, D. W., Pilkington, J. G., Smith, J. A. & Pemberton, J. M. (1999). Parasite-mediated selection against inbred Soay sheep in a free-living, island population. *Evolution* **53**, 1259-1267.

Coulson, T., Albon, S., Slate, J. & Pemberton, J. M. (1999). Microsatellite loci reveal sex dependent responses to inbreeding and outbreeding in red deer calves. *Evolution* **53**, 1951-1960.

Coulson, T. N., Pemberton, J. M., Albon, S. D., Beaumont, M. A., Marshall, T. C., Slate, J., Clutton-Brock, T. H. & Guinness, F. E. (1998). Microsatellites measure inbreeding depression and heterosis in red deer. *Proceedings of the Royal Society of London B* **265**, 489-495.

Crnokrak, P. & Roff, D. A. (1999). Inbreeding depression in the wild. *Heredity* **83**, 260-270.

Crooks, K. R., Sanjayan, M. A. & Doak, D. F. (1998). New insights on cheetah conservation through demographic modeling. *Conservation Biology* **12**, 889-895.

Dahlgaard, J. & Hoffmann, A. A. (2000). Stress resistance and environmental dependency of inbreeding depression in *Drosophila melanogaster*. *Conservation Biology* **14**, 1187-1192.

Eldridge, M. D. B., King, J. M., Loupis, A. K., Spencer, P. B. S., Taylor, A. C., Pope, L. C. & Hall, G. P. (1999). Unprecedented low levels of genetic variation and inbreeding depression in an island population of the black-footed rock-wallaby. *Conservation Biology* **13**, 531-541.

Elgar, M. A. & Clode, D. (2000). Genetic diversity of animals in fragmented populations: implications for conservation management. *Australian Biologist* **12**, 155-163.

Falconer, D. S. & Mackay, T. F. S. (1996). *An Introduction to Quantitative Genetics*, 4th edn. Longman, Harlow, Essex.

Frankel, O. H. & Soulé, M. E. (1981). *Conservation and Evolution*. Cambridge University Press, Cambridge.

Frankham, R. (1995a). Inbreeding and extinction: a threshold effect. *Conservation Biology* 9, 792-799.

Frankham, R. (1995b). Conservation genetics. *Annual Review of Genetics* 29, 305-327.

Gilpin, M. E. & Soulé, M. E. (1986). Minimum viable populations: processes of species extinction. In *Conservation Biology: The Science of Scarcity and Diversity* (Ed. M. E. Soulé), pp. 19-34. Sinauer Associates, Sunderland, MA.

Gomendio, M., Cassinello, J. & Roldan, E. R. S. (2000). A comparative study of ejaculate traits in three endangered ungulates with different levels of inbreeding: fluctuating asymmetry as an indicator of reproductive and genetic stress. *Proceedings of the Royal Society of London B* 267, 875-882.

Jiménez, J. A., Hughes, K. A., Alaks, G., Graham, L. & Lacy, R. C. (1994). An experimental study of inbreeding depression in a natural habitat. *Science* 266, 271-273.

Kalinowski, S. T. & Hedrick, P. W. (1999). Detecting inbreeding depression is difficult in captive endangered species. *Animal Conservation* 2, 131-136.

Keller, L. F. (1998). Inbreeding and its fitness effects in an insular population of song sparrows (*Melospiza melodia*). *Evolution* 52, 240-250.

Lacy, R. C. (1997). Importance of genetic variation to the viability of mammalian populations. *Journal of Mammalogy* 78, 320-335.

Lacy, R. C., Alaks, G. & Walsh, A. (1996). Hierarchical analysis of inbreeding depression in *Peromyscus polionotus*. *Evolution* 50, 2187-2200.

Lacy, R. C. & Ballou, J. D. (1998). Effectiveness of selection in reducing the genetic load in populations of *Peromyscus polionotus* during generation of inbreeding. *Evolution* 52, 900-909.

Laikre, L., Andren, R., Larsson, H-O. W. & Ryman, N. (1996). Inbreeding depression in brown bear *Ursus arctos*. *Biological Conservation* 76, 69-72.

Laikre, L. & Ryman, N. (1991). Inbreeding depression in a captive wolf (*Canis lupus*) population. *Conservation Biology* 5, 33-40.

Madsen, T., Shine, R., Olsson, M. & Wittzell, H. (1999). Restoration of an inbred adder population. *Nature* 402, 34-35.

Margulis, S. W. (1998). Differential effects of inbreeding at juvenile and adult life-history stages in *Peromyscus polionotus*. *Journal of Mammalogy* 79, 326-336.

Marshall, T. C., Slate, J., Kruuk, L. E. B. & Pemberton, J. M. (1998). Statistical confidence for likelihood-based paternity inference in natural populations. *Molecular Ecology* 7, 639-655.

Marshall, T. C. & Spalton, J. A. (2000). Simultaneous inbreeding and outbreeding depression in reintroduced Arabian oryx. *Animal Conservation* 3, 241-248.

Meagher, S., Penn, D. J. & Potts, W. K. (2000). Male-male competition magnifies inbreeding depression in wild house mice. *Proceedings of the National Academy of Sciences USA* 97, 3324-3329.

Mills, L. S. & Smouse, P. E. (1994). Demographic consequences of inbreeding in remnant populations. *American Naturalist* 144, 412-431.

Montgomery, M. E., Duckett, R. J., Houlden, B. A. & Taggart, D. A. (2000b). Inbreeding depression in the koala, addendum to *Proceedings of the 47th Annual*

Meeting of the Genetics Society of Australia. Australian National University, Canberra.

Montgomery, M. E., Woodworth, L. M., Nurthen, R. K., Gilligan, D. M., Briscoe, D. A. & Frankham, R. (2000a). Relationships between population size and loss of genetic diversity: comparisons of experimental results with theoretical predictions. *Conservation Genetics* 1, 33-43.

Newman, D. & Pilson, D. (1997). Increased probability of extinction due to decreased genetic effective population size: experimental populations of *Clarkia pulchella. Evolution* 51, 354-362.

Pemberton, J. M., Albon, S. D., Guinness, F. E., Clutton-Brock, T. H. & Dover, G. A. (1992). Behavioral estimates of male mating success tested by DNA fingerprinting in a polygynous mammal. *Behavioral Ecology* 3, 66-75.

Pemberton, J. M., Coltman, D. W., Coulson, T. N. & Slate, J. (1999). Using microsatellites to measure the fitness consequences of inbreeding and outbreeding. In *Microsatellites: Evolution and Application* (Eds. D. B. Goldstein & C. Schlötterer), pp. 151-164. Oxford University Press, New York.

Peterson, R. O., Thomas, N. J., Thurber, J. M., Vucetich, J. A. & Waite, T. A. (1998). Population limitation and the wolves of Isle Royale. *Journal of Mammalogy* 79, 828-841.

Pray, L. A., Schwartz, J. M., Goodnight, C. J. & Stevens, L. (1994). Environmental dependency of inbreeding depression: implications for conservation biology. *Conservation Biology* 8, 562-568.

Ralls, K., Ballou, J. D. & Templeton, A. (1988). Estimates of lethal equivalents and the cost of inbreeding in mammals. *Conservation Biology* 2, 185-193.

Reed, D. H. & Bryant, E. H. (2000). Experimental tests of minimum viable population size. *Animal Conservation* 3, 7-14.

Saccheri, I., Kuussaari, M., Kankare, M., Vikman, P., Fortelius, W. & Hanski, I. (1998). Inbreeding and extinction in a butterfly metapopulation. *Nature* 392, 491-494.

Sherwin, W. B., Timms, P., Wilcken, J. & Houlden, B. (2000). Analysis and conservation implications of koala genetics. *Conservation Biology* 14, 639-649.

Slate, J., Kruuk, L. E. B., Marshall, T. C., Pemberton, J. M. & Clutton-Brock, T. H. (2000). Inbreeding depression influences lifetime breeding success in a wild population of red deer (*Cervus elaphus*). *Proceedings of the Royal Society of London* B 267, 1-6.

Tanaka, Y. (2000). Extinction of populations by inbreeding depression under stochastic environments. *Population Ecology* 42, 55-62.

Vrijenhoek, R. C. (1994). Genetic diversity and fitness in small populations. In *Conservation Genetics* (Eds. V. Loeschcke, J. Tomiuk & S. K. Jain), pp. 37-53. Birkhauser Verlag, Basel, Switzerland.

Westemeier, R. L., Brawn, J. D., Simpson, S. A., Esker, T. L., Jansen, R. W., Walk, J. W., Kershner, E. L., Bouzat, J. L. & Paige, K. N. (1998). Tracking the long-term decline and recovery of an isolated population. *Science* 282, 1695-1698.

Worthington-Wilmer, J. M., Melzer, A., Carrick, F. & Moritz, C. (1993). Low genetic diversity and inbreeding depression in Queensland koalas. *Wildlife Research* 20, 177-188.

6

Impacts of inbreeding on components
of reproductive success

KAREN KOENINGER RYAN, ROBERT C. LACY &
SUSAN W. MARGULIS

INTRODUCTION AND OBJECTIVES

Although inbreeding depression may reduce individual fitness at all life-history stages, empirical investigations have been largely limited to studies of juvenile survival in captive mammals. Numerous studies (e.g. Ralls *et al.*, 1979; Ballou & Ralls, 1982; Ralls & Ballou, 1982; Ralls *et al.*, 1988; Lacy *et al.*, 1993, reviewed by Thornhill, 1993) have demonstrated a reduction in the survival of offspring produced by related mates. This narrow focus, however, has led some scientists (e.g. Shields, 1982) to speculate that inbreeding depression is less important than it appears from the size of the effects found. First, if some offspring will usually be lost due to sib–sib competition, losses due to inbreeding depression may not drastically affect the parent's fitness. Second, it is possible (but still largely untested) that inbreeding could result in enhancements to other components of fitness, thereby offsetting reductions in juvenile survival.

It is not clear, however, that inbreeding depression affects mainly juvenile life-history traits (Charlesworth & Charlesworth, 1987). Rather, the effects of inbreeding on early stages of reproduction and other adult life-history traits have been little investigated, especially in non-domesticated animals. Inbred individuals that survive to adulthood may still suffer reduced fitness via reduced adult survival, poor performance in mating competition, reduced fecundity and less capable parental care. The paucity of data regarding the effect of inbreeding on these adult traits may lead biologists to underestimate the total cost of inbreeding for sexually reproducing species.

The current literature offers little evidence regarding the proximate behavioural and physiological mechanisms underlying inbreeding avoidance and inbreeding depression. However, such data would provide an invaluable resource to biologists who manage small captive and wild populations. In addition to the current practice of using pedigrees to avoid matings between closely related individuals, an understanding of such proximate mechanisms might provide further options for controlling the effects of inbreeding when managers cannot avoid it. Furthermore, mechanisms used by the animals themselves to avoid inbreeding may depress reproduction in small populations consisting largely of related animals, even if no inbreeding occurs. While this would not be inbreeding depression *per se*, it is yet another way in which processes that relate to inbreeding and kinship could have important consequences for managed breeding and conservation programmes.

This chapter has three specific goals. First, we will provide a brief overview of the extensive literature concerning the effects of inbreeding on juvenile life-history traits in non-domesticated vertebrates. Second, we will identify other components of fitness that we consider both important and under-investigated with regard to inbreeding effects. We will provide a more thorough review of the current knowledge in these crucial areas, highlighting our own work concerning inbreeding and fitness in *Peromyscus* mice. Finally, we will suggest priorities for the direction of future research, with the specific aim of providing additional information to conservation biologists who are charged with the task of managing the reproductive effects of inbreeding in small populations of vertebrates.

TERMINOLOGY

We begin with a brief review of the relevant terminology, specifically highlighting the distinction between inbreeding and kinship. The inbreeding coefficient (f) specifies the relatedness of an individual's parents. Inbreeding coefficient describes the proportion of an individual's loci that are homozygous for genes that are identical by descent. The kinship coefficient (k) is a relative property of a pair of individuals. Kinship coefficient describes the probability that a pair of alleles, chosen at random from the same loci in the two individuals, are identical by descent. Kinship, therefore, is a measure of the relatedness between individuals and is equivalent to the inbreeding coefficient of their potential offspring. A brother and sister, for example, would have a kinship coefficient (k) = 0.25; the inbreeding coefficient of their potential offspring would be $f = 0.25$.

Inbreeding and kinship have often been used interchangeably in the conservation literature, and geneticists sometimes describe populations with high average kinship as being inbred. This confusion of terminology results from the fact that inbreeding and kinship effects are often confounded in small isolated populations. When a population has descended from only a few founders, its constituents would typically have large inbreeding coefficients because their ancestors were related. Furthermore, if the population has remained small and isolated, its constituents would also have high kinship coefficients relative to each other. However, if there is inbreeding avoidance or preferential inbreeding, then the extent of inbreeding in individuals can be decoupled from the average kinship among individuals. The poor reproductive performance commonly observed in small populations may result from inbreeding effects, kinship effects or both. Identifying the separate effects of inbreeding and kinship, however, may suggest targeted solutions to reproductive problems faced by small vertebrate populations.

COMPONENTS OF FITNESS

Decreased reproductive rates commonly observed in small isolated wild populations have generally been attributed to inbreeding depression. While this is broadly accurate, the various avenues by which kinship and inbreeding may have led to low population growth rates remain largely unexplored. Fitness can be organised into several components (outlined in Figure 6.1): survival to sexual maturity; adult survival; mate acquisition; fecundity; and parental care. We shall organise our discussion below according to these components.

INBREEDING DEPRESSION OF JUVENILE SURVIVAL

The negative impact of inbreeding on juvenile survival is well documented. In their seminal studies, Ralls and Ballou reported increased juvenile mortality due to inbreeding for many captive mammal populations using data from zoological records (Ralls *et al.*, 1979, 1988; Ballou & Ralls, 1982; Ralls & Ballou, 1982). Individuals were scored as either surviving or not surviving half the estimated time to sexual maturity. Inbred offspring suffered increased mortality during this period. Similar trends have been reported in channel catfish, common iguana, great tits, oldfield mice and many other vertebrates (reviewed by Thornhill, 1993).

COMPONENTS OF LIFETIME REPRODUCTIVE SUCCESS

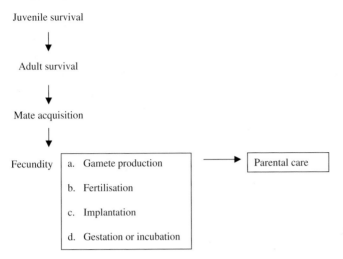

Figure 6.1 In this chapter we review the literature regarding the effects of inbreeding and kinship at each of these components of fitness, drawing attention to those components of lifetime reproductive success that are particularly under-studied.

The sheer volume of evidence that inbreeding can negatively impact juvenile survival has led many scientists to assume prematurely that this is its primary effect. In other words, inbred individuals that survive to adulthood are typically assumed not to suffer from inbreeding depression (Margulis, 1998a). On the contrary, there is still much to learn regarding the importance of inbreeding and kinship for the early stages of reproduction and other adult life-history traits.

INBREEDING DEPRESSION OF ADULT SURVIVAL

Those inbred individuals that survive to adulthood may still suffer inbreeding depression via reduced adult survival. Although the consequences of inbreeding for the survival of inbred adults have received relatively little attention, evidence is building (Pusey & Wolff, 1996). Chen (1993), for example, released inbred and outbred adult land snails into the field. Inbred snails were less likely to be recaptured than their outbred counterparts. Similarly, Keller *et al.* (1994) found that inbred song sparrows were less likely to survive a natural population crash resulting from severe winter weather.

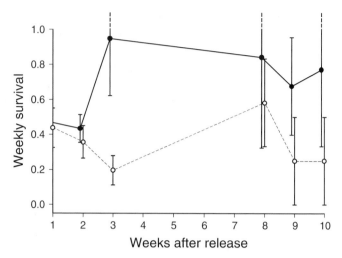

Figure 6.2 Survival of inbred and non-inbred mice (*Peromyscus leucopus*) over 10 weeks. Solid circles represent the mean survivorship values for non-inbred mice, and open circles represent values for inbred mice. Bars represent standard errors of the estimates. Symbols and error bars are slightly offset to show the area of overlap. Non-inbred animals had higher survival than inbred animals during all six time intervals. The ratio of inbred survival to non-inbred survival is 0.558 ± 0.121, averaged over the six estimates shown. None of the survival estimates from single time periods differs significantly between inbred and non-inbred individuals. When the estimates are used as repeated measures of survival for groups of inbred and non-inbred individuals, the overall difference is statistically significant. (From Jiménez *et al.*, 1994.)

Inbred white-footed mice (*Peromyscus leucopus*) also suffered inbreeding depression via reduced adult survival. Jiménez *et al.* (1994) released marked inbred and non-inbred adult white-footed mice into a forested area following several generations of captive breeding. Traps were set on 27 occasions during the 10 weeks following their release. All recaptured mice were identified, weighed and re-released. Inbred males lost body mass throughout the experiment, while non-inbred males regained body mass lost during the first few days following their release. Furthermore, the weekly survival of inbred mice (both male and female) was only 56% of the survival of non-inbred mice (Figure 6.2).

MATE ACQUISITION

Both inbreeding and kinship can affect mate acquisition in small vertebrate populations. Inbred adults may be at a disadvantage in direct intrasexual competition over mates if they are less vigorous than their outbred counterparts. Additionally, 'choosy' members of the opposite sex may prefer outbred mates. Under these competitive circumstances, inbreeding depression might be much more severe than otherwise expected. Kinship between potential mates would affect mate acquisition in systems where individuals actively avoid inbreeding. Specifically, individuals would be expected to choose the least-related mate available. In severe cases, where all available mates are close relatives, animals may delay mating or refuse to mate entirely. Such behaviours could have severe consequences for the growth of small populations.

Effect of inbreeding on mate acquisition

Those inbred individuals that survive to adulthood and remain alive long enough to reproduce may still suffer inbreeding depression if they are less able to acquire a mate. Maynard-Smith (1956) and Sharp (1984) suggested that mate choice and intrasexual competition may favour outbred individuals in many species. If this is indeed a common phenomenon, it represents an additional cost of inbreeding to the reproductive success of inbred adults. Inbreeding reduces competitive male mating ability in *Drosophila melanogaster* (Simmons & Crow, 1977; Miller *et al.*, 1993) and decreases male display rates in guppies (*Poecilia reticulata*) (Farr, 1983). Yet the effect of inbreeding of adults on mate choice and intrasexual competition has received little attention elsewhere, with at least one exception which we describe below.

In a recent study of house mice (*Mus domesticus*), Meagher *et al.* (2000) demonstrated an 81% reduction in male reproductive success due to inbreeding. Inbred ($f = 0.25$) and outbred ($f = 0$) adult mice were released into semi-natural enclosures, and their behaviour and offspring production were monitored. Inbred males had only 19% as many pups that survived to weaning compared with outbred males. The reduced reproductive success of inbred males was attributed to their inability to obtain breeding territories. Fewer inbred males became territorial compared with outbred males. Furthermore, those few inbred males that did secure territories acquired suboptimal territories containing fewer female residents and later producing fewer pups. This inbreeding depression would not have been detected if investigators had focused only on survival of inbred juveniles.

Effect of kinship on mate acquisition

Many animals are known to bias social behaviour according to differences in their kinship to conspecifics (reviewed by Fletcher & Michener, 1987, and Hepper, 1991). Numerous species avoid mating with their first order (parents, full sibs) or second order (half-sibs, aunts/uncles) relatives (e.g. McGuire & Getz, 1981; Dewsbury, 1982; Barnard & Fitzsimons, 1989). Such incest avoidance can sometimes be useful to population managers if it allows sexually mature, opposite-sex relatives to be housed together with little risk of unwanted births.

Although the abilities of animals to detect smaller differences in their kinship to potential mates have been largely untested (but see Slater & Clements, 1981; Bateson, 1982; Barnard & Fitzsimons, 1989; Keane, 1990), they could have important implications for managed breeding. If animals delay or withhold sexual responsiveness toward even distantly related conspecifics, this inbreeding avoidance mechanism could slow the growth of small, isolated populations (Lacy, 2000). We illustrate this possibility with an example from our own experimental studies of inbreeding, kinship and reproduction in a captive population of the monogamous oldfield mouse (*Peromyscus polionotus*) (Ryan, 2000; Ryan & Lacy, 2002). In this population, males chose between distantly related unfamiliar females according to very small differences in their kinship to these potential mates. Moreover, these mate preferences had consequences for their subsequent reproductive success.

Male oldfield mice were allowed to express a social preference between two distantly related, unfamiliar potential mates. The mean kinship coefficient of the choosing male to either of the females was less than the kinship of first cousins. The two females also differed only slightly in their kinship to the choosing male. The mean difference between the two females in their kinship to the choosing male was less than the difference between first cousins and first-cousins-once-removed. Despite these small kinship differences, males consistently favoured the less related of the two females.

These male social preferences between potential mates had further consequences for their subsequent reproductive success (Ryan & Altmann, 2001). Immediately following the social preference tests (above), choosing males were paired either with the female they had preferred or with the female they had rejected. Males that had been paired with their preferred female sired more offspring compared with males that had been paired with their rejected female. Moreover, several of the pairs containing rejected females never produced any offspring, and two of these involved serious fights resulting in the death of one of the mice.

These results suggest an important role for both kinship and mate choice in the design of captive breeding programmes and in the conservation of small natural populations. Not only did oldfield mouse males discriminate based on remarkably small kinship differences, but they apparently used this information to choose the more suitable mate. These unexpected results call for similar investigations in other species (see McLain, 1998; Drickamer *et al.*, 2000). Moreover, they serve as preliminary evidence of the potential benefits of including opportunities for mate choice in managed breeding programmes.

FECUNDITY

Both inbreeding and kinship between mates could affect fecundity in sexually reproducing species. Fecundity is defined here as the number of offspring produced per unit time. Inbred adults may suffer reduced fecundity if they have inferior gamete production, if they are physiologically less capable of fertilisation or implantation, or if they exhibit inadequate gestation (mammals) or incubation (many other vertebrates). Similarly, kinship between mates could affect fecundity if related mates exhibit inferior fertilisation, implantation, gestation or incubation.

Effect of inbreeding on fecundity

Those inbred adults that remain alive long enough to reproduce, and that acquire a mate, might still suffer inbreeding depression via reduced fecundity. Small isolated populations of lion (Wildt *et al.*, 1987), for example, exhibited reduced genetic variation, lower sperm concentrations in semen and higher incidences of sperm abnormalities when compared with a larger, continuous population. This possible inbreeding depression may have been attributable to lower testosterone concentrations. Male Florida panthers were more likely to be unilaterally or bilaterally cryptorchid (having one or both testicles not descended), had lowered testicular and semen volumes, poorer sperm motility and more morphologically abnormal sperm compared with larger, continuously distributed puma populations (Barone *et al.*, 1994). Additionally, captive inbred gazelles exhibited decreases in semen volume, sperm motility and morphology both within and across species (Roldan *et al.*, 1998; Gomendio *et al.*, 2000). Sperm quality was correlated with fluctuating asymmetry, suggesting that a phenotypic trait could be used by females as an indicator of sperm quality and therefore level of inbreeding during mate choice.

Both female and male *Peromyscus polionotus* adults in our laboratory suffered inbreeding depression via reduced fecundity. Margulis & Walsh (2002) compared the sperm counts and testis size of 93 males. Both testis

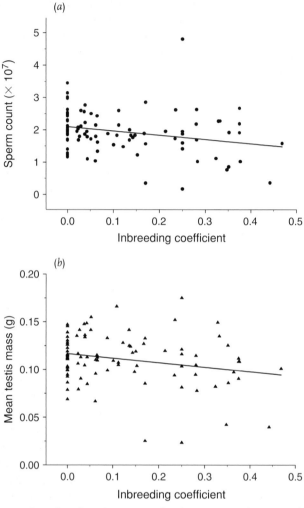

Figure 6.3 Inbreeding depression of male gamete production in oldfield mice (*Peromyscus polionotus*). (a) Sperm count ($F_{1,88} = 6.24$, $P < 0.01$) and (b) testis mass ($F_{1,91} = 5.18$, $P < 0.025$) declined with increasing inbreeding coefficient (f) of adult male oldfield mice. (From Margulis & Walsh, 2002.)

mass and sperm count per gram of testis were negatively correlated with increasing inbreeding coefficient of the male (Figure 6.3). Likewise, inbred female oldfield mice that survived to adulthood also suffered inbreeding depression via reduced fecundity. Inbred dams are less likely to produce litters; when they do reproduce, they are less likely to re-breed to produce a second litter; and the average number of pups born per litter is reduced

(Lacy *et al.*, 1996). In addition, inbred females ($f > 0.10$) displayed a greater latency to the birth of their first litter compared with their outbred ($f < 0.10$) conspecifics, regardless of their kinship to the sire (Margulis & Altmann, 1997; Margulis, 1998a). The specific behavioural or physiological mechanisms responsible for this inbreeding depression in female reproduction have not yet been elucidated. They might include abnormal ovulation, fertilisation, implantation or gestation by inbred females.

Effect of kinship on fecundity

When mates are related (i.e. when their potential offspring are inbred), they often exhibit reduced fecundity. Decreased offspring production by related mates has been demonstrated for several vertebrate species, including geese (Rave *et al.*, 1999), house mice (Krackow & Matuschak, 1991) and oldfield mice (Lacy *et al.*, 1996).

Possible behavioural mechanisms for the reduced fecundity of related mates include latency or refusal to engage in adequate mating behaviour. Those oldfield mice males, for example, that were paired with the (typically less-related) female that they had previously preferred in a social preference test received a greater proportion of receptive lordosis behaviours from their mates (Ryan, 2000).

Possible physiological mechanisms for the reduced fertility of related mates include impaired fertilisation and inferior gestation or incubation. In a small isolated human population, for example, couples sharing alleles at the major histocompatibility complex (MHC) exhibited an increased incidence of recurrent spontaneous abortion (Ober *et al.*, 1992; see Hedrick, Chapter 7, for a discussion of the MHC in relation to breeding). It has been suggested that successful implantation of mammalian embryos requires that the maternal immune system recognise the foetus by its different MHC gene products. Mates that share many MHC alleles by common descent, therefore, would be histoincompatible and more prone to recurrent spontaneous abortion. This maternal–foetal histoincompatibility might provide a mechanism for the reduced fecundity of related mates (reviewed by Jordan & Bruford, 1998).

INBREEDING DEPRESSION OF PARENTAL CARE

Those inbred adults that remain alive long enough to reproduce, that acquire a mate and produce offspring might still suffer inbreeding depression if they exhibit inadequate parental care. Margulis (1998b) observed the parental behaviour of inbred and outbred oldfield mice at regular

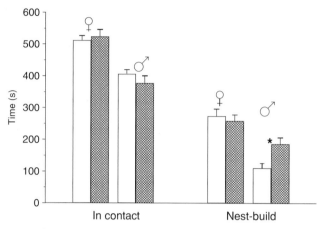

Figure 6.4 The effect of parental inbreeding on parental behaviour during the postpartum period. Seconds (of 600) spent in contact with pups (left) and nest-building (right) for inbred (white) and outbred (hatched) males and females. *P < 0.05. (From Margulis, 1998b.)

intervals following the birth of their litters. Inbred males were less capable fathers compared with their outbred counterparts. Inbred fathers spent less time nest-building compared with outbred fathers; this is an important thermoregulatory function in this monogamous species (Figure 6.4). In contrast, inbred adult females were better mothers than their outbred counterparts; they had shorter latencies to begin nest-building and nuzzled their pups more frequently. However, superior maternal skills only slightly offset the reduced fecundity of inbred females. Inbred females still weaned fewer offspring compared with outbred females.

SUMMARY AND PRIORITIES FOR FUTURE RESEARCH

The deleterious effects of inbreeding for juvenile survival have been known for more than a century (Darwin, 1859). Moreover, the importance of inbreeding depression for the management and conservation of small vertebrate populations has been discussed for more than two decades (e.g. Frankel & Soulé, 1981; Soulé, 1987; Lacy, 1993; Frankham, 1995). Although the primary threats to many species are anthropogenic (e.g. habitat destruction and over-harvesting), inbreeding within the resulting small and isolated populations may increase their susceptibility to these threats and to other stochastic events (Lacy, 1997; Taylor, Chapter 5).

Despite this rather long history, we know surprisingly little regarding the effects of inbreeding on components of fitness other than juvenile survival. Inbred individuals that survive to adulthood might still suffer inbreeding depression via reduced adult survival, inability to obtain mates, reduced fecundity and/or insufficient parental care. The effects of inbreeding on these adult life-history traits have rarely been reported. If inbreeding depression is indeed detrimental to early stages of reproduction and other adult life-history traits, then we have greatly underestimated its impact. In this chapter we have reviewed the limited literature concerning inbreeding depression of these various components of fitness, and we emphasise the need for additional studies of this nature.

Likewise, we still know too little regarding the physiological and behavioural mechanisms that mediate inbreeding avoidance and inbreeding depression. An understanding of such proximate mechanisms might suggest means by which managers can mitigate the deleterious effects of inbreeding when it cannot be avoided. In this chapter we have reviewed the limited literature regarding the proximate physiological and behavioural mechanisms that mediate inbreeding depression, and again we emphasise the need for additional studies of this nature.

The well-documented reduction in juvenile survival with increased inbreeding may represent only a fraction of the risk associated with inbreeding depression. Inbred adults may also suffer reduced survival and reproductive success. There is a need for additional investigations regarding the impact of inbreeding and kinship on adult life-history traits and the mechanisms of these effects. Such studies would provide invaluable information to conservation biologists charged with managing captive and wild populations of threatened species.

ACKNOWLEDGEMENTS

Our studies of kinship and inbreeding in *Peromyscus* have been funded by the Animal Behavior Society, the Chicago Zoological Society, the US National Science Foundation, Sigma Xi and the University of Chicago. We thank Glen Alaks and Allison Walsh for years of animal care and assistance with data collection. We thank the symposium organisers and participants for helpful comments and discussion.

REFERENCES

Ballou, J. & Ralls, K. (1982). Inbreeding and juvenile mortality in small populations of ungulates: a detailed analysis. *Biological Conservation* 24, 239–272.

Barnard, C. J. & Fitzsimmons, J. (1989). Kin recognition and mate choice in mice: fitness consequences of mating with kin. *Animal Behaviour* **38**, 35-40.

Barone, M. A., Roelke, M. E., Howard, J., Brown, J. L., Anderson, A. E. & Wildt, D. E. (1994). Reproductive fitness of the male Florida panther: comparative studies of *Felis concolor* from Florida, Texas, Colorado, Chile, and North American Zoos. *Journal of Mammalogy* **75**, 150-162.

Bateson, P. (1982). Optimal outbreeding. In *Mate Choice* (Ed. P. Bateson), pp. 257-277. Cambridge University Press, Cambridge.

Charlesworth, D. & Charlesworth, B. (1987). Inbreeding depression and its evolutionary consequences . *Annual Review of Ecology and Systematics* **18**, 237-268.

Chen, X. (1993). Comparison of inbreeding and outbreeding in hermaphroditic *Areanta arbustorum* (land snail). *Heredity* **71**, 456-461.

Darwin, C. (1859). *On the Origin of Species by Means of Natural Selection*. Murray, London.

Dewsbury, D. (1982). Avoidance of incestuous breeding between siblings in two species of *Peromyscus* mice. *Biology of Behavior* **7**, 157-169.

Drickamer, L. C., Gowaty, P. A. & Holmes, C. M. (2000). Free female mate choice in house mice affects reproductive success and offspring viability and performance. *Animal Behaviour* **59**, 371-378.

Farr, J. A. (1983). The inheritance of qualitative fitness traits in guppies, *Poecilia reticulata*. *Evolution* **37**, 1193-1209.

Fletcher, D. J. C. & Michener, C. D. (Eds.) (1987). *Kin Recognition in Animals*. Wiley, New York.

Frankel, O. H. & Soulé, M. E. (1981). *Conservation and Evolution*. Cambridge University Press, Cambridge.

Frankham, R. (1995). Inbreeding and extinction: a threshold effect. *Conservation Biology* **9**, 792-799.

Gomendio, M., Cassinello, J. & Roldan, E. R. S. (2000). A comparative study of ejaculate traits in three endangered ungulates with different levels of inbreeding: fluctuating asymmetry as an indicator of reproductive and genetic stress. *Proceedings of the Royal Society of London B* **267**, 875-882.

Hepper, P. (Ed) (1991).*Kin Recognition*. Cambridge University Press, Cambridge.

Jiménez, J. A., Hughes, K. A., Alaks, G., Graham, L. & Lacy, R. C. (1994). An experimental study of inbreeding depression in a natural habitat. *Science* **266**, 271-273.

Jordan, W. C. & Bruford, M. W. (1998). New perspectives on mate choice and the MHC. *Heredity* **80**, 239-245.

Keane, B. (1990). The effect of relatedness on reproductive success and mate choice in the white-footed mouse, *Peromyscus leucopus*. *Animal Behaviour* **39**, 264-273.

Keller, L. F., Arcese, P., Smith, J. N. M., Hochachka, W. M. & Stearns, S. C. (1994). Selection against inbred song sparrows during a natural population bottleneck. *Nature* **372**, 356-357.

Krackow, S. & Matuschak, B. (1991). Mate choice for non-siblings in wild house mice: evidence from a choice test and a reproductive test. *Ethology* **88**, 99-108.

Lacy, R. C. (1993). Impacts of inbreeding in natural and captive populations of vertebrates: implications for conservation. *Perspectives in Biology & Medicine* **36**, 480-496.

Lacy, R. C. (1997). Importance of genetic variation to the viability of mammalian populations. *Journal of Mammalogy* **78**, 320-335.

Lacy, R. C. (2000). Considering threats to the viability of small populations using individual based models. *Ecological Bulletin* **48**, 39-51.

Lacy, R. C., Alaks, G. & Walsh, A. (1996). Hierarchical analysis of inbreeding depression in *Peromyscus polionotus*. *Evolution* **50**, 2187-2200.

Lacy, R. C., Petric, A. M. & Warneke, M. (1993). Inbreeding and outbreeding depression in captive populations of wild species. In *The Natural History of Inbreeding and Outbreeding* (Ed. N. W. Thornhill), pp. 352-374. University of Chicago Press, Chicago.

Margulis, S. W. (1998a). Differential effects of inbreeding at juvenile and adult life history stages in *Peromyscus polionotus*. *Journal of Mammalogy* **79**, 326-336.

Margulis, S. W. (1998b). Relationships among parental inbreeding, parental behaviour and offspring viability in oldfield mice. *Animal Behaviour* **55**, 427-438.

Margulis, S. W. & Altmann, J. (1997). Behavioural risk factors in the reproduction of inbred and outbred oldfield mice. *Animal Behaviour* **54**, 397-408.

Margulis, S. W. & Walsh, A. (2002). The effects of inbreeding on testicular sperm concentration in *Peromyscus polionotus*. *Reproduction, Fertility and Development* **14**, 63-67.

Maynard-Smith, J. (1956). Fertility, mating behavior, and sexual selection in *Drosophila subobscura*. *Journal of Genetics* **54**, 261-279.

McGuire, M. R. & Getz, L. L. (1981). Incest taboo between sibling *Microtus ochrogaster*. *Journal of Mammalogy* **62**, 213-215.

McLain, D. K. (1998). Non-genetic benefits of mate choice: fecundity enhancement and sexy sons. *Animal Behaviour* **55**, 1191-1201.

Meagher, S., Penn, D. J. & Potts, W. (2000). Male-male competition magnifies inbreeding depression in wild house mice. *Proceedings of the National Academy of Sciences USA* **97**, 3324-3329.

Miller, P. S., Glasner, J. & Hedrick, P. W. (1993). Inbreeding depression and male-mating behavior in *Drosophila melanogaster*. *Genetica* **88**, 29-36.

Ober, C., Elias, S., Kostyu, D. D. & Hauck W. W. (1992). Decreased fecundability in Hutterite couples sharing HLA-DR. *American Journal of Human Genetics* **50**, 6-14.

Pusey, A. & Wolff, M. (1996). Inbreeding avoidance in animals. *Trends in Ecology and Evolution* **11**, 201-206.

Ralls, K. & Ballou, J. (1982). Effects of inbreeding on infant mortality in captive primates. *International Journal of Primatology* **3**, 491-505.

Ralls, K., Ballou, J. D. & Templeton, A. (1988). Estimates of lethal equivalents and the cost of inbreeding in mammals. *Conservation Biology* **2**, 185-193.

Ralls, K., Brugger, K. & Ballou, J. (1979). Inbreeding and juvenile mortality in small populations of ungulates. *Science* **206**, 1101-1103.

Rave, E. H., Fleischer, R. C., Duvall, F. & Black, J. M. (1999). Factors influencing reproductive success in captive populations of Hawaiian Geese, *Branta sandviencensis*. *Wildfowl* **49**, 36-44.

Roldan, E. R. S., Cassinello, J., Abaigar, T. & Gomendio, M. (1998). Inbreeding, fluctuating asymmetry and ejaculate quality in an endangered ungulate. *Proceedings of the Royal Society of London B* **265**, 243-248.

Ryan, K. K. (2000). Consequences and causes of mate choice by monogamous male oldfield mice, *Peromyscus polionotus*. Ph.D. dissertation, University of Chicago.

Ryan, K. K. & Altmann, J. (2001). Selection for male choice based primarily on mate compatibility in the oldfield mouse, *Peromyscus polionotus*. *Behavioral Ecology and Sociobiology* **50**, 436–440.

Ryan, K. K. & Lacy, R. L. (2002). Monogamous male mice biased behaviour towards females according to very small differences in kinship. *Animal Behaviour* (in press).

Sharp, P. L. (1984). The effect of inbreeding on competitive male mating ability in *Drosophila melanogaster*. *Genetics* **106**, 601–612.

Shields, W. (1982). *Philopatry, Inbreeding, and the Evolution of Sex*. SUNY Albany Press, Albany, NY.

Simmons, M. J. & Crow, J. F. (1977). Mutations affecting fitness in *Drosophila* populations. *Annual Review of Genetics* **11**, 49–78.

Slater, P. J. B. & Clements, F. A. (1981). Incestuous mating in zebra finches. *Zeitschrift fur Tierpsychologie* **57**, 201–208.

Soulé, M. E. (1987). *Viable Populations for Conservation*. Cambridge University Press, Cambridge.

Thornhill, N. W. (Ed) (1993). *The Natural History of Inbreeding and Outbreeding*. University of Chicago Press, Chicago.

Wildt, D. E., Bush, M., Goodrowe, K. L., Packer, C., Pusey, A. E., Brown, J. L., Joslin, P. & O'Brien, S. J. (1987) Reproductive and genetic consequences of founding isolated lion populations. *Nature* **329**, 328–331.

7

The major histocompatibility complex (MHC) in declining populations: an example of adaptive variation

PHILIP HEDRICK

INTRODUCTION AND OBJECTIVES

Conservation biology has focused on the long-term survival of endangered species. To this end, the primary genetic goals in managed populations of endangered species have been the avoidance of lowered fitness from inbreeding and the maintenance of potentially adaptive genetic variation. Captive breeding programmes of endangered species have specifically been designed both to avoid inbreeding (inbreeding depression) and to retain a given amount of genetic variation for a given period of time, primarily by minimising mean kinship in the population (Ballou & Lacy, 1995). Generally these goals are mutually consistent and may also serve other purposes, such as avoiding adaptation to captive conditions, avoiding accumulation of detrimental variants and maintenance of adaptive variation.

However, as more molecular genetic information accumulates, it is useful to consider whether these new data can be used to manage more effectively genetically captive populations. For example, by using a number of microsatellite loci (over 5000 highly variable genes have been described in humans; Dib et al., 1996), it may be possible to estimate the relationships among founders or other individuals of unknown ancestry. With this information, breeding plans may be modified to reflect previously unknown relationships as well as those known from captive breeding. Relevant to the discussion here, it may be possible to determine the value of maintaining particular genetic variants in a population because of their adaptive significance. Priority could be given to breeding individuals or groups of individuals that would maintain these adaptive variants.

Over the past 30 years, there has been extensive debate about the extent of genetic variation that is maintained by selection. Although there is general agreement that adaptive genetic change is fundamental to evolution and that advantageous variants are selected to high frequency in populations, it appears that most molecular genetic variation is primarily influenced by selection against detrimental variants and non-selective factors, such as genetic drift, mutation and gene flow. Within a population, the extent and pattern of molecular variation is generally consistent with a balance predicted by a reduction by genetic drift from finite population size and an increase by mutation generating new mutations (i.e. the neutral model of evolution). Even if selection is acting on the variation at a given gene, when the population is small, as it is for many endangered species or captive populations, then genetic drift may have a greater effect than selection. In fact, neutrality of genetic variants is generally defined as when the selection coefficient $s < 1/(2N)$ where N is the effective population size (Kimura, 1983). For example, if the selection coefficient is 0.01, say 1% selection against a recessive homozygote, then the above relation suggests that selection is ineffective against this allele when the effective population size is less than 50. Because many captive populations have small effective population sizes, genetic variation may be effectively neutral today, rather than disadvantageous (or perhaps advantageous) as when population sizes were previously larger.

The extensive molecular data available today provide new methods to determine whether selection has operated in the past on a given gene. For example, rather than being able to measure the impact of selection in a single generation by determining differential viability or reproduction (Hedrick & Kim, 2000), the cumulative effect over many generations may be observed in analysis of DNA variation (Satta et al., 1994). I will discuss two such applications below, the rate of non-synonymous (amino-acid changing) to synonymous substitutions and the pattern of sequence variation within and between species, but a number of other such approaches are now available (e.g. Li, 1997; Kreitman, 2000; Nei & Kumar, 2000). However, these techniques evaluate all the variation at a locus and do not generally allow identification of specific selected alleles.

Here I will introduce a system, the genes in the major histocompatibility complex (MHC), for which variation is thought to be adaptive. I will then summarise the various balancing selection models that have been proposed to operate on MHC variation with an emphasis on the role these genes play in pathogen recognition. Then I will give a summary of our data on MHC genes from two endangered species, the Arabian oryx and the Mexican wolf. Finally, I will discuss potential approaches for the maintenance of MHC variation, or other adaptive variation, in captive populations in which matings are determined by management decisions.

Major histocompatibility complex (MHC)

Probably the most widely accepted example of loci that are under adaptive selection are those in the tightly linked genes of the major histocompatibility complex (MHC) (see Hedrick, 1994; Hedrick & Kim, 2000, for summaries of evidence supporting the role of selection for MHC genes). The MHC has been found in all vertebrates except jawless fishes (Flajnik *et al.*, 1999), and in humans (where it is known as the HLA) it includes the most polymorphic loci known (Parham & Ohta, 1996). Recently the complete sequence of the 3.6 megabase base pair HLA region has been completed (MHC Sequencing Consortium, 1999; Beck & Trowsdale, 2000). In this region there are 224 identified genes (128 are predicted to be expressed), the most gene-dense region in the human genome, of which approximately 40% are involved with the immune system. The size, function and complexity of the human MHC are probably indicative of the general properties of the MHC in other mammals.

The best known, and probably the most important, of the MHC genes are the class I and class II genes, originally discovered because of their role in success or failure of organ transplants in humans and also implicated in a number of autoimmune diseases. The fundamental role of class I genes is to recognise antigens from intracellular proteins, including those from viruses. The primary role of class II genes is to recognise antigens from extracellular proteins, including those from bacteria and other pathogens and parasites. These functions allow the immune system to determine whether foreign proteins are present to start an immune response against the pathogens or parasites that have invaded the organism. Although it has long been thought that MHC variation allows recognition of various pathogens, only in recent years has extensive evidence documenting this role been accumulated (Hedrick & Kim, 2000). For example, variants of the HLA (as the MHC in humans is known) have been found to be important in resistance to malaria (Hill *et al.*, 1991), hepatitis (Thurz *et al.*, 1997) and HIV (Carrington *et al.*, 1999).

Obviously resistance to disease is important to endangered species because of the threat of various diseases from introduced (or new) parasites or pathogens, many of which are harboured by livestock, pets, humans or non-endangered species (Lyles & Dobson, 1993; Laurenson *et al.*, 1998; Murray *et al.*, 1999). In addition, O'Brien & Evermann (1988) suggested that low MHC variation in an organism might result in high susceptibility to parasites (however, see Edwards & Potts, 1996; Mikko *et al.*, 1999). Black (1992) also suggested that low HLA in aboriginal peoples might be in part responsible for the devastating effect of diseases introduced by colonising Europeans. To respond effectively to these new infectious disease threats, it is necessary to have the appropriate MHC resistance, whether it is a general level of genetic variation at the MHC or specific alleles that recognise and give resistance to the threatening pathogens.

Balancing selection at the MHC

A number of selection models has been proposed to maintain genetic variation at MHC genes (Hedrick & Kim, 2000; Meyer & Thomson, 2001). Perhaps the most generally accepted ones are those that influence resistance to infectious diseases, primarily heterozygote advantage, frequency-dependent selection and variable selection in time and space. It is not clear which of these models is most appropriate (or if all three have a role at times), and the three types of balancing selection may be overlapping. For example, a frequency-dependent model in which rare alleles have a high fitness, may also have a constant advantage for heterozygotes. With frequency-dependent models a common allele may have been selectively important in the past, so that rarity itself may not be a good indicator of selective relevance. Further, it is likely that the extent of selection on an allele under a heterozygote advantage or a frequency-dependent model varies over both space and time because of spatial and temporal variation in parasites or pathogens.

Various researchers have suggested that genetic variation at MHC loci is maintained by heterozygote advantage because heterozygotes can recognise a larger suite of pathogens than can homozygotes (Doherty & Zingernagel, 1975; Hedrick & Kim, 2000) and therefore have higher fitness. If the constituent alleles were more divergent, then the diversity of pathogens recognised by heterozygotes may be even larger than if the constituent alleles are similar (Ohta, 1991). In other words, the very large amino-acid divergence among the remaining three Arabian oryx MHC alleles or the three groups of Mexican wolf alleles may be advantageous for recognition of a diverse array of pathogens.

There is some evidence that the MHC is important in mate selection (Brown & Eklund, 1994; Penn & Potts, 1999; Genin *et al.*, 2000) and maternal–foetal interactions (Alberts & Ober, 1993; Ober *et al.*, 1998; Fernandez *et al.*, 1999), although other studies do not support the universality of these effects (Hedrick & Black, 1997; Paterson & Pemberton, 1997).

For example, some researchers believe that individuals choose their mates based on MHC differences in order to avoid mating with their kin (Edwards & Potts, 1996; Penn & Potts, 1999). In theory, if the extent of variation at the MHC becomes reduced and individuals were MHC similar, then the factors influencing mate choice might be altered. Also, there is some evidence that for normal implantation and development of the foetus, the mother and foetus should differ at the MHC. If there was low MHC variation, then this process may also be altered.

The fundamental role of variation in the MHC appears to be in pathogen recognition but this high variability may be utilised to identify differences either for mate choice or in foetal recognition. In other words, these secondary aspects of MHC selection may occur, but they may not be fundamental to the maintenance of the high polymorphism at the MHC. For the models that have been used for both mate selection and maternal–foetal interaction, heterozygotes and homozygotes are treated as two homogeneous classes (Hedrick & Thomson, 1988; Hedrick 1992). In other words, maintenance of genetic variation by minimising mean kinship should also maintain the highest level of heterozygosity so that these modes of selection may continue. Of course, mate selection or maternal–foetal interaction may depend on the level of difference, not just difference, of the MHC alleles involved.

STATE OF THE ART

MHC variation in endangered species

Because of their potential adaptive significance, there have been recent efforts to examine MHC variation in various endangered species. Here, recent studies in the Arabian oryx and the Mexican wolf, examining the variation in a class II *DRB* gene, are discussed. For the homologous gene in humans, 221 alleles have been documented (Marsh *et al.*, 2000) and 30 different alleles were identified in a sample of cattle (Mikko & Andersson, 1995). In contrast, for species that have been through known bottlenecks, as in many endangered species, the amount of MHC variation is significantly less. For example, in American bison, which went through a bottleneck at the end of the nineteenth century, Mikko *et al.* (1997) found nine alleles in a sample of 20 animals. In the Przewalski's horse, in which the entire present species is descended from 13 founders, Hedrick *et al.* (1999) observed four alleles at one locus and two alleles at a second locus in a sample of 14 individuals.

Arabian oryx

The Arabian oryx (*Oryx leucoryx*), one of only three species of oryx, historically ranged throughout the deserts of the Arabian Peninsula. However, extensive hunting pressure in the 1960s and 1970s led to its extinction in the wild in 1972 (Henderson, 1974). In the 1960s, a captive breeding programme was initiated, and 18 founders have contributed to the over 2000 animals world-wide today (Marshall *et al.*, 1999). In the captive population there have been several outbreaks of infectious disease, including tuberculosis in 1986 at the Taif, Saudi Arabia facility in which 22 out of 57 (38.6%) Arabian oryx died (Ostrowski *et al.*, 1998) and foot-and-mouth disease in several facilities (Marshall, 1998).

Hedrick *et al.* (2000a) found that, in a sample of 57 Arabian oryx, there were only three different *DRB* alleles in the frequencies 0.737, 0.228 and 0.035. The observed genotypic numbers are not significantly different from that expected under Hardy–Weinberg proportions, although there were slightly more heterozygotes observed than expected. Brown *et al.* (1993) documented the amino-acid positions for a *DRB* molecule in humans thought to be important in the antigen-binding site (ABS). Of the 16 ABS amino-acid positions, 12 (75%) are variable over the three Arabian oryx alleles, while for the remaining 62 amino-acid positions examined, not thought to interact with the antigen-binding site, only nine (14.5%) are polymorphic. Figure 7.1 shows the expected heterozygosity for the variable amino-acid positions based on allele frequencies. The amino-acid positions with highest heterozygosities, 0.404, are three ABS positions with three different amino acids. Overall, the 16 ABS positions have an average heterozygosity of 0.245 per site while the non-ABS positions have an average heterozygosity of 0.045, only 18.4% as much.

For genes that are not under selection, the rate of substitution should be the same for non-synonymous and synonymous substitutions (Li, 1997; Nei & Kumar, 2000). It has been found for ABS positions in the MHC that the rate of non-synonymous substitution is actually higher than the rate of synonymous substitution, suggesting that there is selection favouring new amino-acid variants (e.g. Hughes & Nei, 1988). We also found this pattern for the Arabian oryx sequences; the ratio of non-synonymous to synonymous substitution rates for the ABS positions is 2.78, significantly greater than unity. The importance of this observation, and that of the high heterozygosity for the ABS sites discussed above, is that selection favouring amino-acid differences has been occurring in Arabian oryx for many generations.

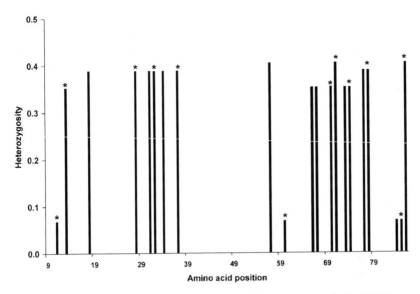

Figure 7.1 The amino-acid heterozygosity for different positions in the MHC molecule for the Arabian oryx (Hedrick *et al.*, 2000a). The polymorphic positions indicated with an asterisk are those that are thought to interact with the antigen binding site.

Although the number of alleles surviving in the Arabian oryx is small, the difference between these alleles is large with an average difference in amino acid sequence of 19.2%. When selection acted to produce these effects is not known, but the reports of disease outbreaks in captive Arabian oryx populations suggest that some of this pattern may be partly the result of selection in recent generations.

Mexican wolf

The grey wolf (*Canis lupus*) once had a distribution throughout much of the Northern Hemisphere. However, hunting and eradication programmes in the late nineteenth and throughout the twentieth centuries resulted in its extirpation from most of its original range. In the United States (excluding Alaska), the remaining wolves have been listed as endangered, and the Mexican grey wolf subspecies, *C. l. baileyi*, was listed as endangered in 1976. Mexican wolves are thought to have been extirpated from the United States, and greatly reduced in Mexico, by 1970. Because there have been no confirmed sightings in 20 years throughout their ancestral range, they are thought to be extinct in the wild.

The extant Mexican wolves are in captivity, except for approximately 25 individuals that have been reintroduced into eastern Arizona and western New Mexico over the past few years. The three captive Mexican wolf lineages – McBride (formerly known as Certified), Ghost Ranch and Aragon – were all found to be authentic Mexican wolves (Garcia-Moreno *et al.*, 1996; Hedrick *et al.*, 1997). The combined captive population is now descended from seven founders – 3, 2 and 2 – from the McBride, Ghost Ranch and Aragon lineages, respectively, although all of the wolves released to date descend entirely from the three founders of the McBride lineage.

In the Mexican wolves, we found two *DRB* alleles in the McBride lineage, one allele in the Ghost Ranch lineage and three alleles in the Aragon lineage. The only overlap in alleles between lineages was the Ghost Ranch allele, which was also the most frequent allele in the Aragon lineage. The observed heterozygosities were larger than that expected for both the McBride and Aragon lineages, although they were not statistically significant. The overall pattern of variation was generally similar to that found in the Arabian oryx in that most of the variation was in the amino acids of the ABS, and the rate of non-synonymous to synonymous substitutions was significantly greater than unity. However, the samples of Mexican wolves, founded from a total of only seven animals, and with a history of inbreeding within lineages, have five different alleles for the *DRB* locus.

For context, MHC variation in samples of grey wolves, red wolves and coyotes were also examined. Figure 7.2 presents a neighbour-joining tree with the 21 *DRB* sequences that we found in these taxa. The sequences from any one taxon are generally widely dispersed in the tree and, in almost all cases, different sequences from other taxa are most closely related to each of the sequences. The five alleles from the Mexican wolf were in three different groups, allele *Calu-1*, alleles *Calu-4* and *Calu-5*, and alleles *Calu-2* and *Calu-3*, spread throughout the tree. Alleles *Calu-4* and *Calu-5* differed by only one amino acid (one nucleotide) while alleles *Calu-2* and *Calu-3* differed by three amino acids (six nucleotides). The average percentage of amino-acid differences between these groups was 16.1% and the average percentage of nucleotide differences was 8.2%.

The intermingling of MHC alleles from different species within a phylogenetic tree from related taxa has been found in multiple organisms (see Edwards & Hedrick, 1998, for discussion). Often the closest sequence for MHC genes is from another species and not from another allele within the same species, as would be expected when there is no differential selection (neutrality). Klein (1987) termed this phenomenon 'trans-species polymorphism' and suggested that the variability from an ancestral species is

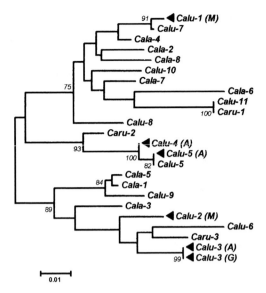

Figure 7.2 A neighbour-joining tree giving the relationships for the 21 sequences found in Mexican wolves and related taxa (Hedrick *et al.*, 2000b). The triangles indicate the six different Mexican wolf sequences, the vertical lines indicate identical sequences found in different lineages of the Mexican wolf (M, McBride; G, Ghost Ranch; and A, Aragon) or taxa, and the numbers indicate bootstrap significance values of 75 or greater.

retained even when the species splits into two or more descendant species. The mechanism thought to be responsible for the retention of ancestral variation is some sort of balancing selection and results in alleles in different species having closest ancestry to alleles in different species. We found this pattern for both the Mexican wolf and the Arabian oryx, providing further evidence that selection has operated in these organisms for an extended period.

Pedigree approaches to maintaining MHC Variation

As mentioned above, the most commonly accepted approach to maintaining genetic variation in a captive population is to minimise mean kinship (Ballou & Lacy, 1995), and this general approach appears to be the best to maintain genetic diversity (Haig *et al.*, 1990), presumably for MHC as well as other loci. However, all populations contain some alleles in low frequency and over the years there have been proposals to maintain such rare alleles in a population. Hedrick *et al.* (1986) warned that a breeding scheme designed to maintain rare alleles would be operationally extremely difficult as well as counter-productive for the maintenance of genetic variation in the rest of the genome. In particular, selection for any specific allele may result in a faster loss of variation at most of the other loci in the genome (Haig *et al.*, 1990). In addition, Hedrick *et al.* (1986) pointed out that it would, in principle, be difficult to determine what rare alleles are advantageous, neutral, or detrimental. Models of neutral evolution predict that populations will have, at low frequency, alleles that are adaptively equivalent to more common ones. Detrimental alleles maintained in a population by a balance between purifying selection and mutation will also be present in low frequency. Advantageous variants may also be in low frequency if the environment in which they are favoured has not been available recently and there is some cost to their advantage in other environments. However, advantageous alleles may be in high frequency because of selection favouring their increase (e.g. Hill *et al.*, 1991). Accordingly, there is no obvious way to differentiate rare alleles that are advantageous, neutral or disadvantageous, or even to know which category is the most common among rare alleles.

Allendorf (1986) suggested that the 'number of alleles remaining is important for the long-term response to selection and survival of populations and species'. Hughes (1991), in a more specific proposal, said that 'the most clear-cut examples of loci illustrating heterozygote advantage are at MHC loci', and as a result he advocated a breeding programme to save any MHC 'alleles declining in frequency by drift by selective breeding'. The wisdom of the suggestion that captive-bred animals be managed for MHC variation was questioned by Gilpin & Wills (1991), Miller & Hedrick (1991) and Vrijenhoek & Leberg (1991).

A major concern of Miller & Hedrick (1991) about Hughes's proposal was that it is hard to determine which MHC alleles are advantageous compared with those that are neutral or even detrimental (many MHC alleles in humans are associated with autoimmune diseases). However, it may be possible to make an educated guess as to the importance of particular MHC alleles given the selection model of Ohta (1991) in which heterozygotes that differ greatly in amino-acid sequence have higher fitness. For example, the three Arabian oryx MHC alleles found by Hedrick *et al.* (2000a) are extremely divergent, and nearly all of the nucleotide differences result in amino-acid differences at the ABS. This suggests a situation in which the different variants contribute differential pathogen resistance, and that maintenance of these variants by selective breeding may be important. In this instance, selection for the increase of the least frequent of the three alleles may be warranted. For the Mexican wolf, the five alleles fell into three groups in which nearly all of the differences were also amino-acid differences in the ABS (Hedrick *et al.*, 2000b). Although two groups of sequences are represented in the McBride lineage, which comprises most of the captive population, the third group (*Calu-4* and *Calu-5* in Figure 7.2) is present only in the Aragon lineage and comprises 50% of that lineage. The Aragon lineage ancestry represents only about 10% of the total population so this sequence group is about 5% of the total. Therefore, a case could be made for a selective increase of this allele group.

Another major concern of Miller & Hedrick (1991) was that selection for MHC variants would sacrifice the maintenance of variation in the rest of the genome. Haig *et al.* (1990), Hedrick & Miller (1994) and Miller (1995) investigated the effects of favouring rare alleles in pedigree management. Taken to the extreme, if the contribution of an individual with a rare allele is greatly increased, then the pedigree will disproportionately reflect the ancestral contributions of that individual. If that individual descends from only a few founders, then the pedigree will retain less diversity than would be possible if the pedigree were managed to maximise mean kinship.

Miller (1995) examined the effect of selecting for a rare allele in the pedigrees of the Przewalski's horse and California condor captive breeding programmes. In neither of these species was there information about the MHC (however, see Hedrick *et al.*, 1999); so as surrogates in the Przewalski's horse population a transferrin allele present in only one individual (and an offspring) was used, and in the California condor population a DNA fingerprint pattern present in only one individual (and two deceased founders) was used. Three management scenarios were compared: the minimisation of mean kinship (the present-day recommended approach), a 'control' (the actual matings that were made in the populations before modern management approaches were employed), and the rare-allele, mean kinship approach. In this last, the individual with the rare allele was mated multiple times in order to increase the representation of the rare allele but was always mated with individuals chosen to minimise mean kinship. In other words, half of the genetic contribution to the progeny represented the strategy of increasing the rare allele with the other half minimising mean kinship.

As an example of the effects of these different management strategies, Figure 7.3 gives the change in mean kinship for the early Przewalski's horse pedigree as one to eight progeny are added to the population (Miller, 1995). Note that using the mean kinship criterion lowers the mean kinship as each individual is added and results in a 19% decrease after eight progeny are added. This can be compared to the control, the next eight progeny actually produced, which resulted in no change in the mean kinship. Selecting for rare alleles was similar in effect to the control, suggesting that the half of

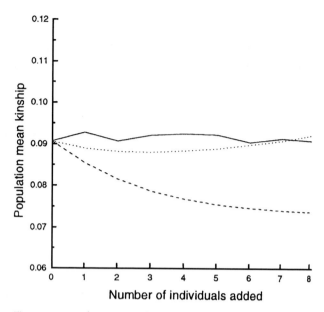

Figure 7.3 Population mean kinship for three management strategies; mean kinship (-----), control (———) and rare-allele, mean kinship (······) as one to eight individuals are added to the Przewalski's horse pedigree (Miller, 1995).

the contribution that increased the rare allele was detrimental to mean kinship, but that the other half selected for mean kinship compensated for this negative effect.

Overall, Miller (1995) found that the rare-allele, mean kinship approach was poorer in maintaining genetic diversity than management for mean kinship. This effect depended upon the depth and complexity of the pedigree and the number of living animals. For example, if the individual with the rare allele also contained ancestral contributions from under-represented founders, then the increase in the rare allele also increased the contributions from these founders. In this case, the management increasing the rare allele appears to have a less negative effect than if the individual with the rare allele had the mean population contribution from the founders. Finally, if it is decided to increase the frequency of a rare allele, such as the MHC alleles discussed in the Arabian oryx and Mexican wolf studies above, Miller (1995) suggested that (1) the mates for the rare allele carrier be chosen on the mean kinship criterion, (2) the programme be limited in scope with only a small number of rare-allele matings and (3) the genetic structure of the pedigree be monitored carefully during the programme.

PRIORITIES FOR THE FUTURE

The extensive molecular data now being accumulated will add a new dimension to management of endangered species. With these data, we may be able to make several important advances in understanding the evolutionary significance of specific genetic variants and consequently modify management actions to reflect this knowledge. For example, we may be able to identify important genetic variants, not only for the MHC, but also for other traits of adaptive significance. In addition, we may be able to identify detrimental alleles (some of these could also be MHC variants) and develop approaches to reduce their contributions (Laikre, 1999; Lacy, 2000). However, all of these applications should be made carefully and in the context of accepted pedigree management.

CONCLUSION

The MHC is widely accepted to contain genes of important adaptive significance. Recently, the complete MHC sequence has been obtained in humans and other studies have examined MHC variation in endangered species. The accepted management approaches for captive populations, such as minimising mean kinship, should also retain MHC diversity. However, if specific MHC alleles are known or suspected to be important for adaptation, then an approach to increase these alleles may be considered. Miller (1995) showed that pairing individuals with a rare allele to mates selected to minimise mean kinship reduces the overall negative effects of increasing rare alleles. The future will present opportunities to utilise molecular genetic data in population management, but this information should be used carefully and in the context of accepted approaches to retain diversity in the remainder of the genome.

ACKNOWLEDGEMENTS
Support of the US National Science Foundation and the Ullman Professorship are appreciated.

REFERENCES
Alberts, S. C. & Ober, C. (1993). Genetic variability in the major histocompatibility complex: a review of non-pathogen-mediated selective mechanisms. *Yearbook of Physical Anthropology* **36**, 71–89.
Allendorf, F. W. (1986). Genetic drift and loss of alleles versus heterozygosity. *Zoo Biology* **5**, 181–190.

Ballou, J. D. & Lacy, R. C. (1995). Identifying genetically important individuals for management of genetic diversity in pedigreed populations. In *Population Management for Survival and Recovery* (Eds. J. D. Ballou, M. Gilpin & T. J. Foose), pp. 76-111. Columbia University Press, New York.

Beck, S. & Trowsdale, J. (2000). The human Major Histocompatibility Complex: lessons from the DNA sequence. *Annual Review of Genomics and Human Genetics* 1, 117-137.

Black, F. J. (1992). Why did they die? *Science* 258, 1739-1740.

Brown, J. H., Jardetzky, T. S., Gorga, J. C., Stern, L. J., Uban, R. G., Strominger, J. L. & Wiley, D. C. (1993). Three-dimensional structure of the human class II histocompatibility antigen HLA-DR1. *Nature* 364, 33-39.

Brown, J. L. & Eklund, A. (1994). Kin recognition and the major histocompatibility complex: an integrative review. *American Naturalist* 143, 435-461.

Carrington, M., Nelson, G. W., Martin, M. P., Kissner, T., Vlahov, D., Goedert, J. J., Kaslow, R., Buchbinder, S., Hoots, K. & O'Brien, S. J. (1999). HLA and HIV-1: heterozygote advantage and B^*35-Cw^*04 disadvantage. *Science* 238, 1748-1752.

Dib, C., Faure, S., Fizames, C., Samson, D., Drouot, N., Vignal, A., Millasseau, P., Marc, S., Hazan, J., Seboun, E., Lathrop, M., Gyapay, G., Morissette, J. & Weissenbach, J. (1996). A comprehensive map of the human genome based on 5,264 microsatellites. *Nature* 380, 152-154.

Doherty, P. & Zingernagel, R. (1975). Enhanced immunologic surveillance in mice heterozygous at the H2 complex. *Nature* 245, 50-52.

Edwards, S. & Hedrick, P. W. (1998). Evolution and ecology of MHC molecules: from genomics to sexual selection. *Trends in Ecology and Evolution* 13, 305-311.

Edwards, S. V. & Potts, W. K. (1996). Polymorphism of genes in the major histocompatibility complex (MHC): implications for conservation genetics of vertebrates. In *Molecular Genetic Approaches in Conservation* (Eds. T. B. Smith & R. K. Wayne), pp. 214-237. Oxford University Press, New York.

Fernandez, N., Cooper, J., Sprinks, M., AbdElrahman, M., Fiszer, D., Kurpisz, M. & Dealtry, G. (1999). A critical review of the role of the major histocompatibility complex in fertilization, preimplantation development and feto-maternal interactions. *Human Reproduction Update* 5, 234-248

Flajnik, M. F., Ohta, Y., Namikawa-Yamada, C. & Nonaka, M. (1999). Insight into the primordial MHC from studies in ectothermic vertebrates. *Immunological Reviews* 167, 59-67.

Garcia-Moreno, J., Roy, M. S., Geffen, E. & Wayne, R. K. (1996). Relationships and genetic purity of the endangered Mexican wolf based on analysis of microsatellite loci. *Conservation Biology* 10, 396-405.

Genin, E., Ober, C., Weitkamp, L. & Thomson, G. (2000). A robust test for assortative mating. *European Journal of Human Genetics* 8, 119-124.

Gilpin, M. &, Wills, C. (1991). MHC and captive breeding: a rebuttal. *Conservation Biology* 5, 554-555.

Haig, S. M., Ballou J. D. & Derrickson, S. R. (1990). Management options for preserving genetic diversity: reintroduction of Guam rails to the wild. *Conservation Biology* 4, 290-300.

Hedrick, P. W. (1992). Female choice and variation in the major histocompatibility complex. *Genetics* 132, 575-581.

Hedrick, P. W. (1994). Evolutionary genetics of the major histocompatibility complex. *American Naturalist* 143, 945-964.

Hedrick, P. W. & Black, F. L. (1997). HLA and mate selection: no evidence in South Amerindians. *American Journal of Human Genetics* 61, 505-511.

Hedrick, P. W. & Kim, T. J. (2000). Genetics of complex polymorphisms: parasites and maintenance of the major histocompatibility complex variation. In *Evolutionary Genetics: From Molecules to Morphology* (Eds. R. S. Singh & C. B. Krimbas), pp. 204-234. Cambridge University Press, Cambridge.

Hedrick, P. W. & Miller, P. S. (1994). Rare alleles, MHC and captive breeding. In *Conservation Genetics* (Eds. V. Loeschcke, J. Tomiuk & S. K Jain), pp. 187-204. Birkhauser, Basel, Switzerland.

Hedrick, P. W. & Thomson, G. (1988). Maternal-fetal interactions and the maintenance of HLA polymorphism. *Genetics* 119, 205-212.

Hedrick, P. W., Brussard, P. R., Allendorf, F. W., Beardmore, J. A. & Orzack, S. (1986). Protein variation, fitness, and captive propagation. *Zoo Biology* 5, 91-100.

Hedrick, P. W., Lee, R. & Parker, K. M. (2000b). Major histocompatibility complex (MHC) variation in the endangered Mexican wolf and related canids. *Heredity* 85, 617-624.

Hedrick, P. W., Miller, P. S., Geffen, E. & Wayne, R. (1997). Genetic evaluation of the three captive Mexican wolf lineages. *Zoo Biology* 16, 47-69.

Hedrick, P. W., Parker, K. M., Gutierrez-Espeleta, G. A., Rattink, A. & Lievers, K. (2000a). Major histocompatibility complex (MHC) variation in the Arabian oryx. *Evolution* 54, 2145-2151.

Hedrick, P. W., Parker, K. M., Miller, E. L. & Miller, P. S. (1999). Major histocompatibility complex variation in the endangered Przewalski's horse. *Genetics* 152, 1701-1710.

Henderson, D. S. (1974). Were they the last Arabian oryx? *Oryx* 12, 347-350.

Hill, A. V. S., Allsop, C. E. M., Kwiatdowski, D., Antsey, N. M., Twumasi, P., Rowe, P. A., Bennett, S., Brewster, D., McMichael, A. J. & Greenwood, B. M. (1991). Common West African HLA antigens are associated with protection from severe malaria. *Nature* 352, 595-600.

Hughes, A. L. (1991). MHC polymorphism and the design of captive breeding programs. *Conservation Biology* 5, 249-251.

Hughes, A. L. & Nei, M. (1988). Pattern of nucleotide substitution at major histocompatibility complex class I loci reveals overdominant selection. *Nature* 335, 167-170.

Kimura, M. (1983). *The Neutral Theory of Molecular Evolution*. Cambridge University Press, Cambridge.

Klein, J. (1987). Origin of major histocompatibility complex polymorphism: the trans-species hypothesis. *Human Immunology* 19, 155-162.

Kreitman, M. (2000). Methods to detect selection in populations with applications to the human. *Annual Review of Genomics and Human Genetics* 1, 539-559.

Lacy, R. C. (2000). Should we select genetic alleles in our conservation breeding programs? *Zoo Biology* 19, 279-282.

Laikre, L. (1999). Hereditary defects and conservation genetic management of captive populations. *Zoo Biology* 18, 81-99.

Laurenson, K., Sillero-Zubiri, C., Thompson, H., Shiferaw, F., Thirgood, S. & Malcom, J. (1998). Disease as a threat to endangered species: Ethiopian wolves, domestic dogs and canine pathogens. *Animal Conservation* 1, 273-280.

Li, W.-H. (1997). *Molecular Evolution*. Sinauer Associates, Sunderland, MA.

Lyles, A. M. & Dobson, A. P. (1993). Infectious disease and intensive management: population dynamics, threatened hosts, and their parasites. *Journal of Zoo and Wildlife Medicine* 24, 315-326.

Marsh, S. G. E., Parham, P. & Barber, L. D. (2000). *The HLA Facts Book*. Academic Press, London.

Marshall, T. C. (1998). Inbreeding and fitness in wild ungulates. Ph.D. thesis, University of Edinburgh.

Marshall, T. C., Sunnucks, P., Spalton, J. A., Greth, A. & Pemberton, J. M. (1999). Use of genetic data for conservation management: the case of the Arabian oryx. *Animal Conservation* 2, 269-278.

Meyer, D. & Thomson, G. (2001). How selection shapes variation of the human major histocompatibility complex: a review. *Annals of Human Genetics* 65, 1-26.

MHC Sequencing Consortium (1999). Complete sequence and gene map of a human major histocompatibility complex (MHC). *Nature* 401, 921-923.

Mikko, S. & Andersson, L. (1995). Extensive MHC class II DRB3 diversity in African and European cattle. *Immunogenetics* 42, 408-413.

Mikko, S., Roed, K., Schmutz, S. & Andersson, L. (1999). Monomorphism and polymorphism at Mhc DRB loci in domestic and wild ruminants. *Immunological Reviews* 167, 169-178.

Mikko, S., Spencer, M., Morris, B., Stabile, S., Basu, T., Stormont, C. & Andersson. L. (1997). A comparative analysis of the Mhc *DRB3* polymorphism in the American Bison (*Bison bison*). *Journal of Heredity* 8, 499-503.

Miller, P. S. (1995). Selective breeding programs for rare alleles: examples from the Przewalski's horse and California condor pedigrees. *Conservation Biology* 9, 1262-1273.

Miller, P. S. & Hedrick, P. W. (1991). MHC polymorphism and the design of captive breeding programs: simple solutions are not the answer. *Conservation Biology* 5, 556-558.

Murray, D. L., Kapke, C. A., Evermann, J. F. & Fuller, T. K. (1999). Infectious disease and the conservation of free-ranging large carnivores. *Animal Conservation* 2, 241-254.

Nei, M. & Kumar, S. (2000). *Molecular Evolution and Phylogenetics*. Oxford University Press, New York.

Ober, C., Hyslop, T., Elias, S., Weitkamp, L. R. & Hauck, W. W. (1998). Human leukocyte antigen matching and fetal loss: results of a 10-year prospective study. *Human Reproduction* 13, 33-38.

O'Brien, S. J. & Evermann, J. F. (1988). Interactive influence of infectious disease and genetic diversity in natural populations. *Trends in Ecology and Evolution* 3, 254-259.

Ohta, T. (1991). Role of diversifying selection and gene conversion in evolution of major histocompatibility complex loci. *Proceedings of the National Academy of Sciences USA* 88, 6716-6720.

Ostrowski, S., Bedin, E., Lenain, D. M. & Abuzinada, A. H. (1998). Ten years of Arabian oryx conservation breeding in Saudi Arabia – achievements and regional perspectives. *Oryx* **32**, 209-222.

Parham, P. & Ohta T. (1996). Population biology of antigen presentation by MHC class I molecules. *Science* **272**, 67-74.

Paterson, S. & Pemberton, J. M. (1997). No evidence for major histocompatibility complex-dependent mating patterns in a free-living ruminant population. *Proceedings of the Royal Society of London B* **264**, 1813-1819.

Penn, D. J. & Potts, W. K. (1999). The evolution of mating preferences and major histocompatibility complex genes. *American Naturalist* **153**, 145-164.

Satta, Y., O'Huigin, C., Takahata, N. & Klein, J. (1994). Intensity of natural selection at the major histocompatibility complex loci. *Proceedings of the National Academy of Sciences USA* **91**, 7184-7188.

Thurz, M. R., Thomas, H. C., Greenwood, B. M. & Hill, A. V. S. (1997). Heterozygote advantage for HLA class-II type in hepatitis B virus infection. *Nature Genetics* **17**, 11-12.

Vrijenhoek, R. C. & Leberg, P. L. (1991). Let's not throw the baby out with the bathwater: a comment on management for MHC diversity in captive populations. *Conservation Biology* **5**, 252-254.

8

When is the birth rate the key factor associated with population dynamics?

TIM COULSON & ELODIE HUDSON

INTRODUCTION AND OBJECTIVES

The role of reproductive technology in conservation biology, and the conditions under which the application of such technology is likely to succeed, will in part depend on the importance of fecundity rates on the dynamics of populations. For example, if a population is declining as a result of depressed fecundity rates, any improvement in the birth rate using reproductive technology may be of benefit. Conversely, if a population is declining because of depressed survival rates or increased emigration rates, then action that reverses these factors would be more relevant.

Birth, death, immigration and emigration generate patterns in the change of size of populations over time. Detecting and describing these patterns using field and statistical techniques are the mainstay of many population ecologists. They are also the first stage in understanding population dynamics well enough to make predictions or generalisations for the purposes of management, exploitation and conservation.

The size of a population in any year equals the size of the population in the previous year plus the number of individuals that have been recruited into the population by birth or immigration, minus the number of individuals that have been removed by death or emigration. The first step in trying to understand the processes associated with variation in the size of a population over time is to identify which vital rate (birth rate, survival rate or dispersal rate) is most strongly correlated with increases or decreases in population size. If a population is declining, or is small enough that random fluctuations in the birth and death rates pose an unacceptably high risk of extinction, identifying the key vital rate or rates is an important first step in developing a strategy to reverse the decline and conserve the population.

In this chapter we consider the influence of fecundity on changes in population size in increasing populations, stable populations and declining populations. We present one case study – a population of red deer living in the North Block on the Isle of Rum, Scotland (Clutton-Brock *et al.*, 1982; Coulson *et al.*, 2000) – to demonstrate how the influence of each of the vital rates can be estimated and to compare the results from two different app-roaches. We also review empirical evidence from a wide range of studies across taxa, which suggests that fecundity is rarely the key factor associ-ated with fluctuations in population size of stable or declining populations. Finally, we suggest that the key factor associated with the population growth rate may depend on whether a population is increasing, stable or declining. We find no apparent associations between key vital rates and taxa or body size.

STATE OF THE ART

Various methods exist to identify the key vital rates associated with the popu-lation growth rate. First, there are those that take observed changes in population size over a time period of several years and directly estimate the relative contributions of each vital rate. To be accurate these methods require detailed information on temporal variation in vital rates and popula-tion size. The first approaches of this kind used key-factor analysis (Varley & Gradwell, 1960), which correlates variation in each of the vital rates, often within different age or stage classes, with changes in the total population size. Royama (1996) identified some technical inadequacies of key-factor analysis and more recent methods, such as lambda contribution analysis (Sibly & Smith, 1997) and structured accounting of the variance of demo-graphic change (Brown & Alexander, 1991) has overcome many of these shortcomings. Despite various problems with key-factor analysis, the results it generates are unlikely to be so inaccurate that they are qualita-tively incorrect. Consequently, in this review we consider results from long-term studies using this method as well as results from analyses using more robust methods.

Another approach uses elasticity analyses of matrix models (Caswell, 1989) and variation around vital rates. The method is termed retrospective matrix analysis. A matrix model is constructed where the probability of av-erage survival and fecundity for each age or stage group is estimated. Each of these values is then independently varied by the same proportion, and the effect of a relative change of each vital rate on lambda, the population growth rate (equal to the dominant eigenvalue of the transition matrix), is estimated (Caswell, 1989). The elasticities are then multiplied by the coefficient of variation of the vital rates. A proportional change in a vital rate that has a large effect on lambda has a high elasticity, while a proportional change in a vital rate with a small effect on lambda has a low elasticity. The rate with the highest elasticity is equivalent to the key factor. This approach does not require such high quality data as key-factor analysis, lambda contribution analysis or structured accounting of the variance of demographic change, but has been more frequently used. Matrix models can be constructed with values for different vital rates estimated from more than one population (e.g. see Saether & Bakke, 2000).

Recent research has shown that there is a negative association between the elasticity of a vital rate and its actual temporal variability (Pfister, 1998; Gaillard et al., 2000; Saether & Bakke, 2000). Vital rates that are strongly associated with variation in lambda (and have high elasticities) tend to show little variation over time. In contrast, those vital rates with low elasticities, that have smaller effects on population dynamics, tend to show greater temporal variability (Caswell, 1997; Saether & Bakke, 2000). There is currently debate about the relative importance of actual temporal variability in a vital rate and its elasticity on population dynamics (Wisdom & Mills, 1997; Crooks et al., 1998; Gaillard et al., 2000; Wisdom et al., 2000). The most thorough empirical study to date, that compares the relative importance of trait variability and elasticity, suggests that for birds, those traits with high elasticites tend to remain the key factor once variability has been included (Saether & Bakke, 2000), although their importance declines. In a review of the population dynamics of large mammals.

The relative effect of each vital rate on the population growth rate can only be estimated if information on all vital rates is known. There are various studies that demonstrate that an environmental, ecological or genetic process can lower the average of a vital rate. For example, inbreeding depression has decreased fecundity rates in the black-footed rock-wallaby (Eldridge et al., 1999). Although this may have a detrimental effect on the population growth rate, its actual importance can only be demonstrated if information on other vital rates is known.

Below is an example of the application of structured accounting of the variance of demographic change in red deer. This analysis is then compared with results from the same population using an elasticity analysis (they give similar results). We then review the literature on other studies that identify key vital rates associated with variation in the population growth rate.

The red deer of Rum

Structured accounting of the variance of demographic change
Since 1971 the population of red deer (*Cervus elaphus*) in the North Block of the island of Rum (Scotland) has been intensively studied (Clutton-Brock *et al.*, 1982; Pemberton *et al.*, 1996; Coulson *et al.*, 2000). Each individual is marked shortly after birth; the reproductive success of each individual is determined by observation and with genetic markers. Consequently, individual life histories are known for over 2000 individuals.

In the early years of the study, the population initially increased following the cessation of culling, reaching carrying capacity in the early 1980s (Albon *et al.*, 2000; Figure 8.1). Thereafter it has been fluctuating around an average of approximately 170 adult females. Because we know which individuals are living in the study area and which individuals were born, bred and died in each year, we can break down the change in population size from one year to the next into the relative contributions of reproduction and survival. This was done using a method devised by Brown *et al.* (Brown & Alexander, 1991; Brown *et al.*, 1993) known as Structured Accounting of the Variance of Demographic Change. In order to assess if the key factor changed depending on whether the population was increasing or was remaining approximately the same size, we divided our data into the three periods 1971–80, 1981–89 and 1990–97 and ran separate analyses on each (Albon *et al.*, 2000). We considered only the population of females,

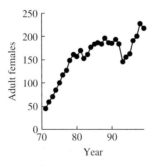

Figure 8.1 The number of adult female deer living in the North Block of Rum in each year between 1971 and 1999.

Table 8.1 *The percentage contribution of recruitment (R),*
mortality (M: adult female survival) and the interaction of
recruitment and mortality (MR) to the variance in relative
population growth rate in the three periods 1971–80, 1981–89
and 1990–97 for red deer (from Albon et al., 2000)

	1971–80	1981–89	1990–97
Recruitment (R)	51.2	32.0	14.7
Mortality (M)	27.6	38.8	40.1
Interaction (MR)	21.2	29.2	45.2

and decomposed the dynamics into contributions from the following
rates:

Recruitment
- Birth rate; the proportion of adult females that gave birth in each year
- Calf summer survival (from birth in May/June to 1 October)
- Calf winter survival (from 1 October to 15 May)
Mortality
- Adult summer survival (from 15 May to 1 October)
- Adult winter survival (from 1 October to 15 May)

As the population increased (1971–1980), 51% of the variance in population growth rate was attributed to recruitment (birth rate and first year
survival), whereas adult female mortality contributed about 28%, with the
remaining 21% due to the covariation between recruitment and mortality
(Table 8.1). In contrast, as the population fluctuated (1981–1989) the relative importance of recruitment declined to 32% while both adult female
mortality and its covariation with recruitment both increased to 39% and
29%, respectively. Finally, from 1990 to 1997, the contribution of recruitment to the variance in relative population growth rate declined to 15%,
while adult female mortality remained relatively unchanged at 40%, and
the covariation with recruitment rose to 45%.

Decomposition of the recruitment component into its contributory
factors (birth rate and first year survival) revealed that from 1971 to 1980
changes in birth rate contributed three times as much as either female calf
summer or female calf winter survival, to the variance in relative population growth rate (29% vs. 9% and 8%, respectively; diagonal of Table 8.2a).
However, in both periods after 1981, variation in birth rate contributed less
than 5% to the variance in relative growth rate (4.8% and 3.6%, respectively;

diagonal of Table 8.2b & c). At the same time, female calf summer mortality declined to account for only 1% of the variance in growth rate, while female calf winter survival accounted for 10% to 15% (diagonal of Table 8.2b & c).

Results from this population show that when it was increasing in size the key factor associated with the population growth rate was the birth rate but, once the carrying capacity was reached, the key factor associated with the population growth rate was mortality. We then assessed whether an elasticity analysis using matrix modelling supports this finding.

Matrix modelling

Benton *et al.* (1995) constructed a stochastic matrix model for the red deer using data between 1971 and 1991. They calculated the mean birth and survival rates for each age group in each year, and averaged these across all years to give one matrix model for the whole time period. Sensitivities (the change in the population growth rate resulting from a fixed change in each matrix element; Caswell, 1989) and elasticities (the change in the population growth rate resulting from a proportional change in each matrix element; de Kroon *et al.*, 2000) were calculated. Between 1971 and 1991 Benton *et al.* (1995) found that survivorship had the highest elasticity and that for each age class up to 13 years, survival had higher elasticity than fecundity.

Albon *et al.* (2000) and Benton *et al.* (1995) used data from the same population but with different time intervals. Qualitatively, the two approaches found similar results: survival appears to be more strongly associated with changes in population size than fecundity. A quantitative comparison between the two methods, although possible, is not presented here.

Several other studies report results from both matrix modelling and key-factor methods which identify the vital rate most strongly associated with variation in population size. However, relatively few studies have good quality data and reliable estimates of vital rates. The majority simply report elasticities from a population. We were able to find three papers that looked for systematic variation in the contribution of a vital rate to the population growth rate across several species. Saether & Bakke (2000) used matrix model methods to analyse populations of passerine birds. They found that fecundity rates were more important in *r*-selected species – those that breed young, produce large broods and have short longevities, than in *k*-selected species – those that delay reproduction for several years, produce small broods and are long-lived. However, even in *r*-selected species survival tended to be the key vital factor. Gaillard *et al.* (2000), reviewing the

Table 8.2 Contribution of vital rates (fitness components) to the variance in relative population growth rate from 1971 to 1980, 1981 to 1989 and 1990 to 1997 combined over all age groups for red deer. Here A represents the contribution of changes in age structure and the recruitment (R: see Table 8.1) is split into its components: B, birth rate (fecundity); s, calf summer survival; w, calf winter survival. The mortality segment of the table includes: S, adult summer survival; W, adult winter survival. In each of the elements of the table there are two values: percentage contribution to the variance in relative population growth and (in parentheses) boot-strap standard errors. The values along the diagonal (shaded) are the percentage contributions attributable simply to the vital rate given by the row/column. The values above the diagonal show the pairwise covariance between the component vital rates and values below the diagonal are the simultaneous independent variation in each pair of vital rates. Third order terms are given separately

	A	B	s	w	S	W
(a) 1971–80 Var δN = 0.00246						
Age (A)	3.4(1.11)	-9.8(5.38)	-2.3(3.62)	2.6(3.27)	2.6(1.51)	-10.4(7.05)
Birth rate (B)	0.5(0.10)	29.9(10.23)	0.0(7.72)	15.3(7.00)	-8.4(3.26)	31.0(11.15)
Summer calf survival (s)	0.3(0.06)	0.8(0.17)	9.4(1.24)	-4.3(0.86)	-1.9(0.35)	-4.5(0.60)
Winter calf survival (w)	0.1(0.02)	0.5(0.06)	0.5(0.04)	8.4(0.47)	-0.8(0.15)	15.3(0.21)
Summer adult survival (S)	0.1(0.01)	.	.	.	1.8(0.11)	0.0(0.33)
Winter adult survival (W)	0.6(0.14)	.	.	.	.	23.3(0.62)

Three way interactions

age.birth.summer calf	-3.03(2.12)
age.birth.winter calf	3.03(1.71)
birth.winter calf.winter adult	4.81(1.34)

(b) 1981–89 Var δN = 0.00575

	A	B	s	w	S	W
Age (A)	0.8(0.18)	0.2(0.92)	−0.7(0.75)	−0.3(2.75)	−0.1(0.56)	4.6(5.04)
Birth rate (B)	0.1(0.02)	4.8(1.85)	1.8(1.23)	6.8(4.44)	−1.7(0.97)	9.2(7.02)
Summer calf survival (s)	.	0.1(0.02)	1.2(0.10)	4.0(0.32)	−0.3(0.09)	−0.5(0.34)
Winter calf survival (w)	0.1(0.02)	0.3(0.02)	0.2(0.01)	14.6(0.99)	0.1(0.05)	21.6(0.92)
Summer adult survival (S)	.	.	.	.	0.8(0.03)	−1.1(0.15)
Winter adult survival (W)	0.3(0.04)	.	.	.	.	35.8(1.07)

Three way interactions
age.birth.winter calf   2.01(0.82)

(c) 1990–97 Var δN = 0.00848

	A	B	s	w	S	W
Age (A)	0.8(0.35)	1.5(1.22)	−1.0(0.60)	0.2(1.81)	0.5(0.33)	2.0(6.32)
Birth rate (B)	0.1(0.02)	3.6(1.60)	−1.1(0.95)	−1.1(3.27)	0.3(0.54)	2.1(7.12)
Summer calf survival (s)	.	0.1(0.01)	0.8(0.04)	0.9(0.15)	−0.4(0.03)	5.3(0.44)
Winter calf survival (w)	0.1(0.02)	0.3(0.04)	0.1(0.01)	10.9(0.74)	−1.1(0.09)	40.1(1.28)
Summer adult survival (S)	.	.	.	.	0.3(0.01)	−1.6(0.01)
Winter adult survival (W)	0.3(0.11)	.	.	.	.	40.3(1.77)

Three way interactions
none

From Albon *et al.* (2000).

literature from studies on large ungulates, found that survival tended to be more strongly associated with population dynamics than fecundity rates, and that for five studies the important association was survival in the juvenile age class. Pfister (1998) analysed 30 field studies and found that in every case, survival or growth rates had higher elasticities than fecundity rates.

We identified 34 studies that assessed the contribution of different vital rates to the dynamics of populations and had good quality data (Table 8.3). Of these, 28 reported temporal trends in the population growth rate. Five were declining, and all reported survival as the key vital rate. In contrast, of the four populations that were increasing, three reported fecundity as the key vital rate. Nineteen studies reported no temporal trend while 14 reported survival as the key factor. Of the remaining 12 studies that reported no information on temporal trend in population size, 11 reported survival as the key vital rate, and one reported fecundity and larval mortality as the key vital rate. There was no obvious systematic variation in the key vital rate across taxa, kingdom or body size.

Generalisations

In the majority of studies, the key factor associated with population fluctuations is survival – either adult or juvenile. Fecundity rates are rarely the key factor. These results lend support to work by Saether & Bakke (2000), Gaillard *et al.* (2000) and Pfister (1998). There is some systematic variation between the importance of fecundity on the population growth rate and life history in passerine birds. However, there was no such association for large mammals, and our review suggests that there is no evidence across orders.

Although there appears to be no systematic variation across taxa, body size or ecological condition (Gaillard *et al.*, 2000; Table 8.3), there may be systematic variation in the key factor across populations that are increasing, decreasing or stable. An increasing population is unlikely to be limited by ecological processes such as food availability or predation – it has probably either recently undergone a change in the regulating factor or may have recently colonised an area. The growth rate of populations in this state is likely to be regulated by the maximum reproductive output of a female per year, and the key factor is probably the birth rate. This is because a relatively high proportion of juveniles survive compared with populations showing no temporal trend. Results from the study of red deer support this (Albon *et al.*, 2000).

In contrast, stable populations tend to be regulated by resource availability (food or territories) or by predation. The key factor is usually

Table 8.3 Results from the literature review. Several of the populations that show no temporal trend fluctuate dramatically from year to year

Species	Key factor	Duration of study (years)	State of population	Reference
Desert tortoise	Adult survival			Heppell (1998)
Sea turtles	Adult survival			Heppell et al. (2000)
Painted turtles	Adult survival			Heppell et al. (2000)
Emperor geese	Adult survival			Schmutz et al. (1997)
Least tern	Juvenile survival			Kirsch (1996)
Wood frog	Fecundity/larval mortality	7–13		Williams & Hero (1998)
Bridled nailtail wallaby	Adult survival	8	Declining	Fisher et al. (2000)
Northern pintails	Adult survival	4	Declining	Fling et al. (1998)
Atlantic croaker	Ocean larva mortality		Declining	Diamond et al. (2000)
Elk	Fecundity/juvenile survival	23	Increasing	Coughenour & Singer (1996)
Kemp's ridley sea turtle	Adult survival		Declining	Heppell (1998)
Spanish ibex	Adult survival		Declining	Escos et al. (1994)
Spanish ibex	Adult survival		Increasing	Escos et al. (1994)
Red deer	Fecundity	7	Increasing	Albon et al. (2000)
House sparrow	Fecundity/juvenile survival	6	Increasing	Saether et al. (1999)
Grey partridge	Adult survival		No temporal trend	Bro et al. (2000)
Red deer	Adult survival	8	No temporal trend	Albon et al. (2000)
Red deer	Adult survival	7	No temporal trend	Albon et al. (2000)
Soay sheep	Adult survival	10	No temporal trend	Coulson et al. (1999)
Passerine bird[a]	Adult survival	> 10	No temporal trend	Saether & Bakke (2000)
Giant columnar cactus	Survival		No temporal trend	Godinez-Alvarez et al. (1999)
Sage grouse	Survival	23	No temporal trend	Johnson & Braun (1999)
Yellow mud turtles	Adult survival		No temporal trend	Heppell (1998)
Big horn sheep	Juvenile survival	21	No temporal trend	Gaillard et al. (2000)
Big horn sheep	Juvenile survival	12	No temporal trend	Gaillard et al. (2000)
Roe deer	Juvenile survival	20	No temporal trend	Gaillard et al. (2000)
Roe deer	Juvenile survival	11	No temporal trend	Gaillard et al. (2000)

[a] Eight species, common names not reported.

either juvenile or adult survival. In the deer, the average birth rate, juvenile survival rate and adult survival rate all tend to be lower for populations that show no temporal trend than for those that are increasing, but the greatest difference tends to be in survival rates (Albon *et al.*, 2000). In these populations relatively few juveniles survive when compared with populations that show an increasing trend.

In populations that are declining, the key factor associated with the population growth rate also tends to be survival. Theoretically, the key factor could also be the birth rate, if the births were strongly depressed compared with a population showing no temporal trend. However, we are unaware of examples where a robust key-factor analysis has been carried out for such a population. There are examples of birth rates being depressed in populations that are small or declining (Eldridge *et al.*, 1999), but this in itself is insufficient to demonstrate that birth rate is the key factor.

Once the key factor associated with the population dynamics has been identified, and if the population is considered to be at risk of extinction, a strategy needs to be devised to help conserve it. For example, if adult survival is the key factor, and adult survival is most strongly affected by poaching, the obvious solution is to target poaching. If the key factor is reproduction, one could attempt to increase the birth rate; how the birth rate should be increased will depend upon why it is depressed. If the birth rate is depressed due to inbreeding depression, as in the rock wallaby (Eldridge *et al.*, 1999), reintroduction of new stock may be appropriate; however, one should first consider the potential risks of introducing individuals from other populations that may be adapted to different ecological and environmental conditions (Cross, 2000). Reproductive technologies such as artificial insemination could also be used to try and increase the birth rate within a population, but several concerns must be addressed before such an approach is undertaken. Individual animals make choices about when to breed, and may only breed when the benefits of reproducing outweigh the risk of death that reproduction may incur (Clutton-Brock, 1988). This pay-off between reproduction and survival is the product of evolution. An artificial increase in the birth rate risks increasing the mortality rate, perhaps hastening the decline of a population.

PRIORITIES FOR THE FUTURE

There is currently much interest in identifying the key factors associated with the population growth rate (Pfister, 1998; Saether & Bakke, 2000;

Gaillard *et al.*, 2000) as this has implications for conservation (Heppell, 1998). Recent advances that allow the inclusion of observed temporal variation in a vital rate to be incorporated into matrix methods (e.g. Caswell, 1997) and the development of empirical decomposition methods (Brown & Alexander, 1991; Brown *et al.*, 1993; Sibly & Smith, 1997) should help to increase our understanding of the way in which populations fluctuate. The development of these new methods, and the increasing number of long-term data sets (e.g. Festa-Bianchet *et al.*, 1997; Gaillard *et al.*, 1998; Coulson *et al.*, 1999; Saether *et al.*, 1999) should provide sufficient data to test our prediction that there is systematic variation between the key factor(s), and whether the population is increasing, decreasing or showing no temporal trend.

To add to this work, new methods also allow the costs of reproduction on survival to be accurately estimated (Benton & Grant, 1999). If this research reveals any systematic variation in the cost of reproduction on survival across taxa, life history or body size, the effects of artificially manipulating the birth rate in wild populations could be assessed in advance.

SUMMARY

Populations of animals are regulated by a variety of factors, and these influence the key factor. In most of the published long-term studies, survival is the key factor. There also appears to be no systematic variation in the contribution of survival and birth rates across taxa, body size or ecological conditions. The only trend we suggest is that increasing populations tend to have the birth rate as the key factor; stable or declining populations tend to have survival as the key factor. This is supported in a study of red deer. More data are required across populations and species to support or refute this hypothesis. The best way to conserve a population is to target processes that are associated with variation in the key factor. However, we caution against approaches that may upset the trade-off between reproduction and survival.

ACKNOWLEDGEMENTS
We wish to thank Tim Clutton-Brock, Steve Albon and Josephine Pemberton for access to the Rum red deer data, and Jean-Michel Gaillard for providing further information on five of the studies reported in Table 8.3 and comments on the manuscript.

REFERENCES

Albon, S. D., Coulson, T. N., Brown, D., Guinness, F. E., Clutton-Brock, T. H. & Pemberton, J. M. (2000). Temporal changes in the key factors influencing the population dynamics of red deer. *Journal of Animal Ecology* **69**, 1096-1109.

Benton, T. G. & Grant, A. (1999). Optimal reproductive effort in stochastic, density-dependent environments. *Evolution* **53**, 677-688.

Benton, T. G., Grant, A. & Clutton-Brock, T. H. (1995). Does environmental stochasticity matter: analysis of red deer life histories in Rum. *Evolutionary Ecology* **9**, 559-574.

Bro, E., Sarrazin, F., Clobert, J. & Reitz, F. (2000). Demography and the decline of the grey partridge *Perdix perdix* in France. *Journal of Applied Ecology* **37**, 432-448.

Brown, D. & Alexander, N. (1991). The analysis of the variance and covariance of products. *Biometrics* **47**, 429-444.

Brown, D., Alexander, N. D. E., Marrs, R. W. & Albon, S. (1993). Structured accounting of the variance of demographic change. *Journal of Animal Ecology* **62**, 490-502.

Caswell, H. (1989). *Matrix Population Models.* Sinauer Associates, Sunderland, MA.

Caswell, H. (1997). Methods of matrix population analyses. In *Structured-population Models in Marine, Terrestrial and Freshwater Systems* (Eds. S. & C. H. Tuljipurkar), pp. 19-58. Chapman & Hall, New York.

Clutton-Brock, T. H. (1988). *Reproductive Success: Studies of Individual Variation in Contrasting Breeding Systems.* University of Chicago Press, Chicago.

Clutton-Brock, T. H., Guinness, F. E. & Albon, S. D. (1982). *Red Deer: Behaviour and Ecology of Two Sexes.* University of Chicago Press, Chicago.

Coulson, T., Albon, S., Pilkington, J. & Clutton-Brock, T. (1999). Small-scale spatial dynamics in a fluctuating ungulate population. *Journal of Animal Ecology* **68**, 658-671.

Coulson, T., Milner-Gulland, E. J. & Clutton-Brock, T. H. (2000). The relative roles of density and climatic variation on population dynamics and fecundity rates in three contrasting ungulate species. *Proceedings of the Royal Society of London B* **267**, 1771-1779.

Coughenour, M. B. & Singer, F. J. (1996). Elk population processes in Yellowstone National Park under the policy of natural regulation. *Ecological Applications* **6**, 573-593.

Crooks, K. R., Sanjayan, M. A. & Doak, D. F. (1998). New insights on cheetah conservation through demographic modeling. *Conservation Biology* **12**, 889-895.

Cross, T. F. (2000). Genetic implications of translocation and stocking of fish species, with particular reference to Western Australia. *Aquatic Research* **31**, 83-94.

de Kroon, H., van Groenendael, J. & Ehrlen, J. (2000). Elasticities: A review of methods and model limitations. *Ecology* **81**, 607-618.

Diamond, S. L., Cowell, L. G. & Crowder, L. B. (2000). Population effects of shrimp trawl bycatch on Atlantic croaker. *Canadian Journal of Fisheries and Aquatic Sciences* **57**, 2010-2021.

Eldridge, M. D. N., King, J. M., Loupis, A. K., Spencer, P. B. S., Taylor, A. C., Pope, L. C. & Hall, G. P. (1999). Unprecedented low levels of genetic variation and inbreeding depression in an island population of the black-footed rock-wallaby. *Conservation Biology* 13, 531-541.

Escos, J., Alados, C. L. & Emlen, J. M. (1994). Application of the stage projection model with density dependent fecundity to the population dynamics of Spanish ibex. *Canadian Journal of Zoology* 72, 731-737.

Festa-Bianchet, M., Jorgenson, J. T., Berube, C. H., Portier, C. & Wishart, W. D. (1997). Body mass and survival of bighorn sheep. *Canadian Journal of Zoology* 75, 1372-1379.

Fisher, D. O., Hoyle, S. D. & Blomberg, S.P. (2000). Population dynamics and survival of an endangered wallaby: a comparison of four methods. *Ecological Applications* 10, 901-910.

Fling, P. L., Grand, J. B. & Rockwell, R. F. (1998). A model of northern pintail productivity and population growth rate. *Journal of Wildlife Management* 62, 1110-1118.

Gaillard, J. M., Andersen, R., Delorme, D. & Linnell, J. D. C. (1998). Family effects on growth and survival of juvenile roe deer. *Ecology* 79, 2878-2889.

Gaillard, J.-M., Festa-Bianchet, M., Yocooz, N. G., Loison, A. & Toigo, C. (2000). Temporal variation in fitness components and population dynamics of large herbivores. *Annual Review of Ecology and Systematics* 31, 367-393.

Godinez-Alvarez, H., Valiente-Banuet, A. & Banuet, L. V. (1999). Biotic interactions and the population dynamics of the long-lived columnar cactus *Neobuxbaumia tetetzo* in the Tehuacan Valley, Mexico. *Canadian Journal of Botany* 77, 203-208.

Heppell, S. S. (1998). Application of life-history theory and population model analysis to turtle conservation. *Copeia* 1998, 367-375.

Heppell, S., Pfister, C. & de Kroon, H. (2000). Elasticity analysis in population biology: methods and applications. *Ecology* 81, 605-606.

Johnson, K. H. & Braun, C. E. (1999). Viability and conservation of an exploited sage grouse population. *Conservation Biology* 13, 77-84.

Kirsch, E. (1996). Habitat selection and productivity of least terns on the lower Platte River, Nebraska. *Wildlife Monographs* 132, 5-48.

Pemberton, J. M., Smith, J. A., Coulson, T. N., Marshall, T. C., Slate, J., Paterson, S., Albon, S. D. & Clutton-Brock, T. H. (1996). The maintenance of genetic polymorphism in small island populations: large mammals in the Hebrides. *Philosophical Transactions of the Royal Society of London B* 351, 745-752.

Pfister, C. A. (1998). Patterns of variance in stage-structured populations: evolutionary predictions and ecological implications. *Proceedings of the National Academy of Sciences USA* 95, 213-218.

Royama, T. (1996). A fundamental problem in key factor analysis. *Ecology* 77, 87-93.

Saether, B. & Bakke, O. (2000). Avian life history variation and contribution of demographic traits to the population growth rate. *Ecology* 81, 642-653.

Saether, B. E., Ringsby, T. H., Bakke, O. & Solberg, E. J. (1999). Spatial and temporal variation in demography of a house sparrow metapopulation. *Journal of Animal Ecology* 68, 628-637.

Schmutz, J. A., Rockwell, R. F. & Petersen, M. R. (1997). Relative effects of survival and reproduction on the population dynamics of emperor geese. *Journal of Wildlife Management* 61, 191-201.

Sibly, R. M. & Smith, R. H. (1997). Identifying key factors using λ contribution analysis. *Journal of Animal Ecology* 67, 17-24.

Varley, G. C. & Gradwell, G. R. (1960). Key factors in population studies. *Journal of Animal Ecology* **29**, 399–401.

Williams, S. E. & Hero, J. M. (1998). Rainforest frogs of the Australian Wet Tropics: guild classification and the ecological similarity of declining species. *Proceedings of the Royal Society of London B* **265**, 597–602.

Wisdom, M. J. & Mills, L. S. (1997). Sensitivity analysis to guide population recovery: prairie-chickens as an example. *Journal of Wildlife Management* **61**, 302–312.

Wisdom, M. J., Mills, L. S. & Doak, D. F. (2000). Life stage simulation analysis: estimating vital-rate effects on population growth for conservation. *Ecology* **81**, 628–641.

PART III

Reproductive techniques for conservation management

An investment in knowledge pays the best interest.   *Benjamin Franklin*

Since the early discovery that eggs could be fertilised in a laboratory Petri dish and that sperm and embryos could be frozen indefinitely, reproductive biologists have been passionate about using these tools in practical ways to produce offspring. Foremost has been the application to human infertility, now a well-recognised problem in adults of prime reproductive age. There now is a potpourri of options for correcting even the most serious cases of reproductive dysfunction. Spermatozoa can be used for artificial insemination, eggs can be recovered and fertilised in the laboratory, spermatozoa can be recovered from the epididymis or even from the testis and injected directly into the egg cytoplasm. As a last resort, couples can opt for donor semen, donor eggs, or even both. These advances have led to massive amounts of media attention and public discourse and have tended to create two serious misdirected impressions. The first is that it is the job of reproductive biologists to produce offspring using an ever increasingly bizarre menu of high-tech infertility 'fixes'. And second, that the creation of life in a test tube is easy.

These notions have caused problems in the conservation community, the first being that traditional conservation biologists are often suspicious of high-tech fixes. Equally naïve managers and the public also often suppose that problems of breeding endangered species can be overcome simply by directly applying human infertility treatments. As has been illustrated in previous chapters, there are many factors to consider before adopting this suite of techniques. Most importantly is the simple truth that we have too little basic information on most species, scholarly capital if you will. How can *in vitro* fertilisation be performed if methods for inducing sperm capacitation or ovulation do not exist? How can assisted breeding proceed if we do not know about the timing of ovulation, the preferred site of sperm deposition or the minimum number of sperm required for conception? These (and many other) real issues must be solved before any high-tech progress can be made with rare wildlife species, and certainly argue the need for many more basic investigations.

The aim of this section is to provide an honest assessment of the current and future potential of reproductive technologies for conservation and genetic management of small populations. Some successes with artificial insemination, *in vitro* fertilisation and embryo transfer have been reported over the past three decades. However, there are few cases where these high profile examples have been consistently repeated to allow improvements in management. One area in particular, interspecies embryo transfer, although showing early promise, has proved to be extremely difficult owing to incompatible placentation mechanisms between even taxonomically related species.

While wildlife enthusiasts continue to investigate the adaptability of human/lab animal technologies to rare species, biomedical science has probed the far reaches of procreation. Cloning has become so routine for domestic livestock, that it now merits little media attention. Nonetheless, some have speculated on the potential value of cloning for wildlife preservation. Why not clone the giant panda or the Iberian brown bear, whose declining numbers are so dramatic as to suggest the need for rather extraordinary remediation measures? We felt it important to evaluate these questions realistically by inviting detailed comment from the most qualified experts in these fields.

If our tone towards assisted breeding seems negative or at least muted, it is worth re-emphasising – the production of offspring alone does not equate with conservation. Indeed, there are examples (including those presented in a later section) where assisted breeding techniques have been valuable to genetic management of endangered species, including *in situ* recovery programmes. But additionally, it is just as important, or even more so, to use these techniques as *tools* to generate badly needed basic knowledge. For this reason, we have included extensive new information on the value of relatively straightforward technologies such as non-invasive hormone monitoring. These simpler technologies, though less newsworthy, are probably far more powerful for producing scholarly knowledge – our highest priority in the reproductive sciences. And, as will be illustrated non-invasive

monitoring is in considerable demand in modern zoo breeding programmes for identifying everything from the causes of infertility in gorillas to
predicting the impending birth of a baby elephant. Particularly significant
and exciting is the value of hormonal monitoring under field conditions,
merging behavioural ecology with explanations of reproductive function
and fitness.

9

Reproductive and welfare monitoring for the management of *ex situ* populations

AMANDA R. PICKARD

INTRODUCTION

Non-invasive reproductive hormone monitoring methods originated many years ago. Urine-based pregnancy diagnosis methods for humans and live-stock species were developed in the 1920s (Cowie, 1948), to measure either gonadotrophins or oestrogens. However, these techniques were non-invasive only for the subject of study and relied on the assessment of physiological changes in other species (usually mice) following injection of the subject's urine. Chemical urinary pregnancy tests followed approximately 10 years later, but at that time were not considered reliable or accurate enough to be routinely used (Cowie, 1948). The advent of specific, immunological tests for identifying and quantifying hormones (Yalow & Berson, 1959) provided new opportunities for reproductive monitoring, allowing the development of the non-invasive techniques used today.

Quantifying hormone concentrations non-invasively has gained popularity within the conservation community over the last 15 to 20 years, as the practical and welfare implications of collecting blood samples from intractable and endangered animals have been recognised. Commonly, steroid hormone metabolite concentrations are measured in excreta, such as urine, faeces, saliva and sweat, by radioimmunoassay or more recently, enzyme immunoassay. In isolation, knowledge of the reproductive status of wild animals in captivity is a useful indicator of individual well-being. However, when integrated with other data it becomes a powerful management tool. As such, predictions about, for example, the outcome of an *ex situ* conservation programme, the success of an assisted reproduction programme, the point when available resources for housing animals will become limiting, or the impact of the environment on an animal's physiology can be made.

One drawback of the wealth of information published about non-invasive hormone monitoring is the diversity of analytical methods adopted

Table 9.1 *Summary of the available literature describing non-invasive hormone monitoring in Rhinocerotidae*

Species	Sample	Metabolites measured	Source of information
White rhinoceros	Urine	20α-hydroxyprogesterone	Hindle & Hodges (1990); Hindle *et al.* (1992)
		Oestradiol-17β	
		Oestrone conjugates	Ramsay *et al.* (1994)
		Pregnanediol-3-glucuronide	
		C19/C21 progesterone metabolites	
	Faeces	20α-hydroxyprogesterone	Strike (1999)
		20-oxo-pregnanes	Schwarzenberger & Walzer (1995); Schwarzenberger *et al.* (1998)
		Progesterone metabolites	Radcliffe *et al.* (1997)
		11α-pregnanedione	Patton *et al.* (1999)
Black rhinoceros	Urine	20α-hydroxyprogesterone	Hindle *et al.* (1992)
		Oestrone	
		Oestrone conjugates	Ramsay *et al.* (1987, 1994)
		Pregnanediol-3-glucuronide	
		C19/C21 progesterone metabolites	
	Saliva	20α-hydroxyprogesterone	Czekala & Callison (1996); Thorne *et al.* (1998)
		Oestradiol	
	Faeces	20α-hydroxyprogesterone	Schwarzenberger *et al.* (1993)
		Pregnandiol-3-glucuronide	
		20-keto-progestagens	
		20-oxo-progestagens	Schwarzenberger *et al.* (1996b)
		Oestrogen metabolites	Berkeley *et al.* (1997)
		Progesterone metabolites	
Sumatran rhinoceros	Urine	Oestradiol	Heistermann *et al.* (1998)
	Faeces	Pregnanediol	Heistermann *et al.* (1998)
		5α-pregnane-3α-ol-20-one	
Indian rhinoceros	Urine	Total immunoreactive oestrogen	Kassam & Lasley (1981)
		Oestrone sulphate	Kasman *et al.* (1986)
		Pregnanediol-3-glucuronide	

by different laboratories. Each publication contributes to our knowledge of wildlife physiology, but frequently information produced by different organisations is difficult to compare. By way of example, Table 9.1 summarises the available literature relating to non-invasive analysis of reproductive hormones in rhinoceros species in captivity. Descriptions of progesterone metabolite analyses alone refer to the quantification of eight different progestagen groups, some of which have been measured by more than one author, but not necessarily using the same antibody or methodology. In many cases, the specific compound being measured by a particular antibody remains uncharacterised. While much can be gained from comparing relative differences, rather than absolute changes in sample concentration, strength will always be added to the conclusions that can be drawn from the data if like can be compared with like. For many conservation programmes financial resources are often limited. Therefore, an internationally coordinated approach to hormone monitoring, with an effort to ensure accurate use of steroid nomenclature and full antibody validation, would minimise duplication of effort and maximise the relevance and significance of each laboratory's output.

The practicalities of non-invasive monitoring procedures and the species to which they have been applied have been reviewed extensively by other authors (see e.g. Heistermann *et al.*, 1995; Schwarzenberger *et al.*, 1996a), and will therefore not be covered in detail in this chapter. There have been a number of integrated investigations, which have used non-invasive monitoring to help understand or explain other observations and enhance our efforts in conservation biology. Examples of these will be given. However, it should be recognised that data from non-invasive monitoring studies may be unable to resolve physiological problems. Nevertheless, the data provide a valuable diagnostic tool to aid our comprehension of biological events. The purpose of this review is to examine how the ability to monitor reproduction and stress non-invasively has contributed to the success of *ex situ* conservation programmes. The methods we use today are still far from ideal. Therefore, this chapter will also address some of their shortcomings and possible ways to overcome these in the future.

STATE OF THE ART

Genetic management

The benefits of applying assisted reproduction techniques in conservation programmes have long been recognised. However, the ease of application and success of these techniques varies greatly among species. As such, net economic considerations should be taken into account when planning a programme of assisted reproduction. Often skilled personnel and specialised equipment are required, which may not be locally available. The cost of bringing these together should be judged against the overall likelihood of success.

Since 1995, the Institute of Zoology (Zoological Society of London) and the Estación Experimental de Zonas Áridas (Consejo Superior de Investigaciones Científicas) have collaborated to develop assisted reproduction and genetic resource bank technologies to support the conservation of the Mohor gazelle (*Gazella dama mhorr*). This species became extinct in the wild in 1968, but has survived in captivity since 1971 when remnant populations were brought together for *ex situ* conservation. Despite originating from just 12 founder individuals, this species has bred well in captivity, and provides a useful model population for investigating approaches to the conservation of endangered ungulates. The success of this *ex situ* programme has resulted in distribution of the population to different geographical locations, i.e. various zoos, where these subpopulations are likely to suffer genetic drift and further inbreeding. Artificial insemination and the establishment of a genetic resource bank were proposed to minimise these inbreeding effects (see Holt *et al.*, Chapter 17).

No data on the reproductive physiology of this or any closely related species were available at the outset of the programme, thus limiting the logical development of artificial insemination protocols. Initial attempts at artificial insemination of Mohor females, without investigations of endocrine physiology, had a limited degree of success (Holt *et al.*, 1996), resulting in 30% conception rates. Frozen-thawed semen was used, and the oestrous cycles of the females synchronised using exogenous progesterone. Therefore, several possibilities were available to increase the success of the manipulations. We undertook to characterise the endocrine attributes of the oestrous cycle by closely monitoring cyclic females in the presence of a vasectomised male, and conception and pregnancy after oestrous synchronisation and natural insemination (Pickard *et al.*, 2001a). Non-invasive faecal hormone analysis was used for this purpose to avoid stressing the animals.

Conception rates using natural mating were similar to those achieved by artificial insemination. The faecal progestagen analyses showed no evidence that the females had conceived and suffered subsequent early pregnancy loss. Investigation of each animal's life history demonstrated that under natural breeding conditions the fertility of the study group was also approximately 30%. Therefore, we can surmise that some form of ovulation or fertilisation failure may occur in this species. Further detailed hormone analyses suggest that successful conception is related to periovulatory steroid hormone excretion. The ratio of faecal oestrogen: progestagen is positively correlated with the mean time to conception ($R^2 = 0.58$; $P = 0.046$) (Figure 9.1).

Using this information we now have the opportunity to revise predictions of future population growth, and the economic impact of undertaking an assisted reproduction programme for this species can now be assessed relative to a known fertility rate. While further investigations may find a way to improve the reproductive output of this endangered species, it is possible that this may only be achieved by undertaking invasive assessments of ovarian function and oocyte competence. These would currently be considered inappropriate.

Behaviour

Ex situ conservation programmes inevitably result in animals being housed in relatively unnatural conditions, which can adversely affect individual behaviour. Hand-reared individuals, or those raised in isolation, may relate better to humans than their conspecifics and may not develop the appropriate social skills to recognise and breed successfully with potential mates. Breeding pairs or groups may also be unable to exhibit their full repertoire of social behaviours due to restrictions in enclosure space. Mating attempts in zoos can be compromised, and in some cases (such as large felids), individuals are at risk of injury if not death owing to mate aggression. In contrast, in the wild, they would normally be able to escape.

In such circumstances, non-invasive hormone assessments can provide an indication of the best time to introduce individuals (e.g. during female sexual receptivity), to minimise risk of injury. Similarly, predicting when a female is likely to give birth allows separation of the father or isolation from the group, in cases where there is a high risk of infanticide. Preparation for intervention, where females have a history of failing to rear their offspring successfully can also be made, improving the likelihood of rearing a subsequent generation.

Behavioural observations are themselves a form of non-invasive monitoring which may have practical use when circumstances preclude the collection and analysis of endocrine samples. To be economically effective, batch sample analysis is usually undertaken, resulting in a retrospective,

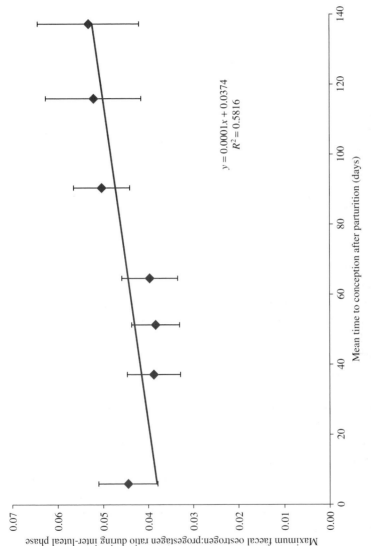

Figure 9.1 Correlation between maximum inter-luteal phase oestrogen:progestagen ratio and mean time to conception for seven female Mohor gazelles. Data are taken from life-history characteristics and represent 26 inter-gestational periods. (From Pickard *et al.*, 2001a.)

rather than real-time indication of an animal's physiological condition. In practical terms, the net benefits of reproductive monitoring are therefore reduced. With this in mind, as part of the investigations of Mohor gazelle physiology described above, we undertook a detailed analysis of the relationship between faecal hormone excretion and the behavioural interactions between cycling female gazelles and a vasectomised male. Our objectives were to quantitatively examine specific reproduction-associated behaviours to ascertain whether they could be used as predictors of reproductive success. Reproduction-associated behaviours were grouped into three categories: exploratory or testing behaviours, courtship behaviours and mounting behaviours.

Our results indicated that the frequency of mounting and copulation is positively correlated with peri-ovulatory faecal oestrogen concentrations ($R = 0.546$; $P = 0.01$) and the frequency of pre-copulatory, exploratory behaviours ($R = 0.744$; $P < 0.0001$) (Pickard et al., 2001b). Since steroid hormone excretion at this time is related to reproductive success, observing the intensity of courtship interactions may provide a useful alternative to faecal hormone assessments for monitoring an individual's fertility.

Inbreeding

The effects of inbreeding are considered to be a major contributing factor to the accelerated decline of small, isolated populations (see Taylor, Chapter 5 and Koeninger Ryan, Chapter 6). Few studies have directly highlighted effects on reproduction in endangered species, but these effects are potentially exacerbated in captivity, where populations can only usually be kept in modest numbers and transfer of genetic material between populations is difficult because of geographical or physical barriers, including behavioural incompatibility. The relationship between inbreeding and population fitness varies considerably among species. A wide variety of factors such as mating strategy, generation time and extrinsically induced variations in population demography also impact on reproductive fitness.

Experimental manipulation of wild, domestic and laboratory species has, however, demonstrated effects of inbreeding on reproductive success. For example, territorial scent-marking behaviour in inbred male Mongolian gerbils is increased when compared with founder generations (Turner & Carbonell, 1984). Although this effect was found to be androgen-independent, the consequences for the reproductive success of outbred individuals might be significant if they were unable to maintain a territory.

Other studies have also shown that mechanisms of steroid biochemistry can vary in inbred versus outbred strains of rabbits (Schwab & Johnson, 1985), and that pituitary function differs in squirrel species which adopt different mating strategies to avoid inbreeding (Boonstra & McColl, 2000). In inbred mice, differences in oocyte maturation have been attributed to differences in the dynamics of ovarian steroid production (Krzanowska & Szoltys, 1996). It is possible, therefore, that the consequences of inbreeding may be detected through the use of comparative non-invasive hormone analysis in some cases.

Environment

Commonly, in *ex situ* conservation programmes the animals are substantially removed from their natural environment. Suitable foodstuffs may be unavailable locally, patterns of daylight and seasonality may be significantly altered and these, together with confinement, may all serve to affect breeding potential adversely. Nevertheless, physiological compensation usually occurs, and most individuals continue to reproduce, although it is difficult to determine whether optimal reproductive rates are achieved.

The negative effects of translocation to captivity may or may not be obvious immediately. For example, large proportions of wild-born Southern white rhinoceros (*Ceratotherium simum simum*) have failed to breed *ex situ*. Furthermore, captive-bred females also suffer from low birth rates (Göltenboth & Ochs, 1997), directly affecting the viability of the *ex situ* population. Rhinoceros managers predict a demographic crisis in coming years (Patton *et al.*, 1999), but the cause of this breeding failure has yet to be determined. However, the ability to compare physiological parameters between animals in their natural environment, with captive populations which have high rates of breeding success and those which suffer substantial reproductive failure, may provide an indication of the source of the problem. Schwarzenberger *et al.* (2000) have undertaken the first such investigation for the Southern white rhinoceros, and found that fertility in the wild is not compromised as it is in captivity. Nutrition, for example, could be a major factor limiting rhinoceros reproduction *ex situ*. Nutritional imbalances may compromise steroidogenesis and ovarian or testicular function and foetal development (see McEvoy & Robinson, Chapter 3). Locally available foodstuffs or synthetic substitutes may contain compounds such as phyto-oestrogens or tannins, which may mildly or severely compromise reproduction in some species. Such effects may be detected or monitored by close examination of data generated through non-invasive reproductive assessments.

Contraception

Most frequently, reproductive monitoring is used to evaluate the success of captive breeding programmes or to diagnose infertility in specified individuals. Nevertheless, some captive breeding programmes are over-successful, resulting in more individuals than the zoo community can reasonably accommodate. Limiting breeding opportunities must then be considered, to prevent the problem being exacerbated. However, merely separating males and females presents its own problems, just as interfering with the social organisation of a breeding group can cause behavioural problems, as described above. Sterilisation represents one alternative, although this is normally considered irreversible and therefore not suitable for many endangered species breeding programmes. As discussed elsewhere in this book (see Rodger, Chapter 18 and Mate & Hinds, Chapter 19), contraception offers a potentially reversible method for limiting breeding.

A non-invasive, urinary assay for the contraceptive agent levonorgestrel was reported by Munro *et al.* (1996) for monitoring breeding in contracepted non-human primates, and Bettinger *et al.* (1997) demonstrated that the use of Norplant implants (which contain levonorgestrel) in chimpanzees did not adversely affect reproductive physiology or oestrogen excretion. However, the majority of studies that have used non-invasive hormone analyses to study the effects of contraception in captive wildlife are those performed within the scope of medical research. Few if any studies have been reported within the conservation literature.

Welfare monitoring in *ex situ* conservation programmes

The preceding discussion has related almost exclusively to the use of non-invasive monitoring techniques for assessing reproduction in threatened species in captivity. Significant attention in the literature and the zoo community has, however, recently focused on the measurement of glucocorticoid hormones for welfare assessment. A recent publication by Wasser *et al.* (2000), reports the use of a non-specific glucocorticoid radioimmunoassay capable of monitoring the excretion of cortisol metabolites in a wide range of mammalian and non-mammalian species, which provides new opportunities to monitor stress in individuals under different management regimes.

The principles of non-invasive glucocorticoid analysis are the same as those for monitoring reproductive hormones. There are significant advantages in monitoring stress by means of non-invasively collected samples. The samples can be collected relatively easily with minimal disturbance to the animals, and provide an integrated measure of the individual's stress physiology over the preceding hours or days, rather than a 'point-in-time' measure as would be generated from a blood sample. Furthermore, measuring glucocorticoid concentrations provides an indication of the sustained stress response to a stimulus, as opposed to the instantaneous response of the sympathetic nervous system, which releases catecholamines very rapidly following stimulation. However, caution should be used when interpreting the data generated from non-invasive glucocorticoid analyses, particularly if it is to be used for welfare assessments and to influence management practice.

Determining whether an individual is exhibiting a stress response is impossible without significant baseline data from each animal. It must be ascertained that the metabolite concentrations measured exceed the normal physiological range for that particular animal. For example, Jurke *et al.* (1997) reported three categories of baseline faecal cortisol metabolite concentrations in unstimulated female cheetahs, and individual sample concentrations approximately 10 times greater than the peak value recorded for an experimentally stressed male. In this example, the two females categorised as 'high in cortisol' also demonstrated impaired reproductive function, providing a reasonable indication that their biology was compromised. Nevertheless, other animals housed under the same conditions had significantly lower faecal cortisol concentrations and reproduced without intervention. In such cases, it would be difficult to advise on the suitability of the management techniques used for the group as a whole.

Glucocorticoid analyses are further complicated by the difference in physiological response to acute versus chronic stress. For example, acute glucocorticoid stimulation (e.g. by injection) can increase locomotor activity, whereas chronic glucocorticoid release (e.g. from a hormone implant) suppresses it. This can be relevant, for example, when studying competitive mating systems where males compete for access to females, and high circulating concentrations of glucocorticoid may, in this case, be positively correlated with reproductive success. Furthermore, the response to repeated stressors differs from that to novel stressful stimuli as the individual begins to exhibit a 'learned response' based on its ability to judge the physiological consequences of the stimulus. It is therefore vitally important to consider the circumstances under which glucocorticoid data are generated before drawing conclusions about an individual's welfare. Researchers undertaking these studies would be best advised to consider their findings in conjunction with other objective physiological measures (such as conception rate or other endocrine measures) when interpreting their observations.

PRIORITIES FOR THE FUTURE

Many Western nations now have facilities for undertaking non-invasive hormone analyses. Improved international communications allow rapid shipment of samples and/or reagents without compromising their integrity, and the available laboratory technologies can provide the accurate, reliable data required by animal managers. However, the laboratories undertaking these analyses are often dedicated to scientific research and method development, and routine sample analysis using established assays is outside the scope of their remit. Unfortunately, there are limited resources to offer what essentially becomes a commercial service once techniques have been established and fully validated for a particular species, at a price that can be afforded by the conservation community. Therefore, there is significant scope for improving the efficiency of sample analysis, either in terms of economics, time or sample throughput, which would greatly increase the availability of this technology to conservation biologists.

Hormone analyses inevitably provide a retrospective indicator of an individual's physiological status. While this information is doubtless useful, in many cases more benefit would be gained from building up an ongoing profile of each animal's endocrine characteristics. The ability for the analysis to be conducted locally, without the need for specific technical expertise or complicated laboratory equipment, would provide significant new opportunities in this field. The need for import/export permits to transfer samples across borders, and the associated courier charges, would be removed, reducing some of the administrative and financial burden of generating the data. Conservation organisations would be in a position to make judgements about the need for, or frequency of, sample analysis depending on the results generated for a particular individual on a long-term basis and their specific data requirements at that time. Where, for example, assisted reproduction or infertility treatments are being attempted, a rapid indication of the efficacy of a protocol greatly improves the quality and relevance of the data resulting from it, and can make the difference between a successful intervention and a 'useful experience'.

The concept of a rapid, cheap 'stick-test' for generating data about endocrine parameters is very appealing to the conservation community.

However, to date little progress has been realised in achieving this aim. Our experiences with non-invasive methods have demonstrated that quantitative assessments of changing hormone concentrations are generally required for a full evaluation of species physiology, and that a simple colour-change, like that of human home pregnancy diagnostic kits, is inadequate. Nevertheless, recent developments in biosensor technology and the miniaturisation of circuits and electronic components may provide novel opportunities to develop equipment to meet our requirements. Preliminary trials (A. R. Pickard & T. T. Mottram, unpublished observations) indicate that biosensors being developed for the in-line analysis of progesterone in the milk of dairy cows (Pemberton *et al.*, 1998) will prove useful for monitoring reproductive status in endangered species. Extracts of faecal material from Mohor gazelles, when analysed by standard ELISA techniques and by prototype biosensor methodology, provide comparable longitudinal profiles, which indicate the future promise of developments in this area. Currently, prototype equipment is still at the bench-test stage, and further developments are required to standardise and automate sample preparation procedures in such a way that they can be undertaken in the zoo or field environment in a reliable and repeatable manner. Nevertheless, the prospect of portable endocrine monitoring equipment is more realistic than it was two years ago.

It should be recognised, however, that the development of biosensor or other real-time monitoring equipment will not necessarily provide an immediate generic system for non-invasive monitoring. Interspecies variability may mean that initial systems are more suited to some species than to others, in the same way that no single immunoassay system can be applied across all species. Furthermore, expert analysis of the data generated will continue to be required to maximise its practical use and value. This presents enhanced opportunities to improve our understanding of biological systems. With modern Internet communications, data could be collated centrally, and databases similar to those used in the genome mapping projects developed. By making this information available to the wider conservation community, new opportunities would arise: for example, to evaluate the positive and negative aspects of different animal husbandry systems, the effect of the environment on productivity or welfare, and to make revised predictions about population viability.

Clearly, current technology in non-invasive monitoring has opened new possibilities for the management of wild animals *ex situ*, but the role of scientists in this field is to press forward with the development of improved analytical techniques and methods for data interpretation. Conservation scientists and reproductive biologists need to remain aware of technological developments in seemingly unrelated fields to be able to take advantage of new technologies as they arise. For example, advances in thermal image capture and analysis have already proved useful as a tool for diagnosing pregnancy in circumstances where non-invasive endocrinology is not readily available (Hilsberg 1998; A. R. Pickard, A. Ferguson & A. Tucker, unpublished observations). Collaboration with scientists in other disciplines will facilitate this and allow the potential of non-invasive monitoring to be fully realised within integrated conservation programmes.

ACKNOWLEDGEMENTS
Sincere thanks go to Drs Teresa Abaigar, Mar Cano and Toby Mottram for ongoing collaborations which contribute to much of the research highlighted in this text, and to Dr Bill Holt for having the inspiration and dedication to bring many conservation disciplines together.

REFERENCES
Berkeley, E. V., Kirkpatrick, J. F., Schaffer, N. E., Bryant, W. M. & Threlfall, W. R. (1997). Serum and fecal steroid analysis of ovulation, pregnancy, and parturition in the black rhinoceros (*Diceros bicornis*). *Zoo Biology* 16, 121-132.
Bettinger, T., Cougar, D., Lee, D. R., Lasley, B. L. & Wallis, J. (1997). Ovarian hormone concentrations and genital swelling patterns in female chimpanzees with norplant implants. *Zoo Biology* 16, 209-223.
Boonstra, R. & McColl, C. J. (2000). Contrasting stress response of male arctic ground squirrels and red squirrels. *Journal of Experimental Zoology* 286, 390-404.
Cowie, A. T. (1948). *Pregnancy Diagnosis Tests: A Review.* Commonwealth Agricultural Bureaux, Reading, Berkshire.
Czekala, N. M. & Callison, L. (1996). Pregnancy diagnosis in the black rhinoceros (*Diceros bicornis*) by salivary hormone analysis. *Zoo Biology* 15, 37-44.
Göltenboth, R. & Ochs, A. (1997). *International Studbook for African Rhinoceroses.* Zoologische Garten Berlin, Berlin.
Heistermann, M., Agil, M., Büthe, A. & Hodges, J. K. (1998). Metabolism and excretion of oestradiol-17β and progesterone in the Sumatran rhinoceros (*Dicerorhinus sumatrensis*). *Animal Reproduction Science* 53, 157-172.
Heistermann, M., Möstl, E. H. & Hodges, J. K. (1995). Non-invasive endocrine monitoring of female reproductive status: methods and applications to captive breeding and conservation of exotic species. In *Research and Captive Propagation* (Eds. U. Gansloßer, J. K. Hodges & W. Kaumanns), pp. 36-48. FI Lander Verlag GmbH, Fürth, Germany.
Hilsberg, S. (1998). Infrared-thermography in zoo animals: new experiences with this method, its use in pregnancy and inflammation diagnosis and survey of environmental thermoregulation in zoo animals. In *Proceedings of the 2nd scientific meeting of the European Association of Zoo and Wildlife Veterinarians*, pp. 397-409. European Association of Zoo and Wildlife Veterinarians, Chester, UK.

Hindle, J. E. & Hodges, J. K. (1990). Metabolism of oestradiol-17β and progesterone in the white rhinoceros (*Ceratotherium simum simum*). *Journal of Reproduction and Fertility* 90, 571-580.

Hindle, J. E., Möstl, E. & Hodges, J. K. (1992). Measurement of urinary oestrogens and 20α-dihydroprogesterone during ovarian cycles of black (*Diceros bicornis*) and white (*Ceratotherium simum*) rhinoceroses. *Journal of Reproduction and Fertility* 94, 237-249.

Holt, W. V., Abaigar, T. & Jabbour, H. N. (1996). Oestrous synchronization, semen preservation and artificial insemination in the Mohor gazelle (*Gazella dama mhorr*) for the establishment of a genome resource bank programme. *Reproduction, Fertility and Development* 8, 1215-1222.

Jurke, M. H., Czekala, N. M., Lindburg, D. G. & Millard, S. E. (1997). Fecal corticoid metabolite measurement in the cheetah (*Acinonyx jubatus*). *Zoo Biology* 16, 133-147.

Kasman, L. H., Ramsay, E. C. & Lasley, B. L. (1986). Urinary steroid evaluations to monitor ovarian function in exotic ungulates 3. Estrone sulfate and pregnanediol-3-glucuronide excretion in the Indian rhinoceros (*Rhinoceros unicornis*). *Zoo Biology* 5, 355-361.

Kassam, A. A. & Lasley, B. L. (1981). Estrogen excretory patterns in the Indian rhinoceros (*Rhinoceros unicornis*), determined by simplified urinary analysis. *American Journal of Veterinary Research* 42, 251-255.

Krzanowska, H. & Szoltys, M. (1996). Preovulatory dynamics of ovarian steroid hormones in two mouse strains differing in the rate of meiotic maturation. *Folia Biologica, Krakow* 44, 111-116.

Munro, C. J., Laughlin, L. S., VonSchalscha, T., Baldwin, D. M. & Lasley, B. L. (1996). An enzyme immunoassay for serum and urinary levonorgestrel in human and non-human primates. *Contraception* 54, 43-53.

Patton, M. L., Swaisgood, R. R., Czekala, N. M., White, A. M., Fetter, G. A., Montagne, J. P., Rieches, R. G. & Lance, V. A. (1999). Reproductive cycle length and pregnancy in the southern white rhinoceros (*Ceratotherium simum simum*) as determined by fecal pregnane analysis and observations of mating behavior. *Zoo Biology* 18, 111-127.

Pemberton, R. M., Hart, J. P. & Foulkes, J. A. (1998). Development of a sensitive, selective electrochemical immunoassay for progesterone in cow's milk based on a disposable screen-printed amperometric biosensor. *Electrochimica Acta* 43, 3567-3574.

Pickard, A. R., Abaigar, T., Green, D. I., Cano, M. & Holt, W. V. (2001b). Hormonal and behavioural predictors of breeding success in the Mohor gazelle (*Gazella dama mhorr*). *Theriogenology* 55, Abstract 396.

Pickard, A. R., Abaigar, T., Green, D. I., Holt, W. V. & Cano, M. (2001a). Hormonal characterisation of the reproductive cycle and pregnancy in the female Mohor gazelle (*Gazella dama mhorr*). *Reproduction* 122, 571-580.

Radcliffe, R. W., Czekala, N. M. & Osofsky, S. A. (1997). Combined serial ultrasonography and fecal progestin analysis for reproductive evaluation of the female white rhinoceros (*Ceratotherium simum simum*): preliminary results. *Zoo Biology* 16, 445-456.

Ramsay, E. C., Kasman, L. H. & Lasley, B. L. (1987). Urinary steroid evaluations to monitor ovarian function in exotic ungulates. 5. Estrogen and pregnanediol-3-glucuronide excretion in the black rhinoceros (*Diceros bicornis*). *Zoo Biology* 6, 275-282.

Ramsay, E. C., Moran, F., Roser, J. F. & Lasley, B. L. (1994). Urinary steroid evaluations to monitor ovarian function in exotic ungulates. 10. Pregnancy diagnosis in Perissodactyla. *Zoo Biology* 13, 129-147.

Schwab, G. E. & Johnson, E. F. (1985). Two catalytically distinct subforms of cytochrome p-450 3b as obtained from inbred rabbits. *Biochemistry* 24, 7222-7226.

Schwarzenberger, F. & Walzer, C. (1995). Oestrous cycle induction in a white rhinoceros (*Ceratotherium simum simum*) monitored by fecal progestagen analysis. *Erkrankungen der Zootiere* 37, 79-83.

Schwarzenberger, F., Francke, R. & Göltenboth, R. (1993). Concentrations of faecal immunoreactive progestagen metabolites during the oestrous cycle and pregnancy in the black rhinoceros (*Diceros bicornis michaeli*). *Journal of Reproduction and Fertility* 98, 285-291.

Schwarzenberger, F., Möstl, E., Palme, R. & Bamberg, E. (1996a). Faecal steroid analysis for non-invasive monitoring of reproductive status in farm, wild and zoo animals. *Animal Reproduction Science* 42, 515-526.

Schwarzenberger, F., Tomasova, K., Holeckova, D., Matern, B. & Möstl, E. (1996b). Measurement of fecal steroids in the black rhinoceros (*Diceros bicornis*) using group-specific enzyme immunoassays for 20-oxo-pregnanes. *Zoo Biology* 15, 159-171.

Schwarzenberger, F., Walzer, C., Jago, M., Reinhardt, P., Mraz, B. & Modler, F. (2000). Faecal steroid analysis in free-ranging female white rhinoceros. In *Proceedings of the Zoological Society of London Symposium 'Reproduction and Integrated Conservation Science'* (Eds. W. V. Holt, A. R. Pickard, J. C. Rodger & D. E. Wildt) p. 19. Zoological Society of London, London.

Schwarzenberger, F., Walzer, C., Tomasova, K., Vahala, J., Meister, J., Goodrowe, K. L., Zima, J., Strauss, G. & Lynch, M. (1998). Faecal progesterone metabolite analysis for non-invasive monitoring of reproductive function in the white rhinoceros (*Ceratotherium simum*). *Animal Reproduction Science* 53, 173-190.

Strike, T. (1999). The application of faecal 20α-hydroxyprogesterone analysis for the non-invasive monitoring of reproduction in female southern white rhinoceros (*Ceratotherium simum simum*). Masters thesis, Royal Veterinary College, University of London.

Thorne, A., Cox, R., Gunn, I., Woods, R., Blyde, D. & Trounson, A. (1998). Characterisation of oestrous cycles and pregnancy in black rhinoceros (*Diceros bicornis*) using salivary hormone analysis. In *Proceedings of the Euro-American Mammal Congress*, Santiago de Compostela, Spain.

Turner, J. W., Jr & Carbonell, C. (1984). A relationship between frequency of display of territorial marking behavior and coat color in male Mongolian gerbils. *Laboratory Animal Science* 34, 488-490.

Wasser, S. K., Hunt, K. E., Brown, J. L., Cooper, K., Crockett, C. M., Bechert, U., Millspaugh, J. J., Larson, S. & Monfort, S. L. (2000). A generalized fecal glucocorticoid assay for use in a diverse array of nondomestic mammalian and avian species. *General and Comparative Endocrinology* 120, 260-275.

Yalow, R. S. & Berson, S. A. (1959). Assay of plasma insulin in human subjects by immunological methods. *Nature* 184, 1648-1649.

Non-invasive endocrine measures of reproduction and stress in wild populations

STEVEN L. MONFORT

INTRODUCTION AND OBJECTIVE

The evaluation of steroid metabolite content and/or profiles in either urine or faeces represents a snapshot of hormone activity and permits the long-term study of reproductive patterns in individuals, populations or species, all without perturbing the animal. By the mid-1980s, non-invasive immunoassay analysis of urine, which was pioneered in captive non-human primates (Hodges *et al.*, 1979), had been adopted for the *ex situ* reproductive study of diverse primate, ungulate and avian species. Steroid monitoring in faeces was first described in the human (Adlercreutz & Martin, 1976) and then applied to the domestic mare (Bamberg *et al.*, 1984) and cow (Möstl *et al.*, 1984), before being used in the first non-domesticated species, the macaque (Risler *et al.*, 1987). The non-invasive measurement of adrenal hormone metabolites was first accomplished in the bighorn sheep (Miller *et al.*, 1991). These technological breakthroughs have revolutionised wildlife endocrinology.

Similar strategies using either urine or faeces also have application to free-living wildlife. The first study was reported in 1984 and investigated musth in male African elephants (Poole *et al.*, 1984). Shortly thereafter, followed a study of female vervet monkeys (Andelman *et al.*, 1985). Since then, more than 50 publications (Table 10.1) have described non-invasive endocrine monitoring of free-living mammals and birds. These studies have assessed longitudinal reproductive patterns (including seasonality, ovarian cyclicity and pregnancy), but more often have evaluated fecundity or hormonal relationships in 'social' species. Recently, non-invasive measures of adrenal status have been used to evaluate stress associated with dominance,

Table 10.1 Reproductive and stress hormones measured in the urine and faeces of free-living wildlife

Group	Species	Reproductive hormones		Stress hormones	Reference
		Urinary	Faecal		
Primates	*Macaca tonkeana*	EC, PdG			Thierry et al. (1996)
	Alouatta seniculus	P	E		Herrick et al. (2000); Clarke et al. (1991)
	Gorilla gorilla	T, EC, PdG, hCG		Urine	Robbins & Czekala (1997); Czekala & Sicotte (2000)
	Cercopithecus aethiops	PdG			Andelman et al. (1985)
	Pan troglodytes	EC			Knott (1993)
	Pongo pygmaeus	EC, hCG, LH			Knott (1993)
	Macaca fascicularis	PRL, T		Urine	van Schaik et al. (1991)
	Brachyteles arachnoides		E, P, T	Faeces	Strier & Ziegler (1994; 1997); Ziegler et al. (1997a, b); Strier et al. (1999)
	Propithecus verreauxi		E, P, T		Brockman & Whitten (1996); Brockman et al. (1998)
	Papio cynocephalus		E, P		Wasser (1996); Stavisky et al. (1995)
	Presbytis entellus		PdG		Ziegler et al. (2000)
	Sanguinus oedipus		EC, PdG		Savage et al. (1997)
	Callithrix jacchus		E, P		Albuquerque et al. (2001)
	Eulemur mongoz		E, P		Curtis et al. (2000)
	Macaca sylvanus			Faeces	Wallner et al. (1999)

Group	Species				References
Carnivores	*Helogale parvula*	EC, T		Urine	Creel et al. (1991, 1992, 1993, 1995)
	Suricata suricatta	EC, PdG, T	E, P, T		Clutton-Brock et al. (2001)
	Lycaon pictus		E,P,T	Faeces	Creel et al. (1997a, b, 1998)
Ungulates	*Loxodonta africana*	T		Faeces	Poole et al. (1984); Foley et al. (2001)
	Equus caballus	EC, PdG, eCG	E, EC, PdG, P		Kirkpatrick et al. (1990, 1991a, 1992a, 1993b, 1995)
	Equus przewalskii	EC			Monfort et al. (1991)
	Bison bison	PdG, EC	E, P		Kirkpatrick et al. (1991b, 1992b, 1993a, 1996)
	Alces alces	E, P	P		Monfort et al. (1993); Schwartz et al. (1995); Berger et al. (1999)
	Cervus elaphus		EC, PdG, P	Faeces	White et al. (1995); Garrott et al. (1998); Stoops et al. (1999); Millspaugh (1999)
	Diceros bicornis		P		Garnier et al. (1998)
	Ovis canadensis		P	Faeces	Borjesson et al. (1996)
Birds	*Cinclus pallasii*		E, T		Kofuji et al. (1993)
	Strigops habroptilus		E, T		Cockrem & Rounce (1995)
	Anser anser		E, T, P	Faeces	Hirschenhauser et al. (1999); Kotrschal et al. (1998)
	Strix occidentalis			Faeces	Wasser et al. (1997)

Group specific terms are used for faecal steroid metabolites: E, oestrogen; EC, conjugated oestrogen; PdG, conjugated pregnanediol derivatives; P, progestagen; T, androgens; hCG, human chorionic gonadotrophin; eCG, equine chorionic gonadotrophin; LH, luteinising hormone; PRL, prolactin.

aggression or human disturbance. Some of the most innovative studies have integrated behavioural, genetic and hormone patterns to understand more fully the evolution of mating systems, including phenomena such as dominance, social stress and reproductive suppression.

This rapidly growing database confirms that non-invasive endocrine monitoring is incredibly useful for increasing our fundamental knowledge of free-living wildlife. Because these measures provide information on reproductive status, health, and the impact of human disturbance on animal well-being, they have important implications for the conservation and management of wildlife species. The objective of this chapter is to review current methods for assessing reproductive and adrenal status in free-living wildlife, providing case studies to illustrate how this information has assisted scientists and managers to understand better the biology of animals living in nature.

STATE OF THE ART

Advantages of endocrine monitoring

Collecting blood from free-living wildlife for measuring circulating hormones requires physical restraint or anaesthesia, which is usually stressful, dangerous, costly and ultimately impractical. Physiological stress resulting from such manipulations may obscure the ability to discern the normal underlying hormonal milieu. Non-invasive endocrine monitoring is also advantageous because pooling of urine (in the bladder) or faeces (in the intestinal tract) dampens episodic secretory patterns that normally occur in blood circulation. Additionally, non-invasive endocrine methods allow frequent (even daily) sampling, thereby permitting longitudinal studies while enhancing statistical power.

Metabolic and technical considerations

Circulating gonadal and adrenal steroids are metabolised in the liver and/or kidney before excretion into urine or bile. Generally, biologically potent steroids (oestradiol, oestrone, progesterone, testosterone, cortisol, corticosterone) are rendered impotent during metabolism through subtle molecular changes and/or through conjugation to highly charged, side chain moieties (e.g. glucuronide or sulphate molecules) before excretion. Conjugated steroids have increased molecular polarity that improves solubility in the aqueous environments of urine or bile. The proportion of steroid excreted in urine or faeces is usually species- or taxon-specific. For example, most felids excrete >90% of gonadal steroids into faeces (Brown *et al.*, 1994), whereas baboons excrete >80% of gonadal steroids into urine (Wasser *et al.*, 1991). Steroids vary in the extent to which they are metabolised before excretion, both within and among individuals and species. The time course of steroid excretion and the degree to which steroids are excreted in urine or faeces can be determined by infusing unlabelled or radiolabelled steroid and quantifying hormone metabolites in excreta. The lag-time from steroid production/secretion to appearance in excreted urine is generally less than 12 hours (African wild dog; Monfort *et al.*, 1997). In contrast, the lag-time for faeces ranges from 12 to 24 hours in ruminants (Morrow & Monfort, 1998), and 24 to 48 hours in primates (Wasser *et al.*, 1994) and hind gut fermenters (Wasser *et al.*, 1996).

Method validation

Steroid metabolites can be quantified using a variety of radiometric or non-radiometric (i.e. enzyme immunoassay [EIA] or fluorescent immunoassay [FIA]) techniques. Regardless of the technique employed, immunoassays must be re-validated for each new species or medium (e.g. serum vs. urine vs. faeces) to demonstrate that they provide reliable and consistent estimates of hormone production (Reimers *et al.*, 1981). There are two steps to validation: (1) laboratory validation (specificity, accuracy, precision and sensitivity; Niswender *et al.*, 1975) to demonstrate that the target hormone(s) is actually being measured, and (2) physiological validation, as it is crucial to demonstrate that hormonal measures accurately reflect the physiological events that one is interested in assessing.

From a practical viewpoint, it is unnecessary to determine the specific molecular structure of the hormones being monitored in each species. However, it is critical to prove that fluctuations in the hormone metabolite being measured provide physiologically relevant information. For example, an ovarian cycle might be validated by comparing two independent measures of the same hormone in matched samples (i.e. faecal vs. urinary oestrogen), or by comparing temporal hormone excretion patterns with external signs of reproductive status (e.g. sex skin swelling, copulatory behaviour). Similarly, showing a predicted rise and fall in a metabolite coincident with pregnancy onset and parturition, respectively, is solid evidence of a hormone's utility for assessing pregnancy status. Administering a drug known to stimulate hormone production (i.e. gonadotrophin releasing hormone [GnRH] or adrenocorticotrophic hormone [ACTH]) is also useful for demonstrating a cause-and-effect relationship between its exogenous administration and the subsequent excretion of the target hormone. This latter approach also clarifies the excretory lag-time between stimulation of an endocrine gland and the appearance of its hormone metabolites in excreta.

Urinary hormone monitoring

Urinary steroids are almost always excreted as conjugates (e.g. oestradiol-sulphate and oestrone-glucuronide). These are sometimes enzymatically or chemically hydrolysed before extraction and/or chromatography, and before using immunoassay techniques. However, urinary steroid monitoring was greatly simplified by the advent of direct conjugate immunoassay procedures (Lasley & Kirkpatrick, 1991). Antibodies raised against specific steroid conjugates simply permit dilution and assaying of urine without further processing, thus minimising sample processing. Urinary steroid measures are typically indexed to creatinine excretion, which is measured using a modified Jaffe reaction (Taussky, 1954). Urinary measures have the advantage over faecal methods by providing a reduced lag-time for steroid excretion (i.e. relative to events in blood circulation), simplified processing, reduced labour and ultimately lower costs. Once collected, urine can be preserved indefinitely by freezing ($-20\,^{\circ}$C) or with 'field-friendly' storage methods, including absorbing urine onto filter paper or storing urine in 10% ethanol at room temperature for up to 12 weeks (see review, Whitten *et al.*, 1998).

Case Study 1: Urinary hormones in the dwarf mongoose (Helogale parvula)
Dwarf mongooses are gregarious, cooperatively breeding mammals, studied extensively in field ecology and behavioural research. Previously, little was known about the endocrine mechanisms associated with this species. However, the advent of non-invasive endocrine monitoring techniques has allowed the physiology of reproduction in packs of the dwarf mongoose free-living in the Serengeti ecosystem to be studied (Creel *et al.*, 1991, 1992, 1993, 1995). Endocrine evaluations were compared with behavioural indices of dominance status, aggression and reproductive activity, including reproductive suppression and spontaneous lactation in non-pregnant females. In addition, it was possible to document short-lived events such as the perioestrual oestrogen surge indicative of ovulation.

Urine collection from truly wild mongooses initially appeared unlikely, if not impossible. However, when one of the pack animals sniffed and then urinated on the researcher's sandals a unique opportunity to exploit normal scent-marking behaviour occurred. Ultimately, every pack member

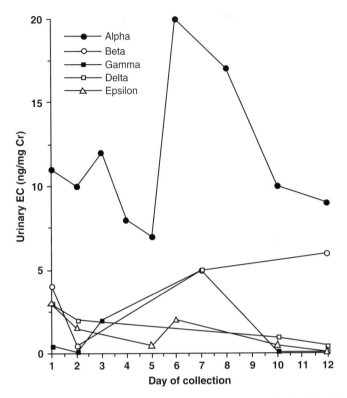

Figure 10.1 Urinary oestrogen conjugate concentrations for five females of a single pack during a synchronised oestrous period. Mating occurred on days 5–9. (Adapted from Creel *et al.*, 1992.)

routinely urinated on a rubber sandal, which was washed between sampling to prevent cross-contamination (this was systematically tested by assaying water flushed off the sandal between each use). Individual identification, using morphometric features, allowed urinary steroid excretion patterns to be correlated with dominance behaviours. Physiological validation was through comparison of endocrine profiles with well-defined mating patterns in males and females. Testicular size also correlates with androgen excretion in males.

The data revealed that a complex of endocrine and behavioural mechanisms reproductively suppressed subordinate females (see Figure 10.1). In contrast, subordinate males appeared to be suppressed through physical aggression, suggesting fundamental differences in how reproductive suppression is mediated between the sexes (Creel *et al.*, 1992). Urinary oestrogen data also helped to document spontaneous lactation, which is believed to increase the evolutionary fitness of lactating females by increasing the inclusive fitness of related young. Litters supplemented by spontaneous lactators were significantly larger at weaning compared with litters in which only the dominant female lactated (Creel et al., 1991).

Faecal hormone monitoring

Urinary hormone monitoring is quick and inexpensive, but samples can be difficult to collect under field conditions. Numerous well-established immunoassay methods are also available for processing, extracting and accurately quantifying faecal steroid metabolites. However, these have disadvantages in terms of increased time, labour and overall cost. Faecal extraction typically relies on an aqueous-based, alcohol containing (10–100%) solvent, with variation as to whether (1) samples are extracted wet or dry, (2) procedural losses are documented and (3) heat is used during processing.

Faecal steroids are typically unconjugated in excreta, in part because bacterial enzymes hydrolyse or deconjugate steroid conjugates in the large intestine. Adopting standardised collection and storage methods can minimise the potential impact of bacterial degradation on steroid metabolites, which continues after defecation. Ideally, samples should be collected as quickly as possible after defecation, followed immediately by treatment to minimise continued bacterial degradation. If samples cannot be collected within 1–2 hours post-defecation, the impact of time from defecation to sample collection on hormone metabolite concentrations should be tested systematically. Faecal storage and preservation methods range from simple freezing (liquid nitrogen tank or household freezer), drying in a portable oven, preservation in alcohol or using simple field extraction methods (see review, Whitten et al., 1998). Surprisingly, no systematic comparisons among preservation methods have been published to date, and so there is no consensus method to recommend for field use. Therefore, preservation methods should be thoughtfully considered and fully validated before large-scale application to a field setting.

Case Study 2: Faecal hormones for pregnancy diagnosis in moose (Alces alces) Faecal steroid measures have been used to provide single-sample pregnancy diagnosis in a variety of ungulates (Table 10.1). In one recent example, faecal progestagen was used to study the relationship between carnivore colonisation and ecological carrying capacity in the Greater Yellowstone Ecosystem (Berger et al., 1999). Following the extirpation of wolves and grizzly bears over 60 years ago, wild herbivore populations have increased in Yellowstone, causing concern that this trend may have detrimental effects on the ecosystem. Conversely, there is concern that the active reintroduction of predators (wolves and grizzly bears) may reduce prey availability for hunters.

Before applying our methods in the field, validations were conducted on semi-free-ranging moose, living in large, fenced enclosures. These included extraction methodology, immunoassay validations, longitudinal assessments of ovarian cycles and sexual behaviour and hormonal evaluations throughout gestation to determine quantitative criteria for diagnosing pregnancy (Monfort et al., 1993; Schwartz et al., 1995). These studies suggested that single-sample faecal progestagen concentrations >7 μg/g faeces were indicative of pregnancy throughout the second half of gestation (mid-December to late April). For field validations, progestagen was assayed 'blind' in faeces collected from anaesthetised cow moose where pregnancy was confirmed independently by rectal palpation. Test subjects were radio-collared to permit tracking of individual females and to provide confirmation that birth occurred.

Once validated, it was possible to use faecal progestagen assessments to conduct an ecological study, specifically distinguishing the relative roles of predation versus food-imposed limitations and juvenile recruitment in the wild population. Faecal hormone data revealed that contemporary pregnancy rates (75%) had declined sharply from 1996 estimates (90%), even though juvenile survival rates were among the highest in North America. Faecal data supported the hypothesis that the decline in juvenile moose numbers was not due to predation. Rather, the most influential factor for this herbivore population appears to be food availability. This study demonstrated that faecal steroid monitoring was useful for developing a broader understanding of predator–prey dynamics while providing a means for assessing long-term trends in fecundity. In the face of growing numbers of carnivore reintroductions, non-invasive endocrine measures can be an important tool for evaluating population dynamics and ecological relationships.

Non-invasive corticosteroid monitoring

Although there is no single definition or physiological measure of 'stress', urinary cortisol determinations have been considered reflective of adrenal status in many species held *ex situ*, as well as those living *in situ* (Table 10.1). Restraint and/or anaesthesia for blood sample collection can itself elicit an adrenal stress response. Furthermore, corticosteroid secretion can be both pulsatile and diurnal. Thus, a primary advantage of non-invasive corticosteroid monitoring is that one can derive a 'pooled' measure of adrenal status in undisturbed individuals.

Little native cortisol (or corticosterone) is found in faeces because these hormones are extensively metabolised before excretion. In addition to laboratory validations for faecal corticosteroid immunoassays, radiolabelled cortisol infusions and/or ACTH challenge studies have been undertaken in the captive African elephant, black rhinoceros, elk, gerenuk, scimitar-horned oryx, sea otter, sun bear, cheetah, clouded leopard, long-tailed macaque, hyaena and Northern spotted owl (Goymann et al., 1999; Wasser et al., 2001). These studies revealed that faecal corticosteroid assays accurately reflected endogenous changes in adrenal activity. Interspecific variation in corticosteroid metabolites makes it impossible to predict which faecal metabolites a species is likely to produce. However, independent laboratories have demonstrated the efficacy of group-specific antibodies for recognising a family of metabolites rather than any specific metabolite (Palme et al., 1998; Wasser et al., 2001).

Case Study 3: Faecal corticosteroids and radiocollaring African wild dogs
(Lycaon pictus)
Wild dogs of the Serengeti ecosystem are difficult to track, and radiocollars are essential for gathering data on demography, population dynamics, ecological processes that limit density, epidemiology and pathology of infectious diseases and behaviours that influence reproduction and species survival (Creel et al., 1997a, b). There has been contentious debate on the potential adverse impacts of handling wild dogs for the placement of radiocollars (Creel et al., 1997a), a concern driven in part by a disease-related decline in East African wild dog populations. One investigator hypothesised that mortality was related to immune suppression caused by the stress of darting, radiocollaring and vaccinations (Burrows et al., 1994). Others countered that short-term handling was unlikely to provoke chronic stress, and that population declines were likely to be related to other factors, including overall small population size and exposure to viral diseases (Creel et al., 1997a).

Faecal corticosteroid monitoring was used in radiocollared versus uncollared dogs to produce an objective, physiological assessment of the potential adverse consequences of short-term handling. Repeated faecal sampling and exogenous hormone challenge studies were impractical in free-living wild dogs. Therefore, the laboratory and physiological validations were conducted in zoo-maintained wild dogs. Physiological validity was demonstrated by documenting a 10- to 30-fold increase in corticosteroid

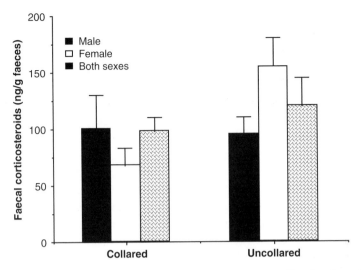

Figure 10.2 Baseline (unstressed) faecal corticosterone in collared and uncollared African wild dogs. Error bars show one standard error; there were no differences ($P < 0.05$) between collared and uncollared individuals. (Adapted from Creel *et al.*, 1997a.)

excretion within 24 hours of administering exogenous ACTH (Monfort *et al.*, 1998).

The technique then was applied to wild dog packs living in nature. After controlling for the effects of rank and sex on corticosteroid concentrations, it was apparent that there was no effect ($P < 0.05$) of radiocollaring on corticosteroid excretion (Figure 10.2). Likewise, there was no difference in corticosteroid concentrations in animals sampled before and after collaring. These data, combined with behavioural and demographic information, supported the conclusion that typical anaesthesia and radiocollaring did not provoke a chronic stress response in African wild dogs. Results not only addressed a question of fundamental scholarly interest, but also had a profound impact on the future of successfully studying this endangered species *in situ*.

PRIORITIES FOR THE FUTURE

Improved field methods for specimen preservation and storage

Appropriate sample preservation is a crucial consideration when designing any field study, because inadequate sample storage can invalidate hormone measures. Specimens can be stored temporarily (i.e. hours) during transport to the field station using portable insulated containers cooled with frozen gel packs. Longer term faecal and urine specimen storage can be readily achieved in household freezers, liquid nitrogen storage tanks or liquid nitrogen dry shippers maintained at the researcher's field station. However, because these methods are sometimes impractical in remote locations, more research is needed to compare alternative sample preservation methods systematically, including drying in portable ovens, fixing samples in alcohol (or other bactericidal media) or adsorbing urine or faecal extracts onto filter paper (or other media). Few studies have been undertaken to determine the efficacy of these storage methods in terms of their ability to maintain the stability and integrity of excreted steroid metabolites (Whitten *et al.*, 1998). Equal attention should be given to evaluating the flexibility and feasibility of each method for use under field conditions, especially when electricity and laboratory chemicals/supplies are lacking.

Simplified extraction and assay methods for field use

There is some evidence that steroid metabolites can be extracted immediately in the field and with minimal equipment (see review, Whitten *et al.*, 1998). A major advantage to such an approach is circumventing concerns about disease transmission. For example, boiling faeces in 100% ethanol for 20 minutes satisfies the US Department of Agriculture's requirements for importing faeces from ungulates originating from countries where foot-and-mouth disease is prevalent. Specimen exportation can be avoided completely if sample processing and immunoassays are conducted in the range countries where specimens were collected. This is quite feasible given the advent of non-radiometric immunoassays and even non-instrumented immunoassays (Kirkpatrick *et al.*, 1993b). Thus, more work is required to make theses technologies portable and transferable to range countries and even remote field sites.

Improved collaboration between zoo biologists and academic scientists

Zoos have tremendous potential for assisting field biologists with conducting essential laboratory and physiological validations required before undertaking any field investigation. However, most zoos are not well positioned to invest significant human and financial resources towards basic research without partners. Yet, zoos routinely seek to connect their exhibit animals to wild counterparts in nature, and scientific investigation is a natural way to achieve this goal. Zoo and academic partnerships can be mutually beneficial with zoos providing animal access and staff with a wealth of knowledge about individual species and endocrine technologies. Likewise, the field researcher brings additional scientific rigour, supplemental financial and human resources and, most importantly, a connection to animals in nature. There is a compelling need for improved cooperation between zoo biologists and academic scientists to increase knowledge of the life history and basic biology of wildlife more effectively, both *ex situ* and *in situ*. Endocrine technologies can serve as the common link of interest between zoos and academia.

CONCLUSIONS

Our understanding of the reproductive physiology of terrestrial mammals is rudimentary at best, and detailed knowledge exists for fewer than 100 species (see Wildt, Chapter 1). Much less is known about birds, reptiles and amphibians. Although we have begun to utilise zoo-based collections to augment our understanding of reproductive biology, especially through the power of non-invasive hormone monitoring, we have been too slow to extend these studies to free-ranging species. The past 20 years have witnessed a revolution in the discipline of wildlife endocrinology. There is now the technological capacity to accumulate detailed reproductive databases for literally hundreds of unstudied mammalian and non-mammalian species. Together with non-invasive adrenal steroid monitoring, we now have the capability to conduct both basic and applied physiological–endocrine research that can be integrated with other disciplines, including genetics, behaviour, nutrition, animal health, ecology and evolution. The information derived from endocrine studies can satisfy our scientific curiosity, but integrating findings with those of other disciplines is key to defining life-history requirements of individuals, populations and species, as well as complex ecological relationships.

It is hoped that the studies reviewed in this chapter will serve as incentive for future investigations, especially those that are multidisciplinary and integrative. The goal should be to generate more holistic perspectives of how animals reproduce, and to develop an improved understanding of population dynamics, the impacts of human disturbance and the wisdom of undertaking animal translocations and reintroductions. The emerging discipline of conservation endocrinology can be used to provide wildlife managers and decision-makers with new and valuable information to ensure the survival of viable wildlife populations in nature.

ACKNOWLEDGEMENTS

Many collaborators contributed to the concepts and findings discussed in this chapter. The author especially recognises Scott and Nancy Creel, Samuel Wasser, Janine Brown, David Wildt, Joel Berger and Chuck Schwartz. Kendall Mashburn and a host of volunteers assisted with laboratory analyses. The Scholarly Studies Program of the Smithsonian Institution and the Friends of the National Zoo partially funded the described projects.

REFERENCES

Adlercreutz, H. & Martin, F. (1976). Oestrogen in human pregnancy faeces. *Acta Endocrinologica* **83**, 410–419.

Albuquerque, A. C. S. R., Sousa, M. B. C., Santos, H. M. & Ziegler, T. E. (2001). Behavioral and hormonal analysis of social relationships between oldest females in a wild monogamous group of common marmosets (*Callithrix jacchus*). *International Journal of Primatology* **22**, 631–645.

Andelman, S. J., Else, J. G., Hearn, J. P. & Hodges, J. K. (1985). The non-invasive monitoring of reproductive events in wild vervet monkeys (*Cercopithecus aethiops*) using urinary pregnanediol glucuronide and its correlation with behavioural observation. *Journal of Zoology (London)* **205**, 467–477.

Bamberg, E., Choi, H. S., Möstl, E., Wurm, W., Lorin, D. & Arbeiter, K. (1984). Enzymatic determination of unconjugated oestrogens in faeces for pregnancy diagnosis in mares. *Equine Veterinary Journal* **16**, 537–539.

Berger, J., Testa, J. W., Roffe, T. & Monfort, S. L. (1999). Conservation endocrinology: a non-invasive tool to understand relationships between carnivore colonization and ecological carrying capacity. *Conservation Biology* **13**, 980–989.

Borjesson, D., Boyce, W. B., Gardner, I. A., DeForge, J. & Lasley, B. (1996). Pregnancy detection in bighorn sheep (*Ovis canadensis*) using a fecal-based enzyme immunoassay. *Journal of Wildlife Diseases* **32**, 67–74.

Brockman, D. K. & Whitten, P. L. (1996). Reproduction in free-ranging *Propithecus verreauxi*: estrus and the relationship between multiple partner matings and fertilization. *American Journal of Physical Anthropology* **100**, 57–69.

Brockman, D. K., Whitten, P. L., Richard A. F. & Schneider, A. (1998). Reproduction in free-ranging male *Propithecus verreauxi*: the hormonal correlates of mating and aggression. *American Journal of Physical Anthropology* **105**, 137–151.

Brown, J. L., Wasser S. K., Wildt, D. E. & Graham, L. H. (1994). Measurement of fecal estrogen and progesterone metabolites for assessing ovarian activity in felids. *Biology of Reproduction* **51**, 776–786.

Burrows, R., Hofer, H. & East, M. (1994). Demography, extinction and intervention in a small population: the case of the Serengeti wild dogs. *Proceedings of the Royal Society of London B* **256**, 281–292.

Clarke, M. R., Zucker, E. L. & Harrison, R. M. (1991). Fecal estradiol, sexual swellings and sociosexual behavior in free-ranging howler monkeys in Costa Rica. *American Journal of Primatology* **24**, 93.

Clutton-Brock, T. H., Brotherton, P. N. M., Russell, A. F., O'Riain, M. J., Gaynor, D., Kansky, R., Griffin, A., Manser, M., Sharpe, L., McIlrath, G. M., Small, T.,

Moss, A. & Monfort, S. (2001). Cooperation, control and concession in Meerkat groups. *Science* **291**, 478-481.

Cockrem, J. F. & Rounce, J. R. (1995). Non-invasive assessment of the annual gonadal cycle in free-living Kakapo (*Strigops habroptilus*) using fecal steroid measurements. *Auk* **112**, 253-257.

Creel, S., Creel, N. M., Mills, M. G. L. & Monfort, S. L. (1997b). Rank and reproduction in co-operatively breeding African wild dogs: behavioral and endocrine correlates. *Behavioral Ecology* **8**, 298-306.

Creel, S., Creel, N. M. & Monfort, S. L. (1997a). Radiocollaring African wild dogs (*Lycaon pictus*) does not cause chronic stress. *Conservation Biology* **11**, 544-548.

Creel, S., Creel, N., Wildt, D. E. & Monfort, S. L. (1992). Behavioural and endocrine mechanisms of reproductive suppression in Serengeti dwarf mongooses. *Animal Behaviour* **43**, 231-245.

Creel, S., Marusha-Creel, N. & Monfort, S. L. (1998). Birth order, estrogens and sex-ratio adaptation in African wild dogs (*Lycaon pictus*). *Animal Reproduction Science* **53**, 315-320.

Creel, S., Monfort, S. L., Marusha-Creel, N., Wildt, D. E. & Waser, P. M. (1995). Pregnancy, oestrogens and future reproductive success in Serengeti dwarf mongooses. *Animal Behaviour* **50**, 1132-1135.

Creel, S. R., Monfort, S. L., Wildt, D. E. & Waser, P. M. (1991). Spontaneous lactation is an adaptive result of pseudopregnancy. *Nature* **351**, 660-662.

Creel, S. R., Wildt, D. E. & Monfort, S. L. (1993). Aggression, reproduction and androgens in wild dwarf mongooses: a test of the challenge hypothesis. *American Naturalist* **141**, 816-825.

Curtis, D. J., Zaramody, A., Green, D. I. & Pickard, A. R. (2000). Non-invasive monitoring of reproductive status in wild mongoose lemurs (*Eulemur mongoz*). *Reproduction, Fertility and Development* **12**, 21-29.

Czekala, N. M. & Sicotte, P. (2000). Reproductive monitoring of free-ranging female mountain gorillas by urinary hormone analysis. *American Journal of Primatology* **51**, 209-215.

Foley, C. A. H., Papageorge, S. & Wasser, S. K. (2001). Non-invasive stress and reproductive measures of social and ecological pressures in free-ranging African elephants. *Conservation Biology* **15**, 134-142.

Garnier, J. N., Green, D. I., Pickard, A. R., Shaw, H. J. & Holt, W. V. (1998). Non-invasive diagnosis of pregnancy in wild black rhinoceros (*Diceros bicornis minor*) by faecal steroid analysis. *Reproduction, Fertility and Development* **10**, 451-458.

Garrott, R. A., Monfort, S. L., Mashburn, K. L., White, P. J. & Cook, J. G. (1998). One-sample pregnancy diagnosis in elk using fecal steroid metabolites. *Journal of Wildlife Diseases* **34**, 126-131.

Goymann, W., Möstl, E., Van't Hof, T., East, M. L. & Hofer, H. (1999). Non-invasive fecal monitoring of glucocorticoids in spotted hyaenas, *Crocuta crocuta*. *General and Comparative Endocrinology* **114**, 340-348.

Herrick J. R., Agoramoorthy, G., Rasanayagam, R. & Harder, J. D. (2000). Urinary progesterone in free-ranging red howler monkeys (*Alouatta seniculus*): preliminary observations of the estrous cycle and gestation. *American Journal of Primatology* **51**, 257-263.

Hirschenhauser, K., Möstl, E. & Kotrschal, K. (1999). Seasonal patterns of sex steroids determined from feces in different social categories of greylag geese (*Anser anser*). *General and Comparative Endocrinology* 114, 67-79.

Hodges, J. K., Czekala, N. M. & Lasley, B. L. (1979). Estrogen and luteinizing hormone secretion in diverse primate species from simplified urinary analysis. *Journal of Medical Primatology* 8, 349-364.

Kirkpatrick, J. F., Bancroft, K. & Kincy, V. (1992b). Pregnancy and ovulation detection in bison (*Bison bison*) assessed by means of urinary and fecal steroids. *Journal of Wildlife Diseases* 28, 590-597.

Kirkpatrick, J. F., Gudermuth, D. F., Flagan, R. L., McCarthy, J. C. & Lasley, B. L. (1993a). Remote monitoring of ovulation and pregnancy of Yellowstone bison. *Journal of Wildlife Management* 57, 407-412.

Kirkpatrick, J. F., Kincy, V., Bancroft, K., Shideler, S. E. & Lasley, B. L. (1991b). Oestrous cycle of the North American bison (*Bison bison*) characterised by urinary pregnanediol-3-glucuronide. *Journal of Reproduction and Fertility* 93, 541-547.

Kirkpatrick, J. F., Lasley, B. L., Shideler, S. E., Roser, J. F. & Turner, J. W. (1993b). Non-instrumented immunoassay field tests for pregnancy detection in free-roaming feral horses. *Journal of Wildlife Management* 57, 168-173.

Kirkpatrick, J. F., Liu, I. K. M., Turner, J. W., Jr, Naugle, R. & Keiper, R. (1992a). Long-term effects of porcine zonae pellucidae immunocontraception on ovarian function in feral horses (*Equus caballus*). *Journal of Reproduction and Fertility* 94, 437-444.

Kirkpatrick, J. F., McCarthy, J. C., Gudermuth, D. F., Shideler, S. E. & Lasley, B. L. (1996). An assessment of the reproductive biology of Yellowstone bison (*Bison bison*) subpopulations using non-capture methods. *Canadian Journal of Zoology* 74, 8-14.

Kirkpatrick, J. F., Naugle, R., Liu, I. K. M., Bernoco, M. & Turner, J. W., Jr (1995). Effects of seven consecutive years of porcine zona pellucida contraception on ovarian function in feral mares. *Biology of Reproduction Monographs* 1, 411-418.

Kirkpatrick, J. F., Shideler, S. E., Lasley, B. L. & Turner, J. W. (1991a). Pregnancy determination in uncaptured feral horses by means of fecal steroid conjugates. *Theriogenology* 35, 753-759.

Kirkpatrick, J. F., Shideler, S. E. & Turner, J. W. (1990). Pregnancy determination in uncaptured feral horses based on free steroids in feces and steroid metabolites in urine-soaked snow. *Canadian Journal of Zoology* 68, 2576-2579.

Knott, C. D. (1993). Monitoring of hormonal profiles of free-ranging chimpanzees (*Pan troglodytes*) and orangutans (*Pongo pygmaeus*). *Bulletin of the Ecological Society of America*, Suppl. 74, 314.

Kofuji, H., Kanda, M. & Oishi, T. (1993). Breeding cycles and fecal gonadal steroids in the Brown Dipper (*Cinclus pallasii*). *General and Comparative Endocrinology* 91, 216-223.

Kotrschal K., Hirschenhauser, K. & Möstl, E. (1998). The relationship between social stress and dominance is seasonal in greylag geese. *Animal Behaviour* 55, 171-176.

Lasley, B. L. & Kirkpatrick, J. F. (1991). Monitoring ovarian function in captive and free-ranging wildlife by means of urinary and fecal steroids. *Journal of Zoo Wildlife Medicine* 22, 23-31.

Miller, M. W., Hobbs, N. T. & Sousa, M. C. (1991). Detecting stress responses in Rocky Mountain bighorn sheep (*Ovis canadensis canadensis*): reliability of cortisol concentrations in urine and feces. *Canadian Journal of Zoology* **69**, 15-24.

Millspaugh, J. J. (1999). Behavioral and physiological responses of elk to human disturbances in the southern Black Hills, South Dakota. Doctoral dissertation, University of Washington, Seattle, WA.

Monfort, S. L., Arthur, N. P. & Wildt, D. E. (1991). Monitoring ovarian function and pregnancy by evaluating excretion of urinary oestrogen conjugates in semi-free-ranging Przewalski's horses (*Equus przewalskii*). *Journal of Reproduction and Fertility* **91**, 155-164.

Monfort, S. L., Mashburn, K. L., Brewer, B. A. & Creel, S. R. (1998). Evaluating adrenal activity in African wild dogs (*Lycaon pictus*) by fecal corticosteroid analysis. *Journal of Zoo and Wildlife Medicine* **29**, 129-133.

Monfort, S. L., Schwartz, C. C. & Wasser, S. K. (1993). Monitoring reproduction in captive moose using urinary and fecal steroid metabolites. *Journal of Wildlife Management*, **57**, 400-407.

Monfort, S. L., Wasser, S. K., Mashburn, K. L., Burke, M., Brewer, B. A. & Creel, S. R. (1997). Steroid metabolism and validation of non invasive endocrine monitoring in the African wild dog (*Lycaon pictus*). *Zoo Biology* **16**, 533-548.

Morrow, C. J. & Monfort, S. L. (1998). Ovarian activity in the scimitar-horned oryx (*Oryx dammah*) determined by faecal steroid analysis. *Animal Reproduction Science* **53**, 191-207.

Möstl, E., Choi, H. S., Wurm, W., Ismail, N. & Bamberg, E. (1984). Pregnancy diagnosis in cows and heifers by determination of oestradiol-17α in faeces. *British Veterinary Journal* **140**, 287-291.

Niswender, G. D., Akbar, A. M. & Nett, T. M. (1975). Use of specific antibodies for quantification of steroid hormones. In *Methods in Enzymology* (Eds. B. W. O'Malley & J. G. Hardman), pp. 119-142. Academic Press, New York.

Palme, R., Robia, C., Messmann, S. & Möstl, E. (1998). Measuring faecal cortisol metabolites: a non-invasive tool to evaluate adrenocortical activity in mammals. *Proceedings of the 2nd International Symposium of Physiology and Ethology of Wild and Zoo Animals*, Berlin, Germany. *Advances in Ethology* **33**, 27.

Poole, J. H., Kasman, L. H., Ramsay, E. C. & Lasley, B. L. (1984). Musth and urinary testosterone in the African elephant (*Loxodonta africana*). *Journal of Reproduction and Fertility* **70**, 255-290.

Reimers, T. J., Cowan, B. A., Davidson, H. P. & Colby, E. D. (1981). Validation of radioimmunoassays for triiodothyronine, thyroxine, and hydrocortisone (cortisol) in canine, feline, and equine sera. *American Journal of Veterinary Research* **42**, 2016-2021.

Risler, L., Wasser, S. K. & Sackett, G. P. (1987). Measurement of excreted steroids in *Macaca nemestrina*. *American Journal of Primatology* **12**, 91-100.

Robbins, M. M. & Czekala, N. M. (1997). A preliminary investigation of urinary testosterone and cortisol levels in wild male mountain gorillas. *American Journal of Primatology* **43**, 51-64.

Savage, A., Shideler, S. E., Soto, L. H., Causado, J., Giraldo, L. H., Lasley, B. L. & Snowdon, C. T. (1997). Reproductive events of wild cotton-top tamarins (*S. oedipus*) in Colombia. *American Journal of Primatology* **43**, 329-337.

Schwartz, C. C., Monfort, S. L., Dennis, P. & Hundertmark, K. J. (1995). Fecal progesterone concentration as an indicator of the estrous cycle and pregnancy in moose. *Journal of Wildlife Management* **59**, 580-583.

Stavisky, R. C., Russell, E., Stallings, J., Smith, E. O., Worthman, C. M. & Whitten, P. L. (1995). Fecal steroid analysis of ovarian cycles in free-ranging baboons. *American Journal of Primatology* **36**, 285-297.

Stoops, M. A., Anderson, G. B., Lasley, B. L. & Shideler, S. E. (1999). Estimating the reproductive potential in a free-ranging herd of elk. *Journal of Wildlife Management* **63**, 561-569.

Strier, K. B. & Ziegler, T. E. (1994). Insights into ovarian function in wild muriqui monkeys (*Brachyteles arachnoides*). *American Journal of Primatology* **32**, 31-40.

Strier, K. B. & Ziegler, T. E. (1997). Behavioral and endocrine characteristics of the reproductive cycle in wild muriqui monkeys, *Brachyteles arachnoides*. *American Journal of Primatology* **42**, 299-310.

Strier, K. A., Ziegler, T. E. & Wittwer, D. J. (1999). Seasonal and social correlates of fecal testosterone and cortisol levels in wild male muriquis (*Brachyteles arachnoides*). *Hormones and Behavior* **35**, 125-134.

Taussky, H. H. (1954). A microcolorimetric determination of creatine in urine by the Jaffe reaction. *Journal of Biological Chemistry* **208**, 853-861.

Thierry, B., Heistermann, M., Aujard, F. & Hodges, J. K. (1996). Long-term data on basic reproductive parameters and evaluation of endocrine, morphological, and behavioral measures for monitoring reproductive status in a group of semifree-ranging Tonkean macaques (*Macaca tonkeana*). *American Journal of Primatology* **39**, 47-62.

van Schaik, C. P., van Noordwijk, M. A., van Bragt, T. & Blakenstein, M. A. (1991). A pilot study of the social correlates of levels of urinary cortisol, prolactin, and testosterone in wild long-tailed macaques (*Macaca fascicularis*). *Primates* **32**, 345-356.

Wallner, B., Möstl, E., Dittami, J. & Prossinger, H. (1999). Fecal glucocorticoids document stress in female Barbary macaques (*Macaca sylvanus*). *General and Comparative Endocrinology* **113**, 80-86.

Wasser, S. K. (1996). Reproductive control in wild baboons measured by fecal steroids. *Biology of Reproduction* **55**, 393-399.

Wasser, S. K., Bevis, K., King, G. & Hanson, E. (1997). Noninvasive physiological measures of disturbance in the Northern spotted owl. *Conservation Biology* **11**, 1019-1022.

Wasser, S. K., Hunt, K. E., Brown, J. L., Crockett, C., Bechert, U., Millspaugh, J., Larson, S. & Monfort, S. L. (2001). A generalized fecal glucocorticoid assay for use in a diverse array of non-domestic mammalian and avian species. *General and Comparative Endocrinology* **120**, 260-275.

Wasser, S. K., Monfort, S. L., Southers, J. & Wildt, D. E. (1994). Excretion rates and metabolites of oestradiol and progesterone in baboon (*Papio cynocephalus cynocephalus*). *Journal of Reproduction and Fertility* **101**, 213-220.

Wasser, S. K., Monfort, S. L. & Wildt, D. E. (1991). Rapid extraction of steroids for measuring reproductive cyclicity and early pregnancy in free-ranging yellow baboons (*Papio cynocephalus cynocephalus*). *Journal of Reproduction and Fertility* **92**, 415-423.

Wasser, S. K., Papageorge, S., Foley, C. & Brown, J. L. (1996). Excretory fate of estradiol and progesterone in the African elephant (*Loxodonta africana*) and pattern of fecal steroid concentrations throughout the estrous cycle. *General and Comparative Endocrinology*, **102**, 255-262.

White P. J., Garrott, R. A., Kirkpatrick J. F. & Berkeley, E. V. (1995). Diagnosing pregnancy in free-ranging elk using fecal steroid metabolites. *Journal of Wildlife Diseases* **31**, 514-522.

Whitten, P. J., Brockman, D. K. & Stavisky, R. C. (1998). Recent advances in non-invasive techniques to monitor hormone-behavior interactions. *American Journal of Physical Anthropology*, Suppl. **27**, 1-23.

Ziegler, T., Hodges, K., Winkler, P. & Heistermann, M. (2000). Hormonal correlates of reproductive seasonality in wild female hanuman langurs (*Presbytis entellus*). *American Journal of Primatology* **51**, 119-134.

Ziegler, T. E., Santos, C. V., Pissinatti, A. & Strier, K. B. (1997a). Steroid excretion during the ovarian cycle in captive and wild muriquis, *Brachyteles aracnoides*. *American Journal of Primatology* **42**, 311-321.

Ziegler, T. E., Scheffler, G. & Carlson, A. A. (1997b). Methods and use of fecal steroid analyses for monitoring reproductive functioning in marmosets and tamarins. *Acta Primatologia* **6**, 269-280.

11

Ultrasound for analysis of reproductive function in wildlife species

THOMAS B. HILDEBRANDT, JANINE L. BROWN,
ROBERT HERMES & FRANK GÖRITZ

INTRODUCTION AND OBJECTIVES

Ultrasonography was used as early as the 1950s to characterise soft tissues in humans, and today is used routinely in human and veterinary medicine in the areas of ophthalmology, cardiology, neurology, nephrology, gynaecology and andrology, obstetrics, organ transplantation, oncology, orthopaedics and dermatology. It is somewhat surprising then that ultrasonography has received so little attention in zoo and wildlife medicine (see review, Hildebrandt & Göritz, 1998). Furthermore, although the number of investigations has increased recently, the focus remains on mammals (69%) with less emphasis on reptiles (19%), birds (12%), fish and amphibians (<1%) (Göritz, 1996).

Reproduction in many zoo-held animals is poor, and infertility caused by physiological disorders or mismanagement prohibits creating self-sustaining populations. Because of limited knowledge of species' reproductive anatomy and physiology, techniques to determine sex, sexual maturity, reproductive tract morphology, the reproductive cycle itself and gestation and foetal growth are critical to successful *ex situ* reproduction and management. This is an exciting time because ultrasonography is finally finding a niche in the study and management of rare wildlife species. Since 1993 we have conducted thousands of ultrasound examinations in more than 100 species, often in collaboration with reproductive biologists, theriogenologists and pathologists. The aim of this chapter is to describe some of our experiences in the use of ultrasonography as a powerful tool for assessing reproductive fitness of captive and free-living wildlife species.

STATE OF THE ART

Advantages of ultrasonography

Assessing urogenital structures over time allows description of reproductive events and generation of new knowledge in females (e.g. ovaries and uterus) and males (e.g. testes and accessory sex glands). Sonographically evaluating the ovary allows observation of ovulation, the impact of exogenous gonadotrophin therapies used with assisted breeding and the progress and/or impact of treatment on naturally occurring pathologies. In contrast to other imaging procedures (e.g. radiography, magnetic resonance, endoscopy), ultrasonography has advantages because it (1) is non-invasive and therefore repeatable; (2) provides real-time information; (3) generates high resolution characterisation of soft tissue and morphometrics of organs, implants or other foreign bodies; (4) produces sectional images of tissues and organ structures; (5) permits examining motion and direction (heartbeat, vascular flow, foetal movement); (6) facilitates documenting and preserving data on storable media and (7) is portable and compatible with zoo and field studies.

Challenges of using ultrasonography for wildlife

Applying ultrasonography to wild animals presents unique challenges. Although some animals such as elephants (Hermes *et al.*, 2000; Hildebrandt *et al.*, 2000a, b) and rhinoceroses (Schaffer *et al.*, 1994; Radcliffe *et al.*, 1997, 2001; Roth *et al.*, 2001) can be trained to accept transrectal ultrasound, most require chemical or mechanical restraint. Birds usually are examined in dorsal recumbency by restraining the wings and legs. Poikilothermal animals (i.e. cold-blooded lizards) can be rendered immobile in a cold environment (e.g. ice-water bath). Carnivores nearly always require sedation or anaesthesia.

Morphological specialisations also produce challenges. For example, acoustic coupling of transcutaneous ultrasound probes can be hampered by body shells, plates, thick leathery skin, feathers or fur. Avian air sacs, subcutaneous fat pads, air-filled intestinal loops and large body size also decrease ultrasonographic effectiveness. Because there is so little reference data on organ sonomorphology, results often require confirmation by postmortem ultrasonographic examinations of intact carcasses and isolated organs. Also, ultrasound equipment sometimes must be customised to accommodate species-specific differences in anatomy. Lastly, the cost of accessory components, such as varied transcutaneous and intraoperative transducers, cable extensions, animal-specific scan head adapters and battery packs for field examinations can be prohibitive, although affordability continues to improve.

Ultrasonography for reproductive assessments

Sex determination
Many species (especially birds) express little or no phenotypic or behavioural variation between the sexes. Thus, basic management for *ex situ* breeding (pairing birds of opposite gender) is often difficult. The two most common sexing methods involve laparoscopy (invasive, requiring anaesthesia) and molecular genetic analysis (requires blood sampling and is highly species-specific). Ultrasonography provides a third, non-surgical alternative that can be used to detect gonadal or intragenital structures. Early problems encountered in birds because of transcutaneous ultrasound transmission through air sacs have been overcome by transintestinal and transcloacal methods that rely on high resolution, miniaturised probes. Transintestinal ultrasonography allows viewing the entire genital tract (including gonads) whereas the transcloacal approach images only the caudal genital tract (Hildebrandt *et al.*, 1994, 1995, 1996; Hildebrandt & Göritz, 1998). Birds as small as the common quail have been successfully examined ultrasonographically in this way (Hildebrandt *et al.*, 1997).

For monomorphic species, transcutaneous ultrasound has been used for sexing invertebrates, fish, amphibians and reptiles, whereas transrectal ultrasound has been used to identify sex in the beaver, sloth and spotted hyaena (Hildebrandt & Göritz, 1998). In studies of species with dense scales (e.g. Komodo dragon), transintestinal ultrasound can be effective.

Reproductive assessments
Fundamental reproductive data are limited for most species (e.g. puberty, oestrous cyclicity, seasonality, pregnancy and reproductive senescence). Longitudinal, sonographic examinations can provide these data and are even more informative when combined with endocrine analyses. For example, two precisely-timed luteinising hormone (LH) surges occur during the elephant's ovarian follicular phase, only one of which induces ovulation (Kapustin *et al.*, 1996; Brown *et al.*, 1999). Ultrasonography has demonstrated that the first non-ovulatory LH peak correlates with a wave of follicular growth and breakdown of vaginal mucus that is distinctive from the subsequent ovulatory surge (Hermes *et al.*, 2000). In the Sumatran rhinoceros, parallel ultrasound and endocrine evaluations have suggested that females may exhibit induced ovulation (Roth *et al.*, 2001). Whereas

regular 21-day luteal cycles are observed after mating, haemorrhagic anovulatory structures develop in the absence of mating. Ultrasonography also has been useful in characterising seasonal growth and activity patterns of ovaries, testes and accessory sex glands and for distinguishing adults from juveniles. Indications of juvenile status include the sonographic visualisation of the bursa fabricii in birds (Hildebrandt *et al.*, 1994, 1996) and a mucus-filled vagina in combination with inactive ovaries in the elephant (Hildebrandt *et al.*, 2000a). Ultrasonography can also detect gonadal inactivity associated with reproductive senescence (Hildebrandt & Göritz, 1998), thus indicating when breeding attempts should cease.

Pregnancy diagnosis is the most widely used application of ultrasound to zoo animals. The historical approach of zoo staff relying on observed mating to predict a species' gestation and to estimate delivery date is often inaccurate. Indirect pregnancy diagnosis via hormone measurements in faeces or urine can be informative, but technical methods and data interpretation are often species-specific (Schwarzenberger *et al.*, 1996; Brown *et al.*, 2001b; see also Monfort, Chapter 10 and Pickard, Chapter 9) or simply insufficiently distinctive (Brown *et al.*, 2001). By contrast, ultrasonography can allow direct viewing of embryonic/foetal morphologies, including number, viability and developmental stage (Figure 11.1), allowing a better estimation of impending parturition. In birds and oviparous reptiles, ultrasonic observation of the extent of calcification of eggs has even permitted prediction of the laying term (Hildebrandt & Göritz, 1998).

Reproductive pathology assessments

Reproductive pathologies can be diagnosed by ultrasonography before proceeding with mating recommendations. This approach has been used to confirm a high incidence of benign uterine muscle tumours (leiomyomas) in Asian elephants (Hildebrandt *et al.*, 2000a) and Asian rhinoceroses (Schaffer *et al.*, 1994), endometrial and ovarian cysts in African elephants (Hildebrandt *et al.*, 2000a), endometriosis in non-human primates (Swenson, 1993) and cystic ovarian and endometrial degeneration in aged carnivores (Seidel *et al.*, 1994), especially felids implanted with progestagens for contraception (Munson *et al.*, 1995). However, it is not always easy to distinguish abnormalities from normal physiological changes (e.g. morphological changes due to purulent endometritis in the macaque appear similar to fluctuations in monthly menstrual pattern).

Whenever possible, pre-breeding fitness examinations by ultrasonography should also include the major thoracic and abdominal organs (e.g. heart, lung, liver, spleen, kidney, adrenal and pancreas) (Seidel *et al.*, 1994).

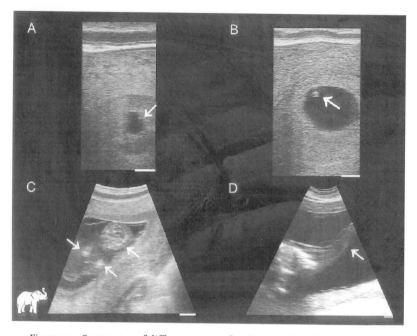

Figure 11.1 Sonograms of different stages of embryo and foetal development in an Asian elephant. (A) Embryonic vesicle in week 9; (B) week 10 embryo, visible as a marked echogenic area in the embryonic fluid; (C) 16-week foetal cross-section through the head, rump and forelimbs showing first signs of mineralisation; (D) trunk of 24-week-old foetus. The bar at the right bottom corner of each sonogram represents 1 cm.

Subclinical changes in these organs could indicate a metabolic disorder that, in the case of a burdensome pregnancy, might have lethal consequences for the dam or foetus. Excessive intra-abdominal fluid has proved to be secondary to chronic tuberculosis, malignant tumour formation and subclinical cardiac, hepatic or renal dysfunctions (Hildebrandt & Göritz, 1998). However, data interpretation is not always straightforward. For example, pericardial fluid is regularly detected in healthy amphibians and turtles, and profuse abdominal fluid is common in clinically healthy white rhinoceroses. These cases reinforce the need to establish a physiological database of sonographic morphology across a diversity of species.

Identifying prenatal pathology

Prenatal pathologies include embryonic and foetal retardation, malformation and death. Clear ultrasonographical signs include no heartbeat or foetal movement, free-floating foetal membranes, reduced volume and/or increased echogenicity of foetal fluid and partial or premature placental separation (Göritz et al., 2001). For the most accurate assessment, the entire genital tract (including conceptus) should be scanned using a low frequency ultrasound probe (2–4 MHz) followed by higher frequency scans (5–11 MHz) for more detailed imaging.

Most embryogenic pathologies occur during implantation. Early embryonic death is generally indicated by structural changes within the endometrium of a slightly enlarged uterus. These patterns often involve an undifferentiated echogenic form in the uterine lumen while embryonic membranes and fluid remain present in the uterus. The time frame in which foetal pathologies can be detected by ultrasonography usually encompasses the first trimester, extending sometimes to the end of the second trimester. Thereafter, the formation of scales, thick skin, fur and skeletal calcification often interfere with imaging. The foetus also can 'descend' into the abdominal cavity later in gestation, becoming hidden by intestines. Changing the dam's position (standing vs. lateral recumbency) can sometimes enhance the view of the gravid reproductive tract. In some cases (e.g. rhinoceros, elephant), assessing the health status of a near-term pregnancy is possible without imaging the foetus. For example, reduced uterine blood flow, cloudy foetal fluid or absence of transferred foetal-induced movements are all indicative of foetal distress or death.

Used repeatedly during gestation, ultrasonography can be powerful for identifying normal foetal growth patterns as well as anomalies such as retardation, malformation and fluid accumulations (e.g. ascites, cystic kidneys, hydrocephalus). Documented abnormalities include 'twin monster syndrome' in the Przewalski horse (Figure 11.2), schistosoma reflexum in red deer, hydrocephaly in the marmoset and anencephaly in the bottlenosed dolphin (Hildebrandt & Göritz, 1998).

Support of assisted reproductive techniques
Ultrasonography has played a significant role in more than 200 assisted reproductive procedures in a wide range of species, including the giant panda, brown bear, Asian and African elephant, Eld's deer, scimitar-horned oryx, numerous felids, yak, swamp deer, European roe deer, European brown hare, African goat, crab-eating macaque, two-toed sloth, spotted hyaena, warthog, tapir and babirusa. Examples include: (1) ultrasonographically-supported collection of uterine blastocysts from *Macaca fascicularis* by transcervical insertion of a two-way catheter; (2) artificial insemination of elephants using ultrasonography to guide a catheter more than 2 metres through the reproductive tract and then deep into the uterus; and

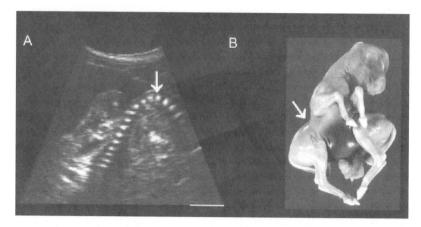

Figure 11.2 Sonogram (A) and post-mortem preparation (B) of a foetal malformation (cephalo-thoraco-omphalopagus) in a Przewalski horse with a high inbred factor (0.7). The 180° bend in the lumbar spinal cord was the intrauterine indicator for the malformed foetus. The bar at the right bottom corner of the sonogram represents 1 cm.

(3) artificial insemination in roe deer, including the monitoring of prostaglandin-induced luteolysis and follicle growth (Göritz, 1996; Hildebrandt & Göritz, 1998; Brown, 2000). In cases of reproductive failure due to a specific pathology, sonographic-assisted follow-up provides the information necessary for evaluating treatment outcomes (e.g. using GnRH analogues or gonadotrophins to treat ovarian cysts or uterine myometrial tumours: Brown, 2000; Hildebrandt & Göritz, 1998).

CASE STUDIES

Case study 1: Fertility challenges in elephants

Asian and African elephant populations *ex situ* are not self-sustaining, owing to naturally low conception rates in captivity and logistical difficulties associated with transporting breeding animals between institutions. To identify potential causes of reproductive failure, more than 2000 ultrasonographic assessments have been conducted in male and female elephants maintained in facilities throughout Asia, Europe, Africa and North America. Results suggest there are several types of infertility related to species, gender and captivity status.

About 250 female elephants have been examined by evaluating the entire urogenital tract using a real-time, B-mode ultrasound scanning system

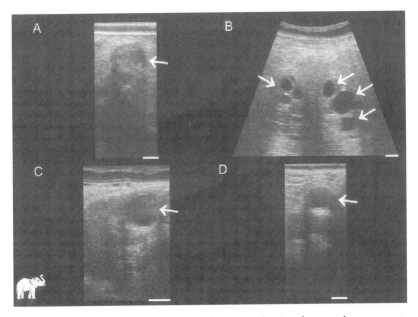

Figure 11.3 Four pathological findings from reproductive ultrasound assessments in female elephants. (A) Uterine leiomyomas in an Asian elephant; (B) multiple uterine cysts in an Asian elephant; (C) an ovarian follicle cyst in an acyclic African elephant; (D) para-ovarian cyst in a normal cycling African elephant. The bar at the right bottom corner of each sonogram represents 1 cm.

equipped with a 3.5-MHz convex, 5.0-MHz microconvex and a 7.5-MHz linear transducer (Hildebrandt *et al.*, 2000a). This system has been modified to incorporate special features, including probe and cable extensions and a monitor helmet with video glasses. In general, female pathologies often involve changes in the internal genital organs, primarily uterine tumours (leiomyomas), endometrial cysts and ovarian cysts (Figure 11.3). There is a higher incidence of genital tract leiomyomas in Asian compared with African elephants, whereas ovarian cysts occur in African but not Asian elephants. Cystic endometrial degeneration has been found in both species. It remains to be determined how these pathologies affect reproduction. Ovarian cysts have been associated with acyclicity in elephants (Brown, 2000), but the impact of uterine cysts or tumours is unclear. Some females with uterine cysts cycle normally and even conceive (T. Hildebrandt, F. Göritz & J. Brown unpublished data). There have been too few studies combining endocrine monitoring with ultrasound to make more definitive conclusions as to the significance of these pathologies. But it now is known that the incidence of these reproductive disorders increases with age and is greater in nulliparous than age-matched, parous individuals. These findings suggest that breeding elephants at a young age (before pathologies develop) should be a high priority and that females be assessed periodically by ultrasound and longitudinal hormonal analyses (usually progesterone) to assess reproductive fitness.

Male elephant infertility appears to be related to poor semen quality and low libido rather than any specific anatomical abnormality. To date, evaluating circulating testosterone has been a non-informative index for diagnosing gonadal dysfunction. Rather, ultrasonography remains the most reliable method of assessing breeding potential in bull elephants. Transrectal ultrasound and manual semen collection of more than 75 bull elephants has characterised the morphology and functionality of the entire urogenital tract, including testes and accessory sex organs (Hildebrandt *et al.*, 2000b). Most bulls were non-breeders (63%), even those exposed to females. The percentage of reproductive tract pathologies detected by ultrasound was low (14%), however, even in older animals. In contrast, semen quality varied markedly, and sperm motility often was less than 50%. Interestingly, more than half of the 'infertile' bulls appeared to be in social situations where they were subordinate to older cows or other bulls. Thus, although many of these bulls could serve as semen donors, they have inconsistently produced good quality ejaculates that could result from physiological disorder(s), behavioural problems or perhaps suboptimal semen collection methods. Regardless, periodic ultrasound examinations combined with semen collection have been recommended as routine management tools to monitor the reproductive value of bull elephants.

Case study 2: Assisted reproduction in the giant panda

The giant panda Bao Bao arrived at the Berlin Zoo in 1981 at the approximate age of 9 years and was maintained without a mate for 13 years. In 1991, as he began approaching reproductive senescence (according to Chinese experts), semen was collected by electroejaculation and frozen for planned artificial insemination of a female giant panda (Ming Ming) at the London Zoo in 1992 and 1993. Both inseminations were unsuccessful, and when Bao Bao was electroejaculated again in January and March 1996, no sperm were obtained. The following year, just before the breeding season (February 1997), he underwent an ultrasonographic examination which indicated that the testes contained multiple hyperechogenic areas within the parenchyma, indicative of connective tissue invasion of spermatogenic tissue (Figure 11.4B). Remaining testicular tissue was moderately echogenic, and the accessory sexual glands were not fully developed (perhaps consistent with the

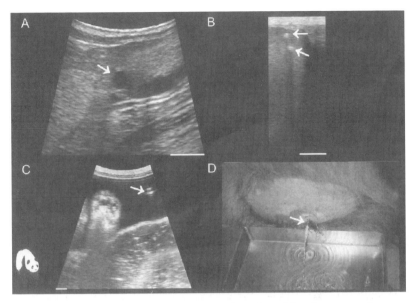

Figure 11.4 Ultrasonographic assessment of a male and female giant panda.
(A) Active ovary with multiple follicles and a low echogenic ovarian cortex after
FSH and LH stimulation of a former acyclic female (arrow indicates a Graafian
follicle); (B) multiple fibrotic foci in the testicular parenchyma in a male
indicating testicular ageing (arrows, two fibrotic regions in the testicular
parenchyma); (C) free-floating intestinal loops indicating a severe abdominal
ascites (arrow, the tip of the needle); (D) abdominal puncture with a 16-gauge
needle performed under transabdominal ultrasound guidance to prevent
perforation of the intestine or other organs (arrow, the cone of the inserted
needle). The bar at the bottom each sonogram represents 1 cm.

examination occurring prior to the peak breeding season in March–May). Of
more concern was the sonographic observation of severe abdominal ascites
that later was determined (via blood analysis) to be due to chronic pancreatic
inflammation (Figure 11.4C). Ultrasound-guided puncture of the peritoneal
cavity with a 16-gauge needle resulted in the recovery of c. 8 litres of clear
transudate (Figure 11.4D). Administering diuretics and broad-spectrum
antibiotics brought about a rapid recovery that was confirmed by a follow-
up ultrasound examination 5 weeks later. A spermic ejaculate was obtained
at that time.

In April 1995, the Berlin Zoo received a wild-born female (Yan Yan,
c. 10 years old) from China. Non-invasive urinary hormone analysis revealed no ovarian cyclicity during her first breeding season in Germany
(Meyer et al., 1997). In 1997, a transrectal ultrasound examination
confirmed that the ovaries were inactive, but indicated the genital tract was
normally developed. Over the next 3 years, three artificial inseminations

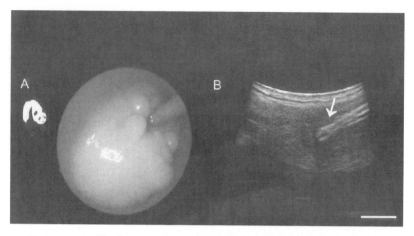

Figure 11.5 Artificial insemination of a giant panda. (A) Endoscopic image of the insemination catheter inserted into the external cervical os; (B) simultaneous guidance of catheter and monitoring of semen deposition by transrectal ultrasound. Seminal fluids were visible in the real-time ultrasound during injection as steadily increasing low echogenic areas below the intrauterine catheter tip. The bar at the right bottom corner of the sonogram represents 1 cm.

were conducted. In each case, ultrasonography was crucial for monitoring ovarian activity after exogenous gonadotrophin treatment (using equine chorionic gonadotrophin [with or without FSH priming] and human chorionic gonadotrophin) and assessing insemination outcome. For each insemination, a disposable catheter (2 mm diameter) was guided into the external cervical os using an endoscope, and then directed into the uterus by transrectal ultrasound (Figure 11.5). One 2 ml quantity of fresh or frozen semen from Bao Bao (0.35–7.5 × 10^9 sperm/ml, 85–95% sperm motility) was deposited into the uterine body.

Ovarian responses at each insemination were relatively uniform, with one to three Graafian follicles (>6 mm diameter) and more than 10 smaller follicles (1–3 mm) forming after gonadotrophin treatment (Figure 11.4A). On each occasion, there was a urinary oestrogen metabolite rise, but no oestrous behaviour. No full-term pregnancies resulted, although ultrasound imaging suggested that a conception followed by embryonic absorption had occurred in 1997. This case study has illustrated the value of combined endocrine monitoring and ultrasonography for collecting substantial new information on a pair of non-reproducing giant pandas. Although the fertility problem has yet to be resolved, certainly ultrasonography is proving helpful in systematically addressing problems facing the management of a high profile endangered species in a zoo collection.

Case study 3: Fertility assessment of European brown hare

European brown hare (*Lepus europaeus*) populations have declined by about 60% in the past 25 years. The species recently was classified as Vulnerable by CITES (the Convention on International Trade in Endangered Species) in four German states. Comprehensive studies on the reproductive fitness of free-living brown hares were initiated in 1998 in the state of Nordrhein-Westfalen. During a 4-year period, 375 brown hares (178 females, 197 males) from 16 areas were assessed using endocrinological, ultrasonographic and seminal evaluations. The female urogenital tract (vulva, vagina, urethra, urinary bladder, cervix, uterus) was scanned transcutaneously using 7.5- and 10-MHz ultrasound probes. In males, the urinary bladder, testes and epididymides were examined transcutaneously using a 10-MHz linear scanner, and the urethra and accessory sex glands were viewed by a transrectal 7.5-MHz microconvex transducer. Additional techniques included (1) colour flow Doppler imaging (5–11 MHz) to measure gonadal, uterine and placental blood flow, and concepti heart rate activity, and (2) three-dimensional ultrasonography to determine stage of pregnancy and foetal health. Most females were pregnant (67%) or lactating (20%) at the time of examination. Even non-reproducing females were experiencing ovarian activity as indicated by the presence of follicles and/or corpora lutea. About two implantation sites were observed per pregnant female. Urogenital tract morphology was normal in males, and good quality semen collected using electroejaculation equipment specifically adapted to this species' anatomy was obtained from most adults. Oligozoospermia was observed in 14% of the males, although flow-cytometric analysis failed to reveal any disruption in spermatogenesis. These males may have mated in the field just before examination; dried ejaculate at the base of the penis supported this view.

Results of this study, using a combination of reproductive technologies, suggest that declining numbers of brown hares is unrelated to any major reproductive disorder(s). Rather it is more likely that species demise is attributable to neonatal loss, enhanced predator pressure and continued habitat loss.

Case study 4: Disrupting pregnancy in bears using anti-progestins

Ironically, excellent zoo housing conditions have led to enhanced reproduction for some species and the need to control fertility artificially in order to avoid overpopulation. Current methods to reduce reproduction in bears (e.g. gonadectomy, progestational implants) either are irreversible or have side-effects that adversely affect behaviour and health. There also is no method for therapeutically terminating pregnancy in ursids. Therefore, a study was conducted to determine the efficacy of an anti-progestin (J956) for interrupting pregnancy in several bear species (Göritz *et al.*, 2001). During a 2-year period, J956 was administered to 11 female bears (European, spectacled and Asiatic black) living in zoos. All animals were proven breeders with a history of mating in the spring. The anti-progestin was administered orally (10 mg/kg) or parenterally (10 mg/kg), with or without ethinyloestradiol (10 μg/kg) and before or after implantation. Bears were examined on the first day of J956 treatment by transrectal ultrasound to confirm the presence of a pregnancy and again 4–6 weeks later to examine treatment effects. After anaesthesia was induced, a 7.5-MHz intraoperative transducer was introduced into the rectum, and the entire urogenital tract was scanned longitudinally.

Oral J956 administration was ineffective in terminating pregnancy. However, when the anti-progestin was injected every female aborted, even those treated post-implantation. Serum and faecal progestogen patterns were also suppressed in parenterally-treated animals, and ultrasonography revealed corpora lutea to be smaller and more hyperechoic than controls. Complete resorptions occurred in four bears treated 2 weeks after implantation (Figure 11.6A). But the conceptus/concepti were incompletely expelled in the two females treated 3 weeks after implantation (Figure 11.6B). Fluid

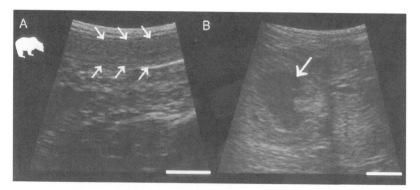

Figure 11.6 Sonograms of the uterus in European brown bears 1 year after contraception treatment with the anti-progestin, J956. (A) No signs of the previous pregnancy (uterus indicated by arrows) when treatment was administered shortly after implantation (<2 weeks post-implantation); (B) signs of embryo resorption (arrow) still present when treatment was given ≥3 weeks post-implantation. The bar at the right bottom corner of each sonogram represents 1 cm.

and foetal tissue remains still were observable in the uterine lumen of these individuals 1 year later.

This study revealed how ultrasonography can be used to develop a method of disrupting pregnancy in species that tend to reproduce too well in zoos. Most importantly, we determined non-invasively that the anti-progestin J956 alone or in combination with ethinyloestradiol was safest and most effective when given prior to implantation. Results also demonstrate the value of ultrasonography for conducting post-treatment follow-up to assess the long-term safety and efficacy of potential contraceptives for captive wildlife.

FUTURE PRIORITIES

This chapter has endeavoured to provide credible examples of the value of ultrasonography as a practical tool for wildlife research. The technology still is vastly under-utilised, and its many advantages (non-invasiveness, re-producible real-time images, cross sectional images of tissues/organs and ability to measure morphometry) certainly argue for more widespread use. In the field of embryology alone, real-time ultrasonography expands our ability to study embryonic development and uterine and ovarian function in ways that are impossible using conventional techniques.

Applying ultrasound to the systematic examination of more zoological species (especially in case-related investigations) will undoubtedly help find new solutions to physiological problems. But it will also promote the technology and provoke the design of new and more specialised, species-specific instruments. Continued miniaturisation of transducer technology and development of micro-probes with compact, contoured shapes will improve the scanning of less accessible anatomical regions. Many new ultrasound systems offer colour flow imaging that allows direct evaluation of blood vessel architecture in reproductive organs. This is a promising area of research because blood supply to the genital tract undergoes marked changes related to seasonality, maturation, sexual activity and pregnancy. Three-dimensional ultrasonography also will further expand our ability to characterise reproductive soundness while facilitating a better understanding of complex physiological processes and creating near-lifelike images.

A high priority is to incorporate this technology into more comprehensive, integrated investigations involving other scientific disciplines. Successful models already exist, especially collaborations amongst ultrasonography specialists, endocrinologists and behaviourists. We predict that more such partnerships will create new scholarly databases, while helping to develop mitigating treatments for overcoming reproductive failure. This chapter has already revealed several of the authors' biases with regard to species priorities. One is the critical challenge of ovarian inactivity in elephants, a problem that affects 15% of Asian and 25% of African females (Brown, 2000). Although well characterised endocrinologically, more ultrasonographic data are needed to determine if this problem relates to specific ovarian or uterine pathologies. When that information is available, treatments can be developed that again can be evaluated by ultrasonography. Rhinoceroses are another group of priority species that also reproduce poorly in captivity. The challenge again is obtaining normative data. For example, faecal progestogen analysis has identified both short and long duration oestrous cycles in the white rhinoceros (Radcliffe *et al.*, 1997; Schwarzenberger *et al.*, 1998; Patton *et al.*, 1999; Brown *et al.*, 2001a), but there is considerable debate about which is 'normal'. Despite numerous hypotheses in favour of each, the mystery will probably only be solved using longitudinal ultrasound examinations.

There are undoubtedly many more examples in which ultrasound technology could be combined with other reproductive technologies to answer questions that directly impact the health and reproductive welfare of wildlife species. Given the resources and access to these very special species, there are no limitations to what can be learned. It is our hope that more scientists will accept the challenge of conducting integrated studies that cross disciplines for the pleasure of pure scientific discovery as well as for developing practical solutions to managing wildlife species.

ACKNOWLEDGEMENTS

The authors thank all IZW collaborators for assistance. We are also grateful to the many institutions associated with these projects, including the European and American Zoo Societies (EAZA and AZA), Faculty of Veterinary Science of Mahidol University (Thailand), National Parks Board (Republic of South Africa) and the National Institute for Wildlife Research. This work was partially funded by the German Research Council (DFG, #HI 753/1-1) and the German Society for Technical Collaboration (GTZ, #95.2172.5-001.00 and #90.2136.1-03.142).

REFERENCES

Brown, J. L. (2000). Reproductive endocrine monitoring of elephants: an essential tool for assisting captive management. *Zoo Biology* **19**, 347-368.

Brown, J. L., Bellem, A., Fouraker, M., Wildt, D. E. & Roth, T. L. (2001a) Comparative analysis of gonadal and adrenal activity in the black and white rhinoceros in North America by non-invasive endocrine monitoring. *Zoo Biology* 20, 463-486.

Brown, J. L., Graham, L. H., Wielebnowski, N., Swanson, W. F., Wildt, D. E. & Howard, J. G. (2001b). Understanding the basic reproductive biology of wild felids through noninvasive faecal steroid monitoring. *Journal of Reproduction and Fertility*, Suppl. 57, 71-82.

Brown, J. L., Schmitt, D. L., Bellem, A., Graham, L. H. & Lehnhardt, J. (1999). Hormone secretion in the Asian elephant (*Elephas maximus*): characterization of ovulatory and anovulatory LH surges. *Biology of Reproduction* 61, 1294-1299.

Göritz, F. (1996). Sonographie bei Zoo- und Wildtieren. D. V. M. Dissertation, Freie Universität Berlin, Germany.

Göritz, F., Quest, M., Hildebrandt, T. B., Meyer, H. H. D., Kolter, L., Elger, W. & Jewgenow, K. (2001). Control of reproduction in captive bears with antiprogestin and oestrogens. *Journal of Reproduction and Fertility*, Suppl. 57, 249-254.

Hermes, R., Olson, D., Göritz, F., Brown, J. L., Schmitt, D. L., Hagan, D., Peterson, J. S., Fritsch, G. & Hildebrandt, T. B. (2000). Ultrasonography of the estrous cycle in female African elephants (*Loxodonta africana*). *Zoo Biology* 19, 369-382.

Hildebrandt, T. B. & Göritz, F. (1998). Use of ultrasonography in zoo animals. In *Zoo and Wild Animal Medicine. Current Therapy 4* (Eds. M. E. Fowler & R. E. Miller), pp. 41-54. W. B. Saunders, Philadelphia.

Hildebrandt, T. B., Göritz, F., Bosch, H., Seidel, B. & Pitra, C. (1996). Ultrasonographic sexing and reproductive assessment of penguins. *Penguin Conservation* 4, 6-12.

Hildebrandt, T. B., Göritz, F., Pitra, C., Thielebein, J., Lücker, H., Schneider, H. E. & Seidel, B. (1994). Transintestinale Ultraschalluntersuchung bei Wildvögeln. *Verhandlungsbericht ber Erkrankungen Zootiere* 36, 127-139.

Hildebrandt, T. B., Göritz, F., Pratt, N. C., Brown, J. L., Montali, R. J., Schmitt, D. L., Fritsch, G. & Hermes, R (2000a). Ultrasonography of the urogenital tract in elephants (*Loxodonta africana* and *Elephas maximus*): an important tool for assessing female reproductive function. *Zoo Biology* 19, 321-332.

Hildebrandt, T. B., Göritz, F., Schnorrenberg, A., Thielebein, J., Heidmann, D., Schmitt, R. M., Seidel, B. & Pitra, C. (1997). Transintestinal sonography [TIS] in common quail. *Proceedings Fourth Conference European Committee Association of Avian Veteterinarians*, United Kingdom, 26-27.

Hildebrandt, T. B., Hermes, R., Pratt, N. C., Fritsch, G., Blottner, S., Schmitt, D. L., Ratanakorn, P., Brown, J. L., Rietschel, W. & Göritz, F. (2000b). Ultrasonography of the urogenital tract in elephants (*Loxodonta africana* and *Elephas maximus*): an important tool for assessing male reproductive function. *Zoo Biology* 19, 333-345.

Hildebrandt, T. B., Pitra, C., Sömmer, P. & Pinkowski, M. (1995). Sex identification in birds of prey by ultrasonography. *Journal of Zoo and Wildlife Medicine* 26, 367-376.

Kapustin, N., Critser, J. K., Olson, D. & Malven, P. V. (1996). Nonluteal estrous cycles of 3-week duration are initiated by anovulatory luteinizing hormone peaks in African elephants. *Biology of Reproduction* 55, 1147-1154.

Meyer, H. H. D., Rohleder, M., Streich, W. J., Göltenboth, R. & Ochs, A. (1997). Sexual steroid profile und Ovaraktivitäten des Pandaweibchen Yan Yan im Berliner Zoo. *Berliner Münchener Tierärztliche Wochenschrift* 110, 143-147.

Munson, L., Harrenstien, L., Haslem, C. A. & Stokes, J. (1995). Update on diseases associated with contraceptive use in zoo animals. *Proceedings of the Annual Meeting, American Association of Zoo Veterinarians*, pp. 396-398. East Lansing, MI.

Patton, M. L., Swaisgood, R. R., Czekala, N. M., White, A. M., Fetter, G. A., Montagne, J. P., Rieches, R. G. & Lance, V. A. (1999). Reproductive cycle length and pregnancy in the southern white rhinoceros (*Ceratotherium simum simum*) as determined by fecal pregnane analysis and observations of mating behavior. *Zoo Biology* **18**, 111-127.

Radcliffe, R. W., Czekala, N. M. & Osofsky, S. A. (1997). Combined serial ultrasonography and fecal progestin analysis for reproductive evaluation of the female white rhinoceros (*Ceratotherium simum simum*): preliminary results. *Zoo Biology* **16**, 445-456.

Radcliffe, R. W., Eyres, A. I., Patton, M. L., Czekala, N. M. & Emslie, R. H. (2001). Ultrasonographic characterization of ovarian events and foetal gestation parameters in two southern black rhinoceros (*Diceros bicornis minor*) and correlation to fecal progesterone. *Theriogenology* **55**, 1033-1049.

Roth, T. L., O'Brien, J. K., McRae, M. A., Bellem, A. C., Romo, S. J., Kroll, J. L. & Brown, J. L. (2001). Ultrasound and endocrine evaluation of the ovarian cycle and early pregnancy in the Sumatran rhinoceros (*Dicerorhinus sumatrensis*). *Reproduction* **121**, 139-149.

Schaffer, N. E., Zainal-Zahari, Z., Suri, M. S. M., Jainudeen, M. R. & Jeyendran, R. S. (1994). Ultrasonography of the reproductive anatomy in the Sumatran rhinoceros (*Dicerorhinus sumatrensis*). *Journal of Zoo and Wildlife Medicine* **25**, 337-348.

Schwarzenberger, F., Möstl, E., Palme, R. & Bamberg, E. (1996). Faecal steroid analysis for non-invasive monitoring of reproductive status in farm, wild and zoo animals. *Animal Reproduction Science* **42**, 515-526.

Schwarzenberger, F., Walzer, C., Tomasova, K., Vahala, J., Meister, J., Goodrowe, K. L., Zima, J., Strauß, G. & Lynch, M. (1998). Faecal progesterone metabolite analysis for non-invasive monitoring of reproductive function in the white rhinoceros (*Ceratotherium simum*). *Animal Reproduction Science* **53**, 173-190.

Seidel, B., Hildebrandt, T. B. & Göritz, F. (1994). Einsatz bildgebender Verfahren in der Diagnostik von Erkrankungen abdominaler Organe. *Verhandlungsbericht ber Erkrankungen Zootiere* **36**, 93-99.

Swenson, R. B. (1993). Endometriosis in nonhuman primates. In *Zoo and Wild Animal Medicine*, 3rd edn (Ed. M. E. Fowler), pp. 339-340. W. B. Saunders, Philadelphia.

12

Role of embryo technologies in genetic management and conservation of wildlife

NAIDA M. LOSKUTOFF

INTRODUCTION AND OBJECTIVES

This review critically evaluates the relative merits of reproductive techniques relating to embryo production and transfer for the genetic management and conservation of rare wildlife species.

The first live calf born following transfer of embryos between two domestic cows was produced by Willett and colleagues 50 years ago (Betteridge, 2000). Since that time, embryo transfer as an assisted reproductive technology (ART) has contributed enormously to the genetic improvement of livestock. In 1999, over half a million *in vivo*-derived, domestic bovine embryos were collected and transferred world-wide; more than half of these embryos were frozen-thawed, and at least another 26 000 bovine embryos were produced *in vitro* and transferred (Thibier, 2000). Embryo technologies have also had a significant impact on human reproduction, especially in treating infertility. In 1997 alone (the most recent data available), 335 fertility clinics in the United States reported the births of more than 24 500 babies (CDC, SART/ASRM and RESOLVE National Report, 1999). In Denmark, more than 4% of all human newborns are conceived by ART methods, including *in vitro* fertilisation (IVF) and sperm microinjection (Skakkebaek *et al.*, 2000).

Certainly, the greatest progress in the development of embryo technologies has occurred in those few species where reproductive biology databases exist (e.g. cattle and primates). In most cases, methods have been developed in the species under study; in some cases, a common 'model' species is studied first before the technology is applied to a wild counterpart (Wildt *et al.*, 1986; Loskutoff & Betteridge, 1992). For example, the well-established

protocols for bovine embryo transfer are being applied to the conservation of
rare breeds of domesticated cattle, buffalo (Solti *et al.*, 2000) and other wild
Bovidae (Pope & Loskutoff, 1999). Correspondingly, the human has served
as an excellent model for applying IVF to the great apes (Loskutoff *et al.*,
1991a, b; Pope *et al.*, 1997). However, for the vast majority of species, there
is (1) insufficient information available on the most fundamental aspects
of their unique reproductive strategies and (2) little, if any, progress on developing customised, reliable and repeatable embryo technologies.

Some well-meaning researchers and practitioners have attempted to
apply some of the most technologically complex methods to 'conserving
endangered species'. Such pronouncements, at best, serve only to draw
attention to the plight of a particular species by the media, who often find
such reports newsworthy. At worst, considerable resources are expended
only to realise that success is thwarted by a lack of knowledge concerning
the most fundamental reproductive biology of the species concerned. These
advanced techniques are highly specialised and call for a level of expertise,
facilities and equipment that are usually unavailable to wildlife managers,
the very people responsible for developing practical conservation strategies.
Thus, there is often a gap between the scientist with the skills (and the
vision) and the manager who is responsible for protecting the species, but
who may well not understand the technology and who may be wary of its
potential benefits to conservation.

STATE OF THE ART

In vitro embryo production from oocytes matured *in vivo* or *in vitro*

In vitro embryo production is the artificial generation of an embryo in culture using gametes (oocytes and sperm) that have been collected in a mature
or immature state. Once fertilisation has occured in the laboratory, the embryo can theoretically be transferred to a surrogate or cryopreserved for later
use. Embryo production *in vitro* offers the opportunity to produce multiple
offspring from genetically valuable individuals, potentially allowing more
rapid expansion of a population than through natural breeding. But successful *ex situ* management of wildlife depends on intensive genetic management. Thus, it is essential that embryos to be used for propagation be
produced from individuals of known provenance. *In vitro* techniques, in
theory, could facilitate genetic management by offering:

1. More offspring from a female than she could produce in a natural
   reproductive lifespan (by using surrogates to gestate transferred
   embryos);

2. The ability to produce viable embryos from prepubertal (Earl *et al.*, 1998) and pregnant (Meintjes *et al.*, 1995) females, from ovarian tissue excised from individuals undergoing damaging therapies (Shaw *et al.*, 2000) or from males (Hopkins *et al.*, 1988) and females (Johnston *et al.*, 1993) after death;
3. The possibility of eliminating certain pathogens from diseased animals by utilising established processing and treatment methods for semen (Wrathall & Sutmoller, 1998) or embryos (Bielanski, 1998; Stringfellow, 1998);
4. The ability to determine or select the sex of embryos directly (Seidel, 1999) or by the flow cytometric-sorting of X- and Y-chromosome-bearing sperm before IVF (Johnson & Welch, 1999);
5. The ability to produce multiple, genetically identical offspring by embryo division (i.e. blastomere separation or embryo splitting; Loskutoff *et al.*, 1993).

Many of these techniques are derived from agricultural research where it may be considered appropriate to collect and use oocytes from pregnant or prepubertal animals. This is unlikely to apply to rare species, where often the managers and keepers prize every individual.

Standard protocols for bovine embryo production are usually effective for producing embryos from immature oocytes in a diversity of non-domesticated ungulate species (Loskutoff, 1998). After recovery (usually from excised ovaries), the oocytes are cultured in the laboratory (to induce maturation) which is followed by IVF and further culture. However, research in common species has revealed inherent problems associated with *in vitro* produced embryos that need to be considered when applying these approaches to wildlife species. Such challenges include (1) an increased incidence of abnormal embryos, as revealed by ultrastructural (Gjorret *et al.*, 2000) and cytogenetic (Iwasaki & Nakahara, 1990) examinations; (2) more spontaneous abortions, perinatal loss and foetal abnormalities (Walker *et al.*, 1998); (3) a higher incidence of dystocias in recipients due to increased birth weights of calves and lambs derived from *in vitro*-produced embryos (Kruip & den Daas, 1997; Walker *et al.*, 1998) compared with natural breeding or the use of *in vivo*-generated embryos; and (4) a potential skewing of sex ratios to favour male offspring (because male embryos develop faster *in vitro* than female counterparts; Xu *et al.*, 1992). Biologists need to be aware of these limitations before applying such technologies to the genetic management of wildlife species. Indeed, to avoid these pitfalls, a research and validation phase should precede any earnest programme to use *in vitro*-derived embryos for propagation.

IN VITRO EMBRYO PRODUCTION BY SPERM
MICROINJECTION

Special microinjection tools are available to insert an individual spermatozoon into an oocyte *in vitro*, which then has the potential to become a viable embryo. Sperm microinjection is useful for overcoming certain problems encountered during conventional IVF. Human and primate oocytes matured *in vitro* may have reduced fertilisability owing to hardening of the zona pellucida that encompasses the ovum. In suids, there is increased incidence of polyspermic fertilisation *in vitro* (Prather & Day, 1998), whereas IVF rates are low in equids because of a difficulty of inducing capacitation or the acrosome reaction *in vitro*. Sperm microinjection could be especially important in cases where (1) only a few males remain, (2) overall semen quality is low or (3) there is a high incidence of teratospermia (e.g. in wild felids; Wildt *et al.*, 1998). Individual sperm, in theory, could first be sorted by flow-cytometry, then injected into oocytes to produce sex-selected offspring. In livestock and/or the human, immotile, non-viable sperm (Goto *et al.*, 1990; Iritani *et al.*, 1998), testicular sperm (Silber *et al.*, 1995; Wright *et al.*, 1998) and even spermatids (Tesarik *et al.*, 1996) have been used to generate embryos by sperm microinjection.

The first mammalian offspring produced by sperm microinjection were from mice (Mann, 1988) and rabbits (Hosoi *et al.*, 1988). Mann (1988) used a technique now referred to as sub-zonal insemination (SUZI), in which a spermatozoon is placed just inside the oocyte's zona pellucida. Hosoi *et al.* (1988) injected sperm directly into the cytoplasm of the oocyte, a technique now known as intracytoplasmic injection (ICSI). ICSI-fertilised embryos have been produced in a number of primate species (Iritani *et al.*, 1998), and offspring have been produced from transferred, ICSI-derived embryos in the human (Palermo *et al.*, 1992), mouse (Ahmadi *et al.*, 1995), sheep (Catt, 1996), horse (Squires *et al.*, 1996) and domestic cat (Pope, 2000). Again, there are notable species specificities. For example, although a live calf has been produced by ICSI using non-viable, immotile sperm (Goto *et al.*, 1990), the technique is not very effective for producing bovine embryos *in vitro*; compared with other species, the cow oocyte is not activated by the ICSI process alone (Keefer *et al.*, 1990).

ICSI has become the treatment of choice world-wide for severe human male factor infertility. However, there are reports of problems associated with ICSI-derived human embryos, including poorer blastocyst development compared with conventional IVF treatment (Griffiths *et al.*, 2000). Aytoz *et al.* (1999) indicated that cryopreserved, ICSI-generated embryos resulted in a higher incidence of miscarriage compared with cryopreserved, IVF-produced embryos. Using a primate model, Hewitson *et al.* (2000) demonstrated that ICSI resulted in embryos with abnormal nuclear remodelling leading to asynchronous chromatin decondensation in the sperm, delaying the onset of DNA synthesis. There are conflicting data on the mental development of children conceived by ICSI. Bowen *et al.* (1998) reported a significantly lower index (Bayley Scale of Infant Development) for ICSI-conceived children at 1 year of age compared with those produced by conventional IVF or natural conception. Using the same index, Bonduelle *et al.* (1998a) reported no differences between 2-year-old ICSI-conceived children and those produced by conventional IVF or naturally. However, there is consensus that, although major abnormalities can be excluded, there are more chromosomal aberrations (especially in the sex chromosomes) in ICSI-conceived children (Bonduelle *et al.*, 1998b). This finding is probably linked to seminal characteristics of the infertile men seeking treatment rather than to the ICSI procedure itself. Nonetheless, this discovery has ramifications when ICSI is being considered for conservation attempts in rare species. Obviously, it is ill advised to propagate individuals that may transmit chromosomal abnormalities or infertilities of genetic origin.

Embryo multiplication and nuclear transfer (cloning)

True cloning, or the production of genetically identical individuals, is a natural phenomenon. The birth of monozygotic multiplets is a common occurrence in many taxa. This can be mimicked artificially by mechanically dividing the embryo through blastomere separation or embryo splitting. By separating the blastomeres of early cleavage stage embryos, as many as four viable calves have been produced from a single, *in vitro*-produced bovine embryo (Loskutoff *et al.*, 1993; Johnson *et al.*, 1995). These clones produced by blastomere separation are identical in nuclear as well as in mitochondrial DNA constitutions. In contrast, clones produced by nuclear transfer can have genetic differences associated with cytoplasmic variation when cytoplasts are used from different donors to produce the reconstructed embryo (Plante *et al.*, 1992; see Critser *et al.*, Chapter 13). There have been no reports of calves produced from embryos containing fewer than one-quarter of the original cell number.

In conservation programmes for rare species, it can be argued that genetically identical offspring are undesirable, since the objective is to maintain and maximise genetic diversity in the extant population. However, for individuals with low mean kinship rankings or founders without living offspring, it might be prudent to produce more than one offspring or, alternatively, to transfer a demi-embryo and cryopreserve the other half as a safeguard for the future. This technical feat has already been demonstrated by Willadsen & Fehilly (1983), who reported the birth of a lamb from a cryopreserved demi-embryo transferred to its adult sibling. There are also certain wildlife species or populations (e.g. cheetah, Asiatic lion, Florida panther) that have severely reduced genomic heterozygosity partially related to population bottlenecks (O'Brien et al., 1985; Wildt et al., 1998). In such cases, producing as many individuals as possible from a single, split embryo would ensure the perpetuation of genes from small, genetically compromised populations. This approach would also be advantageous for wild bovid species where the transfer of multiple embryos of unknown sex could produce sterile freemartins. To achieve the full potential of embryo division, however, improved techniques are needed for cryopreserving micromanipulated embryos, since standard protocols that are effective for whole embryos are significantly less so for demi-embryos (Lucas-Hahn, 1992).

Surrogacy

In ART applications, surrogacy can have several meanings, including the use of temporary recipients for culturing preimplantation stage embryos. For example, sheep and rabbits were first used to transport or overcome developmental blocks in cultured bovine embryos. However, there are several arguments against using animals for temporary *in vivo* culture. These include a serious potential for disease transmission, the difficulty in recovering all embryos from the temporary surrogate and the costs associated with surgery and animal maintenance, as well as animal welfare issues. Modern laboratory improvements in bovine oocyte maturation, fertilisation and embryo culture have generally eliminated the need for animals to serve as culture surrogates.

Tissue cryopreservation or xenogeneic transplantation to immunosuppressed animals has achieved some success in human and domestic animal systems (see Shaw et al., 2000, for review). Human and cow ovarian cortex transplanted into immunosuppressed mice remains viable for up to 12 weeks, and exogenous gonadotrophin treatment stimulates primordial follicles to develop into antral follicles. Similarly, Wolvekamp et al. (2000) have reported that cryopreserved ovarian tissue from wombats transplanted into nude rats survives for 10 weeks with histological evidence of follicular development. Although having potential for preserving female gametes, this approach may provoke criticism from animal welfare advocates about sacrificing animals that serve as 'culture vessels' for another species.

There are several reports of successful interspecies transfer of embryos from wildlife species to domestic, heterospecific species that resulted in living offspring. These include (1) gaur and banteng embryos into domestic cattle, (2) a bongo embryo transferred to an eland, (3) mouflon and Armenian red sheep embryos into domestic sheep, (4) Grant's zebra and Przewalski's horse embryos transferred to domestic horses (reviewed by Loskutoff, 1998) and (5) Indian desert cat and African wild cat embryos into domestic cat recipients (Pope, 2000). However, it must be emphasised that despite these successes, which were well publicised by the media, there have been many more failed than successful attempts to produce viable offspring via interspecies embryo transfer. These failures (illustrated in wild cattle, water buffalo, bison and non-domestic sheep) have been manifested through (1) early resorption of foreign embryos, (2) mid- to late-term abortions, (3) prolonged and complicated pregnancies and (4) inexplicable developmental abnormalities in aborted or stillborn foetuses (Buckrell *et al.*, 1990). Perhaps of greatest significance, most wildlife species simply do not have suitable domesticated counterparts to serve as embryo surrogates, which explains why the limited studies to date generally have been conducted in cattle- or sheep-like species.

The first successful interspecies transfer of an embryo collected from a threatened species (gaur) into a domestic animal was reported by Stover *et al.* (1981). However, of three pregnancies established, one was lost at 5 weeks' gestation and another was stillborn. The placenta from the one live gaur calf contained an abnormally low number of placentomes and abnormal histological architecture (Hradecky *et al.*, 1988). More recently, six gaur calves, derived from *in vitro*-produced embryos, were carried to term in domestic cow recipients (Johnston *et al.*, 1993; Loskutoff *et al.*, 2000). Quite unexpectedly, all of these calves were male, and all died within 1 week of parturition. Although the reason for these losses was inconclusive, the evidence favoured immunological incompatibilities between the dam and the foetus. This was demonstrated by (1) leucocyte infiltration and premature placental detachment (which resulted in gasping *in utero*), (2) significantly fewer placentomes compared with normal pregnancies in both species and (3) presence of anti-gaur antibodies in the dams (Hammer *et al.*, 2001). These results illustrate the physiological, anatomical and medical challenges to be expected from interspecies embryo transfer.

CONCLUSIONS AND PRIORITIES FOR THE FUTURE

To date, embryo technologies have had a limited impact on the genetic management and conservation of wildlife species. There continues to be some potential, but there is a need for both research and development, especially in (1) the fundamental biology of individual species that might benefit from such methods and (2) designing new instrumentation to facilitate embryo collection, creation and development *in vitro*, storage (fresh and cryopreserved) and, ultimately, transfer to produce living, healthy young. Currently, most embryo knowledge, protocols and equipment are derived from, or designed for, common livestock and the human, and are simply inefficient or completely impractical for wildlife species. Therefore, there is a need to fill the enormous gap in information about all aspects of reproductive biology that influences the subsequent ability to use embryos for management and conservation. Data needs are considerable, including reproductive anatomy, oestrous cyclicity and synchronisation, gamete dynamics and interaction and culture *in vitro*, among many other fields of investigation.

A few researchers working in the field of wildlife embryology have also focused too much attention on trying to produce a few offspring rather than emphasising the need to generate new knowledge. Such efforts are likely to continue to fail many more times than they will succeed. Additionally, when the occasional young is born by serendipity, an impression is given through media hyperbole that embryo technologies are somehow contributing to genetic management or large-scale conservation. In reality, such efforts and sporadic accomplishments feed a myth that we are on the edge of using this sophisticated technology on a grand scale. The media's recent attention to the possible role of 'cloning' in preserving endangered species provides an excellent example. The priority is to expend existing resources on fundamental studies of the unique aspects of embryos of the thousands of species that have yet to be studied. Channelling such energy could eventually result in databases that will allow embryo technologies to be used on a practical basis to truly enhance conservation of rare species.

ACKNOWLEDGEMENTS

The author thanks Dr E. G. Crichton and Dr W. V. Holt for assistance in preparation of this chapter.

REFERENCES

Ahmadi, A., Ng, S. C., Liow, S. L., Bonso, A. & Ratman, S. S. (1995). Intracytoplasmic sperm injection of mouse oocytes with 5 mM Ca at different intervals. *Human Reproduction* 10, 431–435.

Aytoz, A., Van den Abbeel, E., Bonduelle, M., Camus, M., Joris, H., Van Steirteghem, A. & Devroey, P. (1999). Obstetric outcome of pregnancies after the transfer of cryopreserved and fresh embryos obtained by conventional *in vitro* fertilization and intracytoplasmic sperm injection. *Human Reproduction* 14, 2619–2624.

Betteridge, K. J. (2000). Reflections on the golden anniversary of the first embryo transfer to produce a calf. *Theriogenology* 53, 3-10.

Bielanski, A. (1998). Potential for disease control or transmission by embryos produced *in vitro*: a review of current literature. In *Manual of the International Embryo Transfer Society*, pp. 45-54. International Embryo Transfer Society, Savoy, IL.

Bonduelle, M., Aytoz, A., Van Assche, E., Devroey, P., Liebaers, I. & Van Steirteghem, A. (1998b). Incidence of chromosomal aberrations in children born after assisted reproduction through intracytoplasmic sperm injection. *Human Reproduction* 13, 781-782.

Bonduelle, M., Joris, H., Hofmans, K., Liebaers, I. & Van Steirteghem, A. (1998a). Mental development of 201 ICSI children at 2 years of age. *Lancet* 351, 1553-1560.

Bowen, J. R., Gibson, F. L., Leslie, G. I. & Saunders, D. M. (1998). Medical and developmental outcome at 1 year for children conceived by intracytoplasmic sperm injection. *Lancet* 351, 1529-1534.

Buckrell, B. C., Garley, C. J., Mehren, K. G., Crawshaw, G. J., Johnson, W. H., Barker, I. K., Balke, J., Coghill, C., Challis, J. R.G. & Goodrowe, K. L. (1990). Failure to maintain interspecific pregnancy after transfer of Dall's sheep embryos to domestic ewes. *Journal of Reproduction and Fertility* 90, 387-394.

Catt, J. W. (1996). Intracytoplasmic sperm injection (ICSI) and related technology. *Animal Reproduction Science* 42, 239-250.

CDC, SART/ASRM & RESOLVE National Report (1999). *Assisted Reproductive Technology Success Rates. National summary and fertility clinic reports.* National Center for Chronic Disease Prevention and Health Promotion. Division of Reproductive Health, Atlanta, GA.

Earl, C. R., Fry, R. C., Maclellan, L. J., Kelly, J. M. & Armstrong, D. T. (1998). *In vitro* fertilization and developmental potential of prepubertal calf oocytes. In *Gametes: Development and Function* (Eds. A. Lauria, F. Gandolfi, G. Enne & L. Gianaroli), pp. 115-137. Serono Symposia, Rome.

Gjorret, J. O., Crichton, E. G., Armstrong, D. L., Loskutoff, N. M. & Hyttel, P. (2000). Oocyte maturation, fertilization and early embryonic development *in vitro* in the Siberian tiger (*Panthera tigris altaica*). *Theriogenology* 53, 334.

Goto, K., Kinoshita, A., Takuma, Y. & Ogawa, K. (1990). Fertilization of bovine oocytes by the injection of immobilized, killed spermatozoa. *Veterinary Record* 127, 517-520.

Griffiths, T. A., Murdock, A. P. & Herbert, M. (2000). Embryonic development *in vitro* is compromised by the ICSI procedure. *Human Reproduction* 15, 1592-1596.

Hammer, C. J., Tyler, H. D., Loskutoff, N. M., Armstrong, D. L., Funk, D. J., Lindsey, B. R. & Simmons, L.G. (2001). Compromised development of calves (*Bos gaurus*) derived from *in vitro*-generated embryos and transferred interspecifically into domestic cattle (*Bos taurus*). *Theriogenology* 55, 1447-1455.

Hewitson, L., Simerly, C., Dominko, T. & Schatten, G. (2000). Cellular and molecular events after *in vitro* fertilization and intracytoplasmic sperm injection. *Theriogenology* 53, 95-104.

Hopkins, S. M., Armstrong, D. L., Hummel, K. C. & Junior, S. M. (1988). Successful cryopreservation of gaur (*Bos gaurus*) epididymal spermatozoa. *Journal of Zoo Animal Medicine* **19**, 195-201.

Hosoi, T., Miyake, M., Utsumi, K. & Iritani, A. (1988). Development of rabbit oocytes after microinjection of spermatozoon. In *Proceedings of the 11th Congress on Animal Reproduction and Artificial Insemination*, Vol. 3, pp. 331-333.

Hradecky, P., Stover, J. & Stott, G. G. (1988). Histology of a heifer placentome after interspecies transfer of gaur embryo. *Theriogenology* **30**, 593-604.

Iritani, A., Hosoi, Y. & Torii, R. (1998). Application of ICSI in domestic and/or zoo animals. In *Gametes: Development and Function* (Eds. A. Lauria, F. Gandolfi, G. Enne & L. Gianoroli), pp. 393-404. Serono Symposia, Rome.

Iwasaki, S. & Nakahara, T. (1990). Cell number and incidence of chromosomal anomalies in bovine blastocysts fertilized *in vitro* followed by culture *in vitro* or *in vivo* in rabbit oviducts. *Theriogenology* **33**, 669-675.

Johnson, L. A. & Welch, G. R. (1999). Sex preselection: high-speed flow cytometric sorting of X and Y sperm for maximum efficiency. *Theriogenology* **52**, 1323-1341.

Johnson, W. H., Loskutoff, N. M., Plante, Y. & Betteridge, K. J. (1995). The production of four identical calves by the separation of blastomeres from an *in vitro*-derived four cell embryo. *Veterinary Record* **137**, 15-16.

Johnston, L., Parrish, J., Monson, R., Leibfried-Rutledge, L., Susko-Parrish, J., Northey, D., Rutledge, J. & Simmons, L. (1993). Oocyte maturation, fertilization and embryo development *in vitro* and *in vivo* in the gaur (*Bos gaurus*). *Journal of Reproduction and Fertility* **100**, 131-136.

Keefer, C. L., Younis, A. I. & Brackett, B. G. (1990). Cleavage development of bovine oocytes fertilized by sperm injection. *Molecular Reproduction and Development* **25**, 281-285.

Kruip, Th. A. M. & den Daas, J. H. G. (1997). *In vitro* produced and cloned embryos: effects on pregnancy, parturition and offspring. *Theriogenology* **47**, 43-52.

Loskutoff, N. M. (1998). Biology, technology and strategy of genetic resource banking in conservation programs for wildlife. In *Gametes: Development and Function* (Eds. A. Lauria, F. Gandolfi, G. Enne & L. Gianoroli), pp. 275-286. Serono Symposia, Rome.

Loskutoff, N. M., Amstrong, D. L., Ohlrichs, C. L., Johnson, D. L., Funk, D. J., VanRoekel, P. V., Molina, J. A., Lindsey, B. R., Looney, C. R., Bellow, S. M., Hammer, C. J., Tyler, H. D. & Simmons, L. G. (2000). Transvaginal ultrasound-guided oocyte retrieval and the developmental competence of *in vitro*-produced embryo *in vitro* and *in vivo* in the gaur (*Bos gaurus*). *Theriogenology* **53**, 337.

Loskutoff, N. M. & Betteridge K. J. (1992). Embryo technology in pets and endangered species. In *Gametes: Development and Function* (Eds. A. Lauria, F. Gandolfi, G. Enne & L. Gianoroli), pp. 235-248. Serono Symposia, Rome.

Loskutoff, N. M., Huntress, S. L., Putman, J. M., Yee, B., Bowsher, T. R., Chacon, R. R., Calle, P. P., Cambre, R. C., Czekala, N. M., Rosen, G. F., Kraemer, D. C. & Raphael, B. L. (1991b). Stimulation of ovarian activity for oocyte recovery in nonreproductive gorillas (*Gorilla gorilla gorilla*). *Journal of Zoo and Wildlife Medicine* **22**, 32-41.

Loskutoff, N. M., Johnson, W. H. & Betteridge, K. J. (1993). The developmental competence of bovine embryos with reduced cell numbers. *Theriogenology* **39**, 95-108.

Loskutoff, N. M., Kraemer, D. C., Raphael, B. L., Huntress, S. L. & Wildt, D. E. (1991a). Advances in reproduction in captive, female great apes: an emphasis on the value of biotechniques. *American Journal of Primatology* 24, 151-166.

Lucas-Hahn, A. (1992). Status of cryopreserving micromanipulated bovine embryos. *Embryo Transfer Newsletter* 10, 18-23. International Embryo Transfer Society, Savoy, IL.

Mann, J. R. (1988). Full term development of mouse eggs fertilized by a spermatozoon microinjected under the zona pellucida. *Biology of Reproduction* 38, 1077-1083.

Meintjes, M., Bellow, M. S., Broussard, J. R., Paul, J. B. & Godke, R. A. (1995). Transvaginal aspiration of oocytes from hormone-treated pregnant beef cattle for *in vitro* fertilization. *Journal of Animal Science* 73, 967-974.

O'Brien, S. J., Roelke, M. E., Marker, L., Newman, A., Winkler, C. A., Meltzer, D., Colly, L., Evermann, J. F., Bush, M. & Wildt, D. E. (1985). Genetic basis for species vulnerability in the cheetah. *Science* 227, 1428-1434.

Palermo, G., Joris, H., Devroey, P. & Van Steirteghem, A. C. (1992). Pregnancies after intracytoplasmic sperm injection of a single spermatozoon into an oocyte. *Lancet* 340, 17-18.

Plante, Y., Schmutz, S. M. & Lang, K. D. M. (1992). Restriction fragment length polymorphism in the mitochondrial DNA of cloned cattle. *Theriogenology* 38, 897-904.

Pope, C. E. (2000). Embryo technology in conservation efforts for endangered felids. *Theriogenology* 53, 163-174.

Pope, C. E. & Loskutoff, N. M. (1999). Embryo transfer and semen technology from cattle applied to nondomestic artiodactylids. In *Zoo and Wild Animal Medicine: Current Therapy*, 4th edn (Eds. M. E. Fowler & R. E. Miller), pp. 597-604. W. B. Saunders, Philadelphia.

Pope, C. E., Dresser, B. L., Chin, N. W., Liu, J. H., Loskutoff, N. M., Behnke, E. J., Brown, C., McRae, M. A., Sinoway, C. E., Campbell, M. K., Cameron, K. N., Owens, O. M., Johnson, C. A., Evans, R. R. & Cedars, M. I. (1997). Birth of a western lowland gorilla (*Gorilla gorilla gorilla*) following *in vitro* fertilization and embryo transfer. *American Journal of Primatology* 41, 247-260.

Prather, R. & Day, B. N. (1998). Practical considerations for the *in vitro* production of pig embryos. *Theriogenology* 49, 23-32.

Seidel, G. E., Jr (1999). Sexing mammalian embryos and sperm - state of the art. *Journal of Reproduction and Fertility*, Suppl. 54, 475-485.

Shaw, J., Oranratnachai, A. & Trounson, A. O. (2000). Fundamental cryobiology of mammalian oocytes and ovarian tissue. *Theriogenology* 53, 59-72.

Silber, S. J., Van Steirteghem, A. C., Lui, J., Nay, Z., Tournaye, G. & Devroey, P. (1995). High fertilization and pregnancy rate after intracytoplasmic sperm injection with spermatozoa obtained from testicle biopsy. *Human Reproduction* 10, 148-152.

Skakkebaek, N. E., Leffers, H., Rajpert-De Meyts, E., Carlsen, E. & Grigor, K. M. (2000). Should we watch what we eat and drink? Report on the International Workshop on Hormones and Endocrine Disrupters in Food and Water: Possible Impact on Human Health. *Trends in Endocrinology and Metabolism* 11, 291-293.

Solti, L., Crichton, E. G., Loskutoff, N. M. & Cseh, S. (2000). Economical and ecological importance of indigenous livestock and the application of assisted reproduction to their preservation. *Theriogenology* 53, 149-162.

Squires, E. L., Wilson, J. M., Kato, H. & Baszczkyk, A. (1996). A pregnancy after intracytoplasmic sperm injection into equine oocytes matured *in vitro*. *Theriogenology* 45, 306.

Stover, J., Evans, J. & Dolensek, E. P. (1981). Interspecies embryo transfer from the gaur to the domestic Holstein. *Proceedings of the American Association of Zoo Veterinarians*, pp. 122-124.

Stringfellow, D. A. (1998). Recommendations for the sanitary handling of *in vivo*-derived embryos. In *Manual of the International Embryo Transfer Society*, pp. 79-84. International Embryo Transfer Society, Savoy, IL.

Tesarik, J., Rolet, F., Brami, C., Sedbon, E., Thorel, J., Tibi, C. & Thebault, A. (1996). Spermatid injection into human oocytes, II. Clinical application in the treatment of infertility due to non-obstructive azoospermia. *Human Reproduction* 11, 780-783.

Thibier, M. (2000). The 1999 statistical figures for the world-wide embryo transfer industry: a data retrieval committee report. *Embryo Transfer Newsletter* 18, 24-28. International Embryo Transfer Society, Savoy, IL.

Walker, S. K., Hartwich, K. M., Robinson, J. S. & Seamark, R. F. (1998). Influence of *in vitro* culture of embryos on the normality of development. In *Gametes: Development and Function* (Eds. A. Lauria, F. Gandolfi, G. Enne & L. Gianoroli), pp. 457-484. Serono Symposia, Rome.

Wildt, D. E., Brown, J. L. & Swanson, W. F. (1998). Reproduction in cats. In *Encyclopedia of Reproduction* (Eds. E. Knobil & J. Neill), pp. 497-510. Academic Press, New York.

Wildt, D. E., Schiewe, M. C., Schmidt, P. M., Goodrowe, K. L., Howard, J. G., Phillips, L. G., O'Brien, S. J. & Bush, M. (1986). Developing animal model systems for embryo technologies in rare and endangered wildlife. *Theriogenology* 25, 33-51.

Willadsen, S. M. & Fehilly, C. B. (1983). The developmental potential and regulatory capacity of blastomeres from two-, four- and eight-cell sheep embryos. In *Fertilization of the Human Egg In Vitro* (Eds. H. Beier & H. Lindner), pp. 353-357. Springer-Verlag, Berlin.

Wolvekamp, M. C. J., MacCallum, C., Cleary, M., Shaw, J., Cox, S., Jenkin, G. & Trounson, A. O. (2000). Novel approach to save the critically endangered northern hairy-nosed wombat (*Lasiorhinus krefftii*). *Theriogenology* 53, 345.

Wrathall, A. & Sutmoller, P. (1998). Potential of embryo transfer to control transmission of disease. In *Manual of the International Embryo Transfer Society*, pp. 17-44. International Embryo Transfer Society, Savoy, IL.

Wright, G., Tucker, M. J., Morton, P. C., Swetzer-Yoder, C. L. & Smith, S. E. (1998). Micromanipulation in assisted reproduction: a review of current technology. *Fertility* 10, 221-226.

Xu, K. P., Yadav, B. R., King, W. A. & Betteridge, K. J. (1992). Sex-related differences in developmental rates of bovine embryos produced and cultured *in vitro*. *Molecular Reproduction and Development* 31, 249-252.

13

Application of nuclear transfer technology to wildlife species

J. K. CRITSER, L. K. RILEY & R. S. PRATHER

INTRODUCTION AND OBJECTIVES

Nuclear transfer (i.e. cloning) is the process whereby the nuclear DNA of a single donor cell is transferred to an enucleated oocyte that, in turn, is activated to produce an embryo which is genetically identical to the original donor cell. Advances in cell and reproductive biology have made the practical application of nuclear transfer theoretically feasible for propagating rare animal species (Campbell *et al.*, 1996; Wilmut *et al.*, 1997; Wakayama *et al.*, 1998, 2000; Wakayama & Yanagimachi, 1999a, b; Colman, 2000; Lanza *et al.*, 2000a). Following successful nuclear transfer in the sheep and the mouse to produce surviving young, a calf from a wild cattle species (*Bos gaurus*) has been produced using nuclear transfer and interspecies embryo transfer (Lanza *et al.*, 2000c). Although it is premature to declare whether nuclear transfer has practical application to wildlife species management or conservation, general interest in this technology is intense, thereby warranting serious and thoughtful consideration. This chapter offers an evaluation of nuclear transfer, distinguishing between what is technically possible, realistic and ethical.

STATE OF THE ART

Technological realities of using nuclear transfer

There is an array of factors limiting the technical feasibility of using nuclear transfer as a routine method of propagating animals, domestic or wild.

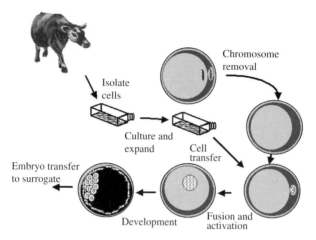

Figure 13.1 Steps involved in nuclear transfer.

Reprogramming the nucleus

Most cells in an animal are genetically identical. Theoretically, each cell's nucleus contains the entire blueprint for that organism, and genes are expressed differentially to construct and maintain the various tissues. During the first week of development, the fertilised mammalian oocyte develops into a blastocyst, which contains two tissue types. One is destined to form the outer layer of the placenta; the other yields the foetus proper. Thus, at this early stage two different sets of genes are turned on to create and maintain these two tissue types. An analogy might be made with falling dominoes. Fertilisation topples the first domino, and a few days later the dominoes diverge along two pathways. Each row has its own repertoire of genes that are being expressed. For cloning to succeed, a nucleus must be taken from the end of one of these rows of dominoes and reprogrammed: that is, the entire row of dominoes must be stood back up to allow them to fall over again. The reprogrammed nucleus must start over again, recapitulating the entire pattern of genes that are turned on and off during development.

Recipient oocyte function

The target nucleus is placed in a recipient oocyte (usually unfertilised). The nucleus of the recipient cell is removed by aspiration with a micropipette and the donor nucleus incorporated into the 'nuclear-free' oocyte via cell fusion or microinjection (Figure 13.1). Because the oocyte is arrested in metaphase II of meiosis, the transferred nucleus condenses and assumes a metaphase configuration. The oocyte is then stimulated to behave as though it were fertilised. A new nucleus is assembled using components from the recipient oocyte's cytoplasm. This nuclear restructuring (or remodelling) is believed to facilitate the required genetic reprogramming. If the structural framework of the new nucleus is derived primarily via components of the recipient oocyte (rather than those transferred with the donor nucleus), then nuclear reprogramming is likely to be successful (Prather, 2000).

One concern when applying nuclear transfer to wildlife species is the availability of appropriate recipient oocytes. What is the appropriate recipient oocyte for DNA from a highly endangered species? A few studies have evaluated cross-species nuclear transfer, including placing pig, sheep, monkey, rat, bison, goat and hamster nuclei into bovine oocytes (Wolf *et al.*, 1990; Dominko *et al.*, 1999). In each instance, a proportion of donor nuclei developed through a few cleavage stages with some advancing to blastocysts, suggesting that certain embryogenic mechanisms may be conserved across mammalian species.

Cytoplasmic inheritance

It is essential that the recipient oocyte for the donor nucleus should originate from the same (or physiologically similar) species because of the need to mimic non-nuclear DNA (i.e. mitochondrial DNA). Cells contain hundreds to thousands of mitochondria, each containing one or more DNA copies that code for RNA and proteins, much the same as nuclear DNA. Proteins produced from mitochondrial DNA must lock and fit precisely with proteins produced under the direction of the nucleus. Thus, there is species-specificity. Although not yet achieved, it is theoretically possible to collect sufficient mitochondria from the donor cell type to allow appropriate reprogramming of the recipient cell before nuclear transfer.

DNA structure

To develop successfully, donor nuclei must negotiate non-reprogrammable and reprogrammable events. The former include gene translocations, amplification, diminution, duplication, rearrangements or other mutations. Additionally, the DNA methylation patterns, believed responsible for establishing paternal imprinting, must be maintained, an event not influenced by nuclear transfer in the mouse (Obata *et al.*, 1998). In contrast, reprogrammable events include redistribution of transcription factors and changes in other epigenetic effectors such as the histone acetylation pattern. Thus the oocyte cytoplasm is capable of inducing some structural changes to the nucleus, but other changes required for normal development remain unalterable.

One important DNA feature that may exhibit species-dependent reprogrammability is telomere length. As cells age *in vivo* or *in vitro*, the telomeres (located on the ends of the chromosomes) shorten. Upon reaching a threshold, the ends of the chromosomes become unstable and degenerate; thus, genes on the chromosomal terminus can be lost. In cattle, shortened telomeres appear to lengthen naturally after nuclear transfer and subsequent embryo development so that genetic problems do not arise (Lanza *et al.*, 2000a). This contrasts with the case in sheep, in which telomere length remains abnormally shortened after nuclear transfer, causing premature ageing and reduced lifespan (Shiels *et al.*, 1999).

Correct ploidy is essential. If the donor cell has not initiated DNA synthesis, then the recipient oocyte can be pre-activated, synchronously activated or post-activated in relation to onset of nuclear transfer. If DNA synthesis has started within the donor cell, then the recipient oocyte must be pre-activated. If in metaphase, the donor nucleus must be transferred to a non-activated oocyte and, upon activation, the correct ploidy re-established with the extrusion of a polar-body-like structure (i.e. a combination of a mitosis and a meiosis) (Prather, 2000).

Oocyte activation

After transfer of the donor nucleus into the recipient cytoplasm, the oocyte must be stimulated to resume meiosis. Ideally, this is accomplished by a mechanism resembling interaction with a spermatozoon at fertilisation (Macháty *et al.*, 1999). Debated theories for activation at fertilisation include (1) sperm binding to an oocyte surface receptor and transducing an initiation signal across the membrane and (2) the spermatozoon introducing an initiation factor into the cytoplasm. In either case, it is likely that integrin–disintegrin binding (Campbell *et al.*, 2000) and a sperm factor (Macháty *et al.*, 2000) are involved. Several methods are available for parthenogenetic activation, including the use of calcium ionophore, protein synthesis inhibition, phosphorylation inhibitors or by injection of calcium. In many cases, these methods are used in combination to enhance the likelihood of oocyte activation.

Gestational surrogates

The same or a very closely related species must serve as the surrogate for cloned embryos. A serious challenge to adapting this technology to wildlife is identifying appropriate surrogates. Before conspecific wild animals can serve as embryo recipients, sufficient basic knowledge about the species' reproductive biology has to be gained to enable oestrous cycle synchronisation and deposition of the manipulated embryo into the uterus at the appropriate time. Such knowledge remains to be elucidated for virtually all wildlife species. Nonetheless, there have been a few encouraging reports of interspecies embryo transfer in domesticated species. For example, some embryological manipulations have resulted in a sheep foetus developing to term in a goat placenta (Polzin *et al.*, 1987). Thus, closely related species that are gestationally mismatched might be made compatible via new technologies.

Development

Surviving the mechanical challenges to nuclear transfer does not ensure subsequent normal development. For example, some genes in cattle do not reprogramme after nuclear transfer (Daniels *et al.*, 2000). This anomaly may occur in up to 5% of identified genes (DeSousa *et al.*, 1999) and it is likely that other genes are similarly adversely affected. Despite abnormal transcription, some embryos continue development *in vivo*. However, there are significant losses of potential offspring from cloned embryos throughout gestation and after birth with half dying shortly after parturition (Kato *et al.*, 1998). Such was the case in the gaur calf born after nuclear and embryo transfer to a domesticated cow (Lanza *et al.*, 2000b; http://www.grg. org/ACTgaur2.htm). Calves produced from nuclear transfer tend to have unusually high birth weights apparently due, in part, to inadequate *in vitro* culture conditions that alter gene expression (Blondin *et al.*, 2000), resulting in excessive growth *in utero* (Farin & Farin, 1995). Other abnormal phenotypes at parturition include placental abnormalities (especially oedema), neonatal respiratory distress, chronic pulmonary hypertension, hydroallantois and cardiopulmonary deformities (Hill *et al.*, 1999).

Thus, there are substantial technical challenges to nuclear transfer that influence its success. Efficiency depends on success of enucleation, fusion, survival after injection, activation, cleavage, development to blastocyst *in vitro*, implantation, live birth and survival to adulthood. The literature suggests that the best offspring production results in cattle have occurred where donor nuclei were recovered from cumulus cells, those cells normally surrounding the follicular or recently ovulated oocyte. Wells *et al.* (1999) used this approach to achieve 88.7% fused oocytes, with 27.5% of these forming blastocysts and 10% foetal term development (based on highest quality blastocysts transferred). The incidence of overall live birth was only 2.4%. Various permutations of success are illustrated in Table 13.1; a low of 0.05% in mice using nuclei recovered from embryonic stem cells is not included in the Table. Thus, even in commonly studied species where

Table 13.1 *Examples of the success of producing offspring from nuclear transfer*

Type of donor cell	Blastocysts from attempted nuclear transfers (%)	Offspring from attempted nuclear transfers (%)	Reference
Mouse Sertoli cell cultured	75% survival; 48% morulae or blastocysts; thus, 36%	3.1% offspring from morulae or blastocysts; thus, 1.1% overall	Ogura *et al.* (2000)
Cow foetal fibroblasts	12% blastocysts	17% offspring from blastocysts; thus, 2.1% overall	Cibelli *et al.* (1998)
Cow cumulus	18% blastocysts	83% offspring from blastocysts; thus, 15% overall	Kato *et al.* (1998)
Goat foetal fibroblasts	? Only cultured to the 2-4-cell stage	5.2% offspring from 2-4-cell stage; cannot predict	Baguisi *et al.* (1999)
Pig foetal fibroblasts	? Only cultured to the 8-cell stage	0.37% offspring from 2-8-cell stage; cannot predict	Onishi *et al.* (2000)
Sheep foetal fibroblasts	64% fused; 24% blastocysts; thus, 15%	6.5% offspring from blastocysts; thus, 0.97%	Wells *et al.* (1997)

reproductive mechanisms are well known and oocyte and embryo culture systems well developed, efficiency remains modest, at best.

Conceptual and practical challenges associated with nuclear transfer in *ex situ* breeding programmes

Small population size

Nuclear transfer's greatest asset to wildlife could involve a situation in which a species is reduced to critically low numbers, a population unlikely to recover from natural mating or other assisted breeding strategies (i.e. last ditch heroics). However, a lack of genetic diversity potentially compromises the ability to rescue a species in this fashion. Offspring will be genetically homozygous to the donor parent, eventually risking inbreeding depression through the expression of deleterious alleles. Regardless, the likely unattractive alternative option is extinction. Whether a population can remain viable into the future depends on the amount of genetic variation in the last remaining founders (i.e. the remaining DNA donors). Wildlife populations have recovered despite few numbers of founders. For example, the contemporary (and generally healthy) black-footed ferret population living *in situ* and *ex situ* was derived from fewer than a dozen founders (see Howard *et al.*, Chapter 16).

Nonetheless, because nuclear transfer results in identical offspring from the single DNA donor parent, its use in modern *ex situ* breeding programmes will require special and vigilant attention. No one individual can become over-represented, and it would be critical that DNA donors be the most genetically valuable, thereby ensuring a healthy, self-sustaining *ex situ* population. This problem is not trivial since reproductive efficiency in terms of offspring production via nuclear transfer is so poor. Benefits to management will arise only when more than the occasional offspring is produced.

In this context there has been much excitement associated with the re-derivation of a single individual from a previously extinct species (i.e. the much discussed woolly mammoth; Stone, 1997). Clearly, such a re-creation would represent a fascinating technical feat; but it is not at all clear how this milestone contributes to conservation. How would this now non-extinct individual reproduce? How would that animal behave without conspecifics? Assuming the donor nucleus was transferred into an oocyte of a 'related' species (e.g. that of an elephant), what would be the impact of mitochondrial inheritance? Finally, would the gut microflora of our contemporary age even sustain the life of a mammoth (like the now presumed extinct microflora of the Pleistocene)?

While many seem focused on such technological possibilities, conservation is more than simply the single or even mass production of rare individuals. The genetic welfare of the subsequent population is crucial to ensuring that future individuals are healthy. Thus, applying nuclear transfer requires weighing the often conflicting, short-term goal of technical achievement with the more favourable, long-term development of genetic integrity and viability (truly the foundations for successful hedge populations of endangered species).

Interfering with other high priorities, especially the need to maintain habitat
A common counter argument to exploring advanced technologies for rare species management is the perception that such strategies reduce attention towards preserving habitats (Wildt & Wemmer, 1999). In the case of nuclear transfer, science seems to be providing 'high-tech' tools to re-create individuals and species, even after extinction. Thus, why be concerned about the

conventional priority of protecting natural habitat when species can be re-derived at will? We can simply collect and cryopreserve cells from extant species and divest ourselves of worrying about living species in nature, or even in zoos.

An interesting, similar scenario has already arisen in the biomedical field. Hundreds of genetically engineered laboratory animals (especially mice) have been produced, and genome resource banks (GRBs) have emerged to freeze-store gametes and embryos from these genotypes as well as somatic cells (Critser & Russell, 2000). The National Institutes of Health (USA) has supported developing these GRBs to allow investigators to discontinue live breeding colonies. However, the differences in applying assisted reproductive technology, including nuclear transfer, to common laboratory animals (where decades of data are available) and to almost totally unstudied wildlife species, are enormous. With current limited technologies, and with little basic knowledge, the chance of re-deriving a rare species using nuclear transfer is remote.

Regardless, the argument that GRBs combined with nuclear transfer could reduce attentiveness to maintaining habitat fails to consider two points. First, most financial support for biomedical research comes from sources which differ markedly from those normally used in funding habitat preservation (Wildt & Wemmer, 1999). Second, scientists who are seriously considering the potential value of nuclear transfer understand that biodiversity is more than individual species propagation. A species is unique because of its interrelatedness to its habitat and to conspecifics as well as other species, animals and plants. The complexity of these 'between-species, within-habitat' interconnections cannot be 'banked' and re-derived at will. In this context, it is remarkable that the number of species on Earth remains unknown to the nearest order of magnitude (Wilson, 1988). For this reason, there is a fundamental first priority need to continue to protect all native habitats: to know what is out there and then to develop strategies to protect it (Wildt, 1997). GRBs provide a useful adjunct for assisting in maintaining genetics and biodiversity, and much progress has been made in identifying their required features (Wildt, 1997, 2000; Wildt *et al.*, 1997; Critser & Russell, 2000; Watson & Holt, 2001; Holt *et al.*, Chapter 17). Hundreds of species have been sampled for gametes, embryos and blood products, but there is now a need to expand these repositories routinely to include somatic cells. Who knows the value of these cells in the future for species propagation via nuclear transfer or a yet-to-be-discovered, more efficient technique.

Ethical and legal issues

The ethics and legalities associated with nuclear transfer and assisted reproduction in humans have received widespread attention (Meslin, 2000; Solter, 2000; Varmus, 2000; Bonetta, 2001; Chougule, 2001; Craft, 2001; Jaenisch & Wilmut, 2001; Murtaugh, 2001; Smaglik, 2001; Vogel, 2001). Issues of most concern include the fundamental ethical aspects of creating cloned individuals as well as critical concerns related to the overall health and well-being of the cloned organisms.

These concerns pertain to the cloning of wildlife species, especially the re-derivation of extinct species. Such re-creations will generate questions about appropriate husbandry of the specimen, an important consideration being the health, safety and welfare of contemporary species, including humans. In fact, microbial pathogens (bacteria and viruses) pose a particularly serious threat to using nuclear transfer for either extinct or extant species. Pathogens present in the donor or recipient cell may be lethal to embryos, result in diseased offspring and potentially spread disease to naïve animal populations (Stringfellow & Givens, 1999). Therefore, using this technology will initially require identifying all potential contaminants followed by continuous screening of donor and recipient cells for already well-recognised microbial pathogens. Polymerase chain reaction techniques are available for sensitive assay of common pathogens found in extant species. However, the characteristics and possible impact of potential contaminating microbes from ancient DNA are unknown. Ostensibly, it may be impossible to screen ancient cells and tissues for unknown viruses or bacteria. Because it has been hypothesised that extinctions during the Pleistocene were due, at least in part, to disease epidemics (MacPhee & Marx, 1997), transmitting microbial pathogens via cloning of extinct populations presents a threat worthy of consideration. When pathogens are detected, current decontamination protocols are inconsistent (Stringfellow & Seidel, 1998), requiring contaminated cells to be destroyed. Thus, more research is required in this area to avoid the loss of invaluable cell lines.

Issues related to ownership of biological materials and animals resulting from nuclear transfer (especially from extinct species) are also controversial. Modern zoos involved in *ex situ* breeding programmes generally avoid commercialism of wildlife. Technically, zoos usually own an individual animal; however, for propagation purposes, zoos share many species in institutional consortia, with animals shipped between zoos to maximise genetic diversity. In the case of multiple young, ownership is often distributed with the young, but the primary goal is always to ensure genetic viability of the species. This collegial relationship is fundamental to the success of *ex situ* breeding programmes. The commercialisation possibilities inherent in re-creating a previously extinct species would, however, generate such enormous publicity and financial incentives that the collegial relationship would almost certainly suffer. Additionally, such offspring would be the product of collaborations amongst zoos, universities and high-tech private industries, including the use of patented methodologies (see e.g. Stice *et al.*, 1999). Property issues would then inevitably arise, providing support for animal activists who argue that zoos do not exist to help protect and manage endangered wildlife. Likewise, even the production of young from extant species using uncommon technologies like nuclear transfer evokes concerns about ownership of these 'special' individuals, with their potential for substantially increasing gate receipts. Therefore, a high priority is to examine the legal implications of this issue *before* initiating such programmes.

CONCLUSIONS AND FUTURE PRIORITIES

The science and technology of nuclear transfer are progressing rapidly in livestock and laboratory animals. Although limited in terms of efficiency and broad-scale applicability across a diversity of species, it is inevitable that nuclear transfer methods will improve. Thus, rather than simply asking, 'is nuclear transfer applicable to wildlife management and conservation?' it is perhaps more useful to ask, 'as the technology evolves, how can nuclear transfer be most appropriately considered as a tool in the repertoire of assisted breeding technology?'. For now, scientists interested in the role of reproductive sciences for wildlife should first consider nuclear transfer as valuable, especially for conducting basic research. It is clear that animal species (mammalian, avian, amphibian, reptilian or fish; vertebrate or invertebrate) differ vastly in reproductive mechanisms. These variations undoubtedly extend to the blueprint genomic material of a cell's nucleus. Thus, nuclear studies across species will provide important, new and scholarly data – a wealth of novel bio-information.

Furthermore, it may be helpful to regard future improvements in nuclear transfer for offspring production as similar to those opportunities offered by other reproductive technologies (artificial insemination, *in vitro* fertilisation, intracytoplasmic sperm injection). In these cases, the techniques are evolving to study challenges specific to a given endangered species; for example, the need to overcome sexual incompatibility, transport genetic material long distances or even combat physiological problems such as teratospermia. Nuclear transfer may also develop as a niche tool, especially in cases of extreme population collapses, where only a few individuals remain. Additionally, we should never underestimate the potential of developing new and startling technologies in the future that will allow nuclear DNA to be used routinely for preserving and propagating animals on a large scale. Regardless, there is a need to be cautious in applying a tool as complicated and controversial as nuclear transfer, a technique that can never be allowed to detract from the primary goal of preserving habitat, genetic diversity and biodiversity. Novel scientific technologies should be seen as powerful opportunities that indeed may have practical application given our ability to remain vigilant and to use these as tools to help, not circumvent, conventional conservation strategies.

ACKNOWLEDGEMENTS

Some concepts and discussion points in the text resulted from a mini-workshop organised through the Conservation Breeding Specialist Group of the IUCN-World Conservation Union's Species Survival Commission on the relevance of nuclear transfer for conservation [Jonathan Ballou, Susie Ellis, JoGayle Howard, Budhan Pukazhenthi, Ulysses Seal, Rebecca Spindler and David Wildt]. The authors also thank Drs Dave Wildt and Bill Holt for their comments and constructive criticisms of this chapter.

REFERENCES

Baguisi, A., Behboodi, E., Melican, D. T., Pollock, J. S., Destrempes, M. M., Cammuso, C., Williams, J. L., Nims, S. D., Porter, C. A., Midura, P., Palacios, M. J., Ayres, S. L., Denniston, R. S., Hayes, M. L, Ziomek, C. A., Meade, H. M., Godke, R. A., Gavin, W. G., Overstrom, E. W. & Echelard, Y. (1999). Production of goats by somatic cell nuclear transfer. *Nature Biotechnology* **17**, 456-461.

Blondin, P., Farin, P. W., Crosier, A. E., Alexander, J. E. & Farin, C. E. (2000). *In vitro* production of embryos alters levels of insulin-like growth factor-II messenger ribonucleic acid in bovine fetuses 63 days after transfer. *Biology of Reproduction* **62**, 384-389.

Bonetta L. (2001) US still lacks human cloning legislation. [News] *Nature Medicine* **7**, 518.

Campbell, K. D., Reed, W. A. & White, K. L. (2000). Ability of integrins to mediate fertilization, intracellular calcium release and parthenogenetic development in bovine oocytes. *Biology of Reproduction* **62**, 1702-1709.

Campbell, K. H. S., McWhir, J., Ritchie, W. A. & Wilmut, I. (1996). Sheep cloned by nuclear transfer from a cultured cell line. *Nature* **380**, 64-66.

Cibelli, J. B., Stice, S. L., Golueke, P. J., Kane, J. J., Jerry, J., Blackwell, C., Ponce de Leon, F. A. & Robl, J. M. (1998). Cloned transgenic calves produced from nonquiescent fetal fibroblasts. *Science* **280**, 1256-1258.

Chougule, G. (2001). Human cloning - not if, but when. *Science* **292**, 639.

Colman, A. (2000). Somatic cell nuclear transfer in mammals: progress and applications. *Cloning* 1, 185-200.

Craft, I. (2001). Source of research embryos for cloning. *Lancet* 357, 1368.

Critser, J. K. & Russell, R. J. (2000). Genome resource banking of laboratory animal models. *Institute for Laboratory Animal Research Journal* 41, 183-186.

Daniels, R., Hall, V. & Trounson, A. O. (2000). Analysis of gene transcription in bovine nuclear transfer embryos reconstructed with granulosa cell nuclei. *Biology of Reproduction* 63, 1034-1040.

DeSousa, P. A., Winger, Q., Hill, J. R., Jones, K., Watson, A. J. & Westhusin, M. E. (1999). Reprogramming of fibroblast nuclei after transfer into bovine oocytes. *Cloning* 1, 63-69.

Dominko, T., Mitalipova, M., Haley, B., Beyhan, Z., Memili, M., McKusick, B. & First, N. L. (1999). Bovine oocyte cytoplasm supports development of embryos produced by nuclear transfer of somatic cell nuclei from various mammalian species. *Biology of Reproduction* 60, 1496-1502.

Farin, P. W. & Farin, C. E. (1995). Transfer of bovine embryos produced *in vivo* or *in vitro*: survival and fetal development. *Biology of Reproduction* 52, 676-682.

Hill, J. R., Roussel, A. J., Cibelli, J. B., Edwards, J. F., Hooper, N. L., Miller, M. W., Thompson, J. A., Looney, C. R., Westhusin, M. E., Robl, J. M. & Stice, S. L. (1999). Clinical and pathologic features of cloned transgenic calves and fetuses (13 case studies). *Theriogenology* 51, 1451-1465.

Jaenisch, R. & Wilmut I. (2001). Developmental biology. Don't clone humans! *Science* 291, 2552.

Kato, Y., Tani, T., Sotomaru, Y., Kurokawa, K., Kato, J.-Y., Doguchi, H., Yasue, H. & Tsunoda, Y. (1998). Eight calves cloned from somatic cells of a single adult. *Science* 282, 2095-2098.

Lanza, R. P., Cibelli, J. B., Blackwell, C., Cristofalo, V. J., Francis, M. K., Baerlocher, G. M., Mak, J., Schertzer, M., Chavez, E. A., Sawyer, N., Lansdorp, P. M. & West, M. D. (2000a). Extension of cell life-span and telomere length in animals cloned from senescent somatic cells. *Science* 288, 665-669.

Lanza, R. P., Cibelli, J. B., Diaz, F., Morales, C. T., Farin, P. W., Farin, C. E., Hammer, C. J., West, M. D. & Damiani, P. (2000b). Cloning of an endangered species (*Bos gaurus*) using interspecies nuclear transfer. *Cloning* 2, 79-90.

Lanza, R. P., Dresser, B. L. & Damiani, P. (2000c). Cloning Noah's Ark. *Scientific American* 283 (5), 84-89.

Macháty, Z., Bonk, A., Kühholzer, B. & Prather, R. S. (2000). Porcine oocyte activation induced by a cytosolic sperm factor. *Molecular Reproduction and Development* 57, 290-295.

Macháty, Z., Rickords, L. F. & Prather, R. S. (1999). Parthenogenetic activation of porcine oocytes following nuclear transfer. *Cloning* 1, 101-109.

MacPhee, R. D. E. & Marx, P. A. (1997). The 40,000-year plague: humans, hyperdisease and first-contact extinctions. In *Natural Change and Human Impact in Madagascar* (Eds. S. Goodman & B. Patterson), pp. 169-217. Smithsonian Institution Press, Washington, DC.

Meslin, E. M. (2000). Of clones, stem cells, and children: issues and challenges in human research ethics. *Journal of Women's Health & Gender-Based Medicine* 9, 831-841.

Murtaugh, C. (2001). Human cloning - not if, but when. *Science* **292**, 639.

Obata, Y., Kaneko-Ishino, T., Koide, T., Takai, Y., Ueda, T., Domeki, I., Shiroishi, T., Ishino, F. & Kono, T. (1998). Disruption of primary imprint during oocyte growth leads to the modified expression of imprinted genes during embryogenesis. *Development* **125**, 1553-1560.

Ogura, A., Inoue, K., Ogonuki, N., Noguchi, A., Takano, K., Nagano, R., Suzuki, O., Lee, J., Ishino, F. & Matsuda, J. (2000). Production of male cloned mice from fresh, cultured and cryopreserved immature sertoli cells. *Biology of Reproduction* **62**, 1579-1584.

Onishi, A., Iwamoto, M., Akita, T., Mikawa, S., Takeda, K., Awata, T., Hanada, H. & Perry, A. C. (2000). Pig cloning by microinjection of fetal fibroblast nuclei. *Science* **289**, 1188-1190.

Polzin, V. J., Anderson, D. L., Anderson, G. B., BonDurant, R. H., Butler, J. E., Pashen, R. L., Penedo, M. C. T. & Rowe, J. D. (1987). Production of sheep-goat chimeras by inner cell mass transplantation. *Journal of Animal Science* **65**, 325-330.

Prather, R. S. (2000). Pigs is pigs. *Science* **289**, 1886-1887.

Shiels, P. G., Kind, A. J., Campbell, K. H. S., Waddington, D., Wilmut, I., Colman, A. & Schnieke, A. E. (1999). Analysis of telomere lengths in cloned sheep. *Nature* **399**, 316-317.

Smaglik, P. (2001). Fears of cults and kooks push Congress towards cloning ban. *Nature* **410**, 617.

Solter, D. (2000). Mammalian cloning: advances and limitations. *Nature Reviews Genetics* **1**, 199-207.

Stice, S. L., Cibelli, J., Robl, J., Golueke, P., Ponce de Leon, A. F. & Jetty, D. J. (1999). Cloning using donor nuclei from proliferation somatic cells. United States Patent 5,945,577.

Stringfellow, D. A. & Givens, M. D. (1999). Infectious agents in bovine embryo production: hazards and solutions. *Theriogenology* **53**, 85-94.

Stringfellow, D. A. & Seidel, S. M. (1998). *Manual of the International Embryo Transfer Society*. International Embryo Transfer Society, Savoy, IL.

Stone, R. (1997). Paleontology. Siberian mammoth find raises hopes, questions. *Science* **286**, 876-877.

Varmus, H. E. (2000). The challenge of making laws on the shifting terrain of science. *Journal of Law, Medicine & Ethics* **28** (Suppl. 4), 46-53.

Vogel, G. (2001). Reproductive science. Human cloning plans spark talk of U.S. ban. *Science* **292**, 31.

Wakayama, T. & Yanagimachi, R. (1999a). Cloning of male mice from adult tail-tip cells. *Nature Genetics* **22**, 127-128.

Wakayama, T. & Yanagimachi, R. (1999b). Cloning the laboratory mouse. *Seminars in Cell & Developmental Biology* **10**, 253-258.

Wakayama, T., Perry, A. C., Zuccotti, M., Johnson, K. R., & Yanagimachi, R. (1998). Full-term development of mice from enucleated oocytes injected with cumulus cell nuclei. *Nature* **394**, 369-374.

Wakayama, T., Tateno, H., Mombaerts, P. & Yanagimachi, R. (2000). Nuclear transfer into mouse zygotes. *Nature Genetics* **24**, 108-109.

Watson, P. F. & Holt, W. V. (Eds.) (2001). *Cryobanking the Genetic Resource: Wildlife Conservation for the Future?* Taylor & Francis, London.

Wells, D. N., Misica, P. M., Day, A. M. & Tervit. H. R. (1997). Production of cloned lambs from an established embryonic cell line: a comparison between *in vivo* and *in vitro* matured cytoplasts. *Biology of Reproduction* 57, 385-393.

Wells, D. N., Misica, P. M. & Tervit, H. R. (1999). Production of cloned calves following nuclear transfer with cultured adult mural granulosa cells. *Biology of Reproduction* 60, 996-1005.

Wildt, D. E. (1997). Genome resources banking: impact on biotic conservation and society. In *Reproductive Tissue Banking: Scientific Principles* (Eds. A. M. Karow & J. K. Critser), pp. 399-439. Academic Press, San Diego, CA.

Wildt, D. E. (2000). Genome resource banking for wildlife research, management and conservation. *Institute for Laboratory Animal Research Journal* 41, 228-234.

Wildt, D. E. & Wemmer, C. (1999). Sex and wildlife: the role of reproductive biology in conservation. *Biodiversity and Conservation* 8, 965-976.

Wildt, D. E., Rall, W. F., Critser, J. K., Monfort, S. L. & Seal, U. S. (1997). Genome resource banks: 'living collections' for biodiversity conservation. *BioScience* 47, 689-698.

Wilmut, I. Schnieke, A. E., McWhir, J., Kind, A. J. & Campbell, K. H. (1997). Viable offspring derived from fetal and adult mammalian cells. *Nature* 385, 810-813.

Wilson E. O. (1988). The current status of biological diversity. In *Biodiversity* (Ed. E. O. Wilson), pp. 3-18. National Academy Press, Washington, DC.

Wolf, B. A., Westhusin, M. E., Levanduski, M. J., Bondioli, K. R. & Kraemer, D. C. (1990). Preimplantation development of embryos produced by intergeneric nuclear transplantation. *Theriogenology* 33, 350.

PART IV

Integrated conservation management

Science has to be understood in its broadest sense, as a method for comprehending all observable reality, and not merely as an instrument for acquiring specialised knowledge.   *Alexis Carrel*

As societies become more conscious of needs for biodiversity conservation, a host of conflicting interests emerge. Investment in wild species preservation may not enjoy high priority in poverty-stricken countries where governments are more concerned with human welfare. Ironically, the poorest countries are often those with the richest biodiversity, a disadvantage that can be turned to advantage when the value of wildlife is transformed into significant tourism revenues. Some countries also may have traditions which do not sit easily alongside wildlife protection; hunting is popular in many societies, even those where some measures of wildlife protection are being introduced. In many cases, wildlife protection comes into conflict with agricultural practices; it certainly is understandable that Nepalese farmers are distraught when a rhinoceros leaves a nearby national park and tramples their crops! Predatory species, especially those regarded as aliens, such as European foxes in Australia, also present a major threat to people, their livelihoods and the success of wildlife reintroduction programmes. Introducing alien species in a foreign environment can wreak havoc, brush-tailed possums introduced into New Zealand being a classic example.

Developing cost-effective practical solutions to these massive problems is akin to squaring the circle. Some situations require nurturing and expanding populations while other, so-called nuisance species must be controlled, preferably by humane approaches. Again, many of the strategies being developed involve regulating reproduction either through prevention (in pest species) or enhancement (in rare counterparts). Under some conditions and in certain habitats, both approaches are needed simultaneously for competing species.

This section contains a compendium of chapters illustrating the complexity of such challenges and of the strategies needed to solve them. This is where 'integration' of the reproductive sciences into conservation policies is most required. For example, several chapters describe how Australia and New Zealand are tackling the protection and reintroduction of native, endangered fauna while simultaneously attempting elimination, or at least control, of rampant, runaway population growth in aliens. For the latter, immunocontraception and poison baits have shown some promise, but routine use is anything but routine or simple. For example, population modelling is critical as scientists explore questions such as 'what proportion of a pest population must be rendered infertile to have an actual impact?' 'What are the likely risks in developing a viral vector for a contraceptive vaccine, and are the risks of affecting a non-target species acceptable to the public?' We felt that this broad sweep of interrelated subjects would be incomplete without a detailed description of the biotechnological approaches currently being investigated; hence, a chapter addressing these issues is included.

For integrated enhancement, we have the example of the black-footed ferret, a species once literally on the verge of extinction, but which has benefited from extensive cooperation amongst managers (*in situ* and *ex situ*) and reproductive scientists. The recovery of the black-footed ferret that suffered due to government policies aimed at eradicating its prey, the prairie dog, exemplifies two important points. Most importantly, a number of individuals and organisations with different skills, knowledge and backgrounds came together to solve a problem of common interest. Admirably, they laid aside their differences of approach and cooperated. They were fortunate to include reproductive biologists with considerable expertise in both the application of technology to animal breeding and the insight to realise that basic investigations of black-footed ferret physiology were an important prerequisite in the action plan. The results are an example to all and demonstrate the considerable benefits that accrue when interdisciplinary action is undertaken.

14

Integrating reproductive sciences into recovery programmes for declining and extinct marsupial populations

PETER D. TEMPLE-SMITH

INTRODUCTION AND OBJECTIVES

Marsupial evolution, diversity and extinction

Australia's marsupials appear to have evolved through colonisation by pro-
genitor species from South America (Szalay, 1982; Temple-Smith, 1987;
Rich, 1991). Land bridges connecting Australia, Antarctica and South
America (c. 45 million years ago) enabled the filtered passage of species from
South America across the Antarctic landmass to Australia. Subsequent evolution and radiation produced a distinct marsupial fauna that adapted to
changing landscapes and habitats. Various palaeontological studies (Archer
et al., 1989; Murray, 1991; Rich, 1991) have described an amazing diversity
of marsupials, including a rhinoceros-sized diprotodontid, a large carnivorous marsupial 'lion' (Thylacoleo; distantly resembling a sabre-toothed
cat), a tapir-like marsupial (Palorchestes sp.), various thylacine species,
rainforest-based marsupial moles and gigantic wombats (Phascolonus and
Ramsayia), wallabies (Protemnodon), kangaroos (Macropus titan) and a
Tasmanian devil (Sarcophilis laniarius), all of which became extinct.

Arrival of humans on the Australian continent started a process of extinctions that was accelerated by the entry of Europeans into the fragile
landscape. Habitat destruction, increased hunting and modern weapons
combined with introductions of the fox, dog, rabbit, goat and cat caused
a rapid loss of species, especially marsupials in the <8 kg weight range. By
the mid-twentieth century, nine marsupial species had been exterminated.
The 2000 IUCN Red List of Threatened Species records five Australian

marsupials as 'Critically Endangered', 17 as 'Endangered' and 22 as 'Vulnerable'. Recent rediscovery of a few 'Extinct' species (i.e. mountain pygmy possum, *Burramys parvus* and Gilbert's potoroo, *Potorous gilberti*) and the down-listing of others following conservation success (e.g. the woylie, *Bettongia penicillata*) have provided a few unexpected additions to Australia's marsupial fauna.

The less diverse, but no less interesting, marsupial fauna of the Americas deserves attention because relatively little is known about the status and biology of these taxa. Of the *c.* 85 species, there is no record of recent extinctions, and only three species are considered 'Critically Endangered', with three 'Endangered' and 18 'Vulnerable'. This assessment, however, may be inaccurate, perhaps reflecting a general lack of interest in, and information on, the status of this group. For example, the 2000 IUCN Red List mentions only the Chilean shrew opossum (*Rhyncholestes raphanurus*), with no reference to the family Caenolestidae, which contains at least six other species. In addition, there are many species in the large Didelphidae family listed as 'data deficient'. This, and the recent discovery of a new caenolestid species in the Andean region of Ecuador, highlights the need for more efforts to survey and study the marsupials of the Americas.

Marsupial recovery and the role of reproductive science

Actions to conserve threatened marsupials in Australia are usually directed by government-approved teams that develop, plan, implement, manage and monitor recovery progress (Male, 1996; Papps, 1996). Recovery teams usually comprise a core group of scientists and representatives from government and wildlife agencies, local government, land managers, community groups and funding organisations. The team sets the agenda for species recovery and decides on priorities, including research. When required, science-based research actions are integrated into the plan (Dickman, 1996; Jarman & Brock, 1996), largely with the objective of providing new knowledge that assists management and population growth.

For many recovery programmes, reproductive biology is an important research priority that assists the team in achieving realistic goals (e.g. enhanced *ex situ* breeding, improved monitoring of breeding activities, increased numbers of offspring and better information about the breeding biology of wild individuals). The temptation for reproductive biologists to direct their initial research efforts into assisted reproductive technologies (ART) is often impractical and neither cost-effective nor appropriate. Since the most obvious measure of recovery programme success is a sustained increase in population size, knowledge of 'fundamental' reproductive biology should be a priority for all programmes. Such information has application to natural captive breeding or, when necessary, developing more intrusive ART. However, ART has not yet been seriously pursued as part of any rare marsupial recovery programme.

This chapter reviews how knowledge about breeding biology and various technologies in the reproductive sciences are being used in marsupial recovery programmes. The potential of using cloning and nuclear transfer to resurrect extinct marsupials or to save those now at the brink of extinction is also discussed.

STATE OF THE ART

ART and marsupials

The most effective means of recovering and expanding rare populations is to ensure suitable conditions in the wild that promote reproduction and progeny survival. The next best strategy is to develop successful *ex situ* (captive) breeding programmes. These views are widely advocated by recovery teams and by zoo staff involved in *ex situ* programmes, but may be overlooked by those whose focus is on developing 'high-tech' offspring production using ART.

The common challenge for recovery teams is trying to breed animals 'artificially' before the natural reproductive processes unique to each species are clearly understood. The most useful approaches for developing breeding databases begin with the least invasive monitoring procedures. These include observations of breeding behaviour and assessing female, or sometimes male, hormonal patterns using faecal steroid analysis. Later, when basic breeding biology is better understood, this is perhaps followed by semen collection, cryopreservation and artificial insemination (AI) with or without ovulation induction (Holt & Pickard, 1999; Wildt & Wemmer, 1999; Monfort, Chapter 10). If unsuccessful, the use of more invasive and complex techniques, such as oocyte recovery and *in vitro* maturation, *in vitro* fertilisation (IVF), intracytoplasmic sperm injection (ICSI), embryo transfer or even cloning (see Critser *et al.*, Chapter 13) may be considered.

Compared with eutherian mammals, knowledge about reproduction in marsupials is rather rudimentary. However, for a few species, such as the tammar wallaby (*Macropus eugenii*), brush-tailed possum (*Trichosurus vulpecula*), koala (*Phascolarctos cinereus*), brown (*Antechinus stuartii*) and agile (*A. agilis*) marsupial mouse, Southern hairy-nosed wombat (*Lasiorhinus latifrons*), striped-faced dunnart (*Sminthopsis macrourus*) and two species of American marsupials, Virginian opossum (*Didelphis virginiana*) and grey short-tailed opossum (*Monodelphis brevicaudata*), the reproductive database is much more comprehensive (see Tyndale-Biscoe & Renfree, 1987; Renfree & Shaw, 1996, 1999). These studies highlight the intricacies of marsupial reproduction and also important differences among families and, sometimes, individual species within families. These species-specificities have contributed to the difficulties of developing suitable practical application of ART in this group.

Semen collection and cryopreservation have received significant attention (Taggart *et al.*, 1996, 1997, 1998; Molinia & Rodger, 1996; Holt *et al.*, 1999; Johnston *et al.*, 2000c), and basic information is now available for representatives from most Australian marsupial families. For the Macropodidae (one of the largest families), although semen collection is relatively simple, successful sperm cryopreservation has not been achieved (Taggart *et al.*, 1996; Holt *et al.*, 1999). Holt *et al.* (1999) have examined techniques for freezing macropodid spermatozoa, demonstrating that these cells survive the freezing process but lose viability during thawing when the temperature exceeds about 22° C.

AI has been attempted in the tammar wallaby (Molinia *et al.*, 1998a; D. Paris, personal communication) and has been successful in the koala (Johnston *et al.*, 2000a), brush-tailed possum (Molinia *et al.*, 1998a; Jungnickel *et al.*, 2000) and more recently in the tammar wallaby (D. Paris, personal communication). Ovulation induction using exogenous gonadotrophins has been tried in a few species (Hinds *et al.*, 1996; Mate *et al.*, 1998, Glazier & Molinia, 1998; Molinia *et al.*, 1998a, b; Glazier, 1999; McLeod *et al.*, 1999; Johnston *et al.*, 2000b; Jungnickel & Hinds, 2000; Jungnickel *et al.*, 2000) and, in conjunction with AI, has resulted in fertilisation and developing embryos (Jungnickel & Hinds, 2000). However, there is no record of these embryos developing to term. Xenografts of ovarian tissue from at least two species have been grafted successfully under the kidney capsule of the SCID mouse (fat-tailed dunnart, *Sminthopsis crassicaudata*; Lamden, 1996) or nude rat (common wombat, *Vombatus ursinus*; Wolvekamp *et al.*, 2001). The objective here has been to develop the xenograft techniques using common species (model analogues) and then apply them to endangered species to provide oocytes for IVF and ICSI.

IVF has been attempted in the tammar wallaby, brush-tailed possum, Virginian and grey short-tailed opossums and striped-faced dunnart, with successful fertilisation in the American species. Oocytes (Mate & Buist, 1999) and embryos (Yousef & Selwood, 1993; Renfree & Lewis, 1996) also have been recovered at various developmental stages and maintained in culture. Renfree & Lewis (1996) reported early cleavage stage development in the tammar wallaby. Yousef & Selwood (1993) described continued embryo development *in vitro* for unilaminar, bilaminar and trilaminar dasyurid embryos, but the *in vitro* conditions failed to support complete or normal development. However, stripe-faced dunnart embryos continued to develop *in vitro* to within 18 hours of birth (Yousef & Selwood, 1993). Although embryo transfer has not yet been achieved in marsupials, the transfer (cross-fostering) of marsupial pouch young (even early neonates 1–5 g in weight; Taggart *et al.*, 2002) between individuals of the same or related species has been successful in common and threatened marsupials (Merchant & Sharman, 1966; Clark, 1968; Smith, 1998; Taggart *et al.*, 1997, 2002). Finally, nuclear transfer has been proposed as a way to save some highly endangered species, in particular the Northern hairy-nosed wombat. However, without detailed knowledge of reproduction for suitable donor and surrogate species, the likelihood of successfully cloning a marsupial will remain a distant possibility.

Case histories

Three cases are offered as examples in which an integrated approach that includes the reproductive sciences is contributing to the recovery of endangered Australian marsupials. This is followed by comments on the recent proposal to 're-create' the extinct Tasmanian tiger (thylacine, *Thylacinus cynocephalis*) by cloning. Justifications for selecting specific reproductive strategies to increase population size, and the success (and sometimes failures) of each are explored.

Breeding success and reintroduction of the Eastern barred bandicoot (EBB)
(Perameles gunnii)
The EBB story is an excellent example of how a 'low-tech' *ex situ* breeding programme can be effective in rebuilding a rare population in conjunction with an *in situ* focus. It also illustrates the need for long-term planning and stewardship of release sites to protect reintroduced individuals. The plan itself has been cited as a prime example of how the endangered species recovery process should be organised, directed and implemented (Clark & Seebeck, 1990; Backhouse *et al.*, 1994).

Originally common throughout the native grasslands of southeastern Australia, the EBB's last stronghold is Tasmania (Myroniuk & Seebeck, 2000). Recent studies have raised concerns about its future even here due

Table 14.1 *Changes in estimated numbers of Victorian eastern barred bandicoots from trapping censuses (1982–1998)*

Year of census	Estimated animal numbers	Comments
1982	1750	Initial *in situ* census
1985	650	Significant *in situ* decline
1988	300	Melbourne Zoo begins *ex situ* breeding programme
1995	800	Peak animal numbers at the Woodlands Historic Park
1998	400	Significant decline in Woodlands Historic Park population

to climate change, continued clearing of grasslands and other destructive agricultural practices, and the recent refarious introduction of the red fox. Nonetheless, the EBB is still sufficiently common in Tasmania to be killed by vehicles on country roads. Decline of the EBB in Victoria is closely associated with late-nineteenth and twentieth century destruction of native grasslands (preferred habitat) which now occupy less than 1% of their former range. By the time government agencies realised the dire status of the species, fewer than 100 individuals remained, mostly around the small rural community of Hamilton in central Victoria (Myroniuk & Seebeck, 2000). The EBB Recovery Team was established in 1991 to develop a species recovery plan, and identified *ex situ* breeding as a high priority action.

This bandicoot breeds year round under captive conditions, produces up to four progeny per cycle, and the females become sexually mature at approximately 4 months of age. In theory, an adult female is capable of producing up to 12 progeny annually. In 1990 a few individuals from the Hamilton site were used to establish an *ex situ* population at the Melbourne Zoo. As with many captive breeding facilities, Melbourne Zoo required a few years of experience to develop reliable husbandry and breeding techniques (Myroniuk, 1995). Within about 2 years, the first *ex situ*-bred individuals were available for release into the wild at Woodland Historic Park on the outskirts of Melbourne. These individuals, and a small EBB population translocated from the wild, had become a genetically robust colony of over 800 individuals by 1995 (Table 14.1). In turn, this population became a source of bandicoots for reintroductions into selected historic sites across the western plains of Victoria (Backhouse *et al.*, 1994). In some years, more than 40 captive-born individuals were released. Two of the three zoos under the umbrella of the Zoological Parks and Gardens Board (Melbourne

Table 14.2 *Decline in eastern barred bandicoot numbers (as shown by change in trapping success) in Woodlands Historic Park during the period of population collapse*[a]

	1996			1997			1998	
Trapping date	Aug	Oct	Dec	Apr	Jul	Oct	Jan	Apr
Animal numbers/100 trap nights	77 (10^b)	19	18	8 (3^b)	5	3	1	0

[a] Data from P. Myroniuk (unpublished).
[b] Numbers in parentheses indicate new recruits to the population caught during the trapping period.

Zoo and Healesville Sanctuary) are now breeding centres for the recovery programme, and the third (Victoria's Open Range Zoo) provides holding facilities for individuals awaiting reintroduction.

Despite a decade of effort, successful *ex situ* breeding has not yet changed EBB status in Victoria because breeding and reintroducing individuals are only part of the process to re-establish and recover a species. Establishing secure reintroduction sites, removing risks that initially caused endangerment and ensuring long-term stewardship are crucial to species recovery success. Two specific examples from the EBB Recovery Programme are informative.

The first example highlights the importance of competent field management of reintroduction sites. The Woodland Park EBB reintroduced population was initially affected by a prolonged drought. There was also an unconstrained expansion of grey kangaroo numbers that caused loss of vegetative cover, reduced food supply for EBBs and increased exposure to predation, especially by foxes. Reproductive activity and recruitment declined. Politics also became an important factor. A change in departmental responsibility by the then State Government resulted in reduced field management of the site. Delay in implementing an active kangaroo culling programme allowed the grey kangaroo population to increase from under 100 to more than 1 300 individuals. The EBB population crashed (Tables 14.1 & 14.2) from over 800 individuals (1995) to fewer than 20 (1999). Culling of kangaroos was finally initiated but too late to save the bandicoot population.

An attempt to capture the remaining EBBs and return them to the *ex situ* breeding programme was unsuccessful. Extensive trapping produced only four individuals, thereby assuring significant loss of genetic diversity from the Victorian population. The overall experiment underscored the importance of coordinated long-term stewardship of reintroduced populations if survival is to be guaranteed beyond the life of political parties in government.

The second experience demonstrates the need for adequate resources and predator control at reintroduction sites. With the success of the EBB captive breeding programme and the large number of EBBs in the Woodlands Historic Park population as a source of animals for reintroductions, additional release sites were required. The Recovery Team rightly identified this as a priority to ensure that EBBs were distributed across a large area in the wild, thereby reducing extinction risk. By 1998, seven habitat sites of varying quality and security, and on government-controlled and private lands had been developed (Myroniuk & Seebeck, 2000). However, with the exception of Woodlands Historic Park and the original Hamilton Community Parklands, predator-proof fences were not constructed around reintroduction sites. For reasons of cost and management, the Recovery Team chose to rely on predator-control programmes directed primarily against the red fox. Because of difficulties in preventing bandicoot predation by foxes, the Team was forced to reduce managed release sites from seven to four. Two successful sites are currently on private land whereas the others are government-owned land at Woodlands Historic Park and Cobra Killuc. At the latter site, two monitored releases of captive-born EBBs demonstrated the devastating effects of insufficient predator control. Of the 20 bandicoots released, foxes killed about half within the first 4 days of introduction. This occurred despite a significant increase in fox baiting and shooting before the second release, which occurred 5 months after the first. Introductions at Cobra Killuc have ceased until security at the site has been improved. Discontinuation of this release programme was supported by the Zoological Parks and Gardens Board of Victoria, which was concerned that its extensive resources in support of the EBB *ex situ* breeding programme were being dissipated as a rather expensive form of 'fox food'.

In contrast to the EBB Recovery Programme, a sister species, the Western barred bandicoot (WBB) has benefited from a different approach. The WBB also experienced severe declines in the nineteenth and twentieth centuries, from predators (e.g. red fox) and poor land use across its Western Australian range. Using a combination of exclusion fencing, fox and cat destruction inside the fenced area and a high natural tolerance of native fauna to Compound 1080 (poisonous, fluoroacetate) baits, this programme had dramatic success. WBB recovery in the Heirisson Prong region of Western Australia has been achieved using on-site and *in situ* breeding from founders taken from a nearby offshore island. Recovery has occurred without the need for an intensively managed *ex situ* breeding programme. The message is that, while fundamental reproduction is crucial, the goals for recovery programmes should always include understanding 'whole' species biology, including the idiosyncrasies of the habitat and the capacity of introduced population to withstand stresses, such as predators and declining habitat quality. Most importantly, long-term stewardship is a critical element.

Saving the 'Shadow': applying ART to conserving the Victorian brush-tailed rock wallaby

Petrogale penicillata, the Victorian brush-tailed rock wallaby (BTRW; known locally as the 'Shadow') is now surviving precariously in its most southerly historic Victorian range. An isolated BTRW population in the Grampians National Park became extinct in 2000 with the placement of its last individual (an aged, greying female with cataracts, a heart murmur and virtually no chance of breeding) into an *ex situ* population. The only remaining populations (totalling perhaps *c.* 20 individuals) are now restricted to far eastern Victoria in a few ravines, amphitheatres and rock buttresses along the Snowy River catchment.

Paradoxically, this species was so numerous along the Snowy River in the early twentieth century that shooting parties killed as many as 20 000 per year until the harvest became unsustainable in the 1920s. At about this time a sudden statewide decline in BTRW populations was noted, but it was already too late to prevent the species sliding from 'Common' to 'Vulnerable' and then 'Endangered'. The Victorian populations are genetically important (Close *et al.*, 1994; Eldridge, 1997) and now 'Critically Endangered'. Larger populations of BTRWs still occur in the central and northern regions of adjacent New South Wales with a few remnants also in southern Queensland. However, the future of the species appears bleak.

The Victorian BTRW Recovery Team (established in 1995) set two breeding priorities: (1) establish an *ex situ* breeding population, and (2) develop a cross-fostering protocol to expand reproductive output rapidly. A small population of six BTRWs, collected from the wild, was first established at Healesville Sanctuary with three additional individuals subsequently translocated to the Adelaide Zoo. The Tidbinbilla Nature Reserve near Canberra joined the Recovery Team to provide additional resources and expertise, and together these three organisations formed a Captive Management Working Group to coordinate the *ex situ* programme.

The Victorian BTRW Recovery Programme has been challenged by a rapid decline in the remaining wild populations, leading to problems in

Table 14.3 *Theoretical difference in reproductive output[a] from a pair of brush-tailed rock wallabies from natural recruitment or after cross-fostering of all pouch young (PY) produced over 6 years*

	Year 0	Year 1.5	Year 3	Year 4.5	Year 6
Natural recruitment	2	3	5	8	13
PY cross-fostering	2	8	32	128	448

[a] Theoretical output assumes equal sex ratios, no mortality over the 6 years, females are sexually mature at about 1.5 years of age, females breed each year (natural recruitment) and have the capacity (by removing PY) to produce six pouch young for cross-fostering (modified from Taggart *et al.*, 2002).

securing breeding stock for the *ex situ* efforts. Also problematic has been the poor breeding success of captured wallabies, and difficulties in obtaining pouch young or juveniles (especially females) from the dwindling wild populations. Poor recruitment in nature, especially of females, has resulted in a demographic shift to an aged population.

It is now critical to increase rapidly the numbers of Victorian BTRWs in captivity and in the wild to preserve the remaining genetic diversity and to prevent extinction. Cross-fostering (the transfer of pouch young from biological dam to a foster mother, usually of a different species) has important potential applications in conserving macropodid marsupials. Lactating macropodid females have a natural tendency to suckle pouch young while carrying a diapausing embryo *in utero*. The embryo reactivates after the pouch young is detached from the nipple, resulting in birth of a new pouch young within about 2 weeks (Tyndale-Biscoe & Renfree, 1987; Renfree & Shaw, 1996, 2000). Merchant & Sharman (1966) pioneered cross-fostering in marsupials. However, the technique's recent inclusion in the BTRW Recovery Plan (Taggart *et al.*, 2002) is the first attempt to use cross-fostering to accelerate reproductive output of an endangered marsupial. Female macropodids have the capacity to increase their normal birth rate from one to at least six young per year by cross-fostering (Table 14.3) but this advantage is taxon-specific. Cross-fostering is not as useful for species such as the wombats that do not appear to have a post-partum oestrus or embryonic diapause.

However, despite the promising modelling calculations that demonstrate the theoretical potential of this technique to increase reproductive efficiency, the practical advantages of cross-fostering still remain to be demonstrated for an endangered macropodid. After 4 years of cross-fostering, there is no measurable change in the size of the three *ex situ* populations of Victorian

BTRWs, and there has only been a minor population increase *in situ*. There is a great need for more basic research to determine the optimal conditions for cross-fostering to be consistently successful. Close cooperation is required among participating wildlife agencies and institutions to ensure that *ex situ* populations consist of fertile and compatible individuals. These latter factors are particularly challenging. Despite extensive field attempts to trap young recruits for *ex situ* breeding, there has been no recent success. There also are worrying signs from the field and zoos that recovery attempts may have started too late. The programme may have one remaining (and excruciating) decision – the issue of a termination (exit) strategy. Ultimately, when dividends are minimal or non-existent in the face of high financial costs, a decision will need to be made on whether to proceed with the recovery or to reallocate vital resources to species with a better chance of survival.

Recovery of the Northern hairy-nosed wombat

The Northern hairy-nosed wombat (NHW), *Lasiorhinus krefftii*, was probably in population decline by the time it had been described in the late nineteenth century. This is one of three extant wombat species in Australia, and is now the second most endangered of Australia's marsupial fauna. The remaining population of *c.* 110 animals is confined to Epping Forest National Park, a *c.* 300 hectare refuge in central western Queensland (Horsup, 1996).

The NHW Recovery Plan includes plans for an *ex situ* population, initially at the Western Plains Zoo (WPZ), largely for the purposes of developing husbandry and breeding protocols and providing individuals for reintroduction. The only recent attempt to establish an *ex situ* population (by translocating a 19 kg subadult male to WPZ in 1996) was unsuccessful, and further action toward this objective has been delayed. The only other NHWs ever held in captivity, a female and male, were successfully maintained for *c.* 30 and 12 years, respectively, in basic enclosures on a property adjacent to the Epping Forest National Park.

With no immediate prospects of resuming *ex situ* breeding, most actions have involved monitoring the breeding status of NHWs in the wild as well as conducting 'model' studies in the sister species, the Southern hairy-nosed wombat (SHW), *Lasiorhinus latifrons*. But progress has been impeded by a general lack of basic reproductive information in wombats in general and in the NHW in particular. Even basic questions about age at maturity, seasonal breeding, oestrous cycle length, mating and mate selection, siring success and recruitment of the NHW remain unanswered.

With these significant challenges in mind, an indirect approach to integrating reproductive sciences for conserving the NHW has been undertaken.

Table 14.4 Research studies into the breeding biology of the common wombat (CW), Southern hairy-nosed wombat (SHW) and Northern hairy-nosed wombat (NHW)

Project	Species	Status	Comment	Reference
Studies using model species for the NHW				
Pouch condition index	SHW	Completed	Index developed to provide relationship between pouch parameters of females at different life and breeding stages. For application to NHW.	V. Steele, D. Taggart & P. Temple-Smith (unpublished data); Tyrell (2001)
Seasonal breeding	SHW/CW	Completed	Clear evidence of seasonal breeding activity in CW and SHW.	Green & Rainbird (1987); C. McCallum (pers. comm.); Hamilton et al. (2000)
Cross-fostering of pouch young	SHW	Completed	Successful cross-fostering of wombat pouch young between SHW females. No evidence of diapausing embryos or post-partum oestrus.	D. Taggart & P. Temple-Smith (unpublished data)
Ex situ breeding	SHW/CW	In progress	Irregular success, outcomes unpredictable. Information from zoo studbook records. Attempts to influence breeding success of SHW by diet manipulation.	No published studies
Assessment of oestrus	CW/SHW	Completed/ in progress	Data on changes in basal body temperature, plasma and faecal progesterone concentrations and oestrus in CW. Study in progress with plasma and faecal progesterone concentrations in SHW.	Peters & Rose (1979); C. McCallum (unpublished data); J. Tyrell, P. Temple-Smith & D. Taggart (unpublished data)
Semen collection	SHW/CW	Completed	Procedure developed successfully.	Taggart et al. (1996, 1998)
Semen cryopreservation	SHW/CW	Completed	Procedure developed successfully.	Taggart et al. (1996, 1998)
Artificial insemination				No published studies

Ovarian xenograft	CW	In progress	Published procedure to produce oocyte maturation stages in wombat xenografts. No evidence of attempts *in vivo*.	Wolvekamp *et al.* (2001)
Superovulation				No published studies
In vitro fertilisation			No published data. Suggested as a possible future ART action.	No published studies
Intracytoplasmic sperm injection				Wolvekamp *et al.* (2001)
Embryo culture				No published studies
Embryo transfer				No published studies
Cloning			Suggested as alternative ART approach. Success unlikely in near future owing to limited data on basic aspects of wombat reproductive biology.	No published studies
Direct studies in the NHW				
Seasonal breeding	NHW	In progress	Inconclusive data.	A. Horsup (pers. comm.)
Ex situ breeding	NHW		No past attempts. Currently no individuals under *ex situ* management.	No published studies
Assessment of oestrus	NHW	In progress	*In situ* pilot study to examine feasibility of monitoring faecal progesterone.	No published studies
Semen collection	NHW	Completed	Pilot study to collect semen partly successful; samples collected and analysed.	P. Temple-Smith, D. Taggart & A. Horsup (unpublished data)
Semen cryopreservation	NHW	Completed		P. Temple-Smith, D. Taggart & A. Horsup (unpublished data)
Cloning	NHW		Suggested as future option. Tissue biopsies from *c.* 40 NHW individuals collected during 1999 trapping census. Fibroblast lines established and cryopreserved for future cloning attempts.	No published studies

With the exception of occasional trapping (for census and animal examination) at the Epping Forest National Park, there is no opportunity for using conventional approaches for collecting field data on NHW breeding biology. For example, it is not possible to collect serial blood samples from individuals to determine seasonal or cyclical changes in reproduction or to monitor physical or physiological reproductive traits, including growth and survival of pouch young. Of more significance to the recovery programme, there is no immediate prospect for such studies in the near future. Two general strategies have, therefore, been adopted by the Recovery Team to develop an improved understanding of wombat breeding biology (Table 14.4). The first is to conduct extensive investigations (*ex situ* and *in situ*) of the SHW and common wombat, *Vombatus ursinus* and apply this new knowledge to NHW conservation. The second strategy involves direct (during trapping) and indirect field monitoring of NHW reproductive activities. Together these strategies are expected to generate useful, practical information and conservation actions. Until access to NHWs is improved and *ex situ* breeding success of wombats is enhanced, there is little probability that ART will play any significant role in the conservation of this species. Although ovulation induction, AI and even IVF, ICSI, embryo transfer and cloning have potential for recovering the NHW, none of these procedures is likely to be useful in the immediate future to improve the status and breeding potential of the NHW.

Re-creating the thylacine

An icon of the devastating footprint of man on the landscape and its fauna, the thylacine (*Thylacinus cynocephalis*) is one of the planet's most recognisable symbols of extinction. Although the last known individual died in captivity in 1936, the extinction process for the thylacine probably began in the late Cainozoic (Rich, 1991). Once widely distributed throughout Australia, its extinction on the mainland has been linked to the arrival of the dingo and its ancestors. The Riversleigh Project (Archer *et al.*, 1989) identified at least two extinct thylacine species in the 25 million years old limestone deposits of northern Queensland. On mainland Australia, the most recent evidence of the thylacine was the discovery of *c.* 5000-year-old desiccated remains in a limestone cave on the Nullarbor Plain of Western Australia.

In Tasmania, the thylacine was isolated for thousands of years from competition, and perhaps predation, by the dingo and, more recently, the red fox which spread rapidly throughout mainland Australia after its introduction in the 1880s. The thylacine survived in Tasmania until hunting, a Government bounty and perhaps canine distemper conspired to cause its rapid, and essentially unnoticed, decline and extinction (Paddle, 2000). Thylacine sightings are still reported from Tasmania, mainland Australia and even Papua New Guinea, but the lack of any genuine evidence (e.g. spoor, hair, skeletal remains, faeces) challenges the veracity of these sightings. Extinction of the thylacine appears, unfortunately, secure – or is it? The almost sacred nature of the thylacine in the Australian memory has created willingness, perhaps a yearning, to seek its re-creation and return to the Tasmanian wilderness. This desire has created ideal conditions for raising public expectations about the potential of cloning to resurrect the thylacine.

A highly publicised plan by two Sydney institutions in 2000 to re-create the thylacine using cloning and tissues from an alcohol-preserved specimen captured the imagination of the world press and public alike. A similarly audacious plan to resurrect the woolly mammoth, using spermatozoa extracted from a frozen specimen in the Siberian tundra and the elephant as the oocyte donor and foster mother, was abandoned long after most scientists had discredited the project. But like the mammoth project, the hyperbole surrounding the thylacine 're-creation' exceeded current scientific capacities, misled the public and challenged the professional esteem of those directly involved. The plan was presented with wild claims that the public would soon be able to obtain thylacines from local pet shops. Not only were the press and public apparently convinced by the cloning rhetoric, but also a state government and a private company provided significant venture capital.

Now the project has become a symbol for issues associated with the concept of cloning extinct species, such as scientific credibility and funding priorities. Since many people (including this author) would like to see and study living thylacines, what is the likelihood that this project will succeed, and what priority should be given to its funding, especially from public/government sources?

Use of scarce resources to determine the efficacy of nuclear transfer to re-create an extinct species, versus technology development to prevent extinction of already living, but endangered, Australasian marsupials deserves more than passing consideration. For example, the Northern hairy-nosed wombat, Scott's tree kangaroo, the long-footed potoroo and Gilbert's potoroo all require immediate attention. At the same time, is there any possibility that this project could succeed in re-creating the thylacine or at least provide significant advancements in scholarly knowledge? What priority and moral/ethical considerations should be given to the project and its potential outcomes?

Despite the optimism of the 're-creation' team, the challenges of cloning a thylacine using existing methods and materials are probably insurmountable. The alcohol-fixed male thylacine pouch young (the DNA donor) is not an ideal source of material for nuclear transfer, unless the meaning of cloning is re-creating parts of the genome rather than re-creating a living individual (as proposed). Although nuclei for transfer are best recovered from fresh or frozen, unfixed tissue, alcohol-fixed tissue is an excellent source of DNA. So far, DNA has been extracted successfully from this specimen using a standard procedure that could be mimicked by any serious molecular biology laboratory. The development of DNA libraries and other DNA-related resources for systematics, evolutionary and gene sequence comparisons across phyla is achievable and has already been accomplished. However, use of this material to create a cloned individual is presently not a viable option and may not be in the future. A graphic illustration of the challenge is the shredded 'Jurassic Park' novel paradigm. In this example, reconstituting DNA extracted from the thylacine pouch young into a form that would support cloning is equated to reconstituting the novel 'Jurassic Park' after it has been shredded into thousands of thoroughly mixed fragments. The resulting minute pieces contain all the word sequences of the book but no obvious keys to the line, paragraph and page sequences. Reconstructing the complete and functional, thylacine genomic sequence using DNA fragments extracted from alcohol-preserved tissue would be as challenging as re-creating the deconstructed novel.

Even assuming that all DNA sequences could be realigned to reconstitute the correct genomic sequence, other extreme challenges follow. These include successfully incorporating the reconstructed DNA into a nuclear structure with appropriate nucleoprotein associations and the capacity to form chromosomes during mitotic divisions of re-created embryos. If nuclear reconstitution were achieved, the next requirement would be to find an oocyte donor with the capacity to activate the thylacine genome appropriately to form a normally developing embryo. Assuming that these hurdles were negotiated, selecting a surrogate recipient species with the capacity to support the normal development, parturition and early care of the clone would be the final challenge. In the case of the thylacine, the breeding biology of the two most frequently mentioned surrogate species, the numbat and Tasmanian devil, is still poorly understood. Thorough knowledge of their reproductive biology is an essential prerequisite to any success.

To set out with failure as the most likely outcome of this venture, especially considering its high profile launch, is not the most constructive approach to developing support from the scientific community and public for the use of cloning in marsupial conservation. Other more feasible options exist, including directing initial cloning studies to species such as the tammar wallaby and striped-faced dunnart, which have well-established genetic, reproduction and developmental databases. Intraspecific embryo transfer using cloned embryos is also sensible. If the technology appears promising, then follow-up attempts at interspecific cloning using transferred nuclei from endangered congeners like the brush-tailed rock wallaby could be investigated in surrogate species such as the tammar wallaby in which cross-fostering already has been successful (Taggart et al., 2002).

CONCLUSIONS AND PRIORITIES FOR THE FUTURE

For the marsupials, the highest priority must be on focused studies of breeding biology. Such an emphasis will ensure that advice on conservation actions for threatened species is supported by a comprehensive database derived from research into those species, their congeners or suitable model analogues. There also is an acute need to generate basic information on the reproductive biology of a wide range of species, genera and families, including those now considered 'safe' and not currently on the IUCN Red List of Threatened Species. We need to take lessons from the past. For most threatened species, the gathering of useful biological information *after* they are recognised as endangered is often extremely difficult (e.g. the Northern hairy-nosed wombat, discussed above) and sometimes impossible.

Finally, there is a compelling need for more investigations of American marsupials, which, with the exception of the grey short-tailed and Virginian opossums, have received even less attention than their Australian counterparts. Most species and their biology, distribution and conservation status remain essentially unknown. Some single-species genera (e.g. *Glironia venusta, Caluromyciops irrupta, Lestodelphys halli*), which are especially vulnerable to land clearing and habitat change, are in danger of becoming extinct even before they are seriously studied. Our goal for marsupials should be to develop comprehensive databases on all species and eliminate the phrase 'data deficient' from the IUCN Red List. A second aim to eliminate marsupials from the Red List altogether, is far more challenging and less realistic in the immediate future!

ACKNOWLEDGEMENTS
I thank Peter Myroniuk, David Wildt, Bill Holt and Meredith Temple-Smith for comments on and assistance with the manuscript. Peter Myroniuk provided information on the Eastern barred bandicoot *ex situ* breeding

programme and data in Tables 14.1 and 14.2. David Taggart provided access to unpublished data, many years of fruitful research collaborations and many hours of discussion on marsupials, ART and conservation.

REFERENCES

Archer, M., Godthelp, H., Hand, S. & Megirian, D. (1989). Fossil mammals of Riversleigh, north western Queensland: preliminary overview of biostratigraphy, correlation and environmental change. *Australian Zoologist* **25**, 29-65.

Backhouse, G. N., Clark, T. W. & Reading, R. P. (1994). The Australian Eastern Barred Bandicoot program, evaluation and reorganization. In *Endangered Species Recovery: Finding the Lessons, Improving the Process* (Eds. T. W. Clark, R. P. Reading & A. I. Clark), pp. 251-271. Island Press, Washington, DC.

Clark, M. J. (1968). Growth of pouch young of the red kangaroo, *Megaleia rufa*, in the pouches of foster mothers of the same species. *International Zoo Yearbook* **8**, 102-106.

Clark, T. W. & Seebeck, J. (1990). *Management and Conservation of Small Populations.* Chicago Zoological Society, Brookfield, IL.

Close, R. L., Eldridge, M. D., Bell, J. N. & Reside, J. (1994). A genetic study of the brush-tailed rock wallaby *Petrogale penicillata* in East Gippsland and relevance for management of the species in Victoria. *Pacific Conservation Biology* **1**, 367-371.

Dickman, C. (1996). Incorporating science into recovery planning for threatened species. In *Back from the Brink: Refining the Threatened Species Recovery Process* (Eds. S. Stephens & S. Maxwell), pp. 63-73. Surrey Beatty & Sons, Chipping Norton, NSW.

Eldridge, M. D. (1997). Rock wallaby conservation: essential data and management priorities. Proceedings of the 1994 National Rock Wallaby Symposium Workshops. *Australian Mammalogy* **19**, 325-330.

Glazier, A. M. (1999). Time of ovulation in the brushtail possum (*Trichosurus vulpecula*) following PMSG/LH induced ovulation. *Journal of Experimental Zoology* **283**, 608-611.

Glazier, A. M. & Molinia, F. C. (1998). Improved method of superovulation in monovulatory brushtail possum (*Trichosurus vulpecula*) using pregnant mares serum gonadotrophin-luteinizing hormone. *Journal of Reproduction and Fertility* **113**, 191-195.

Green, R. H. & Rainbird, J. L. (1987). The common wombat *Vombatus ursinus* (Shaw, 1800) in northern Tasmania - Part 1. Breeding, growth and development. *Records of the Queen Victoria Museum* **91**, 1-19.

Hamilton, R. A, Stanton, P. G., O'Donnell L., Steele, V. R., Taggart, D. A. & Temple-Smith, P. D. (2000). Determination of seasonality in southern hairy-nosed wombats (*Lasiorhinus latifrons*) by analysis of fecal androgens. *Biology of Reproduction* **63**, 526-531.

Hinds, L. A., Fletcher, T. P. & Rodger, J. C. (1996). Hormones of oestrus and ovulation and their manipulation in marsupials. *Reproduction, Fertility and Development* **8**, 661-672.

Holt, W. V. & Pickard, A. R. (1999) Role of reproductive technologies and genetic resource banks in animal conservation. *Reviews of Reproduction* **4**, 143-150.

Holt, W. V., Penfold, L. M., Johnston, S. D., Temple-Smith, P. D., McCallum, C., Shaw, J., Lindemans, W. & Blyde, D. (1999). Cryopreservation of macropodid spermatozoa: New insights from the cryomicroscope. *Reproduction, Fertility and Development* 11, 345-353.

Horsup, A. (1996). The northern hairy-nosed wombat recovery program: trials and triumphs. In *Back from the Brink: Refining the Threatened Species Recovery Process* (Eds. S. Stephens & S. Maxwell), pp.150-154. Surrey Beatty & Sons, Chipping Norton, NSW.

Jarman, P. J. & Brock, M. A. (1996). Collaboration of science and management in endangered species recovery. In *Back from the Brink: Refining the Threatened Species Recovery Process* (Eds. S. Stephens & S. Maxwell), pp. 74-78. Surrey Beatty & Sons, Chipping Norton, NSW.

Johnston, S. D., McGowan, M. R., O'Callaghan, P., Cox, R. & Nicolson, V. (2000a). Studies of the oestrous cycle, oestrus and pregnancy in the koala (*Phascolarctos cinereus*). *Journal of Reproduction and Fertility* 120, 49-57.

Johnston, S. D., McGowan, M. R., O'Callaghan, P., Cox, R. & Nicolson, V. (2000b). Natural and artificial methods for inducing the luteal phase in the koala (*Phascolarctos cinereus*). *Journal of Reproduction and Fertility* 120, 59-64.

Johnston, S. D., McGowan, M. R., Phillips, N. J. & O'Callaghan, P. (2000c). Optimal physicochemical conditions for the manipulation and short-term preservation of koala (*Phascolarctos cinereus*) spermatozoa. *Journal of Reproduction and Fertility* 118, 273-281.

Jungnickel, M. K. & Hinds, L. A. (2000). Hormonal profiles in the tammar wallaby, *Macropus eugenii* following FSH/LH superovulation. *Reproduction, Fertility and Development* 12, 457-464.

Jungnickel, M. K., Molinia, F. C., Harman, A. J. & Rodger, J. C. (2000). Sperm transport in the female reproductive tract of the brushtail possum, *Trichosurus vulpecula*, following superovulation and artificial insemination. *Animal Reproduction Science* 59, 213-228.

Lamden, K. (1996). Development and evaluation of marsupial (*Sminthopsis crassicaudata*) ovarian xenografts in SCID and tolerized mice. Honours thesis, Monash University.

Male, B. (1996). Recovery of Australian threatened species - a national perspective. In *Back from the Brink: Refining the Threatened Species Recovery Process* (Eds. S. Stephens & S. Maxwell), pp. 23-27. Surrey Beatty & Sons, Chipping Norton, NSW.

Mate, K. E. & Buist, J. M. (1999). Timing and regulatory aspects of oocyte maturation *in vitro* in the tammar wallaby, *Macropus eugenii*. *Reproduction, Fertility and Development* 11, 247-254.

Mate, K. E., Molinia, F. C. & Rodger, J. C. (1998). Manipulation of the fertility of marsupials for conservation of endangered species and control of over-abundant populations. *Animal Reproduction Science* 53, 65-76.

McLeod, B. J., Hunter, M. G., Crawford, J. L. & Thompson, E. G. (1999). Follicle development in cyclic, anoestrous and FSH-treated brushtail possums (*Trichosurus vulpecula*). *Animal Reproduction Science* 57, 217-227.

Merchant, J. C. & Sharman, G. B. (1966). Observations on the attachment of marsupial pouch young to teats and on the rearing of pouch young by foster mothers of the same or different species. *Australian Journal of Zoology* 14, 593-609.

Molinia, F. C. & Rodger, J. C. (1996). Pellet-freezing spermatozoa of two marsupials - the tammar wallaby, *Macropus eugenii*, and the brushtail possum, *Trichosurus vulpecula*. *Reproduction, Fertility and Development* **8**, 681-684.

Molinia, F. C., Gibson, R. J., Brown, A. M., Glazier, A. M. & Rodger, J. C. (1998a). Successful fertilization after superovulation and laparoscopic intrauterine insemination of the brushtail possum, *Trichosurus vulpecula*, and tammar wallaby, *Macropus eugenii*. *Journal of Reproduction and Fertility* **113**, 9-17.

Molinia, F. C., Gibson, R. J., Smedley, M. A. & Rodger, J. C. (1998b). Further observations of the ovarian response of the tammar wallaby (*Macropus eugenii*) to exogenous gonadotrophins- an improved method for superovulation using FSH/LH. *Animal Reproduction Science* **53**, 253-263.

Murray, P. (1991). The Pleistocene megafauna of Australia. In *Vertebrate Paleontology of Australasia* (Eds. P. Vickers-Rich, J. M. Monaghan, R. F. Baird & T. H. Rich), pp. 1071-1164. Pioneer Design Studio, Melbourne.

Myroniuk, P. (1995). Captive management of the threatened eastern barred bandicoot: zoos and co-operative conservation. In *People and Nature Conservation: Perspectives on Private Land Use and Endangered Species Recovery* (Eds. A. Bennett, G. Backhouse & T. W. Clark), pp. 63-67. Transactions of the Royal Society of New South Wales. Surrey Beatty & Sons, Chipping Norton, NSW.

Myroniuk, P. & Seebeck, J. (2000). Eastern barred bandicoot. In *Endangered Animals: A Reference Guide to Conflicting Issues* (Eds. R. P. Reading & B. Miller), pp. 89-94. Greenwood Press, Philadephia.

Paddle, R. N. (2000). *The last Tasmanian tiger: the history and extinction of the thylacine*. Cambridge University Press, Cambridge.

Papps, D. (1996). Commonwealth and State Government frameworks for recovery planning for threatened species and communities. In *Back from the Brink: Refining the Threatened Species Recovery Process* (Eds. S. Stephens & S. Maxwell), pp. 28-36. Surrey Beatty & Sons, Chipping Norton, NSW.

Peters, D. G. & Rose, R. W. (1979). The oestrous cycle and basal body temperature in the common wombat (*Vombatus ursinus*). *Journal of Reproduction and Fertility* **17**, 453-460.

Renfree, M. B. & Lewis, A. McD. (1996). Cleavage *in vivo* and *in vitro* in the marsupial *Macropus eugenii*. *Reproduction, Fertility and Development* **8**, 725-742.

Renfree, M. B. & Shaw, G. (1996). Reproduction of a marsupial: from uterus to pouch. *Animal Reproduction Science* **42**, 393-404.

Renfree, M. B. & Shaw, G. (1999). Marsupials. In *Encyclopedia of Reproduction* (Eds. E. Knobil & J. D. Neill), pp. 104-114. Academic Press, London.

Renfree, M. B. & Shaw, G. (2000) Diapause. *Annual Reviews of Physiology* **62**, 353-375.

Rich, T. H. (1991). Monotremes, placentals and marsupials: their record in Australia and its biases. In *Vertebrate Paleontology of Australasia* (Eds. P. Vickers-Rich, J. M. Monaghan, R. F. Baird & T. H. Rich), pp. 893-1071. Pioneer Design Studio, Melbourne.

Smith, M. J. (1998). Establishment of a captive colony of *Bettongia tropicia* (Marsupialia: Potoroidae) by cross-fostering: and observations on reproduction. *Journal of Zoology (London)* **244**, 43-50.

Szalay, F. S. (1982). A new appraisal of marsupial phylogeny and classification. In *Carnivorous Marsupials* (Ed. M.Archer), pp. 621-640. Surrey Beatty & Sons and the Royal Zoological Society of New South Wales, Sydney.

Taggart, D. A., Leigh, C. M., Steele, V. R., Breed, W. G., Temple-Smith, P. D. & Phelan, J. (1996). Collection and cryopreservation of marsupial spermatozoa. *Reproduction, Fertility and Development* **8**, 673–680.

Taggart, D. A., Schultz, D. & Temple-Smith, P. D. (1997). Development and application of assisted reproductive technologies in marsupials: their value for the conservation of rock wallabies. *Australian Mammalogy* **19**, 183–190.

Taggart, D.A., Steele, V. R., Schultz, D. & Temple-Smith, P. D.(1998). Semen collection and cryopreservation in the southern hairy-nosed wombat (*Lasiorhynus latifrons*): implications for the conservation of the northern hairy-nosed wombat (*Lasiorhynus krefftii*). In *Wombats* (Ed. P. Pridmore), pp. 180–191. Surrey Beatty & Sons, Sydney.

Taggart, D. A., Underwood, G., Phillips, K., Whitehead, P. & Schultz, D. (2002). Cross-fostering and marsupial conservation: efforts to accelerate the reproductive rate of the endangered brush-tailed rock wallaby, *Petrogale penicillata* (Marsupialia: Macropodidae). *Australian Journal of Zoology* (in press).

Temple-Smith, P. D. (1987). Sperm structure and marsupial phylogeny. In *Possums and Opossums: Studies in Evolution* (Ed. M. Archer), pp. 171–193. Surrey Beatty & Sons and the Royal Zoological Society of New South Wales, Sydney.

Tyndale-Biscoe, C. H. & Renfree, M. B. (1987). *Reproductive Physiology of Marsupials.* Cambridge University Press, Cambridge.

Tyrell, J. C. (2001). The reproductive biology of the female southern hairy-nosed wombat (*Lasiorhinus latifrons*). Honours thesis, The University of Melbourne.

Wildt, D. E. & Wemmer, C. (1999). Sex and wildlife: the role of reproductive biology in conservation. *Biodiversity and Conservation* **8**, 965–976.

Wolvekamp, M. C. J., Cleary, M. L., Cox, S. L., Shaw, J. M., Jenkin, G. & Trounson, A. O. (2001). Follicular development in cryopreserved common wombat ovarian tissue xenografted to nude rats. *Animal Reproduction Science* **65**, 135–147.

Yousef, A. & Selwood, L. (1993). Embryonic development in culture of the marsupials *Antechinus stuartii* (Macleay) and *Sminthopsis macroura* (Spencer) during preimplantation stages. *Reproduction, Fertility and Development* **5**, 445–458.

15

Captive breeding and predator control: a successful strategy for conservation in Western Australia

TERRY FLETCHER & KEITH MORRIS

INTRODUCTION AND OBJECTIVES

The ultimate goal for captive breeding programmes must be to reintroduce animals to the wild; however, the value of a captive breeding programme is limited if there is no available habitat. Processes threatening native fauna in Australia include loss of habitat from clearing and land degradation, fragmentation of habitat, introduction of domestic stock, introduction of competitors such as rabbits, and predation by foxes and cats (www.environment.gov.au/bg/wildlife/lists/ktp/index). Many of these processes are threats to wildlife anywhere in the world, but integrated *ex situ* and *in situ* conservation programmes in Australia face an unusual habitat management issue, namely the control of introduced predators, in particular foxes and cats. There have recently been major successes where conservation reintroduction programmes have been linked with predator control. Three Western Australian mammal species (woylie, tammar wallaby and quenda) have been removed from State and National Threatened Fauna lists (see http://www.biodiversity.environment.gov.au/wildlife/lists/anzecc/index) as a result of broad-scale fox control and translocations carried out as part of the Western Shield Fauna Recovery Programme of the Western Australia Department of Conservation and Land Management (CALM). Perth Zoo and CALM are working collaboratively to achieve similar outcomes with a range of threatened species. In this chapter we aim to demonstrate the principles involved in this conservation strategy, as readers may be unfamiliar with the dual concept of controlling one wild population to protect another.

Table 15.1 *Comparison of numbers of threatened species in IUCN categories in all of the world with Australia and Western Australia. Data from the IUCN Red Book (Baillie & Groombridge, 1996). Figures in parentheses are species listed by the Australia and New Zealand Environment and Conservation Council (ANZECC) using IUCN criteria*

IUCN category	Mammals of the World	Mammals of Australia		Mammals in Western Australia
Extinct (presumed)	86	(26)	27[a]	10
Extinct in the wild	3	(1)		
Critically Endangered	169	(7)	29	3
Endangered	315	(21)		8
Vulnerable	612	(46)	45	28
Total	1096	(101)	101	49

[a] At the commencement of the Environment Protection and Biodiversity Conservation Act (1999) (EPBC ACT) on 16 July 1999, the National List of Threatened Species consists of those species previously listed under the Endangered Species Protection Act 1992, which is replaced by the new Act. Species are those listed in Wildlife Conservation (Specially Protected fauna) Notice 1999.

STATE OF THE ART

A wave of extinctions

Figures from the IUCN Red Book paint a grim picture when the proportion of extinct and threatened Australian mammals is compared with the rest of the world (Table 15.1). In Australia, the majority of mammals that have become extinct, or are presently threatened with extinction, are in the Critical Weight Range (CWR) of 35 g to 8 kg adult body weight (Burbidge & MacKenzie, 1989). This group is considered to be most vulnerable to introduced predators such as the European red fox and feral cat. The Western Shield Fauna Recovery Programme (www.calm.wa.gov.au/projects/west_shield) aims to recover at least 13 threatened mammals over the next 5–10 years through broad-scale fox control, development of an effective cat control, and translocation.

Predation as a factor in the decline of species in Western Australia

Foxes were originally introduced to Victoria in 1856 for the sport of hunting and are now found throughout most of Australia except the wet tropics (King & Smith, 1985; Coman, 1995). The first experimental evidence

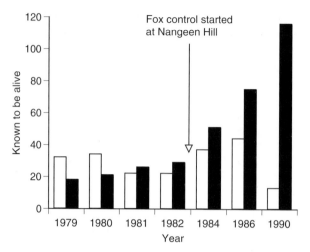

Figure 15.1 Numbers of rock wallabies known to be alive at Sales Rock (open bars) and Nangeen Hill (solid bars) from 1979 to 1990. Data from Kinnear et al., (1988, 1998.) The arrow indicates commencement of fox baiting at Nangeen Hill. Sales Rock, the control site, was not baited.

that fox predation was a problem for mammals in Australia was shown by Kinnear et al. (1988), who controlled foxes and demonstrated an increase in numbers of rock wallabies at Nangeen Hill in Western Australia (Figure 15.1).

The time and mode of arrival of cats in Australia is much less certain. Cats may have been introduced before European settlement, from survivors of Dutch shipwrecks on the west coast of the continent, or from escapees or releases by early European navigators. Cats have contributed to extinctions and declines in arid areas and on islands with arguably less or no impact in more mesic areas (Dickman, 1996).

The effectiveness of predator control in Western Australia is due to 'the gastrolobium advantage'. The toxin sodium monofluoroacetate (Compound 1080 or '1080') occurs naturally in the native pea plants (*Gastrolobium* spp.) of Western Australia. Native animals have co-evolved with these plants and as a result have a high tolerance to 1080 poison (Table 15.2). Calaby (1971) attributed the survival of the woylie (*Bettongia penicillata*) in the wild to its habitation of regions where thickets of *Gastrolobium* species are abundant. Introduced foxes and cats have low tolerance to 1080 (Table 15.2). This tolerance differential allows CALM to control foxes and feral cats selectively. The Western Shield programme for fox and cat control began in 1996 and

Table 15.2 *The gastrolobium advantage: comparison of sensitivity of eastern and western Australian species and fox and cat to fluoroacetate (1080) toxicity*

Species	LD 50 (mg 1080/kg)		Reference
	West	East	
Quolls	7.5	1.5	McIlroy (1981)
Bettong	100–200	1	King *et al.* (1981)
Kangaroos	40–60	0.1–0.35	King *et al.* (1978)
Brushtail possum	>125	0.86	King *et al.* (1978)
Dingo, fox and cat	0.1–0.4		McIlroy (1981)

has an annual budget of $A1.5 million. The programme covers more than 3.5 million hectares of Western Australia's conservation estate.

Captive breeding: action for recovery

The core of the Native Species Breeding Programme (NSBP) at Perth Zoo involves captive breeding of chuditch, dibbler, numbat, djoongari (Shark Bay mouse), greater stick-nest rat, Western swamp tortoise and Lancelin Island skink. Each captive-breeding programme is an action under the relevant Recovery Plan for the species. The greater stick-nest rat is no longer being bred for release, but the breeding programme does illustrate issues for recovery teams which will be addressed later. The Lancelin Island skink and Western swamp tortoise programmes will not be discussed further.

The goals of the NSBP are to provide animals for release, to conduct scientific research into the reproductive biology of the species in the programme and to increase public awareness through the Zoo's Education Programme.

Since captive breeding began at Perth Zoo, 311 chuditch, 86 dibblers, 59 numbats, 126 djoongari and 267 Western swamp tortoises have been produced for release into habitat under regular predator control. Distribution maps, compiled by N. L. McKenzie, A. A. Burbidge, A. Baynes and many other contributors, can be accessed at www.calm.wa.gov.au/science/mupdates. Post-release monitoring of these animals by CALM has shown the occurrence of *in situ* breeding, and those new populations are becoming established in the wild. In each of the programmes reviewed below, predation has been identified as a risk factor for the species' survival. Each species presents unique problems for its captive breeding and has required knowledge of reproductive biology to achieve the successful outcomes reported here.

1. Chuditch (Western quoll, Dasyurus geoffroii)

The chuditch is a carnivorous marsupial (adult body weight 800–1500 g). At the time of European settlement chuditch occupied nearly 70% of the continent (Morris et al., 2000). Over the last 200 years there has been a drastic decline in range with the chuditch retreating to the west (Serena & Soderquist, 1995). In the 1950s chuditch persisted on the Swan coastal plain where it caused problems for poultry farmers. In the 1970s the chuditch, numbering about 6000, were confined to the southwestern part of Western Australia where they were found in the jarrah forest (Serena et al., 1991), and drier woodlands and mallee shrublands of the wheatbelt. Chuditch are listed as 'Fauna that is rare or likely to become extinct' in Western Australia in 1983 and as 'Endangered' by the Commonwealth Government in 1992. The Action Plan for Australasian Marsupials and Monotremes (Kennedy, 1992) listed chuditch as endangered, and the revised plan (Maxwell et al., 1996) listed it as vulnerable under the 1994 IUCN criteria.

The actions of the recovery plan included commencing and maintaining a captive breeding colony and translocating chuditch to areas where they had formerly occurred. The captive breeding programme commenced at Perth Zoo in 1990 to provide animals for CALM's translocation programme. As removing sufficient animals for a translocation from an extant population would have severe consequences on the founder population, captive breeding was a necessary first step. Approximately 15 pairs of chuditch have been maintained as breeding stock each year, and CALM has released over 300 captive-reared chuditch (Figure 15.2). In July 2000 the release of 35 chuditch in Kalbarri National Park marked the end of breeding for subsequent release at the Perth Zoo. CALM officers will continue monitoring chuditch populations for a year to assess their status against the IUCN criteria. Maintenance of a healthy breeding colony has been managed using the Single Population Analysis and Records Keeping System (SPARKS) programme (Wilken & Lees, 1998). Wild-caught animals are introduced into the captive population every year to ensure that genetic variation, indicated by a low inbreeding coefficient (0.013), is maintained.

Research in reproductive biology of the chuditch has provided sufficient information to allow the production of a husbandry manual for the species. Using the method of analysing the pattern of exfoliated vaginal epithelial cells detected in urine samples, the gestation length has been determined at 16–19 days. The female chuditch is polyoestrous, and some females appear

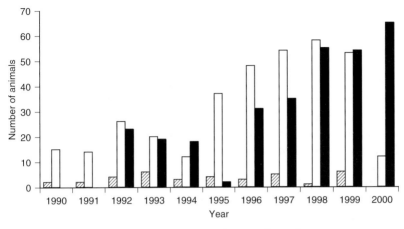

Figure 15.2 Chuditch captive breeding results at Perth Zoo from 1990 to 2000. Hatched bars indicate new animals brought in from the wild, open bars indicate numbers born, and solid bars indicate numbers released into the wild.

to continue cycling for months once mating has finished. The ability to detect oestrus has allowed careful pairing as these animals can be aggressive when inappropriately introduced. The female develops a marked fat collar around the neck before the breeding season to better withstand the male at mating. Recent successful monitoring of oestrogen in chuditch by faecal analysis has provided a hormonal basis for the changes detected in urine cells. This was the first time oestrogen had been measured via the faeces in a female marsupial. Like many marsupials, male chuditch show a large seasonal variation in testis volume and, during the breeding season, void sperm in their urine; consequently, the keeper can easily determine their fertility.

2. Dibbler (Parantechinus apicalis)

The dibbler is a small insectivorous marsupial (adult body weight 75–100 g), believed extinct for over 60 years. It was rediscovered in 1967 at Cheyne Beach in the south of Western Australia by wildlife photographer Michael Morcombe, who was trying to photograph honey possums (Morcombe, 1967). In 1985 dibblers were found on Boullanger and Whitlock Islands in Jurien Bay and Fitzgerald River National Park (FRNP) and have occasionally been recorded from a few pockets on the south coast of Western Australia (Woolley, 1995). Dibblers were once widespread on the mainland, but are now restricted to the FRNP. They are listed as 'likely to become extinct or is rare' (Western Australian Wildlife Conservation Act 1950) and 'Endangered' by the Commonwealth Government (Australian & New Zealand Environment & Conservation Council; ANZECC). The 1996 Action Plan for Australasian Marsupials and Monotremes (Maxwell *et al.*, 1996) listed the dibbler as endangered under the 1994 IUCN criteria.

Dibblers on the islands reportedly exhibit post-mating 'male die-off', where all males die after mating (Dickman & Braithwaite, 1992). However, Fuller & Burbidge (1987) and Woolley (1991) reported survival of island males, while Woolley (1971) has reported that mainland males survive the breeding season. H. Mills (personal communication) has shown that 'male die-off' does not always occur on the islands, and that there is considerable variation in life history between the Boullanger and Whitlock Islands populations in Jurien Bay.

In contrast, little is known of the life history of mainland dibblers. Until very recently, the population in FRNP was too small to permit the required ecological studies. To complicate the situation further, FRNP is in a dieback (*Phytophthora cinnamoni*) control area, and access to the park is prohibited after rainfall to prevent spread of the dieback fungus.

Captive breeding commenced at Perth Zoo in 1997 with two pairs of founding animals from each of the Jurien Bay islands. Introduction of 27, mostly captive-bred dibblers onto a third island, Escape Island, in Jurien Bay was carried out in 1998 and further releases of captive-bred animals occurred in 1999 and 2000 (Figure 15.3). Animals released in 1998 and 1999

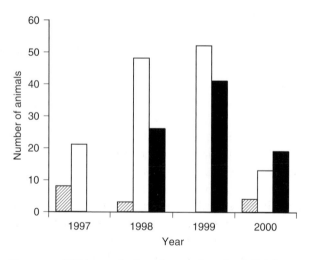

Figure 15.3 Dibbler captive breeding results at Perth Zoo from 1997 to 2000. Hatched bars indicate new animals brought in from the wild, open bars indicate numbers born, and solid bars indicate numbers released into the wild.

have been recaptured in 1999 and 2000, respectively, confirming that a breeding population had been established on Escape Island. Having established a further population in Jurien Bay, the recovery team has turned its attention to mainland dibblers.

Captive breeding studies have shown that males from the island populations can survive and breed a second, and even third time. The dibbler is monoestrous and matings lasting 1-3 days occur from early March to late April. Gestation lasts about 44 days, and females generally have young attached to each of their eight nipples. The urine cell cycle allows detection of oestrus, and appropriate pairings can be planned. Some mate selection is apparent in dibblers; a recent behavioural study showed that females prefer a male bigger than themselves. Males have a short period of fertility, from early February to early June, with a marked seasonal cycle in testis volume.

The Perth Zoo was the first to breed dibblers in captivity, although litters sired in the field had been raised in captivity (Woolley, 1971). In 2000 the NSBP achieved another milestone when a pair of dibblers from FRNP mated in captivity. CALM brought one female and three males into the Zoo and the pair bred about 2 weeks earlier than the island dibblers. The female gave birth after *c.* 55 days, a significantly longer gestation than that of the island animals, although this observation awaits confirmation.

3. Numbat (Myrmecobius fasciatus)
The numbat, Western Australia's faunal emblem, is one of Australia's more threatened mammals. Previously it occurred over most of southern Australia, but now occupies less than 1% of its former range (Friend, 1995). The numbat is a diurnal, terrestrial, termite-eating marsupial (body weight 500-700 g) which has close affinities with the family Dasyuridae, the carnivorous marsupials. Calaby (1960) suggested that anatomical differences between dasyurids and the numbat were the result of its specialised diet. The most important feature of numbat habitat is the abundance of termites in the soil, which in turn defines the most important factor in its captive breeding.

The numbat was listed as 'likely to become extinct or is rare' in Western Australia in 1983, and 'Vulnerable' by the Commonwealth Government (ANZECC 1991, Schedule 1 Part 1 under the Endangered Species protection Act 1992). The 1996 Action plan for Australasian Marsupials and Monotremes (Maxwell *et al.*, 1996) listed the numbat as 'Vulnerable' under the 1994 IUCN criteria. Its status is now 'Vulnerable' following the

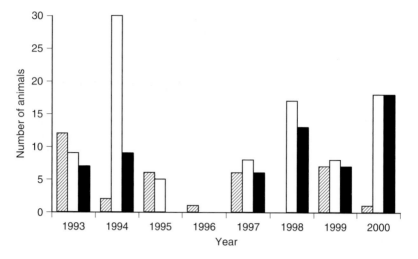

Figure 15.4 Numbat captive breeding results at Perth Zoo from 1993 to 2000. Hatched bars indicate new animals brought in from the wild, open bars indicate number of animals born, and solid bars indicate numbers of animals released.

establishment of six populations in the wild by CALM, some of these from zoo-bred animals.

The numbat was first bred at the CALM Wildlife Research Centre in 1986. Its breeding programme was then transferred to Perth Zoo, where the first breeding success was achieved in 1993. In 1996 the Research Programme was initiated at Perth Zoo after formation of the Marsupial Cooperative Research Centre, CRC (see Rodger, Chapter 18), and the breeding cycle in captivity was characterised. As a result of this work, four of six females gave birth to a total of eight young in 1996–97 (Figure 15.4). Monitoring the urine cell cycle showed that the numbat was seasonally polyoestrous: the female would have three or four oestrous cycles during the breeding season (December–February). The male numbat is also seasonally fertile. In spring the sternal gland becomes developed, and testes volume increases. Males also shed sperm in their urine during the breeding season.

Diet is vitally important to the breeding success of numbats. An artificial 'Numbat Custard' was developed by CALM researchers in an attempt to reduce the requirement for termites. In 1997–98 the effectiveness of the artificial diet was tested in breeding females. The three females fed 50% termite:50% artificial diet raised six young, while the three females fed 100% termite diet produced 11 young. Breeding females are now fed a

100% termite diet. Male numbats, however, are not affected by the artificial diet. Current research is aimed at developing raptor awareness for numbats about to be released in the Stirling Range National Park. When foxes and cats are controlled, raptors are the main predators (J. A. Friend, personal communication). In 1999-2000, seven juvenile captive-bred numbats were monitored for 6 weeks after their release to gain information on their post-release behaviour. Three of the seven died in the period of monitoring, although none appeared to have been taken by raptors. A controlled experiment is planned for this year's (2001) release.

4. Djoongari (Shark Bay Mouse, Pseudomys fieldi)
Djoongari are Australian rodents (adult body weight 50-60 g). Prior to European settlement djoongari occupied most of southwestern Australia (Morris & Robinson, 1995) and became extinct on the mainland late in the nineteenth century. The djoongari is currently listed as 'Vulnerable' (Commonwealth Endangered Species Protection Act 1992), as 'likely to become extinct or is rare' (WA Wildlife Conservation Act 1950) and 'Vulnerable' under the 1994 IUCN criteria.

Up to June 1993, djoongari were found only on Bernier Island in the Shark Bay region of Western Australia (Watts & Aslin 1981; Morris *et al.*, 2000), and the population was estimated at 6000-7000 individuals (Morris *et al.*, 2000). Djoongari appear to prefer coastal sandy areas on Bernier Island, where they construct tunnels and runways in seagrass piled up on the beach (Robinson, 1983), with some use of burrows in the breeding season (Morris *et al.*, 2000). Their ecology on the mainland is unknown. In June 1993 the first translocation was made to Doole Island in Exmouth Gulf, followed in 1994 by translocations to Heirisson Prong, and to North West Island in the Montebello Islands group in 2000. Despite intensive fox and cat control prior to translocation, the translocation to Heirisson Prong appears to have been unsuccessful. Predation by goannas (*Varanus gouldi*) may have been an important factor in this failure. The other populations on Doole and North West Islands are not yet considered self-sustaining (Morris *et al.*, 2000).

Captive breeding commenced at Perth Zoo in January 1996. Several pairs of djoongari were transferred to Perth Zoo from CALM, with the objective of producing large numbers of animals for translocations (Figure 15.5). In the first year 101 offspring were born and in 1997-98, 71 of these were released by CALM on Doole Island. In 1997-98, captive breeding was suspended while a predator eradication programme was implemented on Peron

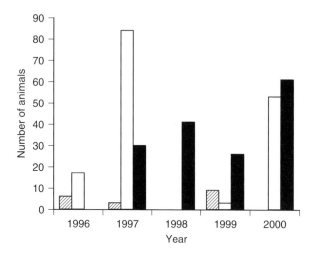

Figure 15.5 Captive breeding of Djoongari at Perth Zoo from 1996 to 2000. Hatched bars indicate new animals brought in from the wild, open bars indicate number of animals born, and solid bars indicate numbers of animals released.

Peninsula (Shark Bay Mainland), a proposed release site. In early 1999 pairing was resumed, without success. Efforts concentrated on supply of a correct diet as it was suspected that a plant-derived compound from fresh shoots (such as gibberellic acid) might stimulate breeding. Providing additional skylights in the building increased light intensity. Twenty-five djoongari from the colony were released on North West Island later in 1999. CALM brought new stock to the Zoo from the founder population on Bernier Island, and breeding began by the end of the year. Twenty-nine Djoongari were released on North West Island in August 2000. Breeding success in captivity seems to be related to replication of the seasonal availability of resources. On Bernier Island, breeding appears to follow a rainfall event by approximately 9 months (P. Speldewinde, personal communication). Fodder bushes have been planted around the breeding facilities to provide appropriate feed, and during pre-release conditioning, free water availability is reduced to harden the animals for the conditions that they will soon experience.

The reproductive biology of the djoongari is not well known. In captivity, impending birth is detected by changes in behaviour, with the female becoming more secretive and increasingly rejecting the male. The oestrous cycle has been reported as 14 days (Watts & Spencer, 1978), but observations in our colony suggest that it may be 28 days, and that mating may occur post-partum. Gestation and lactation each last about 28 days. Djoongari reach sexual maturity at about 60 days, and reach full adult size at 90–100 days. Litter size is normally 3–4, but some females have five young.

5. *Wopilkara (greater stick-nest rat,* Leporilus conditor)

The wopilkara is a medium-sized, social marsupial rodent (adult body weight 180–450 g) with the habit of building large communal nests, hence the name stick-nest rat. The wopilkara is listed as 'Endangered' (ANZECC, 1999), 'Fauna that is rare or likely to become extinct' (Western Australia Wildlife Conservation Act, 1950) and 'Endangered' (South Australia National Parks and Wildlife Act, Schedule 7, 1992).

Formerly distributed across semi-arid zones of Australia, it favoured habitat with succulent or semi-succulent shrubs. The woplikara became extinct on the mainland in the 1930s but persisted on the Franklin Islands of South Australia. It has also been introduced to Salutation Island in Shark Bay, Western Australia and to Reevesby Island in South Australia.

Five pairs of woplikara were transferred to Perth Zoo from the Monarto Zoo (South Australia) in December 1996, to commence a captive breeding programme aimed at providing animals for release in Western Australia. After 12 months breeding with good results (21 births), one animal was diagnosed with small corneal cataracts. The condition of the rat progressively deteriorated as the cataract developed, causing blindness and hindering its ability to forage for food and eventually leading to its death. Other rats (27% of the colony) were also seen to have the problem at this time. When other colonies were examined they too had significant rates of cataract disease. South Australian authorities were contacted, and it was reported that wild populations had about a 7% rate of cataract disease.

Nutritional analysis suggested that the captive diet was similar to the wild diet (N. Costa, personal communication) and unlikely to be a cause of the problem. Urine testing undertaken for diagnosis of diabetes gave negative results. By mid-1999 all the Perth Zoo animals had the disease and some also showed significant kidney pathology upon autopsy. Other animals in the colony also presented with the kidney pathology but without the cataracts. The Monarto Zoo captive breeding data were examined by a geneticist, who suggested that the cataract disease might result from a deleterious recessive gene at high frequency in the captive colonies (D. W. Cooper, personal communication). This may have arisen because the relatively small number of founders originated from an island population with limited gene flow. The Recovery Team subsequently decided not to translocate captive-bred animals, as all of the captive colonies had the problem at rates far exceeding those of the island populations.

Table 15.3 *Preliminary results of analysis of genetic variation in dibblers from Boullanger Island, Whitlock Island and Fitzgerald River National Park (FRNP)*

	Fitzgerald River National Park	Boullanger Island	Whitlock Island
Population size typed	13	22	37
Loci typed	5	5	5
% polymorphic	100	80	20
Mean number of alleles per locus	4.8	3.0	1.4
Allele size variance	14.4	4.4	0.5
Exp H	0.68	0.47	0.14
Obs H	0.71	0.54	0.20

Practical integration of genetics and reproductive biology

Formerly, the mala (*Lagorchestes hirsutus*) was widely distributed through the arid and semi-arid areas of central and western Australia but is now restricted to Bernier and Dorre Islands in Shark Bay, and a 1 km² area in the Northern Territory enclosed by an electrified fence (Johnston & Burbidge, 1995). Genetic differentiation between, and genetic diversity within, the mala were assessed from cytochrome *b* sequences and microsatellite markers which suggested that *L. hirsutus* comprises a single Evolutionarily Significant Unit (ESU) and can be managed as a single species (P. B. S. Spencer, personal communication). The mainland population retained 62% heterozygosity whereas island populations retained 20–30% heterozygosity; the mainland animals were therefore considered more suitable for translocation. Similar microsatellite analyses of mainland and island dibblers indicated greater genetic heterozygosity in the mainland animals (Table 15.3). The Recovery Team has now shifted its focus to the mainland population of the dibbler. Taxonomic relations of the tuan (*Phascogale tapoatafa*), known as wambenger in Western Australia, were determined by microsatellite analyses of DNA extracted from specimens from northern, eastern and western Australia (Soderquist, 1995). As the Western Australian specimens proved significantly different from the other two regions, this population is now being formally described as a new species. This will lead to a reappraisal of the conservation status of the species in the southwest of Western Australia.

Most Australian native species need a sound understanding of their reproductive biology and behaviour in order to produce sufficient animals for reintroduction on request. Much of this information is rudimentary, particularly when dealing with endangered species (Tyndale-Biscoe & Renfree, 1987). This chapter has shown the results of focused, low technology approaches to captive breeding now in place at Perth Zoo. The programmes reviewed here have a number of common elements: (1) genetic health of each colony is maintained via breeding studbooks and regular exchange of wild and captive animals; (2) reproductive biology is characterised and documented in husbandry manuals; (3) suitable microenvironments are developed in the enclosure to allow expression of natural behaviours; (4) a commitment exists to high quality research to address specific questions arising from captive husbandry; (5) research keepers are dedicated to each species participating in the Recovery process, and (6) there is close collaboration with the Western Australian Department of Conservation and Land Management and Recovery Teams. Lessons to be learned from the captive breeding programmes include careful choice of founder animals from a genetically healthy population and the value that genetic analyses can bring to the recovery process.

PRIORITIES FOR THE FUTURE

The Recovery process is an inexact science; of necessity, plans are tailored to each species. A large number of issues are evolving as we gain knowledge in conservation biology. The captive breeding programmes can provide opportunities for studies of reproductive biology and genetic relationships prior to translocation. The establishment of additional wild populations allows studies of the long-term consequences of reintroduction on the ecology and genetic health of the new populations. Application of population genetics can answer questions of success. To mix or not to mix? Questions arise as to the genetic compatibility of different strains of species (e.g. mala). How important is it to maintain genetic purity?

What is the impact of release of captive-bred animals on the ecology of the release area, and what is the impact on the source population of removing animals for translocation? Can behavioural training improve the chances of survival of captive-bred animals? Reintroduction strategies – to rebuild a *fauna*- or a *species-specific* strategy? Both: CALM has fauna reconstruction sites such as Lake Magenta, and also species-specific sites such as the Swamp Tortoise enclosures. An effective feral cat control programme has to be developed. Presently the Western Shield programme is restricted to the wetter parts of the southwest of WA. It has been shown that fox control in the arid zone results in an increase in feral cats which then become a significant problem for native fauna. Until an effective feral cat control method has been developed, fauna recovery will be restricted mainly to the southwest. However, it is the arid zone where most mammal declines have occurred, and it is imperative that the Western Shield programme extends into this area. Current research has focused on developing a palatable cat bait and determining the frequency and intensity of cat-baiting programmes for effective control.

At the present time, only a few native species could benefit from the application of assisted reproductive technology. These approaches are under development for marsupials by the Marsupial CRC and other scientists in Australia. Gilbert's potoroo (*Potorous gilbertii*), in Western Australia is one species which could benefit. This small member of the rat-kangaroo family, restricted to a single site, Mt Gardner in the Two People's Bay Nature Reserve, was rediscovered in 1994 after last being recorded in 1879 (Sinclair *et al.*, 1996). The Gilbert's potoroo population is estimated to be fewer than 100, and they do not breed readily in captivity (J. A. Friend, personal communication). CALM, Perth Zoo and the Marsupial CRC are collaborating to improve captive breeding of Gilbert's potoroo by applying reproductive technology to enhance species survival.

CONCLUSION

The Western Shield Fauna Recovery Programme in Western Australia has been successful, for several reasons. First, many of the mammals that once occurred across Australia are now found only in the southwest of Western Australia or on offshore islands; second, the native fauna has a tolerance to the toxin 1080, allowing fox and cat control; third, captive breeding facilities have been developed, which allow large numbers of founders to be bred for translocation. Collaboration between State and Commonwealth conservation agencies, university and research Institutions and communities is also well developed in Western Australia which has promoted successful conservation outcomes.

ACKNOWLEDGEMENTS

The authors thank Glen Gaikhorst, Vicki Power, Kristen Wolfe, Andrew Lynch, Chris Jones, Cathy Lambert, Harriet Mills, Ernest Stead-Richardson and Peter Spencer for permission to quote their work. The Marsupial CRC is supported under the Australian Government's Cooperative Research Centre Programme.

REFERENCES

Burbidge, A. A. & McKenzie, N. L. (1989). Patterns in the modern decline of Western Australia's vertebrate fauna: causes and conservation implications. *Biological Conservation* **50**, 143-198.

Calaby, J. H. (1960). Observations on the Banded Ant-eater *Myrmecobius fasciatus* Waterhouse (Marsupialia), with particular reference to its food habits. *Proceedings of the Zoological Society of London* **135**, 183-207.

Calaby, J. H. (1971). The current state of Australian Macropodidae. *Australian Zoologist* **16**, 17-29.

Coman, B. J. (1995). Fox *Vulpes vulpes*, Linnaeus 1758. In *The Mammals of Australia* (Ed. R. Strahan), pp. 698-699. Reed Books, Sydney.

Dickman, C. R. (1996). *Overview of the Impact of Feral Cats on Australian Native Fauna.* Australian Nature Conservation Agency, Canberra.

Dickman, C. R. & Braithwaite, R. W. (1992). Postmating mortality of males in the dasyurid marsupials, *Dasyurus* and *Parantechinus. Journal of Mammalogy* **73**, 143-147.

Fuller, P. J. & Burbidge, A. A. (1985). Discovery of the dibbler, *Parantechinus apicalis*, on islands at Jurien Bay. *Western Australian Naturalist* **16**, 177-181.

Friend, J. A. (1995). Numbat *Myrmecobius fasciatus*, Waterhouse 1836. In *The Mammals of Australia* (Ed. R. Strahan), pp. 160-162. Reed Books, Sydney.

Johnston, K. E. & Burbidge, A. A. (1995). Rufous Hare-wallaby *Lagorchestes hirsutus* Gould 1844. In *The Mammals of Australia* (Ed. R. Strahan), pp. 316-318. Reed Books, Sydney.

Kennedy, M. (compiler) (1992). *Australasian Marsupials and Monotremes, an Action Plan for their Conservation.* IUCN, Gland, Switzerland.

King, D. R., Oliver, A. J. & Mead, R. J. (1978). The adaptation of some Western Australian mammals to food plants containing fluroacetate. *Australian Journal of Zoology* **26**, 699-712.

King, D. R., Oliver, A. J. & Mead, R. J. (1981). *Bettongia* and fluoroacetate: a role for 1080 in fauna management. *Australian Wildlife Research* **8**, 529-536.

King, D. R. & Smith, L. A. (1985). The distribution of the European red fox *Vulpes vulpes* in Western Australia. *Records of the Western Australia Museum* **12**, 197-205.

Kinnear, J. L., Onus, M. L. & Bromilow, R. N. (1988). Fox control and rock wallaby population dynamics. *Australian Wildlife Research* **15**, 435-450.

Kinnear, J. L., Onus, M. L. & Bromilow, R.N. (1998). Fox control and rock wallaby population dynamics. II. An update. *Wildlife Research* **25**, 81-88.

Maxwell, S., Burbidge, A. A. & Morris, K. D. (Eds.) (1996). *The 1996 Action Plan for Australian Marsupials and Monotremes.* Wildlife Australia, Endangered Species Project No. 500. Environment Australia, Canberra.

McIlroy, J. C. (1981). The sensitivity of Australian animals to 1080 poison. II. Marsupial and eutherian carnivores. *Australian Wildlife Research* **8**, 385-399.

Morcombe, M. K. (1967). The rediscovery after 83 years of the dibbler *Antechinus apicalis* (Marsupialia, Dasyuridae). *Western Australian Naturalist* **10**, 103-111.

Morris, K. D. & Robinson, A. C. (1995). Shark Bay Mouse *Pseudomys fieldi*. In *The Mammals of Australia* (Ed. R. Strahan), pp. 596-597. Reed Books, Sydney.

Morris, K. D., Speldwinde, P. & Orell, P. (2000). Djoongari (Shark Bay Mouse) Recovery plan, 3rd edn. Western Australian Wildlife Management Program

No. 17. Perth: Western Australia Department of Conservation and Land Management.

Robinson, A. C. (1983). Shark Bay Mouse. In *Complete Book of Australian Mammals* (Ed. R. Strahan), p. 392. Angus & Robertson, Sydney.

Serena, M. & Soderquist, T. R. (1995). Western Quoll *Dasyurus geoffroii*. In *The Mammals of Australia* (Ed. R. Strahan), pp. 62-64. Reed Books, Sydney.

Serena, M., Soderquist, T. R. & Morris, K. D. (1991). The chuditch: *Dasyurus geoffroii*. Wildlife Management Program No. 7, pp. 1-32. Department of Conservation and Land Management, Perth.

Sinclair, E. A., Dansk, A. & Wayne, A. F. (1996). Rediscovery of Gilbert's Potoroo, *Potorous tridactylus*, in Western Australia. *Australian Mammalogy* 19, 69-72.

Soderquist, T. R. (1995). Brush-tailed phascogale *Phascogale tapoatafa*. In *The Mammals of Australia* (Ed. R. Strahan), pp. 104-106. Reed Books, Sydney.

Tyndale-Biscoe, C. H. & Renfree, M. B. (1987). *Reproductive Physiology of Marsupials*. Cambridge University Press, Cambridge.

Watts, C. H. S. & Aslin, H. J. (1981). *The Rodents of Australia*. Angus & Robertson, Sydney.

Watts, C. H. S. & Spencer, L. (1978). Notes on the reproduction of the Shark Bay Mouse, *Pseudomys praeconis*, in captivity. *Western Australian Naturalist* 14, 43-46.

Wilken, J. & Lees, C. (Eds.) (1998). *Managing Zoo Populations: Compiling and Analysing Studbook Data*. Australasian Association of Zoological Parks & Aquaria, Sydney.

Woolley, P. A. (1971). Observations on the reproductive biology of the dibbler, *Antechinus apicalis* (Marsupialia: Dasyuridae). *Journal of the Royal Society of Western Australia* 54, 99-102.

Woolley, P. A. (1991). Reproductive pattern of captive Boullanger Island Dibblers, *Parantechinus apicalis* (Marsupialia: Dasyuridae). *Wildlife Research* 18, 157-163.

Woolley, P. A. (1995). Southern dibbler *Parantechinus apicalis*. In *The Mammals of Australia* (Ed. R. Strahan), pp. 72-73. Reed Books, Sydney.

16

Black-footed ferret: model for assisted reproductive technologies contributing to *in situ* conservation

JOGAYLE HOWARD, PAUL E. MARINARI AND
DAVID E. WILDT

INTRODUCTION AND OBJECTIVES

Assisted reproductive technologies (artificial insemination [AI], *in vitro* fertilisation [IVF], embryo transfer and gamete/embryo cryopreservation) have been postulated for decades as 'high-tech' solutions for helping conserve genetics and biodiversity. There is no doubt that these techniques could offer many advantages for managing small populations, largely by ensuring that all genetically valuable animals reproduce (Howard, 1993, 1999; Wildt & Roth, 1997; Wildt *et al.*, 1997). The potential of assisted reproduction could be enhanced further by developing genome resource banks (repositories of cryopreserved sperm, eggs, embryos), thus preserving valuable genetic material for future generations. The combined use of assisted breeding and germplasm banks also has potential for infusing genetic material from wild-born individuals into genetically stagnant *ex situ* populations or even exchanging genetic material between isolated wild populations (Holt *et al.*, 1996; Wildt *et al.*, 1997).

Despite these advantages, assisted reproduction has not been used consistently in 'practical' wildlife management and *in situ* conservation, largely for one reason: until recently, no wildlife species has been adequately studied, at least to the extent that its reproduction was so comprehensively understood that assisted breeding could become routine.

It commonly is assumed that reproductive knowledge and techniques well established for laboratory rodents, domestic farm species and even humans are readily adaptable to propagating or overcoming infertility in wild animals (Wildt *et al.*, 2000). This is a misperception because all species have naturally evolved 'species-specific' reproductive mechanisms, most of which have not yet been elucidated. Without such scholarly information, no assisted breeding technique can ever become routine.

Thus, although the value of reproductive technologies to *ex situ/in situ* wildlife management has been considered (and touted) for years, there still is a need to demonstrate how such strategies can be used pragmatically. This chapter demonstrates how the management and conservation of an endangered carnivore, the black-footed ferret (*Mustela nigripes*), has benefited from the application of the reproductive sciences, including assisted breeding. We assert that the lessons learned from (1) working in partnership with wildlife managers and *ex situ* breeding institutions, (2) taking a systematic basic and multidisciplinary research approach and (3) integrating knowledge, have led to helping recovery, and reintroduction of this endangered species into nature.

STATE OF THE ART: THE CASE OF THE BLACK-FOOTED FERRET

Decline of black-footed ferrets

The black-footed ferret is one of 65 members in the family Mustelidae and the only ferret native to North America. This species is classified in the subgenus Putorius with the Siberian (steppe) polecat (*M. eversmanni*), European polecat (*M. putorius*) and domestic ferret (*M. putorius furo*). First described by naturalists John Audubon and John Bachman in 1851, this small-sized mustelid historically inhabited grasslands throughout the western Great Plains extending from southern Canada to northern Mexico. In 1967, the black-footed ferret was listed as 'endangered' under a law that preceded the Endangered Species Act of 1973. The demise of the black-footed ferret parallels the loss of the North American prairie ecosystem and the decline of the prairie dog, the ferret's primary prey. Among the world's 17 weasel species, only the black-footed ferret depends on a single prey species for both food and shelter.

As the plains were settled, ranchers claimed that prairie dogs competed with livestock for available forage. It was not then understood that prairie dogs spurn lush grass while thriving in areas overgrazed by cattle. By abusing rangeland, ranchers actually increased prairie dog numbers. This resulted in an extensive, government-sponsored eradication programme in the 1920s and 1930s to poison these 'pest rodents' with strychnine. This large-scale extermination, followed by agricultural and urban development, severely decreased the number of prairie dogs and reduced their habitat from *c.* 100 million acres (40.5 million hectares) to about 1.5 million acres (0.6 m ha). Without the prairie dog, the black-footed ferret had no food source and, by the 1940s, the ferret population had fragmented and severely declined. Black-footed ferrets were believed to be extinct when a small population was discovered in 1964 in South Dakota (Miller *et al.*, 1996; Biggins *et al.*, 1997). Nine animals were captured between 1972 and 1974 and transferred to the US Fish & Wildlife Service's Patuxent Wildlife Research Centre in Maryland. The birth of two litters demonstrated that *ex situ* breeding was possible, but the project failed when the animals died from canine distemper following vaccination with a modified live virus (Carpenter *et al.*, 1976; Hillman & Carpenter, 1983). In 1974, the South Dakota wild population disappeared for unknown reasons, and again the species was believed to be extinct.

Then, in 1981, a ranch dog killed a black-footed ferret, which led to the discovery of another small population near Meeteetse, Wyoming. Intensive field research was conducted to understand the life history, ecology and behaviour of the world's most endangered carnivore. By 1984, this population had increased to nearly 130 individuals. However, in 1985, an outbreak of flea-borne sylvatic plague (*Yersinia pestis*: a disease introduced to North America in the late 1800s) reduced prairie dog numbers (Forrest *et al.*, 1988). In the same year, an epizootic of canine distemper (Morbillivirus) nearly eliminated the last known wild ferret population (Williams *et al.*, 1988). Between the fall of 1985 and spring of 1987, the Wyoming Game and Fish Department, in cooperation with the US Fish & Wildlife Service, captured the last remaining 18 black-footed ferrets – probably the rarest mammals in the world – from the wild (Thorne & Oakleaf, 1991). In the spring of 1987, captive breeding was successful, and two litters of black-footed ferret kits were born.

Species recovery strategy

Given the species' critical status, a recovery plan for *ex situ* propagation and reintroduction was a high priority. A workshop held in 1986 was facilitated by the Conservation Breeding Specialist Group (CBSG) of the IUCN–World Conservation Union's Species Survival Commission. Widespread stakeholder participation was emphasised with representatives from state and federal wildlife and land management agencies as well as experts in mustelids, small population biology, reproduction, nutrition, veterinary medicine and genetics. Using workshop information, the US Fish & Wildlife Service developed an official 'Black-Footed Ferret Recovery Plan' in 1988 that emphasised species preservation through more research, a multi-institutional *ex situ* propagation programme and establishment of multiple reintroduction sites. The goal of the *ex situ* breeding programme was to maintain *c*. 240 ferrets (90 males, 150 females) in captivity, but in multiple institutions in order to avoid a catastrophe that might affect any single facility. The aim of the eventual reintroduction programme was to establish a total of 1500 ferrets in at least 10 self-sustaining, free-ranging populations by the year 2010. The wild populations, scattered geographically within the ferret's former range, each were to be comprised of at least 30 breeding adults.

Discussions of the *ex situ* and (eventually) *in situ* metapopulation structure always stressed the role of sound scientific research, including the potential of reproductive technologies. Managers were especially keen to determine whether such techniques could be useful for evaluating fertility and for developing AI with fresh or cryopreserved spermatozoa, all for the purpose of supporting *ex situ* breeding and especially avoiding further losses in genetic diversity. One early concept was to establish a 'black-footed ferret genome resource bank', a frozen repository of spermatozoa from the most genetically valuable males, especially those that failed to reproduce by natural breeding.

Ex situ natural breeding

Intensive management by the Wyoming Game and Fish Department resulted in offspring production from 1987 into all subsequent years, which allowed dividing the *ex situ* population into a further six subcolonies at numerous zoological institutions in North America. The US Fish & Wildlife Service assumed the responsibility of managing the Wyoming breeding facility in 1996 and renamed it the National Black-Footed Ferret Conservation Center. Since 1987, the multi-institutional *ex situ* breeding programme has produced more than 4000 ferrets while generating extensive knowledge on ferret biology.

For the past decade, the cooperative effort among the breeding facilities has been guided by the Black-Footed Ferret Species Survival Plan (SSP), a population management strategy designed to maintain a self-sustaining *ex situ* population while providing animals for reintroduction. Breeding recommendations also are provided in an attempt to equalise the genetic representation of the few original wild-born founders. The SSP managers determine specific pairs for breeding on the basis of a 'mean kinship' value, a measure of how related an individual is to the remaining population (Ballou & Lacy, 1995; see Ryan *et al.*, Chapter 6). Demographic data, including reproductive lifespan, fecundity, age distribution and ratio of males to females are considered in predicting population stability and growth rate over time. Currently, there are *c.* 250 black-footed ferrets maintained in the SSP.

Reintroduction

The ability to produce ferrets in captivity allowed reintroduction to begin in 1991, initially into the Shirley Basin of southeastern Wyoming (Miller *et al.*, 1993; Biggins *et al.*, 1997). A few animals survived over winter, and additional ferrets were released at this same site in subsequent years. However, in 1995, reintroduction efforts were suspended in Wyoming owing to a sylvatic plague outbreak and the loss of prairie dog colonies. Subsequent ferret reintroduction sites were established at Conata Basin in South Dakota (1994, Badlands National Park and Buffalo Gap National Grasslands) and Montana (1994, Charles M. Russell National Wildlife Refuge; 1996, Fort Belknap Indian Reservation). Arizona became the fourth state in the reintroduction programme in 1996 with ferret releases in Aubrey Valley. Utah and Colorado were added in 1999 when ferrets were released in Coyote Basin near the Colorado border. In the fall of 2000, Cheyenne River Sioux Reservation in South Dakota introduced ferrets. After extensive planning, Mexico became the newest release site in 2001. Successful reproduction and offspring produced in the wild from released ferrets have been documented in Arizona, Wyoming, South Dakota, Montana and Utah. Survival of released ferrets has improved due to 'pre-conditioning', the exposure to large outdoor pens with prairie dog burrow systems and live prey prior to reintroduction. Although success varies, the highest survival recently has occurred at the Conata Basin (South Dakota) with more than 70% of captive-born kits and over 90% of identified wild-born kits surviving over winter and through spring. As of fall 2001, the wild population numbers approximately 350 black-footed ferrets.

Development of reproductive technologies and the value of 'animal models'

Potential benefits of reproductive technologies were recognised from the onset of the recovery programme. The Black-Footed Ferret Recovery Plan of 1988, the original and official guide for species rescue, encouraged developing methods for reproductive assessment and assisted breeding. It was realised that AI with fresh or frozen spermatozoa could help retain genetic diversity by ensuring reproduction in every valuable individual that failed to breed naturally. Additionally, a genome resource bank containing cryopreserved spermatozoa could serve to 'insure' extant genes for the future as well as assist in the genetic management of this small population.

The National Zoological Park's Conservation & Research Center was invited to take a lead role in studying ferret reproductive biology as well as participating in the *ex situ* breeding programme. We began the reproductive investigations using the domestic ferret and closely related Siberian polecat as 'animal models' to first understand general ferret biology and then use that knowledge for developing assisted breeding (Wildt *et al.*, 1986). Molecular analyses have revealed that the common ferret, the Siberian polecat and the black-footed ferret are taxonomically related and genetically similar (O'Brien *et al.*, 1989). All of these species are seasonal breeders with reproductive activity stimulated by long-day photoperiod (Hillman & Carpenter, 1983; Miller *et al.*, 1988; Mead *et al.*, 1990; Miller & Anderson, 1990; Carvalho *et al.*, 1991). Testis size gradually increases beginning in January or February, peaks from March to June and then gradually declines (Neal *et al.*, 1977). The female's breeding season is restricted to the months of March to June and is characterised by changes in vaginal cytology and an increase in vulvar size. Finally, these species are classified as 'induced ovulators', with ovulation occurring *c.* 30 hours after a single copulation or an injection of human chorionic gonadotrophin (hCG) (Mead *et al.*, 1988).

Extensive studies were conducted in common ferrets to develop a reliable approach for collecting, processing and analysing fresh or cryopreserved spermatozoa (Curry *et al.*, 1989; Wildt *et al.*, 1989; Howard *et al.*, 1991; Van der Horst *et al.*, 1991). More than 300 electroejaculates from nine males were collected to address (1) the effect of temporal spermatogenesis patterns on sperm viability; (2) the comparative effectiveness of vaginal versus uterine insemination via an atraumatic laparoscopic approach; (3) the influence of sperm number, dilution medium and time of hCG administration on pregnancy success, gestation interval and number of offspring produced, and (4) the influence of cryodiluent, freezing method and thawing temperature on the biological competence of frozen-thawed ferret spermatozoa (Wildt *et al.*, 1989; Howard, 1999; Howard *et al.*, 1991). Such basic studies were crucial to eventual development of reliable assisted breeding techniques. An effective electroejaculation protocol was developed in the domestic ferret for collection of consistently high quality spermatozoa

Table 16.1 *Mean (± SEM) ejaculate traits, sperm morphology and acrosomal integrity in the domestic ferret, Siberian polecat and black-footed ferret*

	Domestic ferret ($n = 4$ males)[a]	Siberian polecat ($n = 8$ males)[b]	Black-footed ferret ($n = 9$ males)[b]
Sperm motility (%)	80.7 ± 1.0	80.6 ± 2.9	69.4 ± 4.9
Sperm progression (0–5; 5, best)	3.3 ± 0.1	3.0 ± 0.2	2.9 ± 0.3
Sperm motility index[c]	73.6 ± 1.0	72.5 ± 2.4	63.6 ± 4.4
Normal sperm (%)	67.3 ± 1.3[d]	74.5 ± 2.6[d]	50.1 ± 5.1[e]
Normal intact acrosome (%)	92.4 ± 0.5	96.8 ± 1.0	82.1 ± 4.3

[a] Data based on 52 ejaculates from 4 males (Howard et al., 1991).
[b] Data based on 1 ejaculate per male (Howard et al., 1996).
[c] Sperm motility index = [(% sperm motility) + (sperm progression × 20)] divided by 2.
[d,e] Row values with different superscripts are different ($P < 0.05$).

from anaesthetised males (Table 16.1). Vaginal insemination was determined to be ineffective for producing offspring: none of the 10 females became pregnant after depositing spermatozoa intravaginally (Wildt et al., 1989). In contrast, transabdominal-intrauterine sperm deposition via laparoscopy resulted in high pregnancy success. Seventeen of 24 ferrets (70.8%) inseminated in this fashion became pregnant and delivered live young (Wildt et al., 1989). Embryo transfer also was developed in the domestic ferret for non-surgical transfer of preimplantation embryos (Wildt & Goodrowe, 1989; Kidder et al., 1999). Comparative assessments of 12 cryopreservation methods determined that a combination of an egg-yolk/lactose cryodiluent, the 'pellet freezing' method and a 37 ° C thawing temperature was optimal for freeze-thawing ferret sperm and recovering maximal motility and acrosomal integrity (Figure 16.1). Using this cryomethod, seven of 10 females (70.0%) inseminated *in utero* with frozen-thawed ferret spermatozoa became pregnant (Howard et al., 1991). Overall, reproductive efficiency was high (70.6%) after laparoscopic intrauterine AI with fresh or frozen semen (Table 16.2).

The domestic ferret strategy was subsequently applied to the Siberian polecat and finally the black-footed ferret. Although sperm motility traits were similar among the three species, there were significantly fewer structurally normal spermatozoa in the black-footed ferret compared with the domestic ferret and polecat (Table 16.1) (Howard et al., 1991, 1996). After cryopreservation and thawing, sperm motility and membrane integrity also

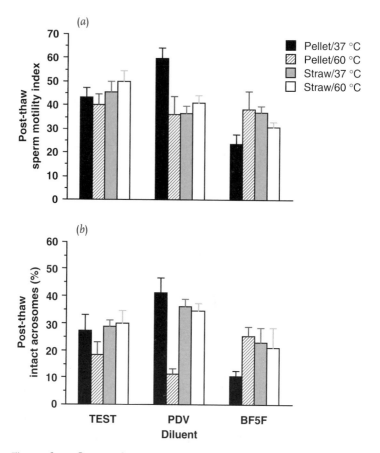

Figure 16.1 Influence of cryodiluent, freezing in pellets or straws and thawing temperature on domestic ferret sperm motility index (*a*) and intact sperm acrosomes (*b*) after thawing (*n* = 36 ejaculates). (From Howard *et al.*, 1991.)

were lower in the black-footed ferret compared with counterpart values (Howard *et al.*, 1991, 1996). These differences in sperm viability were assumed to be related to the restricted founder base and reduced genetic variation in the black-footed ferret. Nevertheless, the laparoscopic intrauterine AI technique, developed in the domestic ferret, proved to be effective in its close relatives. Eight of the 10 (80.0%) Siberian polecats inseminated with fresh or cryopreserved semen became pregnant (Table 16.2), with this high rate providing the confidence to apply the procedure to the rarer black-footed species. Four of six (66.7%) black-footed ferrets inseminated with fresh or frozen-thawed semen became pregnant and delivered live young (Table 16.2) (Howard, 1999; Howard *et al.*, 1996).

Table 16.2 *Laparoscopic intrauterine AI with fresh or frozen-thawed spermatozoa in closely-related ferret species*

	Domestic ferret	Siberian polecat	Black-footed ferret
Number of females inseminated	34	10	6
Number of pregnant females	24	8	4
Pregnancy rate	70.6%	80.0%	66.7%
Number of kits born	116	42	9
Mean number of kits/litter	4.8 ± 0.8	5.2 ± 1.0	2.3 ± 0.6

From Wildt *et al.*, 1989; Howard *et al.*, 1991; Howard *et al.*, 1996.

Assisted technologies for enhancing reproductive efficiency in the black-footed ferret

It soon was realised that the reintroduction goal (1500 breeding ferrets in 10 free-ranging populations by the year 2010) was not achievable at the current rate of propagation in the *ex situ* natural breeding programme. Early experiences revealed that some animals consistently failed to reproduce. Analysis of breeding records indicated that most females (>90%) demonstrated a spring oestrus on the basis of vaginal cytology changes (largely increased numbers of superficial, cornified squamous epithelial cells; Figure 16.2) (Williams *et al.*, 1992; Brown, 1997). However, there was a high incidence (*c.* 40%) of pseudopregnancy whereby matings were observed (via video-camera), and ovulation was confirmed (by an abrupt decrease in superficial cornified cells), but no pregnancy occurred (Williams *et al.*, 1991). Faecal oestradiol and progestogen metabolite profiles in pregnant versus pseudo-pregnant females were similar (Figure 16.2) (Brown, 1997), suggesting that endocrine dysfunction was not contributing to the problem.

Interestingly, records analysis indicated that a remarkably high proportion (>50%) of prime breeding age males (1–3 years old) inexplicably failed to sire offspring in captive breeding situations. In 1995, there were 40 such adult males (54.8% of the breeding age male population) that were exposed to prime age, oestrual females and yet did not produce young. Simultaneous evaluations also revealed a genetic problem, essentially that one of the original wild-born ferret founders was poorly represented in the modern population. This under-represented lineage had only 43 descendants compared with more than 300 descendants from each of the remaining founders. To help preserve original gene diversity, it was imperative to balance founder

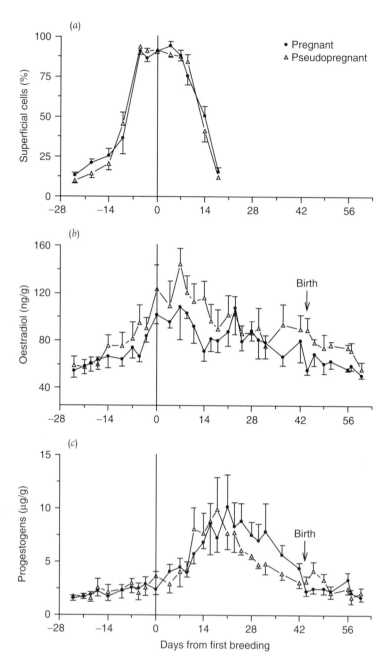

Figure 16.2 Mean (± SEM) percentage superficial cells in vaginal lavages (a) and faecal oestradiol (b) and progestogen (c) metabolite concentrations in pregnant (n = 7) and pseudopregnant (n = 9) black-footed ferrets. Day 0 is the time of first mating. (From Brown, 1997.)

representation. This situation was confounded by another challenge in the under-represented lineage – these males were consistently sexually incompatible with designated mates, expressed largely as aggression. Together, these issues prompted a need to examine the value of reproductive technology and assisted breeding.

At the request of the black-footed ferret managers, we agreed to (1) assess reproductive traits and breeding behaviour in males with proven versus unproven fertility; (2) establish a genome resource bank containing cryopreserved spermatozoa from the most genetically valuable males, and (3) use AI for improving reproductive efficiency in non-breeders for the ultimate purpose of increasing number of kits for reintroduction. A survey was conducted in 1996 and 1997 to determine the precise number of prime breeding age males not siring offspring and the reasons for failed reproduction. As in 1995, a high percentage of 1- to 3-year-old males did not sire young in 1996 (38 of 69 males, 55.1%) or 1997 (35 of 60 males, 58.3%) (Wolf et al., 2000b). Semen evaluations determined that there were no differences in sperm concentration, motility or morphology between proven and unproven breeders (Wolf et al. 2000b). A detailed review of breeding data revealed that males failed to reproduce because of improper breeding positioning, behavioural incompatibility (e.g. aggression) and poor testes development (Wolf et al., 2000b). As much of the problem was 'behaviourally based', we speculated that assisted reproduction could be beneficial for improving reproductive efficiency.

A systematic strategy was used to establish the genome resource bank. Using the computer software programme (SPARKS) developed for SSP programmes, sperm donors could be selected on the basis of founder representation and mean kinship (relatedness among individuals) (Ballou & Lacy, 1995; Johnston & Lacy, 1995). High priority black-footed ferret males were selected for inclusion in the bank, with appropriate amounts of semen collected and cryopreserved for AI (as part of routine management) or for long-term storage (as a hedge repository of valuable genes).

At the National Zoological Park's Conservation & Research Center, the natural breeding programme for black-footed ferrets was adapted to include AI. The goals were to (1) produce offspring from behaviourally incompatible animals, especially non-breeding males, to meet reintroduction demands, and (2) increase founder representation in the under-represented lineage. In achieving these goals, other opportunities arose, including examining the impact of male age on reproductive success. Between 1996 and 2000, non-breeding males of high genetic value were chosen as candidates for assisted reproduction. Overall, 40 females were monitored for natural oestrus

Table 16.3 *Use of laparoscopic AI to enhance propagation in non-breeding founder descendants, 5-year-old males and genetically valuable male black-footed ferrets*

	Founder descendants[a] (n = 3 males)	5-yr-old males[b] (n = 5 males)	Genetically valuable males[c] (n = 11 males)
Number of females inseminated	6	11	23
Number of pregnant females (%)	5 (83.3%)	8 (72.7%)	12 (52.2%)
Number of kits born	16	17	45

[a] Males were descendants of a wild-caught founder whose genetic lineage was under-represented in the *ex situ* population.
[b] Reproductive competence was assessed in older 5-yr-old males.
[c] Despite numerous breeding opportunities, reproductive failure in these genetically valuable males was due primarily to behavioural incompatibility (aggression or shyness) or inappropriate breeding position.

and were administered hCG (to induce ovulation) 5–7 days after maximal vulvar swelling and the presence of over 90% superficial cornified vaginal cells. Twelve to 20 hours later, each female was anaesthetised and, under laparoscopic observation, inseminated *in utero* with fresh or frozen-thawed spermatozoa. Five of six (83.3%) females inseminated with semen from founder descendants became pregnant and produced 16 kits (Table 16.3). Males were found to produce excellent quality semen up to 5 years of age, 2 years longer than the normal female reproductive life span (Wolf *et al.*, 2000a). Eight of 11 females inseminated with semen from 5-year-old males produced 17 kits (Table 16.3). Twelve of 23 females gave birth to 45 kits following AI with semen from genetically valuable, non-breeding males (Table 16.3). Overall, AI resulted in 78 additional black-footed kits, offspring that never would have been born from natural mating.

There were other by-products of this research. For example, we observed that a high proportion of 1-year-old males produced aspermic ejaculates during the breeding season (Howard *et al.*, 1998). These males experienced increases in seasonal testicular tumescence (albeit somewhat slower than their elders: Figure 16.3) and copulated with females. However, systematic seminal evaluations revealed that these yearlings produced spermic ejaculates at least 4 weeks later in the breeding season than older counterparts (Figure 16.3). This asynchrony in sperm production probably influenced the incidence of pseudopregnancy because aspermic males can

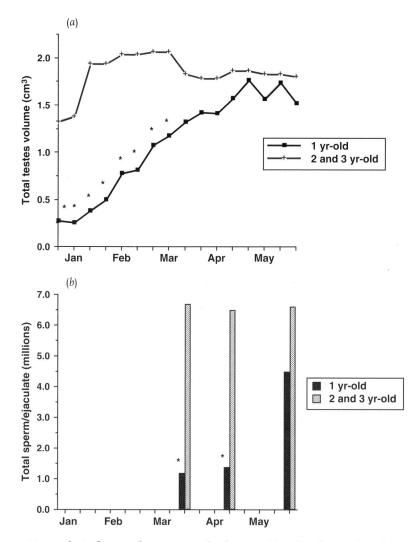

Figure 16.3 Influence of age on testes development (*a*) and total sperm/ejaculate (*b*) in 1-year-old versus 2- and 3-year-old male black-footed ferrets (From Howard *et al.*, 1998; Wildt *et al.*, 2000.)

induce ovulation following copulation. This was an important observation, with significant implications for routine ferret management. Until this finding, males used for breeding had been selected on the basis of enlarged testis size. Now, only males with spermic electroejaculates are allowed access to females for natural breeding. For example, introducing this simple semen assessment technique to the management protocol in 1998 resulted

Table 16.4 *Propagation in the black-footed ferret using enlarged testes versus spermic ejaculate as the criterion for selecting males for natural breeding*

	Enlarged testes	Spermic ejaculate
Number of females bred	84	86
Number of litters	50	69
Pregnancy success	59.5%	80.2%
Number of kits born	190	249

in a striking 20% increase in pregnancy success and 59 additional kits available for reintroduction (Table 16.4).

PRIORITIES FOR THE FUTURE

The black-footed ferret is a provocative example of how reproductive technologies integrated with both *ex situ* and *in situ* management plans can benefit species conservation. The positive results are evidence that reproductive techniques are valuable for (1) generating new knowledge of relevance to natural and assisted breeding and (2) producing living, genetically valuable offspring useful for breeding stock and/or reintroduction. As a result, a high priority is to continue to use these integrated approaches to facilitate management and recovery of this endangered species. The highest research priority is continued development of optimal sperm cryopreservation protocols. Current methods are suboptimal, resulting in excessive post-thaw cellular damage, especially to sperm acrosomal integrity. Therefore, projects are in place that emphasise understanding the biophysical traits and cryobiology of ferret spermatozoa, including membrane sensitivities and permeabilities. Our goal is to improve cryomethods sufficiently to allow production of more offspring using frozen-thawed spermatozoa, thereby continuing to increase kit numbers for reintroduction.

Priorities for this species extend far beyond reproductive biology. For example, adequate survival after reintroduction continues to be essential to the black-footed ferret's future. Urban sprawl and sylvatic plague appear to be never-ending, severe threats. Today, less than 2% of the *c.* 100 million acres (40 m ha) of the original prairie dog ecosystem of the Great Plains remains. Monitoring for presence of sylvatic plague as well as canine distemper is essential for long-term protection of both prairie dogs and ferrets. Research into the development of a sylvatic plague vaccine is ongoing, but not yet near fruition. Even when a vaccine eventually becomes available, there will be enormous distribution challenges to prairie dog colonies. Also, persistent poisoning campaigns and recreational shooting continue to contribute to the collapse of the prairie dog ecosystem.

Finally, a high priority will continue to be the development of education programmes, which play a crucial role in public awareness of black-footed ferret conservation issues. Currently, 27 zoos and wildlife agencies sponsor educational exhibits, often using 'ambassador' black-footed ferrets. Gaining public support, especially from landowners who consider prairie dogs as 'pests', is critical to reintroduction success. Many landowners continue to have serious concerns about endangered species, especially perceived governmental interference and restrictions on land use (Reading & Kellert, 1993). A key factor facilitating landowner support for ferrets has been the designation of the reintroduced population as 'experimental and non-essential' under the Endangered Species Act. Although resulting in a lower level of protection for released ferrets, this strategy has gained local rancher and farmer cooperation while providing some assurance that reintroduced ferrets and traditional land uses can be compatible.

CONCLUSION

It is apparent that reproductive sciences can play a vital role in a holistic, integrated conservation programme to save an endangered species. The contemporary story of the black-footed ferret illustrates the potential of species recovery and reintroduction, but based only upon (1) partnerships and (2) longitudinal, multidisciplinary and sound science. Perhaps most important has been the cooperative feature – collaboration among 35 organisations, including state and federal agencies, conservation groups and zoos that worked together to return ferrets to their former grassland habitats of the Great Plains. Reproductive technologies, including AI and a genome resource bank, have been integrated successfully into the black-footed ferret recovery programme to maintain genetic diversity, enhance reproductive efficiency and produce additional animals for reintroduction.

ACKNOWLEDGEMENTS
The authors acknowledge the US Fish & Wildlife Service and the staff of the National Black-Footed Ferret Conservation Center for continued support.

We thank graduate students Karen Wolf and Rachel Moreland and Dr Janine Brown for generating some of the presented data. We are indebted to Drs Julie Kreeger and Mitchell Bush for animal health and veterinary assistance and Linwood Williamson and the Conservation & Research Center animal keeper staff for animal management and care.

REFERENCES

Ballou, J. D. & Lacy, R. C. (1995). Identifying genetically important individuals for management of genetic diversity in pedigreed populations. In *Population Management for Survival and Recovery* (Eds. J. D. Ballou, M. Gilpin & T. G. Foose), pp. 76-111. Columbia University Press, New York.

Biggins, D. E., Miller, B. J., Clark, T. W. & Reading, R. P. (1997). Conservation management case studies: the black-footed ferret. In *Principles of Conservation Biology* (Eds. G.K. Meffe & C.R. Carroll), pp. 420-426. Sinauer Associates, Sunderland, MA.

Brown, J. L. (1997). Fecal steroid profiles in black-footed ferrets exposed to natural photoperiod. *Journal of Wildlife Management* **61**, 1428-1436.

Carpenter, J. W., Appel, M. J. G., Erickson, R. C. & Novilla, M. N. (1976). Fatal vaccine-induced canine distemper virus infection in black-footed ferrets. *Journal of the American Veterinary Medical Association* **169**, 961-964.

Carvalho, C. F., Howard, J. G., Collins, L., Wemmer, C., Bush, M. & Wildt, D. E. (1991). Captive breeding of black-footed ferrets (*Mustela nigripes*) and comparative reproductive efficiency in 1-year old versus 2-year old animals. *Journal of Zoo and Wildlife Medicine* **22**, 96-106.

Curry, P. T., Ziemer, T., Van der Horst, G., Burgess, W., Straley, M., Atherton, R. W. & Kitchin, R. M. (1989). A comparison of sperm morphology and silver nitrate staining characteristics in the domestic ferret and the black-footed ferret. *Gamete Research* **22**, 27-36.

Forrest, S. C., Biggins, D. E., Richardson, L., Clark, T. W., Campbell, T. M. III, Fagerstone, K. A. & Thorne, E. T. (1988). Population attributes for the black-footed ferret (*Mustela nigripes*) at Meeteetse, Wyoming, 1981-1985. *Journal of Mammalogy* **69**, 261-273.

Hillman, C. N. & Carpenter, J. W. (1983). Breeding biology and behavior of captive black-footed ferrets, *Mustela nigripes*. *International Zoo Yearbook* **23**, 186-191.

Holt, W. V., Bennett, P. M., Volobouev, V. & Watson, P. F. (1996). Genetic resource banks in wildlife conservation. *Journal of Zoology* **238**, 531-544.

Howard, J. G. (1993). Semen collection and analysis in nondomestic carnivores. In *Zoo & Wild Animal Medicine III* (Ed. M. E. Fowler), pp. 390-399. W.B. Saunders, Philadelphia.

Howard, J. G. (1999). Assisted reproductive techniques in nondomestic carnivores. In *Zoo & Wild Animal Medicine IV* (Eds. M. E. Fowler & R.E. Miller), pp. 449-457. W. B. Saunders, Philadelphia.

Howard, J. G., Bush, M., Morton, C., Morton, F. & Wildt, D. E. (1991). Comparative semen cryopreservation in ferrets (*Mustela putorius furo*) and pregnancies after laparoscopic intrauterine insemination with frozen-thawed spermatozoa. *Journal of Reproduction and Fertility* **92**, 109-118.

Howard, J. G., Kwiatkowski, D. R., Williams, E. S., Atherton, R. W., Kitchin, R. M., Thorne, E. T., Bush, M. & Wildt, D. E. (1996). Pregnancies in black-footed ferrets and Siberian polecats after laparoscopic artificial insemination with fresh and frozen-thawed semen. *Proceedings of the American Society of Andrology, Journal of Andrology* Suppl. P-51 (abstract 115).

Howard, J. G., Wolf, K. N., Marinari, P. E., Kreeger, J. S., Anderson, T. R., Vargas, A. & Wildt, D. E. (1998). Delayed onset of sperm production in 1-year old male black-footed ferrets. *Proceedings of the Society for the Study of Reproduction, Biology of Reproduction,* Suppl. **58**, 124 (abstract 170).

Kidder, J., Roberts, P. J., Simkin, M. E., Foote, R. H. & Richmond, M. E. (1999). Nonsurgical collection and nonsurgical transfer of preimplantation embryos in the domestic rabbit (*Oryctolagus cuniculus*) and domestic ferret (*Mustela putorius furo*). *Journal of Reproduction and Fertility* **116**, 235–242.

Johnston, L. A. & Lacy, R. C. (1995). Genome resource banking for species conservation: selection of sperm donors. *Cryobiology* **32**, 68–77.

Mead, R. A., Joseph, M. M. & Neirinckx, S. (1988). Optimal dose of human chorionic gonadotropin for inducing ovulation in the ferret. *Zoo Biology* **7**, 263–267.

Mead, R. A., Neirinckz, S. & Czekala, N. M. (1990). Reproductive cycle of the steppe polecat (*Mustela eversmanni*). *Journal of Reproduction and Fertility* **88**, 353–360.

Miller, B. J. & Anderson, S. H. (1990). Comparison of black-footed ferret (*Mustela nigripes*) and domestic ferret (*M. putorius furo*) courtship activity. *Zoo Biology* **9**, 201–210.

Miller, B. J., Anderson, S., DonCarlos, M. W. & Thorne, E. T. (1988). Biology of the endangered black-footed ferret (*Mustela nigripes*) and the role of captive propagation in its conservation. *Canadian Journal of Zoology* **66**, 765–773.

Miller, B., Biggins, D., Hanebury, L. & Vargas, A. (1993). Reintroduction of the black-footed ferret. In *Creative Conservation: Interactive Management of Wild and Captive Animals* (Eds. G. Mace, P. Olney & A. Feisner), pp. 455–464. Chapman & Hall, London.

Miller, B., Reading, R. P. & Forrest, S. (1996). *Prairie Night: Black-footed Ferrets and the Recovery of an Endangered Species.* Smithsonian Institution Press, Washington, DC.

Neal, J. B., Murphy, B. D., Moger, W. H. & Oliphant, L. W. (1977). Reproduction in the male ferret: gonadal activity during the annual cycle: recrudescence and maturation. *Biology of Reproduction* **17**, 380–385.

O'Brien, S. J., Martenson, J. S., Eichelberger, M. A., Thorne, E.T. & Wright, F. (1989). Biochemical genetic variation and molecular systematics of the black-footed ferret, *Mustela nigripes*. In *Conservation Biology of the Black-Footed Ferret* (Eds. U.S. Seal, E. T. Thorne, S. H. Anderson & M. Bogan), pp. 21–33. Yale University Press, New Haven, CT.

Reading R. P. & Kellert, S. R. (1993). Attitudes toward a proposed reintroduction of black-footed ferrets (*Mustela nigripes*). *Conservation Biology* **7**, 569–580.

Thorne, E. T. & Oakleaf, B. (1991). Species rescue for captive breeding: Black-footed ferret as an example. In *Beyond Captive Breeding: Re-introducing Endangered Mammals to the Wild* (Ed. J. H. W. Gipps), pp. 241–261. Clarendon Press, Oxford.

Van der Horst, G., Curry, P. T, Kitchin, R. M., Burgess, W., Thorne, E. T., Kwiatkowski, D., Parker, M. & Atherton, R. W. (1991). Quantitative light and scanning electron microscopy of ferret sperm. *Molecular Reproduction and Development* **30**, 232-240.

Wildt, D. E. & Goodrowe, K. L. (1989). The potential of applying embryo technology to the black-footed ferret. In *Conservation Biology of the Black-Footed Ferret* (Eds. U. S. Seal, E. T. Thorne, S. H. Anderson & M. Bogan), pp. 160-176. Yale University Press, New Haven, CT.

Wildt, D. E. & Roth, T. L. (1997). Assisted reproduction in managing and conserving threatened felids. *International Zoo Yearbook* **35**, 164-172.

Wildt, D. E., Bush, M., Morton, C., Morton, F. & Howard, J. G. (1989). Semen characteristics and testosterone profiles in ferrets kept in long-day photoperiod, and the influence of hCG timing and sperm dilution on pregnancy rate after laparoscopic insemination. *Journal of Reproduction and Fertility* **86**, 349-358.

Wildt, D. E., Ellis, S. & Howard, J. G. (2001). Linkage of reproductive sciences: from 'quick fix' to 'integrated' conservation. In *Advances in Reproduction in Dogs, Cats and Exotic Carnivores* (Eds. P. W. Concannon, G. C. W. England, W. Farstad, C. Linde-Forsberg, J. P. Verstegen & C. Doberska), pp. 295-307. Journals of Reproduction & Fertility, Ltd., Colchester, UK.

Wildt, D. E., Rall, W. F., Critser, J. K., Monfort, S. L. & Seal, U. S. (1997). Genome resource banks: 'Living collections' for biodiversity conservation. *BioScience* **47**, 689-698.

Wildt, D. E., Schiewe, M. C., Schmidt, P. M., Goodrowe, K. L., Howard, J. G., Phillips, L. G., O'Brien, S. J. & Bush, M. (1986). Developing animal model systems for embryo technologies in rare and endangered wildlife. *Theriogenology* **25**, 33-51.

Williams, E. S., Thorne, E. T., Appel, M. J. G. & Bellitski, D. W. (1988). Canine distemper in black-footed ferrets (*Mustela nigripes*) from Wyoming. *Journal of Wildlife Diseases* **24**, 385-398.

Williams, E. S., Thorne, E. T., Kwiatkowski, D. R., Anderson, S. T. & Lutz, K. (1991). Reproductive biology and management of captive black-footed ferrets (*Mustela nigripes*). *Zoo Biology* **10**, 383-398.

Williams, E. S., Thorne, E. T., Kwiatkowski, D. R., Lutz, K. & Anderson, S.T. (1992). Comparative vaginal cytology of the estrous cycle of black-footed ferrets (*Mustela nigripes*), Siberian polecats (*M. eversmanni*), and domestic ferret (*M. putorius furo*). *Journal of Veterinary Diagnostic Investigations* **4**, 38-44.

Wolf, K. N., Wildt, D. E., Vargas, A., Marinari, P. E., Kreeger, J. S., Ottinger, M. A. & Howard, J. G. (2000a). Age dependent changes in sperm production, semen quality and testicular volume in black-footed ferrets (*Mustela nigripes*). *Biology of Reproduction* **63**, 179-187.

Wolf, K. N., Wildt, D. E., Vargas, A., Marinari, P. E., Ottinger, M. A. & Howard, J. G. (2000b). Reproductive inefficiency in male black-footed ferrets (*Mustela nigripes*). *Zoo Biology* **19**, 517-528.

17

Genetic resource banks for species conservation

W. V. HOLT, TERESA ABAIGAR, P. F. WATSON & D. E. WILDT

INTRODUCTION AND BACKGROUND

Genetic resource banking (GRB) provides potentially useful support for managing and conserving wildlife species. The GRB concept and strategies have received increasing attention over the last two decades (Holt et al., 1996b; Wildt et al., 1997; Holt & Pickard, 1999; Watson & Holt, 2001). This chapter summarises the general ideas presented in these earlier works while outlining new developments and providing examples of how GRBs are being applied to particular species. Specifically, we endeavour to provide a realistic evaluation of the current utility of GRBs, illustrating how to integrate the logistics of the technology into practical conservation programmes.

In terms of focus, this chapter is concerned with wild animal GRBs which are defined as organised collections of stored germplasm, mainly cryopreserved spermatozoa from individuals whose contribution to the gene pool is too valuable to lose. This definition helps to distinguish GRBs from other collections of frozen, dried or fixed biomaterials. Although a useful research resource, such collections have until recently had little practical value in breeding programmes. The GRB discussed here also differs from *ad hoc* collections of germplasm amassed opportunistically over time. By nature such collections are unplanned, containing random assortments of species and individuals. In contrast, a useful GRB is preplanned in some detail, addressing a wide range of organisational issues, from mundane specimen labelling to safe stewardship, to the politics of proprietary rights. One of the most significant considerations is the overall goal of the conservation-breeding programme, and how a GRB can contribute to its success. Species breeding plans generally aim to conserve as much genetic diversity as possible, usually over the next 100–200 years (Ballou & Cooper, 1992). Achieving this aim by natural reproduction involves maintaining large numbers of breeding individuals usually dispersed amongst geographically disparate zoos. Storing germplasm samples from many individuals releases some of the strictures on large space requirements. Fewer living animals are necessary, and more space becomes available for other rare species. Knowledge of genetic histories of the donors allows them to be integrated seamlessly into the planned breeding programmes.

Botanists have already considered the realistic necessities associated with establishing GRBs. The Kew Millennium Seed Bank at Wakehurst Place, UK, is one example. Recognising the impossibility of collecting seeds from every plant species, the programme strives to attain modest and pragmatic goals. One target is to collect and store seeds from 10% (over 24 000 species) of the world's flora and another is to conserve seeds from all native British species. To achieve these aims, a dedicated facility has been built and staffed, supported by a long-term funding plan. No similar facility exists as yet for conserving germplasm from the world's threatened animal species.

Given resource constraints to maintaining such a GRB, and the additional challenge of making germplasm readily accessible to breeding programmes, there is consensus that a 'huge infrastructure–many species approach' is unsuitable for a wildlife GRB. Rather, a single species-collaborative strategy amongst many institutions is likely to be more practical. This, in turn, requires species prioritisation (which to bank and in what order). Furthermore, without a successful managed breeding programme for the 'target' species there is no point in establishing a GRB. Finally, once the biomaterial is banked, its successful utility is tied to knowledge of the reproductive biology of the target species (and manipulating that biology through technology). Sadly, while available for domestic, laboratory and companion animals as well as humans, such information is largely missing for wild species. Paradoxically, the ability to develop suitable background physiological knowledge becomes increasingly difficult as populations diminish. Thus, when they become the focus of a species support programme it may already be too late. Early recognition of the need for reproductive studies in wild species helps ensure that reproductive technologies are available when needed.

Having pointed out the distinguishing features of realistic GRB programmes for wildlife, we present here some models that have been (or are being) developed with explicit conservation goals. We emphasise throughout that the integration of multidisciplinary skills is crucial to the sensible implementation of GRBs. Although the technical details of cell and tissue cryopreservation are important, other wide-ranging issues including the 'non-biological' (e.g. communication) will also be addressed.

STATE OF THE ART

Origins of the GRB concept

The value of cryopreserved germplasm hails back to the mid-twentieth century, to the first discovery of a method for recovering viable spermatozoa after freezing (Polge *et al.*, 1949). In response to this remarkable finding, Sir Alan Parkes (a founder of cryobiology as a discipline) remarked that 'time and space had been abolished for cattle breeding', a phrase that continues to summarise the potential value of the GRB concept for all species. Later studies of frozen mouse embryos (to investigate the potentially damaging effects of background radiation on cryopreserved germplasm) concluded that storage for more than 1000 years would not cause biological problems (Whittingham *et al.*, 1977). In fact, decades of experience in the dairy industry involving extensive freeze-thaw manipulations of semen and embryos confirms that, when suitable technology is used, sperm and embryo viability are unaltered by cryopreservation.

After Polge's original discovery of how to freeze chicken sperm, similar technology for cryopreserving spermatozoa from other common domestic and laboratory animals soon followed. This, in turn, motivated interest in collecting and storing spermatozoa from a wide diversity of species. However, there was a naïve tendency to use the same methods for all species, and it was not surprising that many stored samples, when thawed, failed to retain viability. Early progress in wildlife sperm cryopreservation and reproductive technologies was the topic of a Zoological Society of London symposium (Watson, 1978). Around the same time, Veprintsev & Rott (1979) formulated and published wide-ranging proposals for establishing species-diverse GRBs. Although the goals were unrealistic for the time, their ideas validated the need and value of such repositories. Since the early 1980s various publications have argued the case for GRBs in wildlife conservation (Holt & Moore, 1988; Oldfield, 1989; Sipko *et al.*, 1994, 1997; Holt *et al.*, 1996b; Rott, 1996; Wildt, 1997). Although these papers were persuasive, there are still only a few projects globally that are sufficiently developed to justify recognition as *organised* GRBs. Many *ad hoc* collections of sperm, eggs and embryos are still being amassed, all of which will have little relevance to genetic management or conservation.

GOALS OF GRB PROGRAMMES

The general aim of GRBs for wildlife conservation is to provide another option for enhancing management and protection of genetic diversity. Most target species populations are typically small and fragmented (in nature or zoos) so a primary goal is to prevent the loss of extant genetic diversity (Lacy, 1987). Additionally, because diversity can decline within a population, it also can be restored using cryopreserved sperm, eggs or embryos. The important point here is that stored materials for restoring heterozygosity may be from animals that died generations earlier. This all is contingent on the stored resource being from animals with documented genetic histories. Only then can the GRB material be integrated into managed breeding programmes, where policies are typically designed to maximise genetic diversity and minimise inbreeding effects. Thus, the genetic goals of the GRB coincide exactly with those of the appropriate species management and/or Taxon Advisory Group (TAG). This target is usually to maintain 90% of genetic diversity in a demographically stable population over 200 years. Under such explicit guidelines, population biologists have been able to study models of GRB use, including identifying the most effective theoretical schemes for sample collection and usage (Johnston & Lacy, 1995). Intelligent incorporation of GRBs into managed breeding plans has other advantages, including increasing the generation interval and the effective (reproductively viable) population size. Thus, the cryopreserved samples can be regarded as genetically equivalent to living animals. Coincidentally, and assuming the technology is viable, then such a policy can reduce the amount of space needed for maintaining viable animal populations.

There are significant financial costs to establishing and maintaining a GRB. Realistically, therefore, it makes sense to focus a few programmes on high priority species. These efforts then need adequate resources and underpinning by suitable basic and applied research in reproductive biology. As Wildt (1997, and Chapter 1) points out, there is a paucity of information about the reproductive biology of most animal species. It is irresponsible to wait until a species is 'endangered' before initiating scholarly studies to generate data that may save it. Thus, a strong case can be made for gathering basic information about any species (threatened or not) as opportunities arise.

The species-specific GRB approach runs counter to the earlier expansive visions of GRBs advocated in the 1970s and 1980s. Veprintsev & Rott (1979, 1980), in a series of monographs, promoted biocomplex GRBs comprised of species ranging from viruses, bacteria and fungi to insects and to higher vertebrates (equivalent to the 'frozen zoo' concept often cited in the popular press). This concept is reasonable only if methodologies for collection, storage and use are similar among taxa/species. Perhaps this approach is practical for lower life forms, but it is untenable for species with complex reproductive physiology. Selecting high priority species can be at the discretion of species management programmes. However, it is worth considering the recent comments of Bennett (2001), who considered GRBs across an array of agricultural, biomedical and wildlife species. This author pointed out the importance of supporting species that are culturally or politically significant to nations, localities and individual organisations. The giant panda is the prime example of such symbolism as it is instantly and globally recognised as an icon for the wildlife conservation movement. GRBs for such high profile species would also help promote repository development for the less 'charismatic'.

Management and location of GRBs

A GRB as a major central, stewardship facility for vast species numbers is fraught with difficulties ranging from infrastructure and staffing costs (in perpetuity) to disease control and proprietary issues. A more realistic approach is to use facilities that already exist, or alternatively to implement small targeted initiatives near the populations of interest. In the United Kingdom such a central facility exists: the European Centre for Animal Cell Cultures (ECACC), at Porton Down in southern England. Other countries have similar establishments whose main purpose is to act as a central holding facility for different types of cryopreserved materials. Until recently, ECACC had not received germplasm samples for deposit. However, in 1996, this organisation received sperm samples from Russian Amur tigers as part of an international programme to set up a GRB for this endangered species. The major advantage of an ECACC type facility is the guarantee of safekeeping and security. In contrast, samples held at a non-specialist institution are at greater risk to accidental damage and loss through inadequate maintenance. However, if appropriate stewardship can be ensured, there are advantages to housing stored samples in proximity to the animal populations of interest. Chief among these is minimising accidental transference of microbial contamination from animals to samples or vice versa. Safe storage of potentially contaminated samples has been of concern to the human medical field, one reason why a storage straw has been marketed that provides double packaging to prevent leakage (CBS High Security Straw, IMV Technologies, L'Aigle, France). Such devices may eventually become mandatory for animal gametes, especially those shipped intercontinentally. Likewise, translocating germplasm across international borders requires health status assurances from veterinary authorities in the exporting country. Failure to use appropriately hygienic techniques and materials may well jeopardise the value and future utility of stored samples, an issue considered in detail recently by Kirkwood & Colenbrander (2001).

STATUS OF GERMPLASM CRYOPRESERVATION PROCEDURES

Despite an array of reported successes using frozen sperm and artificial insemination, germplasm cryopreservation procedures are poorly developed and assisted breeding is usually inefficient for wildife species. Cryopreservation itself is a severe stressor to spermatozoa, reducing both functionality and survival. But inefficiency is also a reflection of the diversity of reproductive characteristics among species. For example, differences in female tract physiology and anatomy can affect the timing of ovulation or site of insemination. Additionally, oocyte cryopreservation protocols have so far only been developed for the mouse, hamster, rabbit and cow, and likewise, embryo freezing (while routine in some laboratory and livestock species) has succeeded in only a handful of wildife species.

These *technical* limitations currently drive the practical development of genome banks for conservation. Thus, there is a common argument about the need for appropriate basic research and knowledge before attempting large-scale collection and storage. But there is also a contrary argument that the urgent situation of some species demands attempts to store germplasm even in the face of low expectations of success. Examples include species or populations that have been reduced severely in number to the point of near-extinction. In these cases, saving germplasm as well as tissues and cells is a high priority. Even marginal quality germplasm or somatic tissues may be useful in re-deriving the genotypes of donors in the future once nuclear transfer and microinjection techniques have become more highly developed.

Gametic rescue from tissues has considerable value for spermatozoa, where epididymal spermatozoa are readily obtainable *post mortem*. Because cryopreserving mammalian oocytes is so difficult, there has been considerable interest in the freeze-storage of slices of ovarian tissue as a feasible alternative (Sztein *et al.*, 1998; Candy *et al.*, 2000). Although recovery and maturation of primordial follicles from cryopreserved ovarian tissue remains a technical challenge, some success has been achieved (Carroll *et al.*, 1990). A novel approach to cryopreserving testicular tissue has been used experimentally whereby isolated rat spematogenic cells were transferred to mouse testis that, in turn, produced rat spermatozoa (Clouthier *et al.*, 1996). Interestingly, the spermatogonial preparations had been frozen-thawed prior to transplantation. Thus, cryopreserving testicular cell suspensions is feasible and, in theory, cell suspensions from a rare species could be used to populate the testes of common species, thus permitting the eventual harvesting of spermatozoa from the former. Of course, the fertility of these cells remains unknown because of their development in a 'foreign' endocrine and epididymal environment. Further, although technically attractive, it is unlikely that such technologies will ever become common for the routine management of endangered species, but rather as a last resort to re-derive rare DNA or to avoid species/population extinctions.

GRB PROGRAMMES IN ACTION

Given the complexities defining a genuine GRB, one may ask whether this concept has practical implications for conservation? In fact only a few projects, scattered around the world, have been developed. The most successful integrated GRB and assisted reproduction project is the Smithsonian's National Zoological Park's support of the Black-Footed Ferret Recovery Programme in North America, and even this effort largely relies on fresh rather than cryopreserved spermatozoa (see Howard *et al.*, Chapter 16). Here, and for other species, it is noteworthy that these successes have been based upon substantial basic research often over periods of years and involving 'model' species (e.g. domestic ferret as an experimental model for the black-footed species).

A systematic approach to GRB development to help conserve threatened native fauna has been implemented in Australia. A consortium involving Monash University and Taronga Zoo (Sydney) has formed the Animal Gene Storage and Resource Centre of Australia (AGSRA). One high priority has been a broad policy of opportunistically salvaging gametes and tissues *post mortem*. These samples are documented in detail and information about the collection widely disseminated. The consortium has recognised the inadequate status of reproductive information about most threatened species and thus has focused on a few specific projects, one aimed at developing methods to cryopreserve kangaroo and wallaby semen. Despite substantial efforts, no more than 10% of thawed kangaroo and wallaby sperm exhibit post-thaw motility. Although actively conserving germplasm, the AGSRA is not yet coordinating a truly integrated GRB programme that actively enhances managed breeding of wildlife.

A similar GRB approach has been adopted in southern Africa, where the Wildlife Breeding Resources Centre (WBRC) concentrates on salvaging gametes and tissues from African wildlife, especially from harvested or hunted populations. Located near Pretoria, the WBRC has obtained financial support to collect both semen and oocytes from dead animals, generally using a 'mobile laboratory' approach (caravans converted to laboratories that can be taken directly to field sites). Once cryopreserved, samples are stored at a central repository near Pretoria. Although significant amounts of raw materials have been stored from an impressive array of species, this scheme is insufficiently supported by the background technology that allows cryopreserved gametes to be integrated into breeding programmes.

The Mohor gazelle GRB, a working example

To appreciate the issues associated with putting GRBs into practice, our laboratory at the Institute of Zoology (IOZ) in London collaborated with the Estación Experimental de Zonas Aridas (EEZA) in Almería, southeastern Spain. The aim has been to support conservation breeding programmes for three endangered gazelle species that have bred successfully in Almería since 1971. These are the Mohor gazelle (*Gazella dama mhorr*), Cuvier's gazelle (*Gazella cuvieri*) and Dorcas gazelle (*Gazella dorcas neglecta*), as well as the Saharan Barbary sheep (*Ammotragus lervia sahariensis*). Breeding activities are based within the Parque de Rescate de la Fauna Sahariana (PRFS). However, another long-term goal has been reintroduction of both gazelles and Barbary sheep into original areas of their distribution. To accomplish this, studbooks were established for all species and subspecies. Additionally, biological, behavioural and veterinary research programmes were initiated for these poorly studied species, largely to generate knowledge applicable to developing successful captive breeding. The offspring produced have been distributed to zoos and other breeding centres as a hedge against a catastrophe striking the Almería populations.

Since being founded more than 30 years ago, the populations have flourished. However, genetic management has been challenging, especially development of strategies to minimise inbreeding. The overarching demographic objective has been to maintain an overall 'global' *ex situ* population comprised of individuals of appropriate sex ratio and age classes, one that is healthy and self-sustaining.

The GRB programme in Almería for one of the target species, the Mohor gazelle, commenced as a pilot study funded by the European Union. This particular species was chosen because there was an extant population of several hundred animals with sound and known genetic histories. Some research into the reproductive biology of the Mohor gazelle had already occurred, and there were enough animals to support a meaningful project. Finally efforts devoted to reintroduction into Tunisia, Morocco and other north African countries meant that there was an important *in situ*-related motive for maximising genetic diversity in the founder (source) herd.

It could be argued that the criteria for selecting the Mohor gazelle were equally applicable to the Dorcas and Cuvier's gazelles. However, the former species was chosen largely in relation to practical issues, including a more detailed understanding of the basic reproductive physiology of the species. For example, although semen collection was possible in all three species by electroejaculation of anaesthetised males, initial trials revealed that Dorcas and Cuvier's gazelles consistently produced smaller volumes of less concentrated semen than the Mohor gazelle. This was considered important because large volumes of spermic ejaculates were needed initially to test the feasibility of various semen cryopreservation protocols. Minimal semen quantities in the Cuvier's and Dorcas gazelles severely limited the number of variables (e.g. egg-yolk or glycerol concentration) that could be investigated. Another practical reason for choosing the Mohor gazelle was its overall 'calmness' and tractability compared with Dorcas or Cuvier's gazelles. Thus, we anticipated less risk in handling animals using this particular species.

In terms of actual semen cryopreservation logistics, the first important decision was to choose between the use of straw or pellet freezing/container methods. Discussions led to the realization that this factor might not only influence post-thaw viability, but also hygiene and disease control, especially if samples were ultimately exported. We reviewed the semen freezing literature in ungulates to identify laboratory protocols that showed promising results. As the TEST-yolk diluent had met with some success in most species examined, a decision was made to use this combination as a basic diluent. However, decisions concerning diluent composition were impossible to evaluate without some practical experimentation. For example, what egg-yolk and glycerol concentrations would be best for gazelle semen? Evidence from other species had indicated that glycerol in either too high (e.g. pig and mouse) or too low (e.g. marsupials) concentrations could be damaging to spermatozoa. Because bovid spermatozoa usually survive freezing best when the glycerol concentration is 6–8% (v/v), a decision was taken to use 6% glycerol in initial semen freezing experiments, and to investigate the effects of varying the egg-yolk concentration. This approach resulted in what appeared to be acceptable post-thaw survival with minimal sperm damage (for data, see Holt *et al.*, 1996a).

However, *in vitro* assays are only the first step to ensuring that frozen biomaterial is viable. The best way to test cryopreserved sperm viability is via an AI trial. In this study, we selected 13 test females, but to avoid producing offspring of no value, it was necessary to choose females that would produce calves of genetic value, including low inbreeding coefficients. Because it is known that fertility is related to sperm viability, we subjectively imposed an additional requirement – females would be inseminated only if thawed sperm showed at least 30% motility.

However, for the AI trial to have a chance of success, it was also necessary to make some intelligent guesswork in designing a procedure for oestrus synchronisation. This was accomplished by the use of progesterone-releasing controlled internal drug release (CIDR) devices, routinely used for oestrous synchronisation in goats and deer, but never before used for gazelles. The CIDR devices were placed intravaginally for 12 days, then removed. The females were expected to respond to the sudden fall of circulating progesterone by entering oestrus and ovulating. Intra-uterine sperm deposition of anaesthetised females with thawed sperm eventually resulted in four of 13 females producing conceptions (Holt *et al.*, 1996a). Although the incidence of pregnancy success was not as high as might be expected in domesticated species of ungulates (e.g. cattle), the point is that the *in vivo* viability of frozen-thawed sperm was demonstrated. Such an accomplishment provides the confidence to begin a large-scale banking programme from the most genetically valuable males.

This GRB programme was developed from scratch, beginning with a wild species in which there was little information on basic reproductive biology. The programme has been successful because a systematic research approach was taken in a partnership that involved scientists working together with the species managers. A major advantage was the availability of a dedicated captive breeding facility and the recognition that this programme would only be successful in the face of long-term support. Even so, for this programme to continue to contribute to the overall genetic management of this species, there must be continued devotion to the overall enhanced understanding of Mohor gazelle biology. Additional knowledge not only in reproductive biology but in genetics, nutrition, behaviour, animal health and *ex situ* husbandry is crucial to ensuring that the bank is maximally beneficial to species protection. Finally, although this particular GRB now is most useful for supporting the *ex situ* breeding programme, there is a need to define and then illustrate how the bank can yet contribute to the conservation of Mohor gazelles *in situ*.

PRIORITIES FOR INTEGRATING GRBS INTO
CONSERVATION PROGRAMMES

There is no doubt that the concept and utilitarian value of GRBs for wildlife has moved forward during the past decade. This can partly be attributed to significant amounts of world-wide discussions, published papers and now a few practical initiatives to integrate GRBs into actual breeding programmes. This, in turn, has prompted the opportunity to face the many organisational issues related to establishing, implementing and ensuring the long-range success of GRBs. An 'action plan' for the establishment of a GRB in support of tiger breeding and management (Wildt *et al.*, 1993) presents a particularly valuable reference for anyone interested in understanding the enormously complex issues associated with the banking of biological materials from a rare species.

These decade-long discussions certainly have helped the scientific community focus on the specific challenges that lie ahead. We have gone from the broad-scale idea of large buildings containing samples from thousands of species to the notion that maximal effectiveness will be achieved by targeting high priority species at a grass roots level. There is a need to continue advocating this 'targeted species' approach combined with more integrative scientific research. The key, of course, continues to lie in convincing wildlife managers that basic research is crucial to allowing better natural and assisted breeding, including using banked sperm (and eventually embryos). Such a goal needs to be clearly understood by all stakeholders, especially decision-makers in charge of species conservation programmes.

Once a priority species has been identified and the decision made that a GRB will be useful, organisational issues become extremely important. Sample collection and handling techniques must be consistent, but consideration must also be given to collecting parallel tissue and blood samples. These biomaterials hold a wealth of information for genetic, disease and as yet unknown future studies. In all cases, one of the highest priorities as GRBs are incorporated into the future of conservation is avoiding unintentional disease transmission (Kirkwood & Colenbrander, 2001). More studies are needed to assess the dangers of microbial contamination, especially developing effective methods of screening samples, monitoring the health of banks and decontaminating infected samples.

This chapter has been heavily biased towards mammals, and it is noteworthy that gamete and embryo cryopreservation research is in progress for other non-mammalian vertebrate taxa (Watson, 2000). Progress in poultry production and aquaculture has allowed the successful cryopreservation of wild bird and fish sperm, respectively. Embryo cryopreservation should theoretically provide a strategically important and useful method for conserving rare wild fish species and populations. No embryo transfer techniques would be necessary and methods for embryo production in culture are relatively well developed. However, fish embryo cryopreservation remains elusive primarily because of an impermeable membrane layer of the fish embryo that prevents cryoprotectant penetration. Similar challenges have been observed in invertebrate embryos and have been partially overcome by permeabilising the outer mucous coat of the embryo. In 1997, at a workshop on genome conservation (Reñaca, Chile), Professor Claudio Barros reported high survival (*c.* 70%) of cryopreserved sea urchin larvae frozen using DMSO as a cryoprotectant (C. Barros, unpublished data). Many such basic studies need to be directed at a host of non-mammalian wildlife species.

Finally, although the purpose of GRBs for species conservation is to help preserve and distribute genes from rare individuals, these banks are incredibly useful sources of biomaterials for basic research. Many investigators worldwide are interested in studying materials from wildlife but have no access to gametes, embryos, tissues, blood and DNA. We need to determine how banks can be developed to allow distributing 'excess' materials to our scientific colleagues. This, in turn, entails the need to develop databases where information within banks can be easily shared, especially electronically, while being compatible with widely used genetic management software. Finally, the ultimate success of a GRB will rely on an integrative approach, not only amongst the scientists but also the managers of wildlife species living in nature as well as in zoos. The list of stakeholders is impressive, ranging from field biologists and curators to studbook keepers and registrars. Thus, effective GRBs will be those with an interdisciplinary, broad-scale ethic and a devotion to incorporating all available tools to conserving and managing small populations.

REFERENCES

Ballou, J. D. & Cooper, K. A. (1992). Genetic management strategies for endangered captive populations: the role of genetic and reproductive technology. In *Biotechnology and the Conservation of Genetic Diversity* (Eds. H. D. M. Moore, W. V. Holt & G. M. Mace), pp. 183–286. Oxford University Press, Oxford.

Bennett, P. M. (2001). Establishing animal germplasm resource banks for wildlife conservation: genetic, population and evolutionary aspects. In *Cryobanking the Genetic Resource. Wildlife Conservation for the Future?* (Eds. P. F. Watson & W. V. Holt), pp. 47–67. Taylor & Francis, London.

Candy, C. J., Wood, M. J. & Whittingham, D. G. (2000). Restoration of a normal reproductive lifespan after transplantation of cryopreserved mouse ovaries. *Human Reproduction* **15**, 1300-1304.

Carroll, J., Whittingham, D. G., Wood, M. J., Telfer, E. & Gosden, R. G. (1990). Extraovarian production of mature viable mouse oocytes from frozen primary follicles. *Journal of Reproduction and Fertility* **90**, 321-327.

Clouthier, D. E., Avarbock, M. R., Maika, S. D., Hamma, R. E. & Brinster, R. L. (1996). Rat spermatogenesis in mouse testis. *Nature* **381**, 418-421.

Holt, W. V. & Moore, H. D. M. (1988). Semen banking - is it now feasible for captive endangered species? *Oryx* **22**, 172-178.

Holt, W. V. & Pickard, A. R. (1999). Role of reproductive technologies and genetic resource banks in animal conservation. *Reviews in Reproduction* **4**, 143-150.

Holt, W. V., Abaigar, T. & Jabbour, H. N. (1996a). Oestrous synchronization, semen preservation and artificial insemination in the Mohor gazelle (*Gazella dama mhorr*) for the establishment of a genome resource bank programme. *Reproduction, Fertility and Development* **8**, 1215-1222.

Holt, W. V., Bennett, P. M., Volobouev, V. & Watson, P. F. (1996b). Genetic resource banks in wildlife conservation. *Journal of Zoology (London)* **238**, 531-544.

Johnston, L. A. & Lacy, R. C. (1995). Genome resource banking for species conservation: selection of sperm donors. *Cryobiology* **32**, 68-77.

Kirkwood, J. K. & Colenbrander, B. (2001). Disease control measures for genetic resource banking. In *Cryobanking the Genetic Resource. Wildlife Conservation for the Future?* (Eds. P. F. Watson & W. V. Holt), pp. 69-84. Taylor & Francis, London.

Lacy, R. C. (1987). Loss of genetic diversity from managed populations: interacting effects of drift, mutation, immigration, selection and population subdivision. *Conservation Biology* **1**, 143-158.

Oldfield, M. F. (1989). *The Value of Conserving Genetic Resources*. Sinauer Associates, Sunderland, MA.

Polge, C., Smith, A. V. & Parkes, A. S. (1949). Revival of spermatozoa after vitrification and dehydration at low temperatures. *Nature* **164**, 166.

Rott, N. N. (1996). The organization of genetic cryobanks and the use of developmental biology methods for the conservation of rare animals. II. Obtaining and cryoconservation of embryos of wild animals. *Russian Journal of Developmental Biology* **27**, 245-255.

Sipko, T. P., Abilov, A. I., Shurkhal, A. V. & Rott, N. N. (1994). Creation of a bison sperm cryobank as a means of conserving genetic polymorphism in this species. In *Soviet Genetics* pp. 1516-1520. Plenum Publishing, New York.

Sipko, T. P., Rautian, G. S., Udina, I. G. & Strelchenko, N. S. (1997). Conservation of genetic material from endangered and economically important ungulate species in establishment of cryobanks. *Physiology & General Biology Reviews* **13**, 35-98.

Sztein, J., Sweet, H., Farley, J. & Mobraaten, L. (1998). Cryopreservation and orthotopic transplantation of mouse ovaries: New approach in gamete banking. *Biology of Reproduction* **58**, 1071-1074.

Veprintsev, B. N. & Rott, N. N. (1979). Conserving genetic resources. *Nature* **280**, 633-634.

Veprintsev B. N. & Rott, N. N. (1980). *Genome Conservation*, pp. 1-49. Academy of Sciences of the USSR. Puschino.

Watson, P. F. (Ed.) (1978). *Artificial Breeding of Non-Domestic Animals*. Symposia of the Zoological Society of London, No. 43. Academic Press, London.

Watson, P. F. (2000). The causes of reduced fertility with cryopreserved semen. *Animal Reproduction Science* **60-61**, 481-492.

Watson, P. F. & Holt, W. V. (2001). Organizational issues concerning the establishment of a genetic resource bank. In *Cryobanking the Genetic Resource. Wildlife Conservation for the Future?* (Eds. P. F. Watson & W. V. Holt), pp. 113-122, Taylor & Francis, London.

Whittingham, D. G., Lyon, M. F. & Glenister, P. H. (1977). Long-term storage of mouse embryos at −196 °C: the effect of background radiation. *Genetic Research, Cambridge* **29**, 171-181.

Wildt, D. E. (1997). Genome Resource Banking. Impact on biotic conservation and society. In *Reproductive Tissue Banking* (Eds. A. M. Karow & J. Critser), pp. 399-439. Academic Press, New York.

Wildt, D. E., Byers, A. P., Howard, J. G., Wiese, R., Willis, K, O'Brien, S. J., Block, J., Tilson, R. I. & Rall, W. F. (1993). *Tiger Genome Resource Banking (GRB) Action Plan. Global Need and a Plan for the North American Region*. CBSG. Apple Valley, 12101 Johnny Cake Road, MA 55124, USA.

Wildt, D. E., Rall, W. F., Critser, J. K., Monfort, S. L. & Seal, U. S. (1997). Genome resource banks. *BioScience* **47**, 689-698.

18

Fertility control for wildlife

JOHN C. RODGER

INTRODUCTION

Reproductive biology and related technologies have generally been seen as important tools to assist the breeding of threatened species, especially where total numbers are small or restricted to captive-bred populations (see Wildt, Chapter 1). However, over recent years interest has developed in applying knowledge of reproductive biology to the advancement of fertility control tools for managing abundant wild populations (for reviews, see Bomford, 1990; Tyndale-Biscoe, 1994). Increasing public concern for animal welfare and rights, together with a desire to find non-lethal alternatives to established culling methods (shooting, trapping and poisons; for reviews, see Oogjes, 1997; Fitzgerald et al., 2000) have been major drivers of this research. Before discussing fertility control as a tool it is important to identify why there is a need to control populations and to draw distinctions between the types of problems requiring management. These are critical issues because, although generic aspects of reproductive biology and fertility control technology may underpin approaches to fertility-based management, the specifications for an appropriate product and its use may differ profoundly depending on the species concerned, the specific problem and the management goal(s). Abundant wildlife falls into two main categories, (1) introduced species (e.g. rabbit in Australia) which have become pests, and (2) native species (e.g. kangaroos in Australia) which have become overly abundant because of environmental changes. Although the outcomes of such abundance may be similar, the management paradigms are very different. Introduced pests are targets for massive population reduction, and even eradication if possible. Such action usually has broad public support. Control of native species has much more limited and usually local goals. It must not compromise the conservation status of the species and is less well understood or supported by the public.

This chapter aims to set the scene for fertility control in wildlife. The following two chapters will deal in depth with work to date on fertility control vaccines targeting egg and sperm, especially in Australia, New Zealand and the USA. The structure of the following chapters highlights the main points at issue. Firstly, Mate & Hinds (Chapter 19) look at how a vaccine system would work within the animal, that is its physiological effectiveness, how it enters the target animal's system and also consider cost-effectiveness. Cowan *et al.* (Chapter 20) examine how such an agent would work at the field and population level, and what actual effects fertility control will have on the target populations. These three chapters contend that effective fertility-based population management will only be achieved if research work is integrated on these two critical technical aspects of the problem – physiological and ecological effectiveness. However, type of fertility-based population management tools will not be solely a technical decision. Safety of any control strategy and its public acceptability will be the third critical issue.

A result of these complex technological and public agendas is that the work reported in the three chapters involves collaboration among diverse organisations and scientific disciplines. This is particularly evident for the work in Australia and New Zealand which involves two Cooperative Research Centres (CRC) set up specifically by the Australian Federal Government to encourage such outcomes-focused multi-organisational cooperative research (Chapters 19 & 20, and the earlier Chapter 15 on Conservation in Western Australia by Fletcher & Morris).

Australia's Cooperative Research Centres

The Australian Government's Cooperative Research Centres Programme is a relevant case study illustrating one approach to the structuring of research organisations aimed at facilitating integration of research. The CRC Programme supports multi-institutional, multidisciplinary, outcomes-focused research in areas of national need. CRCs are selected via a highly competitive process and are funded for a seven-year period, during which their continued support is subject to major reviews of their science and management (at years 2 and 5). Some 60–70 Centres are supported at any one time with the programme having a broad portfolio in information technology, mining, manufacturing, agriculture, biomedicine and the environment. As the aim of CRCs is to draw together the expertise of universities, research organisations and industry/user organisations and bodies, their basic structures and processes assume integrated research within an applications and commercialisation environment. In the case of environmental CRCs, the industry/ user involvement includes government agencies responsible for areas such as the environment, agriculture, land and water management and relevant commercial industry bodies.

Managing impacts

Traditionally, wildlife population management has meant pest management, and generally this has been seen in terms of wildlife impacts on human activities, especially agriculture. In reality, the situation is far more complex. As well as commercial effects, there are concerns about conservation and animal and human health impacts. This variety of problem situations requires very different solutions. In all cases, however, the aim of population management action should be to mitigate the impacts of the abundant animals, not simply to reduce their numbers. Reduction of animal numbers without evidence that their impacts are reduced significantly, or that the resulting outcome is cost-effective cannot be justified on scientific, animal welfare/rights or economic grounds (see Caughley & Sinclair, 1994, for a major critique of wildlife ecology and management). There are often poor data on (1) the costs of damage and/or control and (2) the relationship between 'pest' animal density and the level of damage. These issues will be increasingly seen as major factors in the design and analysis of all wildlife management programmes and their justification to funding authorities and the public.

Primary production

Impacts on primary production, particularly agriculture and forestry, remain major reasons for wildlife population management in many countries. The wildlife may directly affect crops or seedlings (eating, trampling) or stimulate more complex impacts on pastures, leading to increased grazing pressure and ecosystem damage through erosion or weed growth. Grazing pressure and weed growth issues are major concerns in arid regions of Australia and are an argument for management of certain kangaroo species.

Disease and injury

Abundant wildlife may also be vectors, or reservoirs, of human or animal diseases. The prevalence of such diseases in wild populations is often density-dependent, providing a strong justification for managing the vector species.

The introduced Australian brushtail possum in New Zealand (bovine tuberculosis) or white-tailed deer (Lyme disease) in the USA are examples of such wildlife disease interactions. There can also be very direct impacts on humans that share habitat with wildlife, and these problems are exacerbated as wildlife densities increase. In many African and Asian situations this may involve trampling of homes and attacks on people, but there are similar concerns with white-tailed deer stags in urban fringes in the USA. However, in developed countries abundant wildlife are more likely to be involved in collisions with cars, resulting in financial costs, animal welfare concerns and occasional human injury (deer in USA, kangaroo species in Australia).

Conservation

Although impacts on human interests have been, and remain, important factors there is a growing need for population management to control conservation impacts of abundant wildlife; this relates to both introduced pest species and native species, in altered habitats and ecosystems. These undesirable effects include habitat damage or destruction, predation, ecosystem changes and impacts on threatened plant or animal species. As a result, abundant wildlife often results in multi-factorial and multi-species issues, and thus management goals may be complex and even competing. Impacts may even be on the abundant species itself (e.g. excessive numbers of koalas destroy koala habitat, leading to population crashes). Often the impacts on the abundant species are not themselves conservation issues, but they do raise animal welfare concerns and, in the case of iconic species, strong public concerns. A good example of the need to manage abundant native species for conservation goals concerns kangaroo management in reserves and conservation areas in arid regions of South Australia and Victoria. In these areas, the damaging results of grazing by introduced species (domestic stock and rabbits) have been greatly reduced through control strategies, yet grazing impacts are still significant through continued kangaroo abundance.

Species with multiple impacts

Further complicating the situation is the case where a species has multiple impacts, multiple stakeholders and potentially conflicting management agendas. The Australian brushtail possum in New Zealand is an example of such a situation (see Montague, 2000, for a detailed account of the possum in New Zealand). Arguably the greatest impact of the possum is on conservation, especially of native forests, threatened plants and native birds, and the land area needing possum management is very large. However, the possum also has animal health implications as a major vector of bovine tuberculosis. Strategies to mitigate these conservation and animal health challenges are not necessarily the same, or operational on the same lands. The common feature is the animal pest: management tools may be similar but the goals and measures of success are different. Controlling the disease in the possum population without affecting its size or reducing the possum's conservation impacts could potentially solve the animal health problem.

Target species

Species targeted for control fall into two main groups with substantial implications for product specification. Abundant species problems are often local, rather than 'global', although in some cases the abundant species may be widespread (e.g. white-tailed deer, kangaroo). There may also be an abundance of one species resulting from successful management of a second, especially of introduced predators (e.g. European fox in Australia). There is already concern in Western Australia that local abundance of formerly threatened native prey will have undesirable impacts on habitat (see Fletcher & Morris, Chapter 15). This is a likely outcome in many Australian situations involving reintroduction following predator control, because the available habitat has been greatly reduced or altered through clearance or agriculture, and native predators have been reduced or lost. Koala abundance problems in southeastern Australia are probably partly attributable to loss of native predators.

The other major target group, the introduced pests, poses different demands and requirements. The problems may be local or episodic, e.g. the house mouse in Australia, but more often they are widespread and their control is a major challenge. Wildlife management seems inevitably to bring a single species focus, 'the pest'. But in highly altered habitats the damage being mitigated may be due to several species and involve non-wildlife factors such as the altered habitat itself. Depending on the species involved, there may or may not be related native species, so the non-target characteristics of the control agent will depend on the situation. As mentioned earlier, since no land mammals are native to New Zealand (except two species of bat) a marsupial-specific agent should suffice from a conservation perspective, although undesirable effects on domestic animals would be a concern.

Approaches to fertility control

Not surprisingly, thinking and research on the development of fertility control for wildlife has been based on the human contraceptive paradigm. This has meant the availability of a considerable literature on which to base wildlife-targeted work. However, it has also been a limitation. Work on wildlife fertility control has tended to remain constrained by product specifications more appropriate for a human contraceptive agent, such as reversibility and low acceptance of pathology. However, irreversibility and local pathology may well be perfectly appropriate for a wildlife control agent especially if the target is an introduced pest species. Thus a focus on interfering in conception itself, say by targeting the egg or sperm, may not always be optimal for wildlife. At a technical level this is perhaps best illustrated by the focus on zona pellucida (ZP)-based vaccines for human contraception, on induction of B-cell but not T-cell responses (e.g. Rhim et al., 1992). This work involves mapping the B- and T-cell stimulatory regions (epitopes) of the ZP molecule. The aim is to produce a human vaccine which maximises transient blocking antibody B-cell responses and minimises, or eliminates, T-cell responses which tend to target tissues and cause pathology. In the case of ZP the result is unacceptable ovarian damage. Arguably, in many wildlife management scenarios, ovarian damage leading to permanent or long-term sterility would be the preferred outcome.

Fertility control for wildlife has had some success stories and some failures. There have been examples in captive animals, of effective fertility control using surgical sterilisation, hormonal agents such as agonists and antagonists, and vaccines (especially using porcine zona pellucida (PZP); e.g. Gao & Short, 1994; Ladd et al., 1994; Kirkpatrick et al., 1996; Nie et al., 1997; Nave et al., 2000; Fayrer-Hosken et al., 2000). These approaches have even been extended to wild populations. However, their major limitation is that all require the animal to be held and directly treated, usually by injection. Even if the agent can be delivered by a dart system this still requires close proximity to the target animal and involves high delivery costs. Arguably the major challenge for fertility control of wildlife is not to develop systems that work under such optimum conditions. The challenge is to deliver the agent remotely and, in the case of pest species, to do it cost effectively over very large land areas to a very high percentage of the population.

Reproductive targets

Because of its central role in reproduction the endocrine system was the first to be targeted in wildlife control (Bomford, 1990). Endocrine processes have been targeted using agents which act either centrally, depressing all reproductive activity (e.g. releasing hormone agonists), or peripherally (e.g. steroid hormones). Hormonal disruption often alters reproductive behaviour, and this may or may not be an advantage, depending on the species. If, for example, endocrine suppression of deer stags leads to failure of antler formation and rut, this may help reduce threats to humans and cars where deer habitat and urban areas overlap. However, there may be undesirable behavioural effects (e.g. in elephants; Fayrer-Hosken *et al.*, 2000) or, if suppression of dominant animals led to breeding by normally suppressed subordinates, increased rather than reduced breeding (e.g. Caughley *et al.*, 1992). Most endocrine control systems are drug-based, requiring direct delivery of an effective dose of the agent. Such agents could potentially be delivered orally if appropriate packaging systems were used, but the cost of such approaches and the need for dose regulation pose serious concerns. There are also problems of making the system specific. Releasing hormones are very simple peptides and highly conserved amongst mammals, while steroids are ubiquitous. Specificity may be enhanced, and non-target effects minimised, via the features of the delivery vehicle or delivery process. This is currently achieved with non-specific toxins such as '1080' for possum control in New Zealand (colour and bait size to reduce native bird uptake) and fox control in eastern Australia (burial to reduce native carnivore uptake). However, the agent itself would still pose significant risks if taken by non-target species.

Vaccine systems are promising alternatives but pose the significant challenge of generating an effective immune response. Although delivery of the effective dose of vaccine is important, low dose *per se* is not likely to be a major constraint because the immune system can respond to very small amounts of vaccine if presented appropriately. Many targets have been considered, including releasing hormones (GnRH), protein hormones and, in particular, gamete antigens (see Mate & Hinds, Chapter 19).

The challenge of delivery

There have been successes thus far in the application of fertility control to wildlife as a management tool. However, this has been limited to icon species, captive animals or relatively small island populations. The technology, although effective, is hands-on, involving surgery, implants and direct injection. However, for a population management tool to be of practical use it must be deliverable to the species at an ecological level. That is, it must reach, and affect, sufficient numbers of animals to achieve the required level of population control, while being cost-effective and safe. These are not insubstantial challenges, and they are not faced in the development of human contraceptives or fertility manipulation agents for domestic animals.

Candidate delivery systems fall into two broad classes: (1) non-disseminating systems, which are essentially orally active bait-delivered systems (Bradley et al., 1997), and (2) disseminating, or live vector, systems which can spread naturally through the target population (Williams, 1997). Non-disseminating systems will almost certainly be the first to be used at the field level because they pose fewer, and more defined, risks that do not necessarily involve living, genetically modified organisms (GMO). (For an extensive discussion of these issues, see Mate & Hinds, Chapter 19).

Field application

As discussed earlier, fertility control for wildlife management is far more than the development of a technological 'magic bullet': it also poses enormous ecological challenges (see Cowan et al., Chapter 20). There has been considerable work to examine the potential of fertility-control agents as population management tools at the field level. This has involved extensive long-term ecological experiments and mathematical modelling. These studies helped to define the characteristics of potentially effective agents and indicated that fertility control can work especially if used in conjunction with conventional control systems. An important outcome of this ecological work has been the clear indication that fertility control is a very slow means to reduce populations, especially of long-lived species. However, this has helped to define relevant questions. It has also suggested that fertility control can be an effective means to restrict population growth or recovery in cases such as mouse plagues, or following conventional control. Ecological issues currently being addressed include the impact of contraception at the population level on compensation in breeding or survival, behaviour, immigration and recruitment of young to the adult population.

CONCLUSIONS

Work to date indicates that developing effective fertility control vaccines for wildlife management is not an unreasonable goal. In particular, ZP-based virally-vectored vaccines can induce contraceptive immune responses, and oral vaccine systems are proving effective (Mate & Hinds, Chapter 19). It has yet to be established whether such systems will be effective in the field, on other than confined populations, or meet acceptable levels of safety. However, ecological experiments and modelling suggest such agents can be useful management tools (Cowan et al., Chapter 20).

The major constraint on the adoption of such technology may be public acceptability. Non-living, but gene technology produced, agents may be acceptable because they produce therapeutic agents that have had wide community acceptance. Live GMO-mediated fertility control, especially if viruses are involved, is far more problematic. However, new ways of dealing with abundant wildlife are urgently needed, and fertility control itself has wide community support. Broad-based community involvement, understanding and support will be essential elements in application of fertility control for wildlife management. The experience of GMO foods would suggest that these processes of communication and involvement must be initiated early when technologies are under development and not when they are ready for use.

ACKNOWLEDGEMENTS

This work was supported by the Australian Government's Cooperative Research Centres Programme. My colleagues (Phil Cowan and Karen Mate) made very helpful suggestions in the preparation of this chapter. I am indebted to Peter Bayliss, Steve McLeod and David Choquenot, who allowed me to report on their unpublished population modelling.

REFERENCES

Bomford, M. (1990). *A Role for Fertility Control in Wildlife Management?* Bureau of Rural Resources Bulletin No. 7, Canberra.

Bradley, M. P., Hinds, L. A. & Bird, P. H. (1997). A bait-delivered immunocontraceptive vaccine for the European red fox (*Vulpes vulpes*) by the year 2002? *Reproduction, Fertility and Development* **9**, 111–116.

Caughley, G. & Sinclair, A. R. E. (1994). *Wildlife Ecology and Management*. Blackwell Scientific, Boston, MA.

Caughley, G., Pech, R. & Grice, D. (1992). Effect of fertility control on a population's productivity. *Wildlife Research* **19**, 623–627.

Fayrer-Hosken, R. A., Grobler, D., Van Altena, J. J., Bertschinger, H. J. & Kirkpatrick, J. F. (2000). Immunocontraception of African elephants. *Nature* **407**, 149.

Fitzgerald, G., Wilkinson, R. & Saunders, L. (2000). Public perceptions and issues in possum control. In *The Brushtail Possum: Biology, Impact and Management of an Introduced Marsupial* (Ed. T. L. Montague), pp. 187–197, Manaaki Whenua Press, Lincoln, New Zealand.

Gao, Y. & Short, R. V. (1994). Fertlity control in wild mice after feeding with RU486 or methyl testosterone. *Journal of Reproduction and Fertility* **101**, 483–487.

Kirkpatrick, J. F., Turner, J. W., Liu, I. K. M. & Fayrer-Hosken, R. (1996). Applications of pig zona pellucida immunocontraception to wildlife fertility. *Journal of Reproduction and Fertility*, Suppl. **50**, 183–189.

Ladd, A., Tsong, Y. Y., Walfield, A. M. & Thau R. (1994). Development of an antifertility vaccine for pets based on active immunization against luteinizing hormone-releasing hormone. *Biology of Reproduction* **51**, 1076-1083.

Montague T. L. (Ed.) (2000).*The Brushtail Possum: Biology, Impact and Management of an Introduced Marsupial*. Manaaki Whenua Press, Lincoln, New Zealand.

Nave, C. D., Shaw, G., Short, R. V. & Renfree, M. B. (2000). Contraceptive effects of levonorgestrel implants in a marsupial. *Reproduction, Fertility and Development* **12**, 81-86.

Nie, G. Y., Butt, A. R., Salamonsen, L. A. & Findlay, J. K. (1997). Hormonal and non-hormonal agents at implantation as targets for contraception. *Reproduction, Fertility and Development* **9**, 65-76.

Oogjes, G. (1997). Ethical aspects and dilemmas of fertility control of unwanted wildlife: an animal welfarist's perspective. *Reproduction, Fertility and Development* **9**, 163-168.

Rhim, S. H., Millar, S. E., Robey, F., Luo, A. M., Lou, Y. H., Yule, T., Allen, P., Dean, J. & Tung, K. S. K. (1992). Autoimmune disease of the ovary induced by a ZP3 peptide from the mouse zona pellucida. *Journal of Clinical Investigation* **89**, 28-35.

Tyndale-Biscoe, C. H. (1994). Virus-vectored immunocontraception of feral animals. *Reproduction, Fertility and Development* **6**, 9-16.

Williams, C. K. (1997). Development and use of virus-vectored immunocontraception. *Reproduction, Fertility and Development* **9**, 169-178.

19

Contraceptive vaccine development

KAREN E. MATE & LYN A. HINDS

INTRODUCTION AND OBJECTIVES

Public acceptability of conventional strategies for the management of over-abundant wild animal populations (e.g. shooting, trapping, poisoning) is continuing to decline, particularly as they are not sustainable in the long term, especially for large, free-ranging populations. Significant interest is being shown in an ecologically-based approach to management of pest populations which recognises that a thorough understanding of the biology and ecology of the species is essential before integrated management of the species can be implemented (Singleton *et al.*, 1999).

This chapter, which should be read in conjunction with Rodger's commentary (Rodger, Chapter 18) focuses on the development of contraceptive vaccines that are highly effective, long-lasting and that can be delivered to large, free-ranging populations in an environmentally safe and publicly acceptable manner. Progress will be reviewed for (1) the identification of appropriate contraceptive targets, (2) the strategies employed to increase the magnitude and longevity of the immune response to specifically target the reproductive tract and ensure species specificity and (3) the delivery of the vaccine via both disseminating and non-disseminating systems. We also address some of the issues relating to public acceptance of some of the proposed methods for delivery of fertility control and future priorities for research.

STATE OF THE ART

Contraceptive targets

A long-term contraceptive effect has been achieved in several animal species following immunisation with reproductive hormones (Cowan *et al.*,

Chapter 20). There has been a concern, however, that endocrine interference for contraception in wildlife may disrupt normal mating behaviour and social structure with counter-productive results. Modelling indicates that the effectiveness of sterilisation as a means of population control is dependent on social structure and mating system, and that productivity could even increase if the sterilisation strategy removed dominance behaviour in a species where dominants normally suppress the breeding of subordinates. Therefore the major targets considered for contraception of wildlife are largely based on the disruption of fertilisation or early embryonic development. Although hormonal and non-hormonal agents involved in early implantation could be targeted (Nie *et al.*, 1997), the greatest interest has been in the use of egg and sperm antigens.

Zona pellucida antigens

The most effective structure studied for immunologically-based fertility control thus far is the zona pellucida (ZP), an extracellular matrix secreted around mammalian oocytes during the early stages of ovarian follicular development. The ZP is crucial to the success of fertilisation and pre-implantation embryonic development, and performs vital functions including sperm recognition, induction of the acrosome reaction and prevention of polyspermy (reviewed by Mate *et al.*, 2000).

Whole porcine ZP (PZP) was the first immunologically-based contraceptive effectively used for control of wildlife (Kirkpatrick *et al.*, 1992), and it continues to find practical application in the management of a broad range of captive and wild populations (reviewed by Kirkpatrick *et al.*, 1996; Barber & Fayrer-Hosken, 2000). The success of PZP vaccine results from its high contraceptive effectiveness (usually >90%) in a broad range of species, its lack of side-effects and the ability to deliver it via darts (Kirkpatrick *et al.*, 1996). Most recently, PZP has been used for fertility control of the free-living African elephant (Fayrer-Hosken *et al.*, 1999).

Despite its success in controlling some wildlife populations, PZP is not applicable for the control of large, wide-ranging pest species, such as the fox and rabbit in Australia and the brushtail possum in New Zealand. Fertility control for these types of pest populations demands a species-specific vaccine that can be remotely delivered. To minimise risk to non-target species, it would be preferable if specificity could be built into the vaccine at several levels including the target antigen and the delivery vector. Thus a major disadvantage of PZP is its effect across a broad range of species as well as a need to deliver at least two vaccinations.

The ZP matrix consists of only three major glycoproteins, ZP1, ZP2 and ZP3, and has therefore been relatively easy to characterise among species (reviewed by Epifano & Dean, 1994; Mate *et al.*, 2000). Since the ZP3 glycoprotein is (1) expressed uniquely in growing oocytes, (2) responsible for mediating initial order-specific sperm–egg binding and (3) is immunogenic, it has been identified as a potentially specific target for immunocontraceptive development (Epifano & Dean, 1994). The function of the ZP3 protein can, in multiple species, be blocked with antibodies resulting in infertility (Prasad *et al.*, 1996).

The contraceptive effects of immunisation with ZP antigens are due either to circulating antibodies, which prevent interaction of the sperm and egg at fertilisation, or cytotoxic T-cell mediated destruction of developing ovarian follicles causing permanent sterility (Lou *et al.*, 1996). This has prompted close examination of the T- and B-cell epitopes present in the ZP3 molecule (Rhim *et al.*, 1992; Lou *et al.*, 1996), motivated primarily by the requirement of a safe and reversible contraceptive for human application. Although any kind of ovarian pathology is undesirable for humans, and some wildlife species, the permanent sterility achieved by depletion of ovarian follicles would be a highly desirable outcome for the control of feral pest populations. One of the most divergent regions within the ZP3 protein consists of overlapping T- and B-cell epitopes and is believed to be involved in fertilisation.

The future of ZP-based vaccines depends upon detailed dissection of the ZP proteins, so that the most effective region(s) for manipulation of the immune responses in each particular target species can be identified. This may also be the only means of achieving the necessary level of species-specificity to meet regulatory requirements for registration of the final product for field use. Thus a further refinement to the use of single species-specific epitopes from the ZP proteins is the identification of species-specific epitopes from other reproductive antigens (implantation antigens, reproductive hormones, oviductal proteins, among others) and construction of polyepitope antigen genes encoding various combinations of these specific antigens and immune-enhancing elements. This approach may also address the need to induce an immune response in all recipients. By presenting several epitopes which will cause infertility, the proportion of non-responders to an individual epitope within a population should be reduced. Work of this nature is being conducted within the Pest Animal Control CRC for the mouse with the intention of assessing effectiveness in the mouse recombinant cytomegalovirus system (C. M. Hardy, unpublished data).

Sperm antigens

Immunisation with whole sperm preparations has induced infertility in the females of several mammalian species (McLaren, 1966; Duckworth *et al.*, 1998), and the presence of naturally occurring anti-sperm antibodies is known to cause infertility in women (Bronson *et al.*, 1984). However, the sperm surface is a complex structure. As hundreds of proteins are present, the identification of those involved in fertilisation and that are immuno-logically active has been a difficult process (reviewed by Frayne & Hall, 1999). To be effective as a contraceptive target, a sperm antigen must (1) be exclusively expressed in the male reproductive tract, (2) be accessible on the sperm surface and (3) either have a critical role in sperm function or cause sperm agglutination in the presence of antibody. Several sperm antigens have been identified that show promise as contraceptive vaccine targets. Despite much effort, however, immunisation trials with single sperm antigens have in general been unsuccessful in terms of contraceptive efficacy.

There are several possible explanations for the problems encountered with sperm antigens: (1) the inability to translate a successful native anti-gen into a successful synthetic or recombinant antigen; (2) the species-specificity of some sperm antigen effects; (3) the failure of antibodies to reach the female reproductive tract and (4) the redundancies built into the fertilisation process. Dozens of sperm proteins have been implicated in sperm–egg interaction; they presumably act in some cooperative manner to achieve maximum fertilising ability.

Manipulating and targeting the immune response

Unlike vaccines directed against infectious diseases, immunocontraceptive vaccines are directed against 'self' antigens that would not normally be re-cognised as foreign. Therefore, the 'self' antigen to be used in the vaccine must be presented in a 'foreign' or 'non-self' form to elicit an immune response that will also lead to infertility. Results from studies using viral-vectored immunocontraception indicate that presentation by a replicating virus effectively stimulates an immune response against the reproductive antigen. For example, presentation of mouse ZP3 in either ectromelia virus or mouse cytomegalovirus induces sustained and specific systemic anti-bodies after a single infection with the recombinant virus (Jackson *et al.*, 1998; M. Lawson, personal communication).

Oral delivery of fertility control agents requires induction of an appro-priate response by the mucosal immune system. In principle this should stimulate other parts of the mucosal immune system (including the reproductive tract), and elicit systemic immune responses. Among the inductive sites of the common mucosal system, the intestine has the greatest amount of lymphoid tissue. However, antigens must be protected from the acidic and proteolytic environment of the gut if they are to reach these inductive sites and initiate an immune response. Packaging the antigens in synthetic coating material such as microspheres, or in biological material such as plant cells, offers improved resistance to denaturation and better ability to stimulate the mucosal immune system (see Non-disseminating delivery systems, below).

Delivery mechanisms for immunocontraceptive vaccines

The delivery of any anti-fertility vaccine to wild animal populations over large areas raises unique challenges. It is essential to consider the distribution of the species under study, whether large-scale or localised control is desired, and the possible consequences for non-target species. The genetic heterogeneity of the wildlife population should also be considered since individual variability in immune responses to a vaccine could be significant. Effective application of a fertility control vaccine requires that a high level of sustained immunity be achieved amongst exposed individuals. Three potential delivery mechanisms for immunocontraceptive vaccines are under development. These include (1) disseminating genetically modified organisms (GMOs) such as recombinant viruses or bacteria, (2) non-disseminating, non-GMO product packaged in synthetic delivery systems and (3) non-disseminating GMOs in baits.

Disseminating GMOs have the greatest theoretical potential for use as vectors. A viral vector could potentially overcome problems associated with the distribution of an immunocontraceptive to control wild populations (Bomford, 1990). Some advantages of a disseminating, virally-vectored immunocontraceptive agent over a bait-delivered, non-disseminating immunocontraceptive agent are: (1) a replicating virus may induce a stronger immune response and greater immunological memory; (2) an infective agent can potentially spread rapidly through a population and be transmissible at low densities of host population; (3) a self-perpetuating, infectious agent is cheaper than baits, which must be manually applied; (4) a viral vector can be chosen for its species-specificity; (5) the agent overcomes problems associated with bait aversion or bait shyness; (6) it overcomes the precise timing necessary for bait delivery relative to the target animal's breeding cycle; (7) it reduces wastage associated with inadvertent multiple baiting of some individuals; (8) it should be more humane in use, and (9) it will be more cost-effective.

There are, however, several advantages of bait-delivered, non-disseminating agents, and for many pests, bait delivery may be the method of choice for political, social, economic and ecological reasons. For example, a bait-delivered immunocontraceptive might be more acceptable to the public than the use of a disseminating GMO and more easily managed for control activities because it can be readily withheld or withdrawn from use.

Disseminating delivery systems

Any vector chosen for delivery of an immunocontraceptive must possess a range of essential and desirable characteristics (Shellam, 1994; Chambers et al., 1999). Some of these include a requirement for high species-specificity, effective transmission between individuals, ability to be engineered to carry foreign DNA and an excellent understanding of the epidemiology of the proposed vector in the target population. Considerable research may be required to confirm the suitability of a vector.

The use of recombinant mouse viruses expressing mouse ZP3 is particularly promising. Proof of concept of the approach was achieved using ectromelia virus as a model development system for immunocontraceptive vaccines delivered by virus (Jackson et al., 1998). Mice inoculated with recombinant ectromelia virus expressing mouse ZP3 became infertile after 3 weeks and remained infertile for 5–9 months. Some mice became fertile again as their anti-ZP3 serum antibodies declined, but if re-inoculated with the recombinant virus they again became infertile. When the ovaries of these mice were examined two mechanisms of infertility were apparent. Approximately half of the animals showed some disruption to folliculogenesis, and thus lacked mature follicles and oocytes, but oophoritis was not observed. The remaining animals showed apparently normal development of follicles and oocytes. Ovarian immunohistochemistry demonstrated antibody binding to the oocytes, suggesting that after ovulation, spermatozoa would be unable to bind to the eggs (Jackson et al., 1998).

However, ectromelia virus does not occur naturally in the Australian environment and, therefore, would be more difficult to introduce for mouse control, as the political, social and regulatory hurdles would be more stringent. By contrast, another virus, mouse cytomegalovirus (MCMV), does occur in the Australian environment (Singleton et al., 1999) and demonstrates many of the characteristics defined by Shellam (1994) as essential and desirable for a vector. Laboratory strains of mice and wild-derived mice become infertile for periods greater than 6 months when inoculated with recombinant MCMV expressing ZP3 (Chambers *et al.*, 1999; M. Lawson *et al.*, unpublished data). A high level of prolonged infertility can also be induced in mice previously infected with a non-recombinant strain of MCMV (M. Lawson *et al.*, unpublished data). The mechanism of infertility has not been determined although histological changes are apparent in the ovaries.

Thus, although promising disseminating pathogens suitable for delivery of reproductive antigens have been identified for some pest species, exhaustive surveys have been unable to identify suitable pathogens in species such as the fox (Bradley *et al.*, 1997) and brushtail possum. Recently, however, research in the fox has commenced to determine the potential of canine herpes virus; this has previously been used to deliver recombinant vaccines to dogs (Xuan *et al.*, 1998). Results to date show that foxes can be experimentally infected with canine herpes virus and that immune responses to the virus are sustained over several months. Further work, to construct a recombinant canine herpes virus expressing a fox antigen, has commenced (G. Reubel, unpublished data).

Although the technical feasibility of viral-vectored vaccination with a contraceptive antigen has already been demonstrated for the laboratory mouse and rabbit, there is considerable debate over the safety of such a system by a public that is increasingly concerned about the release of any genetically modified organisms (see below). Thus, although a disseminating system may offer the most long-term promise for effective population control, it is likely that the less controversial non-disseminating agents will provide the first delivery mechanism for widespread delivery of contraceptive vaccines to wildlife.

Non-disseminating delivery systems

Successful vaccination of foxes against rabies in Europe using a recombinant vaccinia virus expressing a rabies-derived G protein, has been achieved using oral bait (Brochier *et al.*, 1991). When chewed, the bait releases the recombinant virus which is taken up by the tonsils. Many other species also take this vaccinia bait and become protected against rabies. For fertility control delivered via baits, the specificity of the target antigen will be critical as the bait may also be taken by non-target species. Bait design and formulations that selectively attract the target species will need to be developed. Furthermore, the nature of the included agent will define the most suitable method for production and packaging of the oral bait so that it either is effective as an aerosol or is protected until absorbed in the small intestine.

Synthetic packaging

Pharmaceutical companies have developed a range of oral particulate delivery systems based on immunostimulatory complexes (e.g. Quil A, cholesterol, phospholipid constructs), polymer matrix microspheres or liposomes that are designed to avoid digestion in the gut and to stimulate the immune system (Davis, 1996). The ability of microspheres containing a recombinant sperm antigen to stimulate a mucosal immune response in rats demonstrates the potential of these agents, but their current cost of production is not suited to broad-scale application to wildlife populations.

DNA vaccines

DNA vaccines contain genes encoding antigens which, upon delivery orally, nasally or by intramuscular or intravenous injection, are expressed *in situ* leading to an antigen-specific immunity. Although not currently suited to broad-scale use, DNA vaccines may contribute to a fundamental understanding of antigen processing and how the form of antigen (including the presence of DNA sequences *per se*) affects immunogenicity (Koide *et al.*, 2000).

Salmonella

Non-disseminating GMOs, such as AroA deletion mutants of Salmonella, are currently being developed and tested (Bradley *et al.*, 1997). Selected mutant strains of *Salmonella typhimurium* have the advantage that they are apathogenic without decreasing their immunogenicity, and they are not disseminating. Furthermore, the introduction of a 'suicide' plasmid into this system would have the added advantage of degrading the foreign DNA, thus making it more acceptable to regulatory bodies because the bait-delivered product would be devoid of foreign genetic material. Salmonella and *E. coli* are also being developed as infectious clones for delivery of other agents expressing foreign antigens (reviewed by Liljeqvist & Stahl, 1999).

Bacterial ghosts

Vaccination with killed microorganisms enables the immune system to come into risk-free contact with an otherwise harmful pathogen. Non-living vaccines can easily be produced by chemical or physical inactivation of pathogenic bacteria. Bacterial hosts have also been widely used for production and delivery of foreign proteins, including contraceptive antigens, with the bacterial proteins acting as immune potentiators. A recently developed alternative to the use of killed bacteria is the bacterial ghost system. Expression of cloned PhiX174 gene E in bacteria results in lysis of the bacteria by introducing a transmembrane tunnel structure through the cell envelope complex (Szostak *et al.*, 1996). The resulting bacterial ghosts have intact envelope structures devoid of cytoplasmic content including genetic material. Recombinant ghosts can be produced by insertion of foreign proteins into the inner bacterial membrane via specific N-, or C-, or N- and C-terminal anchor sequences prior to lysis. The advantages of recombinant bacterial ghosts as a production and delivery system include (1) full retention of immunogenic determinants as chemical or physical denaturation is not required; (2) insertion of the recombinant protein(s) into a highly immune stimulatory environment; (3) ability to present multiple antigenic determinants simultaneously; (4) inexpensive production costs and (5) a stable product that does not require specialised storage (reviewed by Szostak *et al.*, 1996; Lubitz *et al.*, 1999).

Plant vaccines

Plants offer a promising approach for both production and oral delivery of immunocontraceptive vaccines. The greatest advantage of a plant-based system is the possibility of utilising the plant material directly as a feed, thus generating a cheaply produced and edible vaccine.

A plant-based vaccine delivery system can be constructed in two ways: (1) establishment of plants that have the vaccine gene of interest stably integrated into their genome, or (2) utilisation of modified plant viruses to carry and express the vaccine gene in infected plants (Smith *et al.*, 1997). The recombinant plant virus system allows rapid transient expression that may find greatest application in the rapid screening of plant-produced peptide vaccines. Because of their relatively small size, plant viruses would be less suitable for expression of large complex antigens or the co-expression of immunomodulators or oral adjuvants (Smith *et al.*, 1997). The stable plant expression systems are, therefore, probably more suited to widescale production and delivery of contraceptive vaccines. Stable expression of hepatitis B surface antigen (Mason *et al.*, 1992) and Norwalk virus capsid protein (Mason *et al.*, 1996) was first achieved in potato and tobacco plants. A range of other vaccines for animal health and human health have since been produced in transgenic plants and have demonstrated to be immunogenic (reviewed by Hood & Jilka, 1999).

Public acceptance of GMOs

The development of fertility control agents that are delivered using GMOs, whether disseminating or non-disseminating, engenders an array of divergent responses from members of the public. Some take the view that disseminating systems will never be acceptable or adopted as a control strategy for wild pest populations in Australia or New Zealand. However, it is important in this debate to weigh the risks of genetically modified or engineered organisms against the inherent risks in conventional control methods. It is also imperative to separate the perceived and real risks of GMOs and balance this against the benefits gained in reducing the damage caused by the pests (Chambers *et al.*, 1997). The strategy adopted by the Vertebrate Biocontrol CRC, its successor the Pest Animal Control CRC, and the Marsupial CRC is that research should proceed incrementally with public discussion at each step so that its potential use can be weighed against the risks.

Most risks are not related to technical aspects associated with the development of fertility control, but to the issues of public acceptability of GMOs and maintaining the species-specificity of the control agent. Recent surveys conducted by Biotechnology Australia (Yann Campbell Hoare Wheeler, 1999) indicate that the level of public understanding of biotechnology is generally limited, but that attitudes over the last 3 years are changing in favour of GMO products as understanding increases. Similar surveys in New Zealand found that biological control in a generic sense was more appealing to the public than conventional control strategies, and the use of a GMO was considered the most acceptable of the biological methods (Fitzgerald *et al.*, 2000). The New Zealand public was most accepting of fertility control for possums (considered acceptable by 83% of respondents; Fitzgerald *et al.*, 2000). However, where GMO food products are concerned the public wants labelling information to be provided so that the consumer can make informed choices. In a similar manner, the public acceptability of immunocontraceptive vaccines will be heavily influenced by media interpretation of the technology (Williams, 1997). Many have argued for informed, public debate long before the release of an immunocontraceptive, whether it is a disseminating or non-disseminating agent (e.g. Oogjes, 1997).

FUTURE PRIORITIES

Antigen development

Single antigen products delivered in non-toxic baits may be the first generation product for fertility control. However, the subsequent development and use of multiple epitope vaccines, such as multiple antigen peptides, may increase species-specificity and could potentially overcome any problems of immunological non-response encountered in an outbred population. They may also stimulate higher, more sustained immune responses if coupled with immune modulators, such as cytokines, or other adjuvants such as cholera toxin, diptheria or tetanus.

Species-specificity

Attaining species-specificity will depend on the target animal, the ecosystem, the delivery system, local non-target species and, in general, the aims of the fertility control programme. Species-specificity can be defined at several levels: the reproductive target antigen, the delivery system and the social factors influencing or governing the spread of any disseminating agent (Tyndale-Biscoe, 1994). Ideally, all levels of specificity should be satisfied.

Oral delivery

For oral delivery of fertility control to be highly effective, any putative agent must induce an appropriate and sustained mucosal and/or systemic immunity that is then effective in the reproductive tract. Breaking tolerance in the intestinal tract to induce a sufficient immune response will be challenging. Bacterial artificial chromosomes, which are being designed to deliver recombinant vectors to specific immune sites in the gut, inclusion of potent mucosal stimulants and improved physical and biological packaging systems may provide a solution. It is also critical that the oral bait is designed to optimise acceptance by the target population (Cowan et al., Chapter 20).

Disseminating delivery vectors

For disseminating viral vectors, sustained immunity is required, and depending on the chosen vector, immunity may be boosted by reinfection or resurgence of latent virus. Continuing studies of the epidemiology of chosen vectors in the field and laboratory are required. The major prerequisite for any disseminating vector is species-specificity. Where a disseminating vector expressing the anti-fertility agent does not induce a productive infection in a non-target species, can it still produce an immune response (however small) resulting in infertility? Demonstration of species-specificity to the satisfaction of the public and regulatory authorities will be challenging.

CONCLUSION

Many scientific challenges face researchers as they continue the development of fertility control agents. Although the basic principles of design and delivery are similar among species, the final contraceptive vaccine must be specifically tailored for each target species and application. However, there are also native species that are considered pests in some areas, or in particular seasons, which require a very different management approach. Developing a variety of fertility control agents to meet these needs is essential if we are to reduce the impacts of these pests.

REFERENCES

Barber, M. R. & Fayrer-Hosken, R. A. (2000). Possible mechanisms of mammalian immunocontraception. *Journal of Reproductive Immunology* **46**, 103-124.

Bomford, M. (1990). *A Role for Fertility Control in Wildlife Management?* Bulletin No. 7, Canberra, Bureau of Rural Resources.

Bradley, M. P., Hinds, L. A. & Bird, P. H. (1997). A bait-delivered immunocontraceptive vaccine for the European red fox (*Vulpes vulpes*) by the year 2002? *Reproduction, Fertility and Development* **9**, 111-116.

Brochier, B., Kieny, M. P., Costy, F., Coppens, P., Bauduin, B., Lecocq, J. P., Languet, B., Chappuis, G., Desmettre, P., Afiademanyo, K., Libois, R. & Pastoret, P.-P. (1991). Large scale eradication of rabies using recombinant vaccinia-rabies vaccine. *Nature* **354**, 520-522.

Bronson, R. G., Cooper, G. & Rosenfield, D. (1984). Sperm antibodies: their role in infertility. *Fertility and Sterility* **42**, 171-182.

Chambers, L., Lawson, M. & Hinds, L. A. (1999). Biological control of rodents - the case for fertility control using immunocontraception. In *Ecologically-based Rodent Management* (Eds. G. R. Singleton, L. A. Hinds, H. Leirs & Z. Zhang), pp. 215-242. ACIAR, Canberra.

Chambers, L. K., Singleton, G. R. & Hood, G. M. (1997). Immunocontraception as a potential control method of wild rodent populations. *Belgian Journal of Zoology* **127**, 145-156.

Davis, S. S. (1996). Vaccine delivery systems: particulate delivery systems. *Vaccine* **14**, 672-680.

Duckworth, J. A., Buddle, B. M. & Scobie, S. (1998). Fertility of brushtail possums (*Trichosurus vulpecula*) immunised against sperm *Journal of Reproductive Immunology* **37**, 125-138.

Epifano, O. & Dean, J. (1994). Biology and structure of the zona pellucida: a target for immunocontraception. *Reproduction, Fertility and Development* **6**, 319-330.

Fayrer-Hosken, R. A., Bertschinger, H. J., Kirkpatrick, J. F., Grobler, D., Lamberski, N., Honneyman, G. & Ulrich, T. (1999). Contraceptive potential of the porcine zona pellucida vaccine in the African elephant (*Loxodonta africana*). *Theriogenology* **52**, 835-846.

Fitzgerald, G., Wilkinson, R. & Saunders, L. (2000). Public perceptions and issues in possum control. In *The Brushtail Possum: Biology, Impact and Management of an Introduced Marsupial* (Ed. T. L. Montague), pp. 187-197. Manaaki Whenua Press, Lincoln, New Zealand.

Frayne, J. & Hall, L. (1999). The potential use of sperm antigens as targets for immunocontraception; past, present and future. *Journal of Reproductive Immunology* **43**, 1-33.

Hood, E. E. & Jilka, J. M. (1999). Plant-based production of xenogenic proteins. *Current Opinion in Biotechnology* **10**, 382–386.

Jackson, R. J., Maguire, D. J., Hinds, L. A. & Ramshaw, I. A. (1998). Infertility in mice induced by a recombinant ectromelia virus expressing mouse zona pellucida glycoprotein 3. *Biology of Reproduction* **58**, 152–159.

Kirkpatrick, J. F., Liu, I. K. M., Turner, J. W., Jr, Naugle, R. & Keiper, R. R. (1992). Long-term effects of porcine zonae pellucidae immunocontraception on ovarian function of feral horses. *Journal of Reproduction and Fertility* **94**, 437–444.

Kirkpatrick, J. F., Turner, J. W., Liu, I. K. M. & Fayrer-Hosken, R. (1996). Applications of pig zona pellucida immunocontraception to wildlife fertility. *Journal of Reproduction and Fertility*, Suppl. **50**, 183–189.

Koide, Y., Nagata, T., Yoshida, A. & Uchijima, M. (2000). DNA vaccines. *Japanese Journal of Pharmacology* **83**, 167–174.

Liljeqvist, S. & Stahl, S. (1999). Production of recombinant subunit vaccines: protein immunogens, live delivery systems and nucleic acid vaccines. *Journal of Biotechnology* **73**, 1–33.

Lou, Y.-H., Bagavant, H., Ang, J., McElveen, M. F., Thai, H. & Tung, K. S. K. (1996). Influence of autoimmune disease on ZP3 contraceptive design. *Journal of Reproduction and Fertility*, Suppl. **50**, 159–163.

Lubitz, W., Witte, A., Eko, F. O., Kamal, M., Jechlinger, W., Brand, E., Marchart, J., Haidinger, W., Huter, V., Felnerova, D., Stralis-Alves, N., Lechleitner, S., Melzer, H., Szostak, M. P., Resch, S., Mader, H., Kuen, B., Mayr, B., Mayrhofer, P., Geretschlager, R., Haslberger, A. & Hensel, A. (1999) Extended bacterial ghost system. *Journal of Biotechnology* **73**, 261–273.

Mason, H. S., Ball, J. M., Shi, J.-J., Jiang, X., Estes, M. K. & Arntzen, C. J. (1996). Expression of Norwalk virus capsid protein in transgenic tobacco and potato and its oral immunogenicity in mice. *Proceedings of the National Academy of Sciences USA* **93**, 5335–5340.

Mason, H. S., Lam, D. M. & Arntzen, C. J. (1992). Expression of hepatitis B surface antigen in transgenic plants. *Proceedings of the National Academy of Sciences USA* **89**, 11745–11749.

Mate, K. E., Harris, M. S. & Rodger, J. C. (2000). Fertilisation in Monotreme, Marsupial and Eutherian Mammals. In *Fertilisation in Protozoa and Metazoan Animals* (Eds. J. J. Tarin & A. Cano), pp. 223–275. Springer-Verlag, Berlin.

McLaren, A. (1966). Studies on the isoimmunisation of mice with spermatozoa. *Fertility and Sterility* **17**, 492–497.

Nie, G. Y., Butt, A. R., Salamonsen, L. A. & Findlay, J. K. (1997). Hormonal and non-hormonal agents at implantation as targets for contraception. *Reproduction, Fertility and Development* **9**, 65–76.

Oogjes, G. (1997). Ethical aspects and dilemmas of fertility control of unwanted wildlife: an animal welfarist's perspective. *Reproduction, Fertility and Development* **9**, 163–168.

Prasad, S. V., Wilkins, B. & Dunbar, B. S. (1996). Molecular biology approaches to evaluate species variation in immunogenicity and antigenicity of zona pellucida proteins. *Journal of Reproduction and Fertility*, Suppl. **50**, 143–149.

Rhim, S. H., Millar, S. E., Robey, F., Luo, A. M., Lou, Y. H., Yule, T., Allen, P., Dean, J. & Tung, K. S. K. (1992). Autoimmune disease of the ovary induced by a ZP3 peptide from the mouse zona pellucida. *Journal of Clinical Investigation* **89**, 28–35.

Shellam, G. R. (1994). The potential of murine cytomegalovirus as a viral vector for immunocontraception. *Reproduction, Fertility and Development* **6**, 401-409.

Singleton, G. R., Leirs, H., Hinds, L. A. & Zhang, Z. (1999). Ecologically-based management of rodents - re-evaluating our approach to an old problem. In *Ecologically-based Rodent Management* (Eds. G. R. Singleton, L. A. Hinds, H. Leirs & Z. Zhang), pp. 17-29. ACIAR, Canberra.

Smith, G., Walmsley, A. & Polkinghorne, I. (1997). Plant-derived immunocontraceptive vaccines.*Reproduction, Fertility and Development* **9**, 85-89.

Szostak, M. P., Hensel, A., Eko, F. O., Klein, R., Auer, T., Mader, H., Haslberger, A., Bunka, S., Wanner, G. & Lubitz, W. (1996). Bacterial ghosts: non-living candidate vaccines. *Journal of Biotechnology* **44**, 161-170.

Tyndale-Biscoe, C. H. (1994). Virus-vectored immunocontraception of feral animals. *Reproduction, Fertility and Development* **6**, 9-16.

Williams, C. K. (1997). Development and use of virus-vectored immunocontraception. *Reproduction, Fertility and Development* **9**, 169-178.

Xuan, X., Tuchiya, K., Sato, I., Nishikawa, Y., Onoderaz, Y., Takashima, Y., Yamamoto, A., Katsumata, A., Iwata, A., Ueda, S., Mikama, T. & Otsuka, H. (1998). Biological and immunogenic properties of rabies virus glycoprotein expressed by canine herpes virus vector. *Vaccine* **16**, 969-976.

Yann Campbell Hoare Wheeler (1999). Research report into public attitudes towards biotechnology. Biotechnology Australia Report viewed at http://www.isr.gov.au/ba/index.html.

20

Field applications of fertility control for wildlife management

PHIL COWAN, ROGER PECH & PAUL CURTIS

INTRODUCTION AND OBJECTIVES

Reducing fertility, as opposed to increasing mortality, is an increasingly accepted approach to managing wildlife problems. New immunologically-based approaches (immunocontraception) are often coupled with new technologies for delivery, some of which involve biotechnology (Rodger, 1999). This has created an interesting situation where there is often public support for fertility control for ethical reasons but strong antipathy to genetic engineering (Fitzgerald *et al.*, 2000).

Significant progress has been made with the technical aspects of contraceptive vaccine development for wildlife management (Mate & Hinds, Chapter 19). The development and application of such vaccines, however, require that biotechnology runs in parallel with ecological, behavioural and modelling studies so that criteria established for successful applications in the field help define vaccine and delivery system design and efficacy targets (Sinclair 1997).

Equally, important political and societal concerns about these new approaches need to be considered right from the start. The potential use of transmissible delivery systems, such as genetically modified viruses, also raises international concerns about the risk of natural or illegal spread (Williams, 1997).

This chapter provides an overview of recent pen and field studies and modelling exercises to define the criteria for successful application of immunologically-based fertility control and the likely outcome of deployment of this technology. The chapter focuses on management of key mammal pests in three regions – house mouse, rabbit and fox in Australia, brushtail possum in New Zealand and white-tailed deer in North America. The first four species are introduced, the last is indigenous. The introduced species all impact primarily on agriculture and conservation, while the issues concerning white-tailed deer are driven largely by urban–wildlife conflicts. Because use of these technologies will ultimately be a decision for society, the chapter also reviews initiatives to identify community concerns and develop systems for promoting informed dialogue on the issues.

STATE OF THE ART

Brushtail possums in New Zealand

Brushtail possums (*Trichosurus vulpecula*) were introduced to New Zealand from Australia about 150 years ago to establish a fur industry. They now have serious impacts on native plants, animals and forest communities, and are the principal wildlife vector of bovine tuberculosis, TB (Montague, 2000). Direct costs of possum damage and control are estimated at NZ$80–100 million per annum, but non-tariff trade barriers against TB in livestock could cost up to NZ$1.3 billion (Montague, 2000). About NZ$65 million is spent annually controlling possums, mostly using toxic baits broadcast aerially or deployed in bait stations. Increasing pressure for alternative approaches comes from national and international concerns about killing as a means of management, environmental contamination and risks to non-targeted wildlife (Fitzgerald *et al.*, 2000). About NZ$5 million is spent annually on a wide range of approaches to possum biocontrol, with most aimed at immunologically-based fertility control (Cowan, 2000).

Delivery of fertility control is likely to be initially by bait or possibly aerosol. Transgenic plants, virus-like particles and bacterial ghosts are currently being evaluated as the bases for fertility control baits (Rodger, 1999). A bait-delivered system is also seen as a key step towards possible use of transmissible delivery. Possum-specific viruses and intestinal nematode parasites, particularly *Parastrongyloides trichosuri*, are being evaluated as potential biocontrol vectors (Cowan, 2000).

Ecological research and modelling both play key roles in the research programme. Modelling has been used to (1) identify the general requirements for efficacy of a fertility control vaccine (Barlow, 2000); (2) compare the efficacy of fertility control and culling (Barlow *et al.*, 1997); (3) assess the efficacy of transmissible and non-transmissible delivery systems (Barlow, 2000; Bayliss & Choquenot, 1999), and (4) identify how biological control can be best integrated with conventional control (Bayliss & Choquenot, 1999).

Figure 20.1 Predicted reduction in possum numbers resulting from transmissible immunocontraception in relation to percentage of infected females sterile at mating and contact rate for vector transmission (number of potentially infectious contacts per infectious possum per unit time). (From Barlow, 2000.)

The criterion for successful fertility control of possums is qualitatively similar to that applying to any population (Barlow, 2000). Basically, the birth rate must be reduced to match the minimum or density-independent death rate for possums, when about 66% of females are sterile at mating. For a disseminating system, modelling confirms that a genetically modified vector must attain high prevalence in the face of competition with existing native strains, it must persist, and it must result in a high proportion of animals becoming permanently sterile (Figure 20.1). Inherited non-response can be controlled by appropriate combinations of biological and conventional control (Bayliss & Choquenot, 1999). Overall, modelling suggests that fertility control for possums is theoretically possible in ecological terms (Barlow, 2000). The slow decline in possum numbers predicted under the action of fertility control alone, however, highlights the need for its integration with conventional control as the most effective strategy (Bayliss & Choquenot, 1999).

Field- and pen-based projects have used surgical sterilisation (castration, ovariectomy, tubal ligation) to assess responses that might reduce the efficacy of fertility control (Jolly et al., 1998; Ramsey, 2000). A 5-year population study of free-living possums, where 0%, 50%, or 80% of females were sterilised by tubal ligation, confirmed that sterility exceeding 50% is

needed to reduce *in situ* recruitment of young sufficiently to produce negative population growth. However, immigration had the potential to swamp
effects of fertility control, emphasising the need for application of fertility control over large areas. Possible density-dependent changes in survival
and recruitment are still being analysed. Tubal ligation did not significantly
influence patterns of movement or interactions between possums (Jolly
et al., 1998; Ramsey, 2000). However, prevalence of a socially transmitted,
possum-specific bacterium (*Leptospira interrogans* serovar *balcanica*) was
elevated where 80% of females were tubally ligated, probably because of increased frequency of oestrus and associated social contacts. Fertility control
could thus lead indirectly to higher transmission rates of vectors or diseases such as TB. Sterility (by castration or ovariectomy) altered the movement patterns of adult male possums to resemble those of females
(D. S. L. Ramsey, unpublished data) with possible implications for vector transmission. Movements of females were unaffected by ovariectomy.
Genetic analysis of the possum mating system found little evidence for
strong structuring (Taylor *et al.*, 2000), so effects of social structure on vector transmission are likely to be minor. In general, the results of all ecological and behavioural research suggest that few of the problems hypothesised
for fertility control are likely to result in significant reductions in predicted
efficacy. Public attitudes to possum management in New Zealand are reasonably well defined (Fitzgerald *et al.*, 2000; Parliamentary Commissioner
for the Environment, 2000). Some clear messages emerge from these studies. Doing nothing about the possum problem is not acceptable to most New
Zealanders. Short- and long-term safety and specificity of control methods
are key concerns, and this was reflected in the greater acceptability of shooting and trapping relative to the use of toxins or biological control. Among
proposed methods of biological control, those that did not involve genetic
technologies were more acceptable. Contraception was favoured over other
approaches that targeted embryos or pouch young. Genetic modification (in
general) and of native plants (in particular) was strongly opposed by the
Maori. There is an urgent need for education, communication and partici-
patory decision-making to help the public form considered opinions about
both ongoing research and the ultimate application of fertility control technology for possum management.

Foxes, rabbits and house mice in Australia

The introduced species, the European red fox (*Vulpes vulpes*), the European
rabbit (*Oryctolagus cuniculus*) and the house mouse (*Mus domesticus*) are

all agricultural and environmental pests. Rabbits cause most agricultural damage and major, though largely unquantified, impacts on native plants and animals (Williams *et al.*, 1995). House mice are serious pests in the cereal production areas of southeastern Australia, with eruptions occurring more frequently since the 1980s (Singleton & Brown, 1999). In contrast, foxes are managed mainly to protect native fauna, although lamb predation can also be significant locally (Saunders *et al.*, 1995). New control techniques for foxes, rabbits and house mice are needed that are species-specific, humane and cost-effective.

Field studies and modelling have been used to assess the potential effectiveness of fertility control. A study using tubal ligation to mimic permanent immunocontraception in female rabbits was conducted at sites in eastern Australia and southwest Western Australia (Twigg & Williams, 1999; Twigg *et al.*, 2000). Sterility (0%, 40%, 60% and 80%) was maintained over 3 years in rabbit populations isolated by cleared buffer zones. High levels of sterility, *c.* 80%, effectively prevented increases in rabbit numbers during the breeding season. Fertile animals on the treated sites did not show compensatory breeding, but the rabbit populations showed strong compensation through density-dependent juvenile survival and higher survival rates of sterile rabbits.

Rates of increase of house mice in pens were reduced substantially when 67% of females were sterilised, but with little difference between sterilisation by tubal ligation and ovariectomy (Chambers *et al.*, 1999). This suggests there is no requirement to maintain hormonal competence for fertility control to be effective for mice. The pen trials provided little opportunity, however, to assess possible compensatory changes in survival rates.

Equivalent experiments with foxes have not been feasible for logistical reasons, but behavioural changes that might be induced by sterilisation were assessed. Surgically sterilised vixens tolerated greater territorial overlap with similarly treated animals (compared with intact vixens), but there was little indication of any behavioural changes that would compensate for fertility control (G. Saunders, J. McIlroy & M. Berghout, unpublished data). Potential compensation related to a dominance hierarchy in reproductive performance (Caughley *et al.*, 1992) is yet to be assessed in areas of high fox density, but is unlikely to be significant in most of semi-arid Australia.

The field experiments and modelling highlight the important influences of spatial and temporal environmental variability on the optimal timing and effectiveness of fertility control (Pech & Hood, 1998; Pech *et al.*, 1999; Hood *et al.*, 2000). For example, even without demographic compensation, environmentally induced fluctuations in the abundance of foxes could easily mask the impact of bait-delivered fertility control unless relatively high levels of bait uptake are achieved (Pech *et al.*, 1997).

Damage caused by rabbits, foxes and mice frequently occurs over large regions, where labour-intensive control is not feasible or cost-effective. Consequently, disseminating immunocontraception appears to have substantial advantages. Murine cytomegalovirus (MCMV) is the most promising disseminating vector for mice (Robinson *et al.*, 1999). MCMV recombinants expressing a mouse zona pellucida protein induce high levels of infertility in wild mice (Mate & Hinds, Chapter 19). MCMV already exists in wild mice in Australia, is species-specific, highly infectious and can reinfect mice previously infected with MCMV. Improved models of mouse plagues (Pech *et al.*, 1999) are being used to define the criteria for success of immunocontraceptive MCMV in suppressing plagues.

Myxoma virus was selected originally as the candidate vector for wild rabbits because its epidemiology is relatively well understood, it is now endemic in Australia, and there are no native lagomorphs in Australia. However cross-strain immunity is a major hurdle because a high proportion of rabbits can survive infection by field strains and become immune (Kerr *et al.*, 1998). Maximum suppression of rabbits is predicted if a benign strain is used as a vector, but less than 50% probability of persistence for a sterilising strain competing with equivalent field strains (Hood *et al.*, 2000). Tactical reinfection of rabbit populations remains an option but would require further epidemiological studies to determine suitable times for inoculation (Robinson *et al.*, 1999).

Bait delivery is the preferred option for foxes. Provided the technique is fox-specific, the baits could be spread from aircraft, a technique currently used highly successfully with lethal baits in Western Australia (Thomson *et al.*, 2000). The predicted slow decline in fox abundance with fertility control (Pech *et al.*, 1997; Figure 20.2) could be enhanced by combination with lethal control in a buffer zone (Thomson *et al.*, 2000).

Although fewer pests is the direct outcome of fertility control, the fundamental aim is a reduction in damage to a level that is cost-effective. For rabbits, acceptable thresholds for agricultural damage do not necessarily coincide with conservation objectives, because rabbits also support populations of introduced predators that threaten native species (Pech & Hood, 1998). Beneficial levels of fox control will depend on the prey species requiring protection and the ability of the habitat to provide refuge from predation (Sinclair *et al.*, 1998; R. P. Pech & T. Arthur, unpublished data). Some information is available on damage to crops by house mice (P. R. Brown &

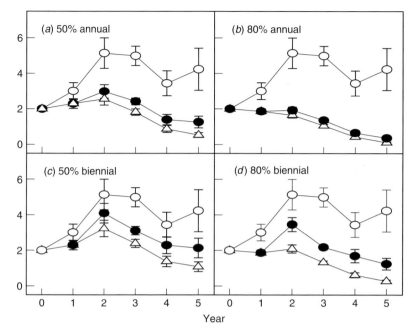

Figure 20.2 Simulation of experiments manipulating fox fertility by bait delivery, showing the density of female foxes with (a) 50% treated every year, (b) 80% treated every year, (c) 50% treated every second year and (d) 80% treated every second year. The control group (no reduction in fertility) is the same in each "experiment" (○, no treatment; ●, temporary infertility; △, permanent infertility. Error bars indicate the standard error of the mean). (From Pech et al., 1997.)

G. R. Singleton, unpublished data), but further data are required to determine fully the benefits of fertility control.

Apart from rabbits (Morgan, 1995), there have been few surveys in Australia of public attitudes to methods of mammal pest management. Johnston & Marks (1997) found reasonably strong support (58%) for biological control for some pest species, particularly rabbits. Species-specific toxins were the preferred option for control of foxes and feral cats, but fertility control was also strongly supported for a number of species. The survey did not, however, canvass opinions about biological controls or delivery methods that involved genetic modification.

White-tailed deer in the USA

White-tailed deer (*Odocoileus virginianus*) have reached unprecedented numbers in the last decade. More than 1 million deer–vehicle collisions occur annually, with costs exceeding US$1.1 billion (Conover *et al.*, 1995). White-tailed deer host the vectors of Lyme and other human diseases, cause crop damage exceeding US$100 million p.a. (Conover, 1997) and impact on commercial forestry (Conover *et al.*, 1995).

Safety concerns and ethical issues have rendered recreational hunting impractical in many residential areas and have sparked interest in fertility control (e.g. Turner *et al.*, 1997). Boone & Weigert (1994) found that sterilisation could be effective as a deer control strategy only following an initial population reduction. Seagle & Close (1996) suggested that contraception may curb population growth over a long time horizon; however, fertility control may be ineffective for reducing herd size with low mortality rates. Modelling by Hobbs *et al.* (2000) suggested that the proportion of infertile females, efficacy of techniques and persistence of reproductive inhibition were critical factors to be assessed in a full evaluation of fertility control for deer management.

Because annual mortality rates for suburban deer herds are often very low, a large proportion of female deer (>50% and possibly up to 90%) needs to be effectively treated to curb or reduce population growth (Hobbs *et al.*, 2000; Rudolph *et al.*, 2000). The primary vaccine for deer immuno-contraception contains porcine zona pellucida (PZP), the most commonly used antigen for fertility control in female mammals. A second approach has used gonadotrophin-releasing hormone agonists (GnRH) (Miller *et al.*, 1997). Both PZP and GnRH vaccines have reduced fawning rates by about 90% in captive (Miller *et al.*, 2000) and free-ranging white-tailed deer (Curtis *et al.*, 2002). Currently, the long-term costs of GnRH and PZP treatments for deer are prohibitive because of the need for booster vaccination on a regular schedule (Rudolph *et al.*, 2000; Miller *et al.*, 2000).

Safe and cost-effective delivery techniques continue to be the most important research need. Although anti-fertility agents have been successfully administered using both darts and biobullets, oral application of anti-fertility agents is needed for practical application to larger deer populations or areas. The cost of labour and materials and the practicality of treating an adequate number of deer are likely to limit the use of contraceptives to small insular herds that are habituated to humans (Rudolph *et al.*, 2000). If short-term population reduction is the management goal, herds will need to be reduced to an acceptable density with some form of lethal control and then treated with contraceptive vaccines to stabilise herd growth (Nielsen *et al.*, 1997).

Deer–human conflicts are socially defined. In some cases, it may not be possible to achieve community consensus for a single deer management approach, and the best outcome may be to achieve consent for management from key stakeholder groups (Curtis & Hauber, 1997). Solving deer conflicts may involve changing stakeholder attitudes or behaviours, as well as modifying deer behaviours or reducing herd size (Curtis et al., 2000).

PRIORITIES FOR THE FUTURE

Population-level efficacy

For most mammal pests, the relationships between pest abundance and damage are only poorly known, if at all. Without that information, the required reduction in pest abundance to mitigate damage to acceptable levels cannot be defined – and without definition of damage thresholds, it is difficult to assess the most effective control strategies and tools, or how to integrate fertility inhibition most efficiently with other methods. Fertility control needs to be assessed in the context of alternative management options. For example, Hood et al. (2000) constructed a 'pay-off' function to determine the conditions where immunocontraceptive myxoma virus would add value to the impact of endemic lethal field strains on rabbit numbers.

For field application, demographic compensation is the most important issue. More experiments are needed to allow better predictions of the ability of pests like possums, foxes, rabbits, house mice and deer to compensate for control. Because the pests involved are often being managed, co-research with pest managers within an adaptive management framework is likely to be an efficient way forward.

Field data and modelling can be used iteratively to improve confidence in the outcomes of fertility control. Two priorities are modelling of pest control under conditions of environmental variability and spatial models of population dynamics, impacts and management. Modelling and experimental analysis are also needed to address issues relating to possible selection for non-response to fertility control vaccines and/or infection with vectors (Bayliss & Choquenot, 1999) that are likely to impact on the long-term effectiveness of fertility control.

Cost-effective delivery systems

Delivery systems need to be appropriate for the particular species and problem. Research, therefore, needs to continue on a range of options including direct delivery by biobullet or darting, oral delivery by baits or aerosols from stations or aerially broadcast, and transmissible delivery. For bait delivery, social and other factors can limit access to baits, and so research will be needed to ensure that the target bait acceptance level is achievable for the desired population reduction. The development of effective baiting strategies for wildlife vaccination against rabies provides a useful model.

Like conventional biological control, the use of transmissible fertility control offers the prospect of low-cost, self-sustaining pest control. However, understanding of vector epidemiology, and hence the ability to predict the effectiveness of biocontrol agents, is severely limited. Significant progress has been made in modelling the epidemiology of immunocontraceptive myxoma virus (Hood *et al.*, 2000), but critical data on the dynamics and spread of field strains of myxoma virus (P. J. Kerr, unpublished data), MCMV and the parasite *P. trichosuri* (M. Ralston & P. Cowan, unpublished data) are only beginning to emerge. Epidemiological data also need to be better integrated with ecological data to improve predictive models.

Acceptability and use

Product development research will be a key to ensuring acceptability and use of fertility control products by management agencies. Factors that influence cost and ease of use, such as longevity of infertility, single versus multiple dose vaccination, and remote delivery, will be critical areas for research.

Safety is a major factor influencing likely acceptability of field application of fertility control technologies. Research is needed to maximise species-specificity of fertility control (Mate & Hinds, Chapter 19) and species-specificity of delivery so that effects on non-target species, environmental contamination and food-chain flow-on effects are minimised. For field application to species such as deer that are hunted for food, it will also be critical to show that treated animals pose no secondary hazards if consumed. Social research will also be needed to address political and societal concerns about these new approaches to controlling wildlife abundance, particularly where they involve genetic modification.

CONCLUSION

Immunologically-based fertility control holds great promise as another tool for controlling wildlife abundance. Technically, much remains to be achieved, and it is likely to be 3–5 years before prototype products are fully developed. Ecological and behavioural research that has run in parallel with vaccine development for possums, rabbits, foxes, mice and deer is providing both input to the criteria for success of the vaccines in the field and confidence that field applications of the vaccines will produce reductions in wildlife populations sufficient to mitigate pest impacts. The development of cost-effective delivery systems and the acceptability of such vaccines by the public and management agencies will be major challenges for successful implementation.

ACKNOWLEDGEMENTS

P. Cowan was funded by the NZ Foundation for Research, Science & Technology, Contract C09X009. P. Curtis acknowledges the contributions of Lowell Miller, USDA National Wildlife Research Center, Fort Collins; Milo Richmond and Robert Pooler, USGS/Biological Resources Division – Cooperative Fish and Wildlife Research Unit, Cornell University; and Dr George Mattfeld and John O'Pezio, New York State Department of Environmental Conservation. Lyn Hinds, Janine Duckworth and Dave Ramsey commented on the manuscript, which was edited by Anne Austin.

REFERENCES

Barlow, N. D. (2000). Models for possum management. In *The Brushtail Possum: Biology, Impact and Management of an Introduced Marsupial* (Ed. T. L. Montague), pp. 208-219. Manaaki Whenua Press, Lincoln, New Zealand.

Barlow, N. D., Kean, J. M. & Briggs, C. J. (1997). Modelling the relative efficacy of culling and sterilisation for controlling populations. *Wildlife Research* **24**, 129-141.

Bayliss, P. & Choquenot, D. (1999). Ecological modelling and possum biocontrol in New Zealand. In *Advances in the Biological Control of Possums*, Royal Society of New Zealand Miscellaneous Series 56 (Ed. G. Sutherland), pp. 19-23. Royal Society of New Zealand, Wellington, New Zealand.

Boone, J. L. & Wiegert, W. G. (1994). Modelling deer herd management: sterilization is a viable option. *Ecological Modelling* **72**, 175-186.

Caughley, G., Pech, R. & Grice, D. (1992). Effect of fertility control on a population's productivity. *Wildlife Research* **19**, 623-627.

Chambers, L. K., Singleton, G. R. & Hinds, L. A. (1999). Fertility control of wild mouse populations: the effects of hormonal competence and an imposed level of sterility. *Wildlife Research* **26**, 579-591.

Conover, M. R. (1997). Monetary and intangible valuation of deer in the United States. *Wildlife Society Bulletin* **25**, 298-305.

Conover, M. R., Pitt, W. C., Kessler, K. K., DuBow, T. J. & Sanborn, W. A. (1995). Review of human injuries, illnesses, and economic losses caused by wildlife in the United States. *Wildlife Society Bulletin* **23**, 407-414.

Cowan, P. E. (2000). Biological control of possums: prospects for the future. In *The Brushtail Possum: Biology, Impact and Management of an Introduced Marsupial* (Ed. T. L. Montague), pp. 262-270. Manaaki Whenua Press, Lincoln, New Zealand.

Curtis, P. D. & Hauber, J. R. (1997). Public involvement in deer management decisions: Consensus versus consent. *Wildlife Society Bulletin* **25**, 399-403.

Curtis, P. D., Decker, D. J. & Schusler, T. M. (2000). Beyond citizen task forces: the future of community-based deer management. In *Proceedings of the 19th Vertebrate Pest Control Conference*, San Diego, California (Eds. T. P. Salmon & A. C. Crabb), pp. 175-179.

Curtis, P. D., Pooler, R. L., Richmond, M. E., Miller, L. A., Mattfeld, G. F. & Quimby, F. W. (2002). Comparative effects of GNRH and porcine zona pellucida immunocontraceptive vaccines for controlling reproduction in white-tailed deer. *Reproduction*, Suppl. **60**, 131-141.

Fitzgerald, G., Wilkinson, R. & Saunders, L. (2000). Public perceptions and issues in possum control. In *The Brushtail Possum: Biology, Impact and Management of an Introduced Marsupial* (Ed. T. L. Montague), pp. 187-197. Manaaki Whenua Press, Lincoln, New Zealand.

Hobbs, N. T., Bowden, D. C. & Baker, D. L. (2000). Effects of fertility control on populations of ungulates: general, stage-structured models. *Journal of Wildlife Management* **64**, 473-491.

Hood, G. M., Chesson, P. & Pech R. P. (2000). Biological control using sterilising viruses: host suppression and competition between viruses in non-spatial models. *Journal of Applied Ecology* **37**, 914-925.

Johnston, M. J. & Marks, C A. (1997). *Attitudinal Survey on Vertebrate Pest Management in Victoria.* Department of Natural Resources and Environment Report Series No. 3. Agriculture Victoria, Melbourne.

Jolly, S. E., Scobie, S., Spurr, E. B., McCallum, C. & Cowan, P. E. (1998). Behavioural effects of reproductive inhibition in brushtail possums. In *Biological Control of Possums*, Royal Society of New Zealand Miscellaneous Series 45 (Ed. R. Lynch), pp. 125-127. Royal Society of New Zealand, Wellington.

Kerr, P. J., Twigg, L. E., Silvers, L., Lowe, T. J. & Forrester, R. I. (1998). Serological monitoring of the epidemiology of myxoma virus to assess the effects of imposed fertility control of female rabbits on myxomatosis. *Wildlife Research* **25**, 123-131.

Miller, L. A., Johns, B. E. & Elias, D. J. (1997). Comparative efficacy of two immunocontraceptive vaccines. *Vaccine* **15**, 1858-1862.

Miller, L. A., Johns, B. E. & Killian, G. J. (2000). Long-term effects of PZP immunization on reproduction in white-tailed deer. *Vaccine* **18**, 568-574.

Montague, T. L. (Ed.) (2000). *The Brushtail Possum: Biology, Impact and Management of an Introduced Marsupial.* Manaaki Whenua Press, Lincoln, New Zealand.

Morgan, R. (1995). *Rabbit Problem Survey.* Report prepared for the Australian and New Zealand Rabbit Calicivirus Disease Program. Roy Morgan Research Centre.

Nielsen, C. K., Porter, W. F. & Underwood, H. B. (1997). An adaptive management approach to controlling suburban deer. *Wildlife Society Bulletin* **25**, 470-477.

Parliamentary Commissioner for the Environment (2000). *Caught in the Headlights: New Zealanders' Reflections on Possums, Control Options and Genetic Engineering.* Wellington: Parliamentary Commissioner for the Environment – Te Kaitiaki Taiao a Te Whare Paremata.

Pech, R. P. & Hood, G. M. (1998). Foxes, rabbits, alternative prey and rabbit calicivirus disease: ecological consequences of a new biological control agent for an outbreaking species in Australia. *Journal of Applied Ecology* **35**, 434-453.

Pech, R. P., Hood, G. M., McIlroy, J. C. & Saunders, G. (1997). Can foxes be controlled by reducing their fertility? *Reproduction, Fertility and Development* **9**, 41-50.

Pech, R. P., Hood, G. M., Singleton, G. R., Salmon, E., Forrester, R. I. & Brown, P. R. (1999). Models for predicting plagues of house mouse (*Mus domesticus*) in Australia. In *Ecologically-based Management of Rodent Pests* (Eds. G. Singleton, H. Leirs, Z. Zhang & L. Hinds), pp. 81-112. Australian Centre for International Agricultural Research, Canberra.

Ramsey, D. S. L. (2000), The effect of fertility control on the population dynamics and behaviour of brushtail possums (*Trichosurus vulpecula*) in New Zealand. In *Proceedings of the 19th Vertebrate Pest Control Conference*, San Diego, California (Eds. T. P. Salmon & A. C. Crabb), pp. 212-216.

Robinson, A. J., Jackson, R. J., Merchant, J. C., Kerr, P. J., Holland, M. K., Lawson, M. A. & Shellam, G. R. (1999). Biological control of pest mammals in Australia - progress towards virally vectored immunocontraception for the mouse and rabbit. *Recent Advances in Microbiology* **7**, 63-98.

Rodger, J. C. (1999). Delivery, arguably the major challenge for possum biocontrol. In *Advances in the Biological Control of Possums*, Royal Society of New Zealand Miscellaneous Series 56 (Ed. G. Sutherland), pp. 16-18. Royal Society of New Zealand, Wellington.

Rudolph, B. A., Porter, W. F. & Underwood, H. B. (2000). Evaluating immunocontraception for managing suburban white-tailed deer in Irondequoit, New York. *Journal of Wildlife Management* **64**, 463-473.

Saunders, G., Coman, B., Kinnear, J. & Braysher, M. (1995). *Managing Vertebrate Pests: Foxes*. Canberra: Bureau of Resource Sciences, Australian Government Publishing Service.

Seagle, S.W. & Close, J. D. (1996). Modelling white-tailed deer *Odocoileus virginianus* population control by contraception. *Biological Conservation* **76**, 87-91.

Sinclair, A. (1997). Fertility control of mammal pests and the conservation of endangered marsupials. *Reproduction, Fertility and Development* **9**, 1-16.

Sinclair, A. R. E., Pech, R. P., Dickman, C. R., Hik, D., Mahon, P. & Newsome, A. E. (1998). Predicting the effects of predation and the conservation of endangered prey. *Conservation Biology* **12**, 564-575.

Singleton, G. & Brown, P. R. (1999). Management of mouse plagues in Australia: integration of population ecology, bio-control and best farm practice. In *Advances in Vertebrate Pest Management* (Eds. D. P. Cowan & C. J. Feare), pp. 189-203. Filander Verlag, Fürth, Germany.

Taylor, A. C., Cowan, P. E., Fricke, B. L. & Cooper, D. W. (2000). Genetic analysis of the mating system of the common brushtail possum (*Trichosurus vulpecula*) in New Zealand farmland. *Molecular Ecology* **9**, 869-879.

Thomson, P. C., Marlow, N. J., Rose, K. & Kok, N. E. (2000). The effectiveness of a large-scale baiting campaign and an evaluation of a buffer zone strategy for fox control. *Wildlife Research* **27**, 465-472.

Turner, J. W., Jr, Kirkpatrick, J. F. & Liu, I. K. M. (1997). Immunocontraception in white-tailed deer. In *Contraception in Wildlife Management*, APHIS Technical Bulletin Number 1853 (Ed. T. J. Kreeger), pp. 147-159. USDA National Wildlife Research Center, Fort Collins, CO.

Twigg, L. E. & Williams, C. K. (1999). Fertility control of overabundant species; can it work for feral rabbits? *Ecology Letters* **2**, 281-285.

Twigg, L. E., Lowe, T. J., Martin, G. R., Wheeler, A. G., Gray, G. S., Griffin, S. L., O'Reilly, C. M., Robinson, D. J. & Hubach, P. H. (2000). Effects of surgically imposed sterility on free-ranging rabbit populations. *Journal of Applied Ecology* **37**, 16–39.

Williams, C. K. (1997). Development and use of virus-vectored immunocontraception. *Reproduction, Fertility and Development* **9**, 169–178.

Williams, C. K., Parer, I., Coman, B. J., Burley, J. & Braysher, M. L. (1995). *Managing Vertebrate Pests: Rabbits*. Canberra: Bureau of Resource Sciences / CSIRO Division of Wildlife and Ecology, Australian Government Publishing Service.

PART V

Reproduction science in non-mammalian species

My own suspicion is that the universe is not only queerer than we suppose, but queerer than we can suppose.

J. B. S. Haldane (essay, 'Possible Worlds', 1927)

A cursory glance at reproductive biology textbooks is enough to confirm that most biologists are exclusively mammal aficionados! Even then, most research is directed at the common mammals – domestic livestock, laboratory rodents and primates, and humans. There is a danger to this provincial approach, that is, that conventional wisdom on reproductive mechanisms is derived from a very few and (in the case of livestock and laboratory animals) genetically homogeneous groups of species. Thus, we teach the science of reproduction to our students on the basis of learned knowledge from an embarrassingly few and (in the opinion of the editors) rather boring, uni-dimensional species. As our text has emphasised, there are thousands of species that have never been studied. To do so would require armies of postdoctoral fellows and vastly expanded sources of funding. Take fishes as a prime example: rich diversity in taxonomy but also in the ways in which they reproduce. In this section a striking picture of this unbeliev-able diversity is presented. For species conservation, where knowledge of reproduction can be crucial to the appropriate design and implementation of conservation measures, how are we to prioritise studies on fish repro-duction? Given that there are 24 000 species, should we only study those that can be used for food production? Will funding bodies provide grants for the acquisition of knowledge that has no immediate application? There are incredible subtleties in fish reproduction that only emerge from de-tailed studies; how do salmon know that they must return to their native rivers in order to breed? Why do eels breed only in the Sargasso Sea? Per-haps funding bodies can be persuaded to support basic studies if they are presented as investigations into direction finding mechanisms, perhaps related to olfaction and navigation.

The situation is similar with reptiles and amphibians, and we provide important, contemporary reviews of reproductive strategies in these taxonomic groups. These groups highlight the dearth of knowledge that exists and the enormous challenges to conducting even the simplest of studies. For example, how can we study the reproductive cycles of reptiles that spend much of their time in the oceans? There is considerable topical concern about global declines in amphibian populations, and many species appear to have been extinguished for reasons still unclear. Again, the solutions to such questions will come from novel strategies developed across disciplines.

Reproduction in birds has benefited from years of agriculturally based studies of domestic poultry. Some chicken and turkey strategies have been applied to certain birds of prey, in part, because raptors are charismatic predators and due to a long, traditional interest in falconry. However, there is often little depth of biological knowledge, although there are now several intensive efforts to develop artificial insemination for some species. Even here, investigators are learning the consequences of ignorance and the need for more fundamental studies such as those involving the use of DNA fingerprinting to demonstrate that extra-pair copulations in house sparrows account for a sizeable proportion of offspring produced. Furthermore, female birds have inherent, fascinating abilities to store sperm long-term in specialised glands, perhaps even the ability to store sperm from different males selectively in different glands. Does such wondrous knowledge have any relevance to conservation? We assert that it certainly does. More importantly, perhaps this strange new bit of information lends further credence to our, by now, quite familiar credo – the key is more basic knowledge about unstudied species. Who knows the value of these intriguing findings for rare birds, other threatened species or frankly to the health and welfare of humankind? It is dangerous to continue to ignore the biology of 97% of the vertebrate species on Earth. We continue to do so at our peril.

21

Reproductive technologies and challenges in avian conservation and management

ANN M. DONOGHUE, JUAN MANUEL BLANCO,
GEORGE F. GEE, YVONNE K. KIRBY, & DAVID E. WILDT

INTRODUCTION AND OBJECTIVES

From a conservation perspective, bird species represent some of the most tragic as well as encouraging examples of efforts to preserve the world's biodiversity. Rachel Carson's classic book *Silent Spring* (1962) was a resounding alarm showing how humans can destroy ecosystems and the avian diversity within them. Carson dramatically described the severe loss in songbirds and raptors (birds of prey) throughout the 1940s–1960s, offering convincing arguments for how indiscriminate use of organochlorine pesticides caused eggshell thinning and infertility.

There now are an estimated 9672 bird species on the planet, widely distributed across a great number of habitats. Little is known about the basic biology of most birds, a matter of concern given that 321 species are listed as 'Endangered' and another 182 as 'Critical' (IUCN, 2000) (Table 21.1). There have been 104 documented bird extinctions world-wide. One of the best known examples is the dodo, discovered in 1598 by Portuguese sailors on the island of Mauritius. With no known predators and lacking fear of humans, the dodo was slaughtered for its meat and was extinct by 1681. Commercial hunting a little more than a century ago reduced the passenger pigeon, then the most numerous bird species on Earth, to 250 000 birds by 1896. Most of this flock was subsequently destroyed on a single day. The last passenger pigeon died on 1 September 1915 at the Cincinnati Zoo and Botanical Garden, perhaps the only time in history when the exact moment an extinction occurred was recorded.

Table 21.1 *Threatened avian species with current IUCN status, numbers of species with genetic management plans (GMP[a]) and numbers of peer-reviewed reproductive biology research publications*

Order	Common names	Total	Critical	Endangered	Vulnerable	GMP	Research[b]
Anseriformes	Duck/Geese	26	5	7	14	2	49[c]
Apodiformes	Swifts/Hummingbirds	35	9	12	14	-	-
Apterygiformes	Kiwis	4	0	1	3	-	1
Caprimulgiformes	Nighthawk	8	3	2	3	-	-
Casuariiformes	Cassowaries	2	0	0	2	1	1
Charadriiformes	Shore birds	34	6	7	21	-	14
Ciconiiformes	Herons	21	4	8	9	6	3
Columbiformes	Pigeons	60	12	14	34	3	18
Coraciiformes	Kingfishers	26	2	3	21	4	1
Cuculiformes	Cuckoos	11	2	2	7	-	-
Falconiformes	Hawk/Eagles	39	9	4	26	1	69[d]
Galliformes	Pheasants/Game birds	73	7	14	52	5	36
Gruiformes	Cranes	54	5	20	29	8	10
Passeriformes	Sparrows/Song birds	563	74	166	323	2	138
Pelecaniformes	Pelicans/Cormorants	15	2	2	11	1	5
Piciformes	Woodpeckers	15	3	4	8	-	3
Podicipediformes	Grebes	4	2	0	2	-	-
Procellariiformes	Petrels	55	13	9	33	-	-
Psittaciformes	Parrots	94	15	34	45	23	10
Rheiformes	Rheas	0	0	0	0	-	-
Sphenisciformes	Penguins	10	0	3	7	3	12
Strigiformes	Owls	27	7	9	11	-	15
Tinamiformes	Tinamous	7	2	0	5	-	-

[a] GMP: Species Survival Plan administered by the American Zoo & Aquarium Association, Australasian Species Management Program and European Association of Zoos & Aquaria.

[b] Reproductive journals surveyed (1978–2000) included: *Journal of Raptor Research*; *Zoo Biology*; *Journal of Wildlife Management*; *Journal of Reproduction & Fertility*; *Biology of Reproduction*; *Endocrinology*; *General & Comparative Endocrinology*; *Journal of Zoo & Wildlife Medicine*; *Reproduction, Fertility & Development*; and *Theriogenology*.

[c] Majority of reports were on mallards.

[d] Majority of articles focused on nesting behaviour.

In contrast, there are outstanding examples of avoiding extinction through collaborative efforts to recover bird numbers followed by reintroduction into nature. These include some of the raptors (birds of prey) that exist near the top of the food chain. Raptors play an essential role in stabilising ecosystems and as indicator species on the cumulative effects of environmental contaminants. The bald eagle and peregrine falcon have made remarkable recoveries since 1972, in part following restrictions on pesticide use. *Ex situ* breeding also has played a role in species recovery. For example, non-profit institutions produced and released 6000 captive-bred peregrine falcons in 34 US states from 1974 to 1997. That, combined with organised protection of nest sites and foraging habitats, resulted in one of the most successful species restoration programmes ever (Hoffman, 1998). Currently, other breeding programmes are returning similarly spectacular species to nature (e.g. California condor, Mauritius kestrel, Imperial eagle, amongst others; Table 21.2).

These keynote successes are only beginning to fulfil a vast need to direct more science at the conservation and management of thousands of unstudied bird species. An intricate, complex and fascinating web of mechanisms controls reproductive success in birds, and a necessary first step is to unravel reproductive strategies that are often species-specific. Among many variables are seasonality, photosensitivity, migratory patterns, pairing behaviour, semen volume, sperm concentration and quality, sperm storage capability of the female, sperm competition, fertility duration, numbers of eggs laid, incubation and hatchability. Diversity in reproductive anatomy, behaviour, physiology and endocrinology all contribute to successful reproduction. In this chapter, we review reproductive strategies for birds, including useful tools and priorities for aiding the conservation and management of threatened avian species.

STATE OF THE ART

Endocrine characteristics of avian species

Endocrine mechanisms have been widely studied among bird species, largely by analysing serially collected blood samples. External cues responsible for modulating the timing of reproduction (e.g. photoperiod, rainfall) pass through neural pathways to the hypothalamus which, in turn, drives reproductive-endocrine pathways (Bronson, 1989). Testosterone is produced by Leydig cells in the male and secondary follicles in the female (Paster, 1991). In the male, testosterone and FSH promote spermatogenesis

Table 21.2 *Status of endangered avian species and in situ reproduction programme progress*

Location	Species	Estimated number at lowest population and year	Current captive population	Number of birds reintroduced	Current *in situ* population	Personal communication source
Island of Mauritius	Mauritius kestrel	9 (1974)	<30		750–800	John Hartley
	Pink pigeon	15–20 (1985)	180		400	John Hartley
New Zealand	Kakapo	50 (1995)	62			Kakapo Recovery Programme
	Takahe	118 (1992)	247			Kakapo Recovery Programme
North America	Attwater prairie chicken	42 (1996)	130–135	400	50	Terry Rosignol
	California condor	27 (1987)	116	50	256	Los Angeles Zoo
	Hawaiian crow	c. 30 (1970–90s)	27	24	2	Dave Ledig
	Masked bobwhite quail	0 (1960s)	800	22 000	300–500	Sally Gall
	Mississippi sandhill crane	30–35 (1960–80s)	40	300	110–120	Scott Hereford
	Peregrine falcon	648 (1975)		6000		Bill Heinrich
	Whooping crane	15 (1941)	120		265	George Gee
Saudi Arabia	Houbara bustard	59–90 (1981)	580	300	100–200	Phil Seddon
Spain	Imperial eagle	60 (1960s)	36	0	296	Juan Blanco

and modulate sexual behaviour and secondary sex characteristics (Paster, 1991). Testosterone also regulates aggressive territorial behaviours in both male and female birds. Peak testosterone secretion generally occurs coincident with copulatory behaviour, intensive mate-guarding by the male and egg-laying in the female (Paster, 1991).

Stress associated with handling is a major concern in many avian species. Corticotrophic releasing factor from the hypothalamus stimulates adrenocorticotrophic hormone from the anterior pituitary which, in turn, releases corticosterone from the adrenals. Increased plasma corticosterone helps an individual adapt to acute change, but also can adversely impact reproduction as a physiological stressor in birds (Liptrap, 1993). Accurate assessment is difficult because circulating corticosterone in blood changes rapidly (within minutes) due to handling stress (Wingfield et al., 1982). Corticosterone is elevated during egg-laying in the female and during the mating season in male passerines (Wingfield & Farner, 1980). In some species, corticosterone declines to basal concentrations in both sexes during the non-breeding season with possible influences on photorefractoriness and gonadal regression, as well as pre-migratory fattening and migration (Wingfield & Farner, 1980).

Endocrine evaluations in birds have been constrained historically by the need for physical restraint and/or anaesthesia to collect blood samples. Contemporary, non-invasive methods for tracking steroidal metabolites in faeces offer extraordinary opportunities for studying reproductive-endocrine interrelationships without stressful manipulations. Excreted hormones can be superior to blood data because values represent pooled averages over time rather than a single point-in-time measure. Monitoring hormonal metabolites in faeces provides the potential for studying the effects of different exhibits, social settings and husbandry practices (including behavioural enrichment) on reproductive performance and well-being. Furthermore, this tool could be useful for evaluating optimal restraint, anaesthesia and translocation tactics to minimise reproductive disturbance. Faecal steroid analyses are useful for evaluating changes in the reproductive cycle, including onset of puberty, duration of sexual receptivity, seasonality, onset of reproductive senescence and impact of environmental disrupters (pollutants, toxins) on reproduction and health (see Pickard, Chapter 9; Monfort, Chapter 10).

Faecal steroid monitoring has been used successfully for sex determination in monomorphic avian species (Czekala & Lasley, 1977; Bercovitz et al., 1982; Tell & Lasley, 1991), as well as for tracking gonadal function and seasonality in captive (Lee et al., 1995) and free-living (Cockrem & Rounce,

1995; Kofuji *et al.*, 1999) birds. The only longitudinal endocrine study in a raptor demonstrated that female bald eagles experienced faecal oestrogen peaks at the time of nest-building, whereas faecal testosterone concentrations increased prior to semen production in males (Bercovitz *et al.*, 1982). Faecal corticoids also have been measured in free-living, Northern spotted owls as an accurate indication of physiological stress related to habitat disturbance (Wasser *et al.*, 1997).

Semen collection

Unlike the situation in domesticated birds, where improved management and genetics have extended the natural period of reproduction, many wild birds experience a short (30–60 day) reproductive season. This restricts the time available for semen collection, making it important to condition birds to the handling and collection process prior to the onset of semen production (Gee, 1995). Three semen collection methods have been used successfully in birds: cooperative, electroejaculation and massage. Cooperative semen collection was pioneered by falconers using sexually imprinted birds of prey (Hammerstrom, 1970). In this method, birds voluntarily copulate on special devices in response to a behavioural stimulation. Because they are not handled, stress and risk of trauma to the animal or handler are minimised. Semen volume varies significantly among individuals. In some cases, birds perform copulatory behaviour but fail to ejaculate or produce only seminal fluid or low sperm concentrations. Better results have been achieved by modifying the method and using an artificial vagina (Muscovy duck; Gvaryaku *et al.*, 1984) or a 'dummy' female (Houbara bustard; Saint Jalme *et al.*, 1994).

Electroejaculation has been used as a semen collection method for ducks and geese, pigeons and a variety of psittacines (see the review by Gee, 1995). Although safe if conducted properly, anaesthesia is required, and ejaculates are frequently contaminated with urine.

In 1936, Quinn and Burrows described a non-invasive 'abdominal massage' method for collecting poultry semen. The male is restrained, followed by gentle but rapid stroking of the back region from behind the wings towards the tail. Most males respond with phallic tumescence at which time the handler gently squeezes the cloaca, expressing semen through the external papilla of the ductus deferens. Collecting semen in this fashion from small passerines is relatively easy. During the reproductive season, most songbirds have a well-developed cloacal protuberance, a small pea-like swelling on the dorsal cloacal lip where the semen is stored (Howell & Bartholomew, 1952). Small quantities of semen can be obtained by applying

Figure 21.1 Restraining device used for semen collection and artificial insemination in parrot species. The rigid clear tube allows for the bird to be handled while minimising the opportunity for biting.

gentle, steady pressure to the protuberance. Adaptations to the massage collection method have been made for waterfowl, ratites, guans and tinamous because these species have a penis-like copulatory appendage (Cooper, 1977). For birds producing small seminal volumes, the operator must evert the phallus early in the collection process, and a suction device often is used to avoid losing semen on the phallic surface (Gee, 1995). Semen from larger birds (i.e. cranes, storks, eagles) are collected with the animal in a standing position (Gee, 1995). Clear, rigid plastic tubes, slightly larger than a bird's body, have been modified for parrots (Gee, 1995), largely eliminating serious bites to handlers or to themselves. The bird is placed head-first into a tube that is sufficiently long to ensure that the head remains completely protected (Figure 21.1). The bird's tail and cloaca are accessible from the contralateral end with the feet restrained with jesses through holes in the tube bottom. This positioning still allows the male to be adequately stroked. Birds are easily released through the tube front after collection.

Ejaculate quality, spermatozoa characteristics, metabolism and evaluation

There is significant variation in ejaculate volume and sperm concentration and quality among bird species (Gee, 1995), even those of similar size. American kestrels produce small volume (10–15 μl) ejaculates containing few spermatozoa (<0.03 million sperm/ml), whereas the domestic turkey ejaculate averages 200–300 μl with average sperm numbers of 8 billion/ml. Collection method and frequency or natural mating influence ejaculate volume. Although small seminal quantities are generally observed early or late in the breeding season, low volumes are not uncommon during the peak breeding season due to frequent copulation (Birkhead & Fletcher, 1995). Larger seminal volumes have been collected from males in a pair with lower fertility compared with smaller volumes from the male of a highly fertile pair (Gee, 1995). Collection attempts earlier in the morning also can improve seminal yields and, therefore, is standard protocol for domestic turkey stud farms as well as for some wild species (e.g. piping guans; DeMatteo *et al.*, 1998).

Interspecies differences in sperm morphology, mitochondria numbers, metabolism, motility and duration of storage in the female are also significant. Sperm morphology varies from a simple sauropsid form (e.g. domestic poultry), to a complex helical type with an exterior ribbon-like membrane and long flagellum (e.g. passerine), to a rounded, flattened shape (e.g. American kestrel; McFarlane, 1971). Avian sperm size (head-to-tail length) ranges from 30 to 300 μm and is unrelated to bird mass (McFarlane, 1962). Within the ejaculate, pleiomorphisms are uncommon, although a recent study of Houbara bustards revealed that as many as 64% of sperm had large nuclei, perhaps as the result of aberrant spermatogenesis (Lindsay *et al.*, 1999). The midpiece appears to be the most variable component of the avian spermatozoon (McFarlane, 1971), especially in numbers of mitochondria that provide the energy for cellular motility. Although similar in ultrastructural appearance, Japanese quail spermatozoa contain more than 1400 mitochondria compared with only 20–30 per cell for the turkey (Korn *et al.*, 2000). Fowl and turkey spermatozoa have similar morphology and mitochondrial numbers, yet the former are capable of anaerobic glycolysis, whereas the latter depend on aerobic oxidation (Wishart, 1989). This suggests that there may be variations in energy requirements for sperm motility or survival within the female reproductive tract.

Female birds, unlike their mammalian counterparts, have sperm storage tubules (SST) that allow viable spermatozoa to be retained for extended periods in the reproductive tract. Thus, avian spermatozoa have evolved mechanisms to survive the harsh environment of the vagina and to reside in an orderly array in a quiescent state until needed for fertilisation. Duration of storage varies among species. Fertile eggs have been produced several days after a single or final insemination in songbirds, but it is well established that viable sperm are stored for months in the turkey.

ARTIFICIAL INSEMINATION

Artificial insemination (AI) has long been considered a potentially valuable tool for helping to manage avian species breeding. Although commonly used to enhance the efficient distribution of valuable genes in poultry, AI with fresh or frozen semen has also been used successfully to overcome natural breeding failure in about 20 non-domestic species. Samour (1986) reported the production of more than 90 peregrine falcon chicks over an 8-year period using AI. Cooperative and massage semen collection methods have been adapted for inseminating females. Sexually imprinted females respond to the handler by everting the cloaca to expose the oviduct, thus allowing insemination. Cloacal eversion can cause stress, however, reducing or stopping egg production. In such cases, the oviduct is located by digital palpation or an inseminating device, and semen is deposited into the vagina (Watanabe, 1957). Vaginal insemination, although challenging in some wild species for behavioural or anatomical reasons, generally results in the highest fertility. The cloacal approach is most effective after frequent inseminations. For example, fertility success has been in excess of 80% in cranes after twice-weekly cloacal inseminations (50 000 sperm per insemination) following oviposition.

Knowledge of natural reproductive behaviours and cyclicity is useful in increasing the success rate of AI. For example, inseminating domestic turkeys before the onset of egg production maximises sperm filling of the SST, resulting in higher fertility throughout the egg production period (McIntyre & Christensen, 1985). This was discovered by noting that wild turkeys begin copulating before the onset of egg production. Inseminating just before or after oviposition decreased fertility, possibly because of fewer sperm reaching the SST or being lost in the egg-laying process.

Cryopreservation of avian spermatozoa

Fowl spermatozoa were the first animal gametes to be frozen-thawed and used to produce live offspring. This milestone occurred after the serendipitous discovery that glycerol was an effective cryoprotectant (Polge, 1951). Since then, glycerol has been used widely for the frozen storage of both poultry and wild bird spermatozoa. However, glycerol also has a contraceptive effect on bird sperm, requiring a series of troublesome steps to remove it during thawing to avoid sperm death (Hammerstedt & Graham, 1992). In general, fewer than 2% of thawed poultry spermatozoa are capable of fertilisation *in vivo* (Wishart, 1989), and similar problems have been encountered with the spermatozoa of wild species. Greater sandhill crane spermatozoa cryopreserved in 6% dimethylsulfoxide (DMSO) yielded 50% fertile eggs upon AI (Gee *et al.*, 1985) compared with 95% fertility in the same number of freshly collected cells. Likewise, there is a 50% reduction in fertility in the American kestrel using sperm frozen with the cryoprotectant dimethylolacetamide (DMA; 12.3% concentration) compared with fresh spermatozoa (Brock & Bird, 1991). This low fertility is probably due to a combination of sensitivity to freeze-thawing and suboptimal cryopreservation technology (Hammerstedt & Graham, 1992). Additionally, sperm function, transport and storage in the hen's reproductive tract appear compromised after either refrigeration or freeze-thawing (Donoghue & Wishart, 2000).

Despite more limited fertility with cryopreserved spermatozoa, such procedures have been adapted to many non-domesticated birds, including the Aleutian goose, seaside sparrow (Gee, 1995), piping guan (DeMatteo *et al.*, 1998), Magellanic penguin (O'Brien *et al.*, 1999) and golden, Imperial and Bonelli's eagles (Blanco *et al.*, 2000) (for a recent review of semen cryopreservation and AI in birds, see Wishart, 2001).

Case study 1: Multidisciplinary science in the restoration of cranes
One of the best examples of cooperative, reproductive and integrative science to restore wild bird populations has involved the cranes, which represent an ancient avian family that has graced the planet for at least 40 million years (Meine & Archibald, 1996). These birds are depicted on the temple walls of the ancient Egyptians, and Chinese imperial royalty long maintained cranes and considered them symbolic of long life (Ellis *et al.*, 1996). However, following grassland and wetland loss/degradation, seven of the 15 crane species living today are threatened with extinction, and several subspecies are critically endangered. In 1941, the migratory population of the whooping crane was estimated at just 15 birds. Through collaborations of the Patuxent Wildlife Centre, US Fish & Wildlife Service, the Canadian Wildlife Service and the International Crane Foundation, substantial progress has been made in recovering this species. There now are about 190 whooping cranes in the Aransas–Wood Buffalo population, 75 in the Florida non-migratory flock and about 120 adult birds in captivity. This population growth has largely been the result of systematic studies to understand bird behaviour, genetics, husbandry, chick rearing and medical requirements as well as basic and applied reproductive biology (Ellis *et al.*, 1996). Especially important has been the development of semen collection and AI that have been essential to the effective management of many species, but particularly to the Mississippi sandhill crane (Gee *et al.*, 1985; Ellis *et al.*, 1996).

Case study 2: Importance of species specificity
In general, in most non-domesticated birds fertility success with cryo-preserved spermatozoa is less than half that obtained with fresh semen and AI. However, success has been highly variable, largely owing to the lack of systematic, cryobiological studies that include analysing the influence of cryoprotectant, duration of equilibration, sperm concentration/quality and timing/frequency of deposition. Especially important is species-specificity, which often varies remarkably even among closely related taxa. For example, we recently reported remarkable variation in sperm sensitivities to freeze-thawing in a comparative study of the chicken, turkey and four raptor species. Rapid cooling was detrimental to Bonelli's eagle, golden eagle, pere-grine falcon and turkey spermatozoa, yet was advantageous to cryopreserv-ing spermatozoa from the chicken and endangered Imperial eagle (Figure 21.2). These findings are significant because they dispel the no-tion of a 'magic bullet' for resolving the mysteries of how better to cryo-preserve avian spermatozoa. Futhermore, domestic bird species protocols are used routinely for non-domestic species. Yet this recent study clearly demonstrates that bird species (even related eagle species) vary strikingly in fundamental sperm biology. One of the many results, then, is that dif-ferences in cryo-sensitivities are of sufficient magnitude to require signifi-cant basic, species-specific research before sperm cryopreservation can be effective. Likewise, we predict that, as in the crane studies, the enhanced management and conservation of all threatened wild bird species will de-pend on a merging of *in situ* and *ex situ* management issues with disciplines across the reproductive sciences, including the fields of behaviour, genetics, nutrition, veterinary medicine, population biology, reproductive physiology, endocrinology and cryobiology.

REPRODUCTIVE PRIORITIES FOR AVIAN CONSERVATION

Indeed there has been progress in understanding some of the fascinating reproductive strategies inherent to wild birds. Yet when one considers that (1) there are far more than 9000 bird species in existence, (2) only a handful has been systematically studied and (3) early studies have recognised a re-markable variation in reproductive mechanisms among species, the magni-tude of the challenge becomes apparent. Birds have evolved to survive in many micro-environments around the world. These adaptations brought changes in reproductive strategies and physiological functions that ensure self-perpetuation. However, without a comprehensive understanding of

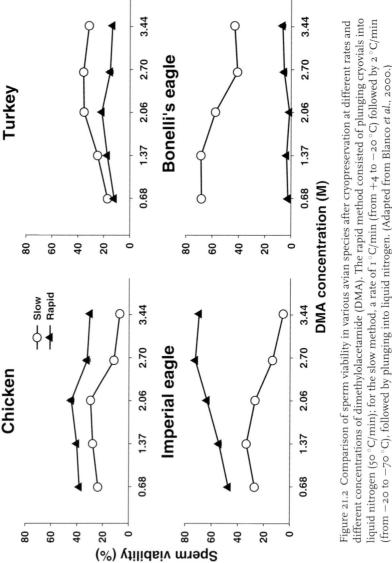

Figure 21.2 Comparison of sperm viability in various avian species after cryopreservation at different rates and different concentrations of dimethylolacetamide (DMA). The rapid method consisted of plunging cryovials into liquid nitrogen (50 °C/min): for the slow method, a rate of 1 °C/min (from +4 to −20 °C) followed by 2 °C/min (from −20 to −70 °C), followed by plunging into liquid nitrogen. (Adapted from Blanco *et al.*, 2000.)

these specialities in natural reproduction, we risk missing valuable knowledge, information which is not only of scholarly importance but also useful for making management and conservation decisions, and for taking action.

This is an exciting time to marshal forces and create new paradigms for avian research. We now have very powerful tools for collecting data from *ex situ* and *in situ* populations. Advances, especially through the availability of non-invasive hormonal metabolite evaluation (via urine or faeces), open up enormous opportunities for assessing longitudinal reproductive changes in wild as well as in captive birds. The value of these techniques is perhaps most substantial for assessing the importance of adrenal function, especially in species where stress may be suppressing reproduction and preventing or reducing offspring production. This area of research is a high priority for (1) evaluating the impact of human disturbance (similar to the studies of Wasser *et al.* (1997), who first confirmed the value of this strategy in the free-living Northern spotted owl) and (2) determining how captive environments can be 'enriched' to reduce stress and promote consistent reproduction.

Thus, the reproductive physiology of birds has value beyond scholarship to assist directly in improving species management. These benefits can range from simply providing knowledge, which helps animal curators to improve husbandry, to developing better 'assisted breeding' especially through AI. This priority will circumvent the common problem of birds failing to copulate in captivity owing to behavioural incompatibilities. Combined with effective sperm storage (cryopreservation), AI would permit easy movement of genes between distant breeding facilities, avoiding the need to transport stress-sensitive birds while ensuring that every genetically valuable individual has the chance to reproduce. In theory, it also may be possible in the future to inseminate wild birds (from small, fragmented populations) using spermatozoa from unrelated males, thereby promoting genetic diversity. However, for now, fundamental sperm cryobiology is another priority. A better understanding of how spermatozoa respond to different cryoprotectants is especially needed. It is also time to consider how to preserve the female gamete, so studies should begin using domestic poultry as a 'model' species. Finally, the routine storage of gametes from endangered birds through the development of genome resource banks would provide a hedge against extinction in the face of unforeseen catastrophes (e.g. disease epidemics, loss of prey, drought or flood). Similar systematic banks of spermatozoa have been established for certain mammals, both domesticated and wild.

CONCLUSIONS

An intricate web of endocrinological and physiological mechanisms controls reproductive success in birds. Several notable examples exist (peregrine falcon, California condor, whooping crane) whereby reproductive knowledge combined with breeding technologies (including assisted breeding) and intensive management contributed to restoration of birds into nature. These species serve as models of incentive for expanding efforts to understand basic reproductive biology and to develop AI with fresh and thawed sperm for other rare aves. Other phenomena and novel technologies deserve exploration. For example, many wild-caught raptors produce ejaculates with low sperm concentrations and high proportions of malformed sperm. Ejaculates from some Spanish Imperial eagles (a critically endangered species with 148 pairs remaining) contain more than 90% abnormally shaped spermatozoa. Non-invasive monitoring of hormonal patterns in excreted faeces is ongoing to examine potential aetiologies as well as to develop a scholarly database relevant to natural and assisted breeding. For example, we have recently developed an intramagnum insemination method to compensate for abnormally low numbers of ejaculated spermatozoa. Offspring have been produced using this approach in the peregrine falcon and golden eagle, even in cases where ejaculate was contaminated with urine. To continue achieving such applied success, priorities for basic reproductive research in birds include: understanding the regulators of seasonality, endocrine relationships to reproductive behaviour, especially timing of copulation, sperm quality, semen storage in the female and mechanisms of fertilisation. Perhaps the greatest challenge with this taxonomic group lies in understanding how species-specific mechanisms determine successful reproduction.

ACKNOWLEDGEMENTS

Special thanks for financial support to the USDA Foreign Agricultural Services Project # SP 33, the Patuxent Wildlife Research Center, USGS, the Junta de Comunidades de Castilla-La Mancha, the Smithsonian Women's Committee and the Smithsonian Institution/British Airways Partnership.

REFERENCES

Bercovitz, A. B., Collins, J., Price P. & Tuttle, D. (1982). Noninvasive assessment of seasonal hormone profile in captive Bald Eagles (*Haliaeetus leucocephalus*). *Zoo Biology* 1, 111–117.

Birkhead, T. R. & Fletcher, F. (1995). Depletion determines sperm numbers in male Zebra Finches. *Animal Behavior* 49, 451–456.

Blanco, J. M., Gee, G., Wildt, D. E. & Donoghue, A. M. (2000). Species variation in osmotic, cryoprotectant, and cooling rate tolerance in Poultry, Eagle, and Peregrine Falcon spermatozoa. *Biology of Reproduction* **63**, 1164-1171.

Brock, M. K. & Bird, D. M. (1991). Prefreeze and postthaw effects of glycerol and dimethylolacetamide on motility and fertilizing ability of American Kestrel (*Falco sparverius*) spermatozoa. *Journal of Zoo and Wildlife Medicine* **22**, 453-459.

Bronson, F. H. (1989). *Mammalian Reproductive Biology*, pp. 28-89. University of Chicago Press, Chicago.

Carson, R. (1962). *Silent Spring*. Houghton Mifflin, Boston, MA.

Cockrem, J. F. & Rounce, J. R. (1995). Noninvasive assessment of the annual gonadal cycle in free-living Kakapo, *Strigops habroptilus*, using fecal steroid measurements. *The Auk* **112**, 253-257.

Cooper, D. M. (1977). Artificial insemination. In *Poultry Diseases* (Ed. R. F. Gordon), pp. 302-307. Baillière Tindall, London.

Czekala, N. M. &. Lasley, B. L. (1977). A technical note on sex discrimination in monomorphic birds using fecal steroid analysis. *International Zoo Yearbook* **17**, 209-211.

DeMatteo, K. E., Asa, C. S., Macek, M. S. & Snyder, T. L. (1998) Artificial insemination and semen preservation of the common Piping Guan. *Cracid Specialists Group, Piple Symposium*. American Ornithologists Union, St Louis, MI.

Donoghue, A. M. & Wishart, G. J. (2000). Storage of poultry semen. *Animal Reproduction Science* **62**, 213-232.

Ellis, D. H., Gee, G. F. & Mirande, C. M. (Eds.) (1996). *Cranes: Their Biology, Husbandry and Conservation*. US Department of the Interior, National Biological Service, Washington DC; International Crane Foundation, Baraboo, WI, in cooperation with the US Fish & Wildlife Service.

Gee, G. F. (1995). Artificial insemination and cryopreservation of semen from non-domestic birds. In *First International Symposium on the Artificial Insemination of Poultry* (Eds. M. R. Bakst & G. J. Wishart), pp. 262-279. Poultry Science Association. Savoy, IL.

Gee, G. F., Bakst, M. R. & Sexton, T. J. (1985). Cryogenic preservation of semen from the Greater Sandhill Crane. *Journal of Wildlife Management* **49**, 480-484.

Gvaryaku, G., Robinson, B., Meltzer, A., Perek, M. & Snapir, N. (1984). An improved method for obtaining semen from muscovy drakes and some of its quantitative and qualitative characteristics. *Poultry Science* **63**, 548-553.

Hammerstedt, R. H. & Graham, J. K. (1992). Cryopreservation of poultry sperm: the enigma of glycerol. *Cryobiology* **29**, 26-38.

Hammerstrom, F. (1970). *An Eagle in the Sky*. Iowa State University Press, Ames, IA.

Hoffman, C. (1998). Peregrine to soar off endangered species list. *Endangered Species Bulletin* **23**, 20-21.

Howell, T. R. & Bartholomew, G. A., Jr (1952). Experiments on the mating behavior of the Brewer Blackbird. *Condor* **54**, 140-141.

International Union for Conservation of Nature and Natural Resources. (2000). *Threatened Species*. IUCN, Gland, Switzerland.

Kofuji, H., Kanda, M. & Oishi, T. (1999). Breeding cycles and fecal gonadal steroids in the Brown Dipper, *Cinclus pallasii*. *General and Comparative Endocrinology* **91**, 216-223.

Korn, N., Thurston, R. J., Pooser, B. P. &. Scott, T. R. (2000). Ultrastructure of spermatozoa from Japanese Quail. *Poultry Science* **79**, 86-93.

Lee, J. V., Whaling, C. S., Lasley, B. L. & Marier, P. (1995). Validation of an enzyme immunoassay for measurement of excreted estrogen and testosterone metabolites in White-Crowned Sparrow (*Zonotrichia leucophrys oriantha*). *Zoo Biology* **14**, 97-106.

Lindsay, C., Staines, H. J., McCormick, P., McCallum, C., Choulani, F. & Wishart, G. J. (1999). Variability in the size of the nucleus in spermatozoa from Houbara Bustards, *Chlamydotis undulata undulata*. *Journal of Reproduction and Fertility* **117**, 307-313.

Liptrap, R. M. (1993). Stress and the reproduction in domestic animals. *Annals of the New York Academy of Sciences* **697**, 275-284.

McFarlane, R. W. (1962). The taxonomic significance of avian sperm. Masters thesis, University of Florida, Gainesville, FL.

McFarlane, R. W. (1971). Ultrastructure and phylogenetic significance of avian spermatozoa. Doctoral dissertation, University of Florida, Gainesville, FL.

McIntyre, D. R. & Christensen, V. L. (1985). Effect of initial insemination and insemination interval on fertility in turkey hens. *Poultry Science* **64**, 1549-1552.

Meine, C. D. & Archibald, G.W (compilers) (1996). Status Survey and Conservation Action Plans: The Cranes. In *International Union for the Conservation of Nature* & *Natural Resources*, pp. 282. M.O.M. Priority, Ottawa, Canada.

O'Brien, J. K., Oehler, D. A, Malowski, S. P. & Roth, T. L. (1999). Semen collection, characterization, and cryopreservation in a Magellanic Penguin (*Spheniscus magellanicus*). *Zoo Biology* **18**, 199-214.

Paster, M. B. (1991). Avian reproductive endocrinology. *Veterinary Clinics of North America Small Animal Practice* **21**, 1343-1359.

Polge, C. (1951). Functional survival of fowl spermatozoa after freezing at −70 °C. *Nature* **167**, 949-950.

Quinn, J. P. & Burrows, W. H. (1936). Artificial insemination in fowls. *Journal of Heredity* **27**, 31-37.

Saint Jalme, M., Gaucher, P. & Paillat, P. (1994). Artificial insemination in Houbara Bustards (*Chlamydotis undulata*): influence of the number of spermatozoa and insemination frequency on fertility and ability to hatch. *Journal of Reproduction and Fertility* **100**, 93-103.

Samour, J. H. (1986). Recent advances in artificial breeding techniques in birds and reptiles. *International Zoo Yearbook* **24/25**, 143-148.

Tell, L. A. & Lasley, B. L. (1991). An automated assay for fecal estrogen conjugates in the determination of sex in avian species. *Zoo Biology* **10**, 361-367.

Wasser, S. K., Bevis, K., King, G. & Hanson, E. (1997). Noninvasive physiological measures of disturbance in the Northern Spotted Owl. *Conservation Biology* **11**, 1019-1022.

Watanabe, M. (1957). An improved technique of the artificial insemination in ducks. *Journal of the Faculty of Fisheries & Animal Husbandry*, Hiroshima University **1**, 363-370.

Wingfield, J. C. & Farner, D. S. (1980). Endocrinologic and reproductive states of bird populations under environmental stress. *United States Environmental Protection Agency Report*. Contract No.cc699095.

Wingfield, J. C., Smith, J. P. & Farner, D. S. (1982). Endocrine responses of White-Crowned Sparrows to environmental stress. *Condor* **84**, 399-409.

Wishart, G. J. (1989). Physiological changes in fowl and turkey spermatozoa during *in vitro* storage. *British Poultry Science* **30**, 443-454.

Wishart, G. J. (2001). The cryopreservation of germplasm in domestic and non-domestic birds. In *Cryobanking the Genetic Resource; Wildlife Conservation for the Future?* (Eds. P. F. Watson & W. V. Holt), pp. 179-200. Taylor & Francis, London.

22

Reptile reproduction and endocrinology

VALENTINE A. LANCE

INTRODUCTION AND BACKGROUND

The alarming pace of the global decline in amphibians has alerted both biologists and the general public to the accelerating rate of habitat loss, fragmentation and degradation (Roth & Obringer, Chapter 23). However, as
Gibbons *et al.* (2000) recently pointed out, 'Although the amphibian decline
problem is a serious threat, reptiles appear to be in even *greater* danger of
extinction worldwide.' For example, one of the most spectacular and enigmatic reptiles, the leatherback sea turtle (*Dermochelys coriacea*) appears to
be on a direct course for extinction, while little continues to be known of its
unusual physiology and life history (Spotila *et al.*, 1996). In fact, many reptile species are destined to disappear before anything is discovered of their
basic biology, including reproduction.

Reptiles were the first truly terrestrial vertebrates. The evolution of the
amniote egg, 'the most marvelous "invention" in vertebrate history' (Romer,
1967), freed reptiles from dependence on an aquatic environment for reproduction, thus allowing exploitation of terrestrial habitats. The increase
in yolk mass, completion of development within an egg and abandonment
of a larval stage resulted in an explosion of forms that typified the 'age of
reptiles' during which at least 17 orders appeared.

Of this extraordinary diversity, only four orders remain today in the
class Reptilia: Chelonia or Testudinata (turtles and tortoises, 260 species),
Crocodilia (crocodiles, alligators and the gharial, 22 species), Squamata
(snakes, lizards and amphisbaenids, >6800 species) and Rhynchocephalia
or Sphenodontida (represented by the genus *Sphenodon*, the tuatara, two
species). This heterogeneous assemblage exhibits a variety of body shapes,
sizes and life histories that make any generalities about reproduction virtually impossible.

Compared with other amniotes (mammals and birds), reproduction in reptiles differs in one universally important way: it is critically dependent on temperature. Despite this limitation, reptiles have successfully adapted to every available habitat except the polar regions and extreme elevations. There are species that exist solely in trees, underground, mud, fresh water, open ocean or the driest of deserts. Additionally, each reptile species has evolved a reproductive cycle which ensures that young are born at the time of year favourable to their survival (Morafka *et al.*, 2000).

Despite the bewildering array of reproductive modes exhibited by reptiles (including temperature-dependent sex determination, parthenogenesis and viable sperm retention in the female reproductive tract for up to 5 years), there is little information on physiology and hormonal control of reproduction for most species. There is a vast and growing literature on reproductive cycles of lizards and snakes (Fitch, 1970, 1982), most of which is ecologically based, and a substantial literature on morphology of the urogenital system (Fox, 1977). For earlier reviews on hormones and reptile reproduction, the reader is referred to Callard & Ho (1980), Lance & Callard (1980), Lance (1984) and Licht (1984).

This chapter focuses on contemporary information for a few species in each order, especially those species where there is detailed hormonal and physiological information. Future high priority research also is discussed.

STATE OF THE ART

Chelonia

There is substantial molecular evidence that the Chelonia and Crocodilia are not, as previously believed, distantly related separate lineages, but are in fact derived from a common ancestor within the last 200 million years (Mannen & Li, 1999). The Chelonia and Crocodilia are relatively conservative in body form and mode of reproduction, but it is within these two orders that temperature-dependent sex determination is widespread. As explained below, the reproductive biology of the two groups also illustrates some similarities supportive of the common ancestry theory.

There have been extensive field studies on temperate zone Chelonia (Gibbons, 1990) and a few on tropical species (sea turtles in particular) that have emphasised reproduction (see Kuchling, 1999). However, for most species, particularly those that are endangered, there is no information whatsoever on reproductive biology.

The male reproductive cycle appears rather conserved, at least in the few species studied to date (Kuchling, 1999; Table 22.1). Most current

Table 22.1 *Published plasma testosterone data on male Chelonia*

Family	Species	Testosterone (ng/ml)[a]	Reference
Chelidae	*Chelodina oblonga*	0.1–130.0	Kuchling (1999)
Kinosternidae	*Kinosternon odoratum*	2.0–85.0	McPherson et al. (1982)[b]
Chelonidae	*Chelonia mydas*	2.0–33.0	Licht et al. (1985a)[b]
	Lepidochelys kempi	0.65–8.44	Rostal et al. (1998)
	Caretta caretta	0.2–7.5	Wibbels et al. (1990)[b]
Trionchidae	*Pelodiscus sinensis*	0.1–2.1	Mao & Wang (1999)
Chelydridae	*Chelydra serpentina*	2.0–80.0	Mahmoud et al. (1985)[b]
Emydidae	*Chrysemys picta*	0.4–18.0	Licht et al. (1985b)[b]
	Trachemys dorbigni	0.3–1.3	Silva et al. (1984)[b]
	Graptemys flavimaculata	0.20–11.0	Shelby et al. (2000)
Testudinae	*Geochelone nigra*	3.7–28.9	Schramm et al. (1999)
	Testudo hermanni	1.0–22.0	Kuchling et al. (1981)[b]
	Gopherus agassizii	18.4–402.0	Rostal et al. (1994)[b]
	Gopherus flavomarginatus	120.0–1050.0	Gonzalez-Trapága (1995)
	Gopherus polyphemus	80.0–325.5	Ott et al. (2000)

[a] Estimated minimum and maximum means.
[b] The full citations may be found in Kuchling (1999).

information is derived from species inhabiting temperate climates where there is a pronounced seasonal cycle. However, the testes of the turtle *Pseudemys scripta* in tropical Panama exhibit a seasonal cycle virtually identical to that of turtles in the temperate zone. Each species for which there are morphological and histological data reveals the same pattern: spermatogenesis occurs during warm summer months with spermiogenesis and spermiation occurring just before the cooler winter months. Peak plasma testosterone is invariably associated with maximal spermatogenesis. There is good evidence that following spermiation in late summer, spermatozoa are stored in the epididymis until spring when mating occurs. Testis mass also is greatest in late summer just before spermiation and lowest in spring during the mating period. In some species, however, insemination occurs in autumn, and spermatozoa are stored in the female reproductive tract until ovulation and fertilisation in spring (Gist et al., 1990; Rostal et al., 1994).

All species for which there is male hormonal information are listed in Table 22.1 with representative species from seven of the 11 families. It is striking that circulating testosterone ranges from a peak of only 1.3 ng/ml in *Trachemys dorbigni* to over 1000 ng/ml in *Gopherus flavomarginatus*. Individual testosterone values in *G. flavomarginatus* sometimes exceed 1500 ng/ml (P. Licht, personal communication), probably the highest circulating testosterone recorded in any vertebrate (testosterone values in all *Gopherus* species often are >500 ng/ml; V. A. Lance, unpublished data). The reason for species variation in androgen circulation is unknown. Low levels may be caused by holding the animal in captivity for several hours before blood sampling, thus causing stress-induced corticosterone production and testosterone suppression (Lance, 1994; Cash *et al.*, 1997). However, variation in testosterone concentrations among species cannot be attributed to stress alone. Body mass does not seem to be a controlling factor because the largest species, *Geochelone nigra*, has lower testosterone levels than the smallest, *Kinosteronon odoratus*. One possibility is that differences in steroid binding proteins in blood can influence the absolute amount of circulating hormone (more binding protein means more steroid bound and retained in circulation, whereas unbound or 'free' steroids are rapidly cleared). Steroid binding protein concentrations are known to vary among mammals, but such data have been reported for only one turtle species, *Chrysemys picta* (Callard & Callard, 1987). This area clearly requires more research.

The desert tortoise (*Gopherus agassizii*) is one species for which there is a detailed picture of the annual male reproductive/endocrine cycle with a parallel database on haematology and blood biochemistry (Christopher *et al.*, 1999). Seasonal variation in rainfall, temperature, plasma testosterone, total plasma lipid, plasma corticosterone and plasma thyroxine during a 1-year period are illustrated in Figure 22.1*a–c* for male tortoises in the eastern Mojave Desert, Nevada. Data are absent during the cooler months (November–March) because the tortoises remain dormant in underground burrows.

The figure demonstrates that there is (1) significant variation in average monthly temperature and (2) very little rain. Tortoise activity and reproductive cycles closely coincide in this unpredictable, harsh environment. Upon emergence from dormancy in late March and early April (immediately after the winter rain), the tortoises actively feed and mate. Elevated circulating thyroid hormones are associated with intense feeding activity in both sexes (Kohel *et al.*, 2001). As summer temperatures increase, tortoises spend most of the day in burrows, emerging only in the early morning and late afternoon for brief feeding (Ruby *et al.*, 1994). Plasma testosterone, corticosterone and thyroxine decline during this decreased activity period. However, as the testicular cycle resumes in May/June, testosterone and corticosterone rise, peaking in August/September when spermatogenesis is complete and intense male–male combat and autumnal mating occur (Rostal *et al.*, 1994). At this time, a secondary, lower amplitude thyroxine rise also is observed (Figure 22.1*c*). A decline in total plasma lipid with

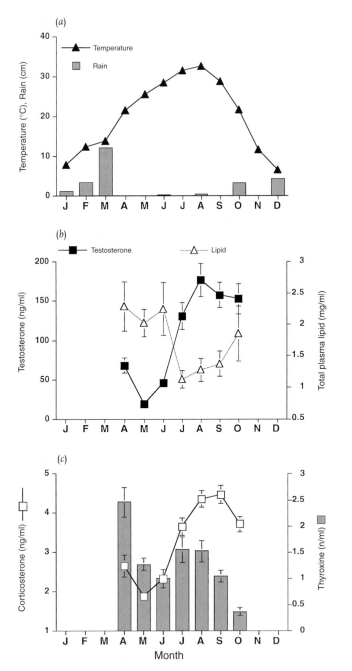

Figure 22.1 (a) A single year of weather data at the Desert Tortoise Conservation Center, Nevada. Solid triangles represent average temperature for each month and the hatched bars the rainfall in cm. (b) Mean plasma testosterone (■) and mean total plasma lipid (△) in the male desert tortoise, *Gopherus agassizii* (n =20) for each month of their activity cycle. (c) Mean plasma corticosterone (□) and thyroxine (hatched bars) in same male tortoises as in (b), above. Lines above and below the symbols = SEM.

increasing testosterone (Figure 22.1*b*) also has been observed in the turtle *Kinosternon odoratus* (McPherson *et al.*, 1982, in Kuchling, 1999) and is believed to result from increased lipid metabolism associated with spermatogenesis (Lance *et al.*, 2002). The annual plasma corticosterone pattern is almost identical to that of plasma testosterone, the relatedness of the two steroids being significant. Furthermore, corticosterone concentrations in the male are higher throughout the year than in the female (Lance *et al.*, 2001).

Table 22.2 presents hormonal data for cycling female chelonians. Sea turtles are well represented because females are easily approached when they haul ashore to nest, but this period represents only a brief window within the entire reproductive cycle. Data on the mating and follicular growth phase (vitellogenesis) are rare. There are notable species differences in hormone concentrations, but fewer extremes compared with male chelonians. Again *Gopherus flavimarginatus* demonstrates unique features, with circulating testosterone in the female (Table 22.2) being higher than in many male turtles (Table 22.1).

Portable X-ray and ultrasonography have greatly increased our ability to monitor the reproductive cycle of female chelonians under field conditions (Figure 22.2). When data from these tools are combined with blood hormonal patterns, a relatively complete picture of the annual reproductive cycle can be produced.

The chelonian ovarian cycle is characterised by a long follicular growth phase during which the follicles increase in diameter and accumulate yolk over several months (Figure 22.3*a*). This prolonged vitellogenic phase is characterised by elevated plasma oestradiol, testosterone, lipids, vitamin E, calcium, iron, zinc, magnesium and phosphorus. Oestradiol secreted from developing follicles drives deposition of lipids, vitamins, minerals and protein in the yolk. Oestradiol acts on the liver to produce the calcium-binding yolk precursor protein, vitellogenin and the low-density lipoproteins that help transport significant amounts of triacylglycerol, phospholipid and cholesterol to the developing follicle (Lance *et al.*, 2002). Similar changes in plasma lipid, phosphorus and calcium can be elicited in males by injecting oestrogen (Ho *et al.*, 1982). The soft-shelled turtle *Lissemys punctata* (Sarkar *et al.*, 1996), however, experiences a short vitellogenic phase and is the one known exception among the Chelonia to this unusual prolonged follicular growth. It is not known if this pattern is unique because there are few data available on the other members of the family Trionchidae.

There is a surge of progesterone near ovulation as the granulosa cells of the preovulatory follicle undergo luteinisation, cease producing oestradiol and testosterone and secrete only progesterone (Figure 22.3*d*). Progesterone

Table 22.2 *Published steroid hormone data on female Chelonia*

Family	Species	Oestradiol (pg/ml)	Testosterone (ng/ml)	Progesterone (ng/ml)	Reference
Kinosternidae	*Kinosternon odoratum*	200–5000	0.25–1.52	0.4–3.5	McPherson et al. (1982)[a]
	Chelonia mydas	> 30	0.26–1.23	0.65–50.0	Licht et al. (1980)[a]
	Caretta caretta	20–195	0.06–0.52	0.08–0.40	Wibbels et al. (1990)[a]
Chelodidae	*Lepidochelys olivacea*	–	–	0.15–16.0	Licht et al. (1982)[a]
	Lepidochelys kempi	0.7–21.4	0.02–0.38	0.27–0.68	Rostal et al. (1998)
Trionchidae	*Lissemys puctata*	23–598	–	0.07–0.86	Sarkar et al. (1996)[a]
Dermochelydae	*Dermochelys coriacea*	79–218	1.25–10.80	1.10–2.87	Rostal et al. (2001)
Chelydridae	*Chelydra serpentina*	13–284	–	0.25–1.44	Lewis et al. (1979)[a]
	Chrysemys picta	10–1366	0.01–5.69	0.10–4.50	Callard et al. (1978)[a]
Emydidae	*Graptemys flavimaculata*	10–195	0.01–0.13	0.01–1.40	Shelby et al. (2000)
	Geochelone nigra	33–160	0.08–1.68	0.26–1.64	Schramm et al. (1999)
Testudinae	*Gopherus agassizii*	60–492	0.38–2.36	0.12–2.36	Rostal et al. (1994)[a]
	Gopherus flavomarginatus	2500–13130	2.54–49.95	1.33–3.53	Gonzalez-Trapága (1995)
	Gopherus polyphemus	90–7000	1.0–20.0	1.0–2.0	Ott et al. (2000)

[a] Complete citation may be found in Kuchling (1999).

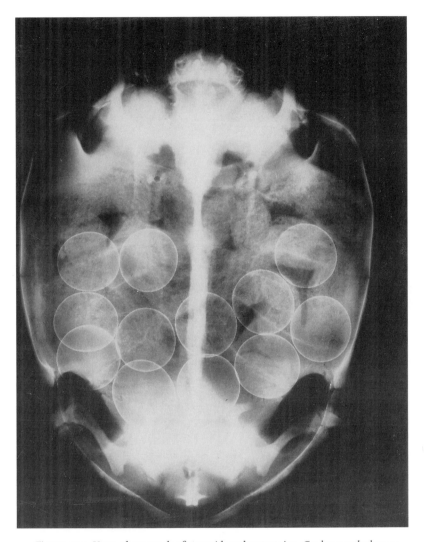

Figure 22.2 X-ray photograph of a gravid gopher tortoise, *Gopherus polyphemus*, in southeastern Georgia, USA (D. Rostal, unpublished data). The exceptionally large clutch of shelled eggs is clearly visible within the oviduct (normal clutch size = 7, range = 2-16).

secretion continues for the first few days after ovulation, rapidly declining with oviposition.

Many of the temperate zone chelonians produce two or three clutches during summer (McPherson *et al.*, 1982 in Kuchling 1999; Rostal *et al.*, 1994), but populations at the northern extreme of the range produce only

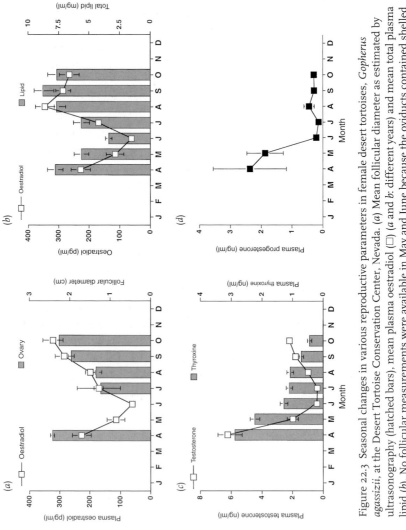

Figure 22.3   Seasonal changes in various reproductive parameters in female desert tortoises, *Gopherus agassizii*, at the Desert Tortoise Conservation Center, Nevada. (*a*) Mean follicular diameter as estimated by ultrasonography (hatched bars), mean plasma oestradiol (□) (*a* and *b*: different years) and mean total plasma lipid (*b*). No follicular measurements were available in May and June because the oviducts contained shelled eggs that obscured the ovary. (*c*) Mean plasma testosterone (□) and thyroxine (□), and (*d*) mean plasma progesterone (■). (Lines above and below the mean = SEM.)

one clutch annually. The leatherback sea turtle, *Dermochelys coriacea*, produces an astounding ten clutches of about 70 eggs every 10 days during the nesting season (Rostal *et al.*, 2001). It is believed that all of these eggs are fertilised from copulations that occur before the nesting season. If true, enormous sperm numbers must be stored in the female reproductive tract so that each successive clutch is fertilised. As each clutch is deposited, circulating oestradiol and testosterone decline. The concentration of these two hormones in circulation, combined with ultrasonography data, is a good index of the stage of the female's nesting cycle. However, the mechanistic role of testosterone in female reptiles is poorly understood. It may be necessary for complete oviductal development (as in birds), but experimental data are lacking.

Substantial calcium is mobilised within days during eggshell formation. Dietary calcium is insufficient to meet demand and, thus, calcium is acquired from structural bone and transported to the oviduct where it is secreted from shell glands. Structural change in the bone as a result of this loss in reproducing females is quantifiable (Edgren, 1960), and depletion is gradually replaced in the months after reproduction by as yet unknown hormonal mechanisms.

Crocodilia

All crocodilians, except the American alligator (*Alligator mississippiensis*), are restricted to the tropics. Species for which there is reproductive cycle information are seasonal breeders. Reproductive patterns in tropical species are usually associated with seasonal rainfall. Substantive hormonal data are available only for the American alligator; the absence of information for other species is related to the difficulty in collecting samples from large, aggressive species. The reproductive cycle of the male and female American alligator in Louisiana has been reviewed by Lance (1987, 1989), as has that of the female alligator of Florida (Guillette *et al.*, 1997).

The reproductive cycle of the American alligator is tightly regulated by seasonal temperature and, unlike that of tropical crocodiles, is less influenced by seasonal rainfall. Dry years, however, result in decreased nesting in American alligators. In years of mild winter and warm spring, nesting and oviposition can occur up to 1 month earlier than in years with a cold winter and cool spring (Joanen & McNease, 1989). The male reproductive cycle may be similarly temperature-dependent, but data on year-to-year variation in spermatogenesis are lacking.

The spermatogenic cycle of the male alligator in Louisiana probably begins during winter, especially if weather is mild. As temperature increases in late March and early April, rate of spermatogenesis increases, and blood testosterone concentrations rise markedly. Spermatogenesis peaks in May when mating intensity increases. Following copulation, testis mass and plasma testosterone decrease precipitously. Testes remain quiescent from June to early August. There is no obvious resumption of the spermatogenic cycle in late August or September, but circulating testosterone increases slightly (Lance, 1989). These temporal events in the male cycle may vary from year to year in cases of extreme weather events. There is no evidence of prolonged sperm storage in the male reproductive tract. Histological examination has revealed empty epididymides in late summer.

The female follicular or vitellogenic phase in Crocodilia is significantly shorter than that of the Chelonia, beginning with temperature increases in early April and being completed by late May. Increased circulating oestradiol, testosterone, lipid, calcium and phosphorus are measured during this period (Lance, 1989). After ovulation in late May, blood oestradiol concentration declines and progesterone increases. An average of 40 hard-shelled eggs is produced 2 to 3 weeks post-ovulation. Only one clutch is laid, usually mid-June, and only 50–60% of mature females nest each year. Inter-nest interval is unknown, but probably is 2 to 3 years. Some crocodiles in captivity have produced two clutches in the same year. There is no evidence of sperm storage in the female reproductive tract (D. Gist, personal communication).

Several peptide hormones have been isolated and sequenced from alligator tissue, and all illustrate the close relationship of crocodilians to birds. For example, the gonadotrophic releasing hormones GnRH-1 and GnRH-2 are identical to those of the chicken (Lovejoy et al., 1991), whereas the structure of alligator prolactin is closely analogous to that of the chicken (Tohohiko et al., 1993).

Squamata

Squamates are the most recently evolved reptiles and exhibit the most diversity in morphology, physiology and life-history traits, including reproductive patterns. The squamate pituitary may secrete only one gonadotrophin with biological properties of both follicle stimulating hormone (FSH) and luteinising hormone (LH) (Licht, 1984). If true, this feature would make snakes and lizards the only amniotes with such an unusual reproductive system. Turtles and crocodiles have two gonadotrophins, an FSH and an LH similar to those of amphibians (anamniotes), birds and mammals. Snakes also have extraordinarily high concentrations of zinc, levels toxic to mammals (Lance et al., 1995). Temperature-dependent sex determination has been described in several lizard families, but not in snakes (Viets et al., 1994). Partheno-genesis also has been reported in at least three lizard families as well as the blind fossorial snake (*Rhamphotyphlops braminis*) and the Arafuran file snake (*Acrochordus arafura*) (Dubach et al., 1997). Viviparity is believed to have evolved independently at least 100 times among the squamates (Shine, 1995). Whether viviparity arose as an adaptation to cool environments (or saline environments, as in the sea snakes) or as an adaptation to favour neonatal fitness continues to be debated (Andrews & Mathies, 2000). It has also been argued that viviparity in reptiles is an ancestral condition whereas oviparity is a 'derived' condition (Webb & Cooper-Preston, 1989). Amongst the crocodilians, chelonians and rhynchocephalians, viviparity is not optional, despite evolutionary pressure that would seemingly favour such an adaptation (Webb & Cooper-Preston, 1989).

Male lizards and snakes express several unusual features not observed in other reptile groups. The copulatory organ (hemipenes) is paired, and each of the pair is used interchangeably (Fox, 1977). A kidney part (the re-nal sex segment) hypertrophies during the mating season (Fox, 1977) due to increased testosterone secretion by testicular Leydig cells. During copu-lation, a complex of lipids and mucopolysaccharides are secreted from the renal segment into the seminal fluid. The function of this material is not fully understood. In some snake species these secretions help to form the copulatory plug that is believed to prevent subsequent males from success-fully mating with the recently inseminated female (Ross & Crews, 1977). Nevertheless, at least one species for which such a function has been pro-posed is known to produce litters with multiple paternity. Genetic testing of females and offspring of the viviparous garter snake (*Thamnophis sirtalis*) has demonstrated that up to 70% of the litters are sired by more than one male, some involving triple paternity (McCracken et al., 1999).

Selected published information on testosterone concentrations in male lizards and snakes is provided in Table 22.3. There is a wide range of val-ues from 3 ng/ml in the snake *Agkistrodon piscivorus* to 400 ng/ml in the lizard *Lacerta vivipara*. This lizard species has unusually high steroid bind-ing protein concentrations in blood of both males and females. No doubt some of the low tabular values result from capture stress and delayed blood collection, resulting in corticosterone suppression of testosterone (Lance, 1994).

The annual testosterone cycle in squamates is similar to that of turtles and crocodiles in that peak concentrations coincide with spermiogenesis.

Table 22.3 *Published plasma testosterone data on male Squamata*

Family	Species	Testosterone (ng/ml)[a]	Reference
Iguanidae	*Anolis sagrei*	1.5–27.0	Tokarz *et al.* (1998)
	Sceloperus undulatus	1.8–46.5	McKinney & Marion (1985)
Agamidae	*Uromastix hardwicki*	3.1–50.8	Arslan *et al.* (1978)[b]
	Amphibolorus caudicinctus	11.6–51.0	Bradshaw *et al.* (1991)
	Amphibolorus nuchalis	7.0–29.0	Bradshaw *et al.* (1991)
	Pogona barbata	2.97–27.58	Amey & Whittier (2000)
Scincidae	*Niveoscincus ocellatus*	0.7–18.6	Jones *et al.* (1997)
	Niveoscincus metallicus	1.7–51.7	Swain & Jones (1994)
Lacertidae	*Podarcis sicula sicula*	5.0–174.2	Ando *et al.* (1990)
	Lacerta vivipara	0.1–390.0	Courty & Dufaure (1980)
Helodermatidae	*Heloderma suspectum*	0.1–8.9	V. A. Lance (unpublished)
Varanidae	*Varanus albigularis*	0.5–95.0	Phillips & Millar (1998)
Colubridae	*Coluber viridiflavus*	3.9–45.0	Bonnet & Naulleau (1996)
	Thamnophis sirtalis concinnus	2.0–88.0	Moore *et al.* (2000)
	Thamnophis sirtalis	2.4–38.3	Weil (1985)
	Nerodia sipedon	0.1–21.5	Weil & Aldridge (1981)
Viperidae	*Agkistrodon contortix*	1.03–103.8	Schuett *et al.* (1997)
	Agkistrodon piscivorus	0.1–3.0	Johnson *et al.* (1982)
	Vipera aspis	0.1–60.0	Naulleau *et al.* (1987)
	Vipera berus	0.51–45.0	Naulleau & Fleury (1988)

[a] Estimated minimum and maximum means.
[b] Full citation in Licht (1984).

There is a second late summer peak in many species, often accompanied by mating just before cooler weather provokes winter denning. Thyroxine also has been measured in a few species with the seasonal pattern reminiscent of that seen in the desert tortoise. Plasma thyroxine has been shown to be maximal in male *Vipera aspis* when the snake emerges in spring (Naulleau *et al.*, 1987).

The spermatogenic cycle has been described for many squamate species (Lance, 1984; Licht, 1984). As with the other reptile groups, testosterone secretion peaks coincide with maximal spermatogenesis. Spermatogenesis may require two seasons to complete in snakes living in cooler extremes of the temperate zone.

Table 22.4 provides published data on plasma steroid hormone concentrations in female lizards and snakes. Most efforts have focused only upon progesterone, although a few studies have measured multiple hormones

Table 22.4 Published steroid hormone data on female Squamata

Family	Species	Oestradiol (pg/ml)	Testosterone (ng/ml)	Progesterone (ng/ml)	Reference
Iguanidae	*Sceloperus jarrovi*	–	–	0.7–3.8	Guillette et al. (1981)[a]
Agamidae	*Agama atra*	–	–	2.1–7.4	Van Wyk (1994)
	Amphibolorus caudicinctus	160–1200	–	0.9–6.3	Bradshaw et al. (1991)
	Amphibolorus nuchalis	110–480	–	1.0–5.0	Bradshaw et al. (1991)
Chamaeleonidae	*Chamaeleo pumilis pumilis*	–	–	0.8–5.0	Veith (1974)[a]
Scincidae	*Niveoscincus ocellatus*	80–1241	–	0.7–6.5	Jones et al. (1997)
	Niveoscincus metallicus	80–714	–	0.5–11.5	Jones & Swain (1996)
Lacertidae	*Lacerta vivipara*	–	–	1.0–400.0	Xavier (1982)
Cordylidae	*Cordylus giganteus*	6.0–650	–	1.8–5.5	Van Wyk (1994)
Varanidae	*Varanus albigularis*	50–1050	0.1–40.0	–	Phillips & Millar (1998)
Colubridae	*Thamnophis elegans*	–	–	1.7–6.2	Highfill & Mead (1975)[a]
	Nerodia (Natrix) sipedon	–	–	1.3–6.9	Chan et al. (1973)[a]
Elapidae	*Naja naja*	10–120	0.05–0.35	1.4–10.5	Bona-Gallo et al. (1980)[a]
Viperidae	*Vipera aspis*	60–4830	–	1.0–25.0	Bonnet et al. (1994)

[a] Full citations in Licht (1984).

(including thyroid hormone and corticosterone; not shown). Species variation in hormonal concentrations is common. Peak oestradiol levels for *V. aspis* are higher than for other reptiles. Elevated concentrations of plasma steroid binding protein (about 20 times above human plasma levels; Martin & Xavier, 1981) may explain the extraordinarily high progesterone of 400 ng/ml in *L. vivipara*. Unfortunately, there are no data on steroid binding proteins in other lizard or snake species that produce low circulating steroid concentrations.

Follicular development in snakes is protracted, requiring 2 to 3 years, and is different from that of crocodiles and turtles. The oocyte is translucent during early follicular growth due to accumulated non-lipid fluid 'yolk'. Such follicles are sometimes referred to as 'hydration stage'. Vitellogenesis proper begins when yellow, lipid-rich yolk is formed in response to oestrogen production from developing follicles. Oestrogen is transported in the blood to the liver where it stimulates vitellogenin synthesis. This phase generally is rapid in squamates, lasting only about 6 weeks, a period that coincides with increased plasma calcium, phosphorus and lipid. The granulosa layer surrounding the oocyte is also unusual in snakes and lizards. Unlike crocodiles, turtles and tuatara that have only a single granulosa cell type, the hydration phase of follicular growth in squamates is associated with three granulosa cell types: small round cells on the basement membrane, intermediate cells and pyriform (nurse or flask) cells. Pyriform cells form cytoplasmic bridges with the developing oocyte and are believed to contribute RNA and unknown proteins to the oocyte's cytoplasm. With oestrogen secretion and vitellogenesis onset, pyriform cells undergo apoptosis, the DNA deconstructs, and the fragments are transferred to the oocyte via intercellular bridges that remain patent until late in cellular breakdown. After this unusual 'recycling', the granulosa is reduced to a single layer (similar to other reptiles) (DeCaro et al., 1998). No other vertebrate is known to exhibit a similar follicular structure.

Rhynchocephalia (Sphenodontia)

The only surviving genus of this order is a small, lizard-like creature that lives on a few windswept islands near the New Zealand coast. The tuatara is considered endangered, even though these islands serve as critical habitat for thousands of individuals. Cree & colleagues (1992, 1995) have demonstrated that this cold-hardy reptile undergoes a reproductive cycle similar to that of the oviparous Chelonia and Crocodilia. Spermatogenesis appears continuous since there is no post-mating testicular regression or seasonal change in testicular mass. Nevertheless, testosterone is elevated (10.8 ng/ml) when spermiogenesis occurs during mid-summer mating. Copulation occurs via cloacal apposition because males lack a copulatory organ. Adult females nest only once every 4 years with vitellogenesis spread over 3 years. Steroid hormone concentrations are in the same range as in squamates (oestradiol, 27 to 327 pg/ml; testosterone, 0.1 to 32.6 ng/ml; progesterone, 2.9 to 57.7 ng/ml).

Eggs are carried in the oviduct of the tuatara for 6 to 8 months before nesting, during which time embryonic development is arrested. Egg incubation is equally slow, from 6 to 12 months (Thompson, 1990), and offspring sex is incubation temperature-dependent (Cree *et al.*, 1995). The upper lethal temperature limit for tuatara eggs (25–26 ° C) is well below that at which embryonic development fails in the eggs of crocodilians and some turtles.

FUTURE PRIORITIES

Endocrine and physiological data have been collected from only a few reptile species, predominately those living in temperate zones. Nothing is known about reproductive cycles or hormones in amphisbaenids, and virtually nothing on tropical lizards and snakes. Without significantly increased efforts to begin studying all readily accessible reptiles, it is inevitable that many genera will disappear before anything is known of their basic biology. The collection of scholarly information, especially in the reproductive sciences, that then is integrated with field ecology studies and *ex situ* breeding programmes, will be essential to helping sustain many reptile species and populations. This is an exciting time to begin new investigations, particularly in nature, given the advent of valuable technologies such as data loggers, satellite tracking, portable X-ray, portable ultrasonography units and pit tags. In addition to fundamental data related to reproductive fitness and fecundity, there is a need to study the intriguing, mysterious reproductive mechanisms in reptiles, including sperm storage, the diversity in absolute hormonal patterns and circulating concentrations and the particular uniqueness of the squamates as a distinctive order. Among such high priorities are: unique follicular structure, apparent lack of two gonadotrophins, presence of venom glands, high circulating zinc in snakes and the multiple times viviparity has evolved. Together the reptiles hold a wealth of information that will serve as rich research resource for years to come. And, due to growing species extinctions, the need for more research action is urgent.

REFERENCES

Amey, A. P. & Whittier, J. M. (2000). Seasonal patterns of steroid hormones in males and females of the bearded dragon, *Pogona barbata*. *General and Comparative Endocrinology* **117**, 335-342.

Andò, S., Panno, M. L., Ciarcia, G. Imbrogno, E., Buffone, M., Beraldi, E., Sisci, D., Angelini, F. & Botte, V. (1990). Plasma sex hormone concentrations during the reproductive cycle in the male lizard, *Podarcis s. sicula*. *Journal of Reproduction and Fertility* **90**, 353-360.

Andrews, R. M. & Mathies, T. (2000). Natural history of reptilian development: constraints on the evolution of viviparity. *BioScience* **50**, 227-238.

Bonnet, X. & Naulleau, G. (1996). Are body reserves important for reproduction in male Dark Green snakes (Colubridae; *Coluber viridiflavus*)? *Herpetologica* **52**, 137-146.

Bonnet, X., Naulleau, G. & Mauget, R. (1994). The influence of body condition on 17β estradiol levels in relation to vitellogenesis in female *Vipera aspis* (Reptilia, Viperidae). *General and Comparative Endocrinology* **93**, 424-437.

Bradshaw, S. D., Saint Girons, H. & Bradshaw, F. J. (1991). Patterns of breeding in two species of agamid lizards in the arid sub-tropical Pilbara region of Western Australia. *General and Comparative Endocrinology* **82**, 407-424.

Callard, I. P. & Callard, G. V. (1987). Sex steroid receptors and non-receptor binding proteins. In *Hormones & Reproduction in Fishes, Amphibians & Reptiles* (Eds. D. O. Norris & R. E. Jones), pp. 355-384. Plenum Press, New York.

Callard, I. P. & Ho, S. M. (1980). Seasonal reproductive cycles of reptiles. *Progress in Reproductive Biology* **5**, 5-38.

Cash, W. B., Holberton, R. L. & Knight, S. S. (1997). Corticosterone secretion in response to capture and handling in free-living red-eared slider turtles. *General and Comparative Endocrinology* **108**, 427-433.

Christopher, M. M., Berry, K. H., Wallis, I. R., Nagy, K. A., Henen, B. T. & Peterson, C. C. (1999). Reference intervals and physiologic alterations in hematologic and biochemical values of free-ranging desert tortoises in the Mojave Desert. *Journal of Wildlife Diseases* **35**, 212-238.

Courty, Y. & Dufaure, J. P. (1980). Levels of testosterone, dihydrotestosterone and androstenedione in the plasma and testis of a lizard (*Lacerta vivipara* Jacquin) during the annual cycle. *General and Comparative Endocrinology* **42**, 325-333.

Cree, A., Cockrem, J. F. & Guillette, L. J. (1992). Reproductive cycles of male and female tuatara (*Sphenodon punctatus*) on Stephens Island, New Zealand. *Journal of Zoology (London)* **226**, 199-217.

Cree, A., Thompson, M. B. & Daugherty, C. H. (1995). Tuatara sex determination. *Nature* **375**, 543.

DeCaro, M., Indolfi, P., Iodice, C., Spagnuolo, S., Tammaro, S. & Motta, C. M. (1998). How the ovarian follicle of *Podarcis sicula* recycles the DNA of its nurse, regressing follicle cells. *Molecular Reproduction and Development* **51**, 421-429.

Dubach, J., Sajewicz, A. & Pawley, R. (1997). Parthenogenesis in the Arafuran file snake (*Acrochordus arafurae*). *Herpetology & Natural History* **5**, 11-18.

Edgren, R. A. (1960). A seasonal change in bone density in female musk turtles, *Sternotherus odoratus* (Latreille). *Comparative Biochemistry and Physiology* **1**, 360-366.

Fitch, H. S. (1970). *Reproductive Cycles of Lizards and Snakes*. University of Kansas Museum of Natural History, Miscellaneous Publication No. 52, pp. 1-247.

Fitch, H. S. (1982). *Reproductive Cycles in Tropical Reptiles*. University of Kansas Museum of Natural History, Miscellaneous Publication No. 96, pp. 1-53.

Fox, H. (1977). The urogenital system of reptiles. In *Biology of the Reptilia*, Vol. 6. *Morphology* (Eds. C. Gans & T. S. Parsons), pp. 1-157. Academic Press, New York.

Gibbons, J. W. (1990). *The Life History & Ecology of the Slider Turtle*. Smithsonian Institution Press, Washington, DC.

Gibbons, J. W., Scott, D. E., Ryan, T. J., Buhlmann, K. A., Tuberville, T. D., Metts, B. S., Greene, J. L., Mills, T., Leiden, Y. Poppy, S. & Winne, C. T. (2000). The global decline of reptiles, déjà vu amphibians. *BioScience* **50**, 653-666.

Gist, D. H., Michaelson, J. A. & Jones, J. M. (1990). Autumn mating in the painted turtle, *Chrysemys picta*. *Herpetologica* **46**, 331-336.

González-Trapága, R. G. (1995). Reproduction of the Bolson tortoise, *Gopherus flavomarginatus*, Legler 1959. Publicaciones de la Sociedad Herpetológica Mexicana No. 2. pp. 32-36.

Guillette, L. J. Jr, Woodward, A. R., Crain, D. A., Masson, G. R., Palmer, B. D., Cox, M. C., Qui, Y.-X. & Orlando, E. F. (1997). The reproductive cycle of the female American alligator (*Alligator mississippiensis*). *General and Comparative Endocrinology* **108**, 87-101.

Ho, S. M., Kleis, S., McPherson, R., Heisermann, G. J. & Callard, I. P. (1982). Regulation of vitellogenesis in reptiles. *Herpetologica* **38**, 40-50.

Joanen, T. & McNease, L. L. (1989). Ecology and physiology of nesting and early development of the American alligator. *American Zoologist* **29**, 987-998.

Johnson, L. F., Jacob, J. S. & Torrance, P. (1982). Annual testicular cycle and androgenic cycles of the cottonmouth (*Agkistrodon piscivorus*) in Alabama. *Herpetologica* **28**, 16-25.

Jones, S. M. & Swain, R. (1996). Annual reproductive cycle and annual cycles of reproductive hormones in plasma of female *Niveoscincus metallicus* (Scincidae) from Tasmania. *Journal of Herpetology* **30**, 140-146.

Jones, S. M., Wapstra, E. & Swain, R. (1997). Asynchronous male and female gonadal cycles and plasma steroid concentrations in a viviparous lizard, *Niveoscincus ocellatus* (Scincidae) from Tasmania. *General and Comparative Endocrinology* **108**, 271-281.

Kohel, K. A., MacKenzie, D. C. Rostal, D. C., Grumbles, J. S. & Lance, V. A. (2001). Seasonality in plasma thyroxine in the Desert tortoise, *Gopherus agassizii*. *General and Comparative Endocrinology* **121**, 214-222.

Kuchling, G. (1999). *The Reproductive Biology of the Chelonia*. Springer-Verlag, Berlin.

Lance, V. A. (1984). Endocrinology of reproduction in male reptiles. *Symposia of the Zoological Society of London* **52**, 357-383.

Lance, V. A. (1987). Hormonal control of reproduction in crocodilians. In *Wildlife Management: Crocodiles and Alligators* (Eds. G. J. W. Webb, S. C. Manolis & P. J. Whitehead), pp. 409-415. Surrey Beatty & Sons, Sydney.

Lance, V. A. (1989). Reproductive cycle of the American alligator. *American Zoologist* **29**, 999-1018.

Lance, V. A. (1994). Life in the slow lane: hormones, stress and the immune system of reptiles. In *Perspectives in Comparative Endocrinology* (Eds. G. K. Davey, R. E. Peter & S. S. Tobe), pp. 529-534. National Research Council of Canada, Ottawa.

Lance, V. & Callard, I. P. (1980). Phylogenetic trends in the hormonal control of gonadal steroidogenesis. In *The Evolution of Vertebrate Endocrines* (Eds. A. Epple & P. Pang), pp. 167-223. Texas Tech Press, Lubbock, TX.

Lance, V. A., Cort, T., Masuoka, J., Lawson, R. & Saltman, P. (1995). Unusually high zinc concentrations in snake plasma, with observations on plasma zinc concentrations in lizards, turtles and alligators. *Journal of Zoology (London)* **235**, 577-585.

Lance, V. A., Grumbles, J. S. & Rostal, D. C. (2001). Sex differences in the plasma corticosterone in desert tortoises, *Gopherus agassizii*, during the reproductive cycle. *Journal of Experimental Zoology* **289**, 285-289.

Lance, V. A., Place, A. & Rostal, D. C. (2002). Variation in plasma lipids during the reproductive cycle of male and female desert tortoises, *Gopherus agassizii*. *Journal of Experimental Zoology* (in press).

Licht, P. (1984). Reptiles. In *Marshall's Physiology of Reproduction*, vol. 1. *Reproductive Cycles of Vertebrates* (Ed. G. E. Lamming), pp. 206-282. Churchill Livingstone, Edinburgh.

Lovejoy, D. A., Fischer, W. H., Parker, D. B., McRory, J. E., Park, M., Lance, V., Swanson, P., Rivier, J. E. & Sherwood, N. M. (1991). Primary structure of two forms of gonadotropin-releasing hormone from the brains of the American alligator (*Alligator mississippiensis*). *Regulatory Peptides* **33**, 105-116.

Mannen, H. & Li, S.-L. (1999). Molecular evidence for a clade of turtles. *Molecular Phylogenetics & Evolution* **13**, 144-148.

Mao, W.-P. & Wang, Z.-X. (1999). Seasonal variation of testicular and epididymal structure and plasma levels of testosterone in the soft-shell turtle (*Pelodiscus sinensis*). *Asiatic Herpetology Research* **8**, 75-80.

Martin, B. & Xavier, F. (1981). High-affinity binding of progesterone, estradiol-17ß and testosterone by plasma proteins of the reptile *Lacerta vivipara*. *Journal of General Comparative Endocrinology* **43**, 299-307.

McCracken, G. F., Burghardt, G. M. & Houts, S. E. (1999). Microsatellite markers and multiple paternity in the garter snake *Thamnophis sirtalis*. *Molecular Ecology* **8**, 1475-1479.

McKinney, R. B. & Marion K. R. (1985). Plasma androgens and their association with the reproductive cycle of the male fence lizard, *Sceloperus undulatus*. *Comparative Biochemistry and Physiology A* **82**, 515-519.

McPherson, R. J. & Marion, K. R. (1982). Seasonal changes in total lipids in the turtle *Sternotherus odoratus*. *Comparative Biochemistry and Physiology A* **71**, 93-98.

Moore, I. T., Lerner, J. P., Lerner, D. T. & Mason, R. T. (2000). Relationship between annual cycles of testosterone, corticosterone and body condition in male red-spotted garter snakes, *Thamnophis sirtalis concinnus*. *Physiology, Biochemistry & Zoology* **73**, 307-312.

Morafka, D. J., Spangenberg, E. K., & Lance, V. A. (2000). Neonatology of reptiles. *Herpetology Monographs* **14**, 353-370.

Naulleau, G. & Fleury, F. (1988) Cycles annuels de la testostéronémie et de la thyroxinémie chez *Vipera berus* L. (Reptilia: Viperidae) en relation avec le cycle sexuel et l'hivernage. *Amphibia-Reptilia* **9**, 33-42.

Naulleau, G., Fleury, F. & Boissin, J. (1987). Annual cycles in plasma testosterone and thyroxine in the male aspic viper *Vipera aspis* L. (Reptilia, Viperidae), in relation to the sexual cycle and hibernation. *General and Comparative Endocrinology* **65**, 254-263.

Ott, J. A., Mendonça, M. T., Guyer, C & Michener, W. K. (2000). Seasonal changes in sex and adrenal steroid hormones of gopher tortoises (*Gopherus polyphemus*). *General and Comparative Endocrinology* **117**, 299-312.

Phillips, J. A. & Millar, R. P. (1998). Reproductive biology of the white-throated savanna monitor, *Varanus albigularis*. *Journal of Herpetology* **32**, 366-377.

Romer, A. S. (1967). Major steps in vertebrate evolution. *Science* **158**, 1629-1638.

Ross, P. & Crews, D. (1977). Influence of seminal plug on mating behaviour in the garter snake. *Nature* **267**, 344-345.

Rostal, D. C., Grumbles, J. S., Palmer, K. S., Lance, V. A., Spotila, J. R. & Paladino, F. V. (2001). Reproductive endocrinology of the leatherback sea turtle (*Dermochelys coriacea*). *General and Comparative Endocrinology* **122**, 139-147.

Rostal, D. C., Lance, V. A. Grumbles, J. S. & Alberts, A. (1994). Seasonal reproductive cycle of the desert tortoise (*Gopherus agassizii*) in the eastern Mojave desert. *Herpetology Monographs* **8**, 72-82.

Rostal, D. C., Owens, D. W., Grumbles, J. S., MacKenzie, D. S. & Amoss, M. S., Jr (1998). Seasonal reproductive cycle of the Kemp's Ridley sea turtle (*Lepidochelys kempi*). *General and Comparative Endocrinology* **109**, 232-243.

Ruby, D. E., Zimmerman, L. C., Bulova, S. J., Salice, C. J., O'Connor, M. P. & Spotila, J. R. (1994). Behavioral responses and time allocation differences in desert tortoises exposed to environmental stress in semi-natural enclosures. *Herpetology Monographs* **8**, 27-44.

Sarkar, S., Sarkar, N. K. & Maiti, B. R. (1996). Seasonal pattern of ovarian growth and interrelated changes in plasma steroid levels, vitellogenesis and oviductal function in the adult female soft-shelled turtle *Lissemys punctata punctata*. *Canadian Journal of Zoology* **74**, 303-311.

Schramm, B. G., Casares, M. & Lance, V. A. (1999). Steroid levels and reproductive cycle of the Galápagos tortoise, *Geochelone nigra*, living under seminatural conditions on Santa Cruz Island (Galápagos). *General and Comparative Endocrinology* **114**, 108-120.

Schuett, G. W., Harlow, H. J., Rose, J. D., Van Kirk, E. A. & Murdoch, W. J. (1997). Annual cycle of plasma testosterone in male copperheads, *Agkistrodon contortix* (Serpentes, Viperidae); relationship to timing of spermatogenesis, mating and agonistic behavior. *General and Comparative Endocrinology* **105**, 417-424.

Shelby, J. A., Mendonca, M. T., Horne, B. D. & Seigal, R. A. (2000). Seasonal variation in reproductive steroids of male and female yellow-blotched map turtles, *Graptemys flavimaculata*. *General and Comparative Endocrinology* **119**, 43-51.

Shine, R. (1995). A new hypothesis for the evolution of viviparity in reptiles. *American Naturalist* **145**, 809-823.

Spotila, J. R., Dunham, A. E., Leslie, A. J., Steyermark, A. C., Plotkin, P. T. & Palladino, F. V. (1996). Worldwide population decline of *Dermochelys coriacea*: are leatherback turtles going extinct? *Chelonian Conservation & Biology* **2**, 209-222.

Swain, R. & Jones, S. M. (1994). Annual cycle of plasma testosterone and other reproductive parameters in the Tasmanian skink, *Niveoscincus metallicus*. *Herpetologica* **50**, 502-509.

Thompson, M. B. (1990). Incubation of eggs of tuatara, *Sphenodon punctatus*. *Journal of Zoology (London)* 222, 303-318.

Tohohiko, N., Swanson, P., Lance, V. A. & Kawauchi, H. (1993). Isolation and characterization of glycosylated and non-glycosylated prolactins from two reptiles, alligator and crocodile. *International Journal of Peptide & Protein Research* 39, 250-257.

Tokarz, R. R., McMann, S., Seitz, L. & John-Alder, H. (1998). Plasma corticosterone and testosterone levels during the annual reproductive cycle of male brown anoles (*Anolis sagrei*). *Physiological Zoology* 71, 139-146.

Van Wyk, J. H. (1994). Physiological changes during the female reproductive cycle of the viviparous lizard *Cordylus giganteus* (Sauria: Cordylidae). *Herpetologica* 50, 480-493.

Viets, B. E., Ewert, M. A., Talent, L. G. & Nelson, C. E. (1994). Sex-determining mechanisms in squamate reptiles. *Journal of Experimental Zoology* 270, 57-70.

Webb, G. J. W. & Cooper-Preston, H. (1989). Effects of incubation temperature on crocodiles and the evolution of reptilian oviparity. *American Zoologist* 29, 953-971.

Weil, M. R. (1985). Comparison of plasma and testicular testosterone levels during the active season in the common garter snake, *Thamnophis sirtalis* (L.). *Comparative Biochemistry and Physiology A* 81, 585-587.

Weil, M. R. & Aldridge, R. A. (1981). Seasonal androgenesis in the male water snake, *Nerodia sipedon*. *General and Comparative Endocrinology* 44, 44-53.

Wibbels, T. Owens, D. W., Limpus, C. J., Reed, P. C. & Amos, M. S. (1990). Seasonal changes in serum gonadal steroids associated with migration, mating and nesting in the loggerhead sea turtle (*Caretta caretta*). *General and Comparative Endocrinology* 79, 154-164.

Xavier, F. (1982). Progesterone in the viviparous lizard *Lacerta vivipara*: ovarian biosynthesis, plasma levels and binding to transcortin-type protein during the sexual cycle. *Herpetologica* 38, 62-70.

23

Reproductive research and the worldwide amphibian extinction crisis

TERRI L. ROTH & AMY R. OBRINGER

INTRODUCTION AND BACKGROUND

This chapter is devoted to stimulating interest in amphibian reproduction and inspiring an appreciation for the challenges and benefits of such research in this largely ignored taxon that is facing a world-wide extinction crisis.

Taxonomic distribution

Amphibia can be divided into three orders: (1) Gymnophiona (caecilians), (2) Caudata (salamanders and newts) and (3) Anura (toads and frogs). Caecilians are worm-like, burrowing, legless amphibians living underground in tropical environments. Little is known about animal numbers within most of the 156 species in this order, but two species are listed by CITES as 'Endangered' or 'Threatened' (IUCN Red Book, 2000). The Caudata comprise 440 species of salamanders and newts that primarily inhabit the Northern Hemisphere. A few species extend to southern Brazil, Bolivia and Southeast Asia. Although there is concern about many of these species, only three are considered 'Critically endangered', eight 'Endangered' and 26 'Vulnerable' (IUCN Red Book, 2000). Anurans are the most broadly dispersed and abundant amphibians with 4360 species identified (about the total number of mammalian species known). Twenty-two anuran species are considered 'Critically endangered', 29 'Endangered' and 56 'Vulnerable' (IUCN Red Book, 2000).

The amphibian extinction crisis

There is a rapid and alarming disappearance of amphibian species in seemingly undisturbed ecosystems. A semi-aquatic lifestyle and a highly permeable skin render amphibians vulnerable to changes in water and/or atmospheric quality. Their dependence on moisture for reproduction also places populations at risk, even during minor perturbations in weather and habitat. This vulnerability makes amphibians popular 'sentinels' for monitoring global environmental health (Weygoldt, 1989; Blaustein & Wake, 1990).

Normal year-to-year fluxes in amphibian populations and the lack of long-term field studies initially made it difficult to establish that the crisis was real (Blaustein et al., 1994). However, in 1997 the Declining Amphibian Population Task Force (IUCN's Species Survival Commission) unanimously confirmed the significant world-wide decline in amphibian populations (Heyer, 1997). Potential causes include habitat degradation, pollution, acid rain, ultraviolet irradiation, pesticides, predators, competition from introduced species, climate changes and disease. Many of these factors probably interact to exert an effect, but disease is emerging as significant and widespread. For example, Chytridiomycosis has been associated with mass amphibian deaths in Latin American and Australian rainforests and parts of North America (Daszak et al., 1999). Ranaviruses can be 100% lethal, especially in tadpoles (Hyatt et al., 1998), but have not been linked to mass deaths. Pesticides are the probable cause of the final demise in the wild of the Wyoming toad (Bufo baxteri; Dickerson, 1999). Ultimately, there appears to have been a change in the global environment that predisposes amphibians to lethal pathogens and/or offers an advantage to pathogens that makes them more deadly. Mattoon (2000) concluded that 'The amphibian crisis is global, but we don't know its full extent. It is the result of human activity but cannot be explained by just one or two causes. It is of deep ecological significance, but we have only a vague sense of what the significance is. When we peer into the amphibian decline, we are looking into the depths of our own ignorance.'

STATE OF THE ART

Diversity of amphibian reproductive mechanisms

Diverse modes of reproduction in amphibians far exceed those observed among other vertebrates and an evolutionary transition towards terrestriality and specialisation that allows species to occupy unambiguous ecological niches. Amphibians can be oviparous, viviparous or ovoviviparous. Fertilisation can occur internally or externally and, if internal, can take place immediately after insemination or up to 2.5 years later. Eggs and/or larvae may occupy aquatic, arboreal or terrestrial environments, or may require some physical attachment to the dam or sire (internally or externally).

Although little studied, all caecilians are presumed to fertilise internally with about 75% bearing live young after a gestation of up to 11 months (Wake, 1977). However, a few species produce eggs in terrestrial environments near water.

Internal fertilisation predominates among caudates. Approximately 90% of salamanders practise this method with just a few species retaining the more primitive external fertilisation. However, copulation *per se* does not necessarily occur. Rather, during an elaborate courtship display, a male deposits a gelatinous spermatophore that the female picks up with her cloacal lips (Propper & Moore, 1991). Spermatozoa are stored in the female's spermatheca in the roof of the cloaca and are expelled by muscular contractions when eggs enter the oviduct. Species such as the fire salamander (*Salamandra salamandra*), that store spermatozoa for up to 2.5 years, may mate with multiple males, resulting in mixed paternity among offspring. Some salamander species can control the developmental stage of offspring. For example, *S. salamandra* and *Mertinsiella caucasica* typically have aquatic larvae, but in montane regions or during drought, they retain their eggs, later giving birth to well-developed young (Duellman & Trueb, 1986).

Anurans mostly fertilise externally. Usually female frogs and toads undertake oviposition in an aquatic environment concurrent with spermiation by males, and fertilisation occurs immediately. Aquatic embryo and larval development follows with eventual metamorphosis to an adult that inhabits both land and water. But there is extensive diversity in reproductive mechanisms and larval development among anurans. For example, the grey treefrog (*Chiromantis xerampelina*) congregates in groups of up to 30 animals that release spermatozoa and eggs on a branch while beating their hind legs to form a foam nest. The arboreal glass frogs, such as *Centrolenella valeriori*, of Latin America attach their eggs beneath tree leaves hanging over running water. Emergent tadpoles drop into the water to begin their aquatic larval development. Others, such as *Dendrobates auratus* and *D. pumilio* produce eggs on land, but the males periodically moisten them by emptying their bladders on the clutch (Wells, 1978; Weygoldt, 1980). The fertilised eggs of the Surinam toad (*Pipa pipa*) become imbedded in the spongy tissue of her flattened back. After several days the eggs hatch, and the tadpoles continue development in pockets on her back until dispersing c. 100 days later as small toadlets. Perhaps most mysterious is the female Australian gastric brooding frog (*Rheobatrachus silus*) that ingests her fertilised eggs, incubates them in her stomach and gives birth 37 days later through her mouth to young toadlets. Unfortunately, we probably will never learn how this fascinating frog turned off gastric digestion to allow brooding, because the species disappeared in the 1980s.

Historical amphibian research

Amphibians have been used in laboratories for decades, but primarily for education. Additionally, of the 115 000 amphibians used by universities and research institutes in the United Kingdom in 1977 (Donnelly, 1980), virtually all were the common *Xenopus laevis* and *Ambystoma mexicanum*. Although there is extensive reproductive research reported in the literature (the Internet's PubMed cites 2376 referenced abstracts on 'amphibian reproduction' since 1964), these references are severely skewed towards basic research involving a few common species.

Historically, sperm–egg interaction and embryo studies were popular because amphibians were readily available, inexpensive and produced large numbers of gametes and embryos. The species' large-sized embryos and aquatic, often brief, larval stages made them ideal for early developmental and cellular differentiation studies. Unfortunately, species conservation is not a concern of most basic scientists, and euthanasia is common practice in research. Therefore, most amphibian conservation studies have been spearheaded by herpetologists and zoological institutions and have resulted in an impressive list of propagated endangered species (Maruska, 1986; Wiese & Hutchins, 1994). Nonetheless, the establishment of consistently successful, genetic-based breeding programmes is lacking. Like mammals, amphibians could benefit from integrating more reproductive studies and technologies into natural and assisted breeding strategies.

Gender determination

Gender determination is typically based on morphometric differences between sexes, but amphibians can be unisexual (Zug, 1993) or, in the case of the crested newt, undergo sex reversal (Wallace *et al.*, 1999). These exceptions aside, most amphibians display sexual dimorphism in body size, glandular development, skin texture, dermal ornamentation, vocal sacs and/or coloration. However, some of these secondary sex characteristics develop in response to gonadotrophic hormones produced during the breeding season (Duellman & Trueb, 1986). Therefore, determining gender during the non-breeding season or in species where breeding cues are unknown can be challenging.

Karyotype analysis is inconclusive. Although available information supports a genetic mechanism for sex determination in amphibians, most species lack morphologically distinguishable sex chromosomes (Hayes, 1998; Wallace *et al.*, 1999), and some species, such as *Rana esculenta*, can be diploid or even triploid (Zug, 1993).

Laparoscopy and ultrasonography have been used to successfully sex hellbenders (*Cryptobranchus alleganiens*) and Chinese giant salamanders (*Andrias davidianus*). The former technique requires anaesthesia and insertion of a 5 mm diameter laparoscope through the peritoneum to view the gonads (Kramer *et al.*, 1983). Ultrasonography can be performed transcutaneously with 3.5–10.0 MHz probes while the animal is physically restrained and submerged in water (Hildebrandt *et al.*, 1997). Neither of these sexing procedures has yet proven useful for determining gender in small-sized amphibians.

Sperm collection

Early gamete research in amphibians generally relied upon macerated testes as a source of spermatozoa, and many scientists still incorporate animal euthanasia into study designs (Browne *et al.*, 1998; Mugnano *et al.*, 1998). This is surprising since non-lethal methods for sperm release have been available since the 1940s, and the ability to induce sperm release repeatedly in the same animal was demonstrated 25 years ago (McKinnell *et al.*, 1976). Furthermore, macerating testes might be inappropriate for some studies because (1) macerates contain a heterogeneous mixture of cell types and (2) a male can be used only once (Waggener & Carroll, 1998b).

Non-lethal sperm collection in amphibians could provide valuable information on reproductive potential, evidence of sexual maturity (in animals of unknown age) and valuable 'genetic resources' that could be cryopreserved and/or used to fertilise eggs from multiple females. Additionally, sperm quality assessments from amphibians either free-living or held in controlled laboratory conditions could be important for monitoring the effects of environmental changes over time (e.g. contaminants, weather fluctuations).

Artificial induction of sperm release in toads dates back to a human pregnancy test developed in the 1940s when spermiation was stimulated by intraperitoneal injection of human chorionic gonadotrophin (hCG) (Galli-Mainini, 1947). Testes of anurans are adjacent to the kidneys, and spermatogenesis occurs in spermatocysts where all sperm cells differentiate synchronously (Zug, 1993). Upon spermiation induction, sperm cells are

Table 23.1 *Sperm characteristics (means ± SEM) in urine collected from five toad species after LHRH treatment*

Species (n = number of animals)	Sperm concentration (×10⁶/ml)	Motile sperm (%)	Morphologically normal (%)
Bufo americanus (American toad) (n = 14)	2.3 ± 0.5	66.8 ± 5.2	91.1 ± 1.7
B. baxteri (Wyoming toad) (n = 4)	1.9 ± 0.9	73.8 ± 3.8	64.0 ± 4.1
P. lemur (Puerto Rican crested toad) (n = 2)	1.8 ± 1.2	35.0 ± 5.0	75.0 ± 1.0
B. marinus (Cane toad) (n = 7)	19.0 ± 9.1	47.9 ± 12.5	88.3 ± 1.9
B. valliceps (Gulf Coast toad) (n = 5)	11.1 ± 3.9	55.0 ± 16.0	82.8 ± 9.0

transported from the efferent ductules of the testes into the kidney collecting tubules and eventually excreted with urine through the Wolffian duct into the cloaca (Duellman & Trueb, 1986). Both gonadotrophin releasing hormone (GnRH) and luteinising hormone releasing hormone (LHRH) are also effective stimulators of spermiation in anurans. Exogenous LHRH induces endogenous LH release, mimicking what occurs in response to amplexus during natural mating (Obringer *et al.*, 2000). Hormone-induced spermiation has already proved successful in eight frog (Waggener & Carroll, 1998b) and five toad species (Table 23.1), suggesting a wide application across a broad range of anurans.

Hormonal stimulation has been incorporated into *ex situ* breeding programmes for some endangered amphibians. For example, to ensure that all captive-produced Wyoming toad tadpoles can be released into the wild in a given location simultaneously, hormones are used to induce breeding synchrony during a narrow time window in the spring. In some years, these captive-held toads produce thousands of tadpoles, whereas reproduction all but fails in other years. This inconsistency may be due, in part, to the lack of standardised protocols backed by sound scientific research. For example, some animals may receive multiple hormone injections within 24 hours or on alternate days for up to a week. Recent data indicate that toads produce spermatozoa within a few hours, and up to 24 hours, after LHRH injection (Obringer *et al.*, 2000). Therefore, there appears to be no rationale for treating male toads more than once in a 24-hour period. Furthermore, sperm depletion can result from multiple hormone treatments at short intervals. Treating cane toads with 4 μg LHRH twice weekly for 4 weeks sharply

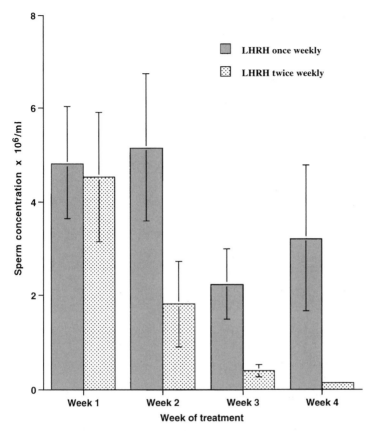

Figure 23.1 Mean sperm concentrations (± SEM) in urine collected from
B. marinus toads treated with LHRH either once (n = 7) or twice (n = 9) weekly
for 4 consecutive weeks.

reduces sperm concentrations in urine compared with once-weekly treatment (Figure 23.1). If multiple treatments are required before a female releases her eggs, it may be wise to alternate males rather than continue to
re-treat a single male whose sperm reserves may be reduced to levels that
affect fertility.

Intraperitoneal hormone injections can be risky, especially if repeated
frequently. An alternative is subcutaneous injection of hormone in the rear
leg (distant from the vital organs) which is less effective (Obringer et al.,
2000). More recently, it has been determined that applying the hormone
in high doses, or in conjunction with an absorptive enhancer (dimethyl-
sulphoxide, DMSO), to the vascular abdominal seat region induces spermiation in c. 70% of toads, thereby offering a non-invasive approach (Rowson
et al., 2001).

Sperm cryopreservation and artificial insemination (AI)

The potential value of sperm cryopreservation and AI to conserving and genetically managing amphibians is significant. Specific situations sometimes arise during *ex situ* breeding that could clearly benefit from the availability of frozen sperm. For example, the use of hormones to induce mating between designated Wyoming toad pairs has occasionally resulted in asynchronous responses. Males have been observed in amplexus with females for several days, yet she releases eggs only after his detachment. In the absence of a male (and thus spermatozoa), the eggs go unfertilised, and that breeding season is lost. If cryopreserved sperm were available, these eggs could be inseminated.

The real-life benefits of sperm cryopreservation are only realised when young are actually produced with thawed samples. For mammals, this requires developing complex *in vitro* fertilisation or intracervical or intrauterine AI procedures. Since amphibians mostly practice external fertilisation, IVF generally is not required. However, developing successful sperm cryopreservation and AI protocols is not without challenges.

Researchers have cryopreserved spermatozoa in an inactivated state by macerating testes directly into isotonic media supplemented with DMSO, glycerol or ethylene glycol (Barton & Guttman, 1972; Beesley *et al.*, 1998; Browne *et al.*, 1998; Mugnano *et al.*, 1998). All of these authors reported some success that, in several cases, was confirmed by successful egg fertilisation post-thaw. Although the information from these studies is valuable, extending these protocols to activated spermatozoa collected in urine of live animals will be difficult. In preliminary studies in our laboratory, spermic urine samples were subjected to published cryopreservation protocols. Although good post-thaw viability was observed (50–70% based on exclusion of the fluorescent vital stain Hoescht 33358), only 15% of the cells were motile when exposed to activating conditions (A. Obringer, unpublished data). Clearly, more basic research is needed on the physiology of activated spermatozoa.

Anuran spermatozoa have an unusual structure that may be essential for both sperm longevity and post-thaw survival. This structure, first identified as an accessory cell on *Lepidobatrachus laevis* spermatozoa by Waggener & Carroll (1998a), is located in the head region of the spermatozoon and easily can be mistaken for a cytoplasmic droplet. However, during spermiogenesis the cytoplasmic droplet is lost by the time spermatozoa reach the Wolffian duct (Sprando & Russell, 1988). Therefore, cytoplasmic droplets may be common on testicular spermatozoa but should not be present on

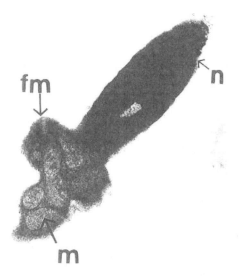

Figure 23.2 Thin section electron micrograph depicting a cross section of the sperm head with attached mitochondrial vesicle (× 16 500). The sperm nucleus (n), mitochondrial vesicle's fragile membrane (fm) and mitochondria (m) are identified.

spermatozoa in the urine. Furthermore, the cell-like structure appears full of mitochondria when examined by transmission electron microscopy (Figure 23.2) and may even contain a nucleus (Waggener & Carroll, 1998a). This mitochondrial vesicle also has been identified on *L. llanensis* (Waggener & Carroll, 1998a), *Bufo americanus, B. baxteri* (Obringer *et al.*, 2000), *B. marinus* and *B. valliceps* spermatozoa and plays a role in sperm motility in *L. laevis* (Waggener & Carroll, 1998a) and *B. americanus* (Vance *et al.*, 2001). Virtually all motile spermatozoa contain this structure, whereas it is lacking in non-motile counterparts. The membrane of the mitochondrial vesicle is fragile and can be observed rupturing spontaneously during microscopic examinations (T. Roth, unpublished observation). This fragility is likely to predispose it to damage during freeze-thawing. In our preliminary observations *c.* 80% of spermatozoa in freshly collected samples contain mitochondrial vesicles, whereas only 1–5% of spermatozoa in post-thaw samples retain them (A. Obringer, unpublished data). The loss of this structure could be the primary reason for poor post-thaw sperm motility.

Although functional spermatozoa have been collected from dead amphibians, such collections traditionally have occurred immediately after planned euthanasia of healthy animals. In mammals, sperm rescue can be successful for at least 24 hours after death if testes are maintained cool.

However, when spermatozoa were recovered from 10 post-mortem Wyoming toads that were kept cool until processed (c. 12–36 h), sperm quality was poor. Percentage of sperm cells that became motile when exposed to activating conditions was low (mean ± SEM, 3.2 ± 1.5%), and only a small percentage of cells (6.4 ± 1.8%) contained intact mitochondrial vesicles (A. Obringer, unpublished data). Similarly, sperm rescue was attempted in two giant Japanese salamanders (*Andrias japonicus*) within 6–18 hours of death. On both occasions, mature sperm cells were recovered but failed to activate (A. Obringer & T. Roth, unpublished data).

Induction of ovulation and spawning

Exposure to environmental changes (e.g. warming temperatures and increased rainfall) can stimulate amphibian breeding. However, in many situations, breeding success depends on the ability to artificially induce ovulation and spawning. For instance, it may be quite difficult to identify or mimic the appropriate cues that induce breeding behaviour in some species. Furthermore, male contact cannot be allowed when AI is planned; therefore, endogenous hormone release is not naturally induced. Additionally, reproductive success can be enhanced if annual seasonal breeders can be induced to mate more than once each year.

Scientists studying amphibian embryogenesis have developed standardised methods that rely upon hCG, frog pituitary homogenate or LHRH injections for inducing ovulation and spawning in commonly studied anurans (i.e. *X. laevis*, *R. pipiens* and *B. japonicus*). Although protocol efficiency is high for these well-studied species, it also depends on females being properly conditioned before treatment. Protocols are not likely to work with similar efficacy in other less well understood species. For example, our experience with Wyoming, Puerto Rican and American toads suggests that hormones alone are not highly effective stimuli and that proper priming and environmental cues still are necessary. Perhaps with additional physiological studies, hormonal regimens that both prime animals and induce ovulation and spawning can be developed, thereby avoiding the need to mimic environmental cues. However, protocol enhancement first requires a more thorough understanding of amphibian endocrinology, and the role of hormones in these taxa appears to differ significantly from that in mammals. For example, rather than inhibiting ovulation as it does in mammals, progesterone stimulates final oocyte maturation and ovulation in amphibians (Rastogi & Iela, 1999).

Oocyte or embryo cryopreservation

Amphibians produce large clutches of eggs. Therefore, an ability to cryo-preserve some of them could greatly reduce the workload involved with raising hundreds or thousands of larval-stage animals to adulthood simul-taneously. Furthermore, reintroduction efforts could benefit by transferring frozen material to release sites and thawing embryos when conditions are optimal for survival. There may be some benefits to reintroducing embryo-stage offspring rather than tadpoles and toadlets. Finally, the ability to pre-serve genetic resources until some of the extinction factors are controlled would provide insurance against the almost certain loss of many amphibian species that is about to occur.

Although a vast majority of early research on sperm–egg interaction and fertilisation was conducted using the amphibian model, gamete or embryo cryopreservation has received negligible attention. Amphibian eggs tend to be large and are surrounded by many protective layers acquired while pass-ing through the oviduct. These include the vitelline membrane that blocks polyspermy and the jelly coat layers that protect eggs from desiccation while assisting in preparing spermatozoa for fertilisation. Therefore, both egg size and permeability resistance are likely to challenge the development of suc-cessful amphibian egg cryopreservation protocols.

The rescue of immature oocytes from valuable, deceased animals also is an area of research worth pursuing. *Xenopus* follicles can be matured *in vitro* by supplementing the medium with progesterone (Ferrell, 1999), but *in vitro* matured oocytes must be fertilisable. For fertilisation and normal embryo development to occur, oocytes must be exposed to secretions of the pars recta section of the oviduct (Miceli, 1986). Although these can be col-lected and later added in a wash to the egg, these proteins lose activity after freezing or lyophilisation (Miceli *et al.*, 1978).

FUTURE PRIORITIES

Amphibian *ex situ* breeding programmes

Although some of the factor(s) responsible for the amphibian crisis are being discovered, we are far from understanding and resolving the phe-nomenon and, until this occurs, species extinctions will continue. When possible, *ex situ* breeding programmes should be established to help pre-serve the most threatened amphibians. Several successful programmes al-ready exist. The Puerto Rican Crested Toad Species Survival Plan (SSP), the first American Zoo and Aquarium Association SSP established for amphibians, was initiated when the southern population of toads had decreased to *c.* 200 individuals. By 1999, 4000 toadlets and 20 000 tadpoles had been released into the wild (Johnson, 1999).

Ex situ breeding also appears responsible for rescuing the Wyoming toad from near-extinction. In the 1990s, the last surviving toads were removed from the wild, and the entire species existed in a captive breeding programme. Since aerial pesticide treatments have been stopped near the species' natural habitat, 10 000 *ex situ*-bred toadlets have been reintroduced (Dickerson, 1999; Spencer, 1999). Unfortunately, these few 'success' stories pale when compared with the number of species that have almost certainly already been extirpated in the cloud forests of Costa Rica, rainforests in eastern Australia and highlands of eastern Brazil (Daszak *et al.*, 1999; Pounds *et al.*, 1999; Rabb, 1999).

For mammalian species, establishing captive breeding programmes can be controversial. Typical arguments against such efforts include financial concerns, potential adverse effects on natural animal behaviours, animal welfare, the limited prospects for successful reintroductions and the misconception that such programmes are a panacea for 'saving' endangered species. Certainly, such concerns warrant consideration but one cannot dispute that *ex situ* breeding has been responsible for saving species, including the American bison, black-footed ferret, California condor, golden-lion tamarin, Arabian oryx, Guam rail and peregrine falcon, all of which exist in the wild today.

Establishing more amphibian *ex situ* breeding programmes is not likely to incite opposition from conservationists or the public. These species are typically small-sized and easy to maintain inexpensively in naturalistic enclosures. Effects of captivity on animal behaviour are only a minor concern because these species are not considered as socially complex as higher vertebrates. Animal rights groups also appear to take little interest in what the public majority considers to be relatively non-charismatic, unevolved species. Perhaps most importantly, reintroductions can be relatively simple because animals can be introduced into nature as larvae and will learn to survive naturally as they undergo metamorphosis. Finally, *ex situ* breeding can provide temporary, if not long-term, solutions to some of the problems implicated in the amphibian crisis. For example, treatment of chytridiomycosis with micondazole is highly successful (Nichols *et al.*, 1998) and could be used to restore health in a captive population that would be impossible to achieve in a wild population. Additionally, contamination can be rectified and land protected, as demonstrated with the Wyoming toad. However, the success of *ex situ* breeding clearly relies upon our ability to breed and efficiently manage the species under captive conditions. For reproductive technologies to play a more significant role, it will be necessary to conduct much more thorough basic science.

Encouraging a conservation ethic in academic researchers

Researchers have used amphibians in basic reproduction studies for more than half a century. Unfortunately, many such scientists view frogs, toads and salamanders simply as a resource for their scientific investigations. If attitudes towards these research subjects would change to embrace an animal welfare and conservation ethic, then euthanasia would become less common and scientists could more effectively contribute new knowledge that actually could facilitate successful *ex situ* breeding. In some cases, researchers may even decide to shift focus from basic, academic studies to whole animal research that may produce many applied benefits to managing and conserving endangered amphibians.

Educating the public and politicians

Public awareness of conservationists' concerns about endangered elephants, giant pandas, rhinoceroses and tigers is high. However, it is much less likely that people have heard or care about the unprecedented world-wide decline in amphibians. Granted, it is more challenging to incite an emotional response from the public over the loss of the Wyoming toad compared to declining populations of elephants, but that does not mean we should stop trying. The tendency for scientists to put aside conservation priorities to focus only on charismatic species is a disturbing pattern. Unfortunately, more than 80% of federal research dollars are spent on military, space and human health research, whereas conservationists must depend upon private donations to support research to save Earth's resources. However, public opinion should not drive conservation activities. Experts in the field should take responsibility for moulding both public and political opinions. The challenge is to encourage people to value all biodiversity, and then they will provide support where it is needed most.

ACKNOWLEDGEMENTS

The authors thank Andrea Lund, Joe Hurst and Michelle McKay for assistance with the cane toad studies and Dr Ann Taylor for her TEM expertise and producing the photomicrographs. Finally, appreciation goes to Cincinnati Zoo & Botanical Garden Director Edward Maruska for supporting CREW's research and his lifelong dedication to preserving amphibians.

REFERENCES

Barton, H. L. & Guttman, S. I. (1972). Low temperature preservation of toad spermatozoa (Genus *Bufo*). *Texas Journal of Science* 23, 363-370.

Beesley, S. G., Costanzo, J. P. & Lee, R. E., Jr (1998). Cryopreservation of spermatozoa from freeze-tolerant and intolerant anurans. *Cryobiology* 37, 155-162.

Blaustein, A. R. & Wake, D. B. (1990). Declining amphibian populations: a global phenomenon? *Trends in Ecology and Evolution* 5, 203-204.

Blaustein, A. R., Wake, D. B. & Sousa, W. P. (1994). Amphibian declines: judging stability, persistence and susceptibility of populations to local and global extinctions. *Conservation Biology* 8, 60-71.

Browne, R. K., Clulow, J., Mahony, M. & Clark, A. (1998). Successful recovery of motility and fertility of cryopreserved cane toad (*Bufo marinus*) sperm. *Cryobiology* 37, 339-345.

Daszak, P., Berger, L., Cunningham, A. A., Hyatt, A. D., Green, D. E. & Speare, R. (1999). Emerging infectious diseases and amphibian population declines. *Emerging Infectious Diseases* 5, 735-748.

Dickerson, K. (1999). Pesticides and the Wyoming toad. In *U.S. Fish & Wildlife Service Endangered Species Bulletin*, vol. 24 (Eds. M. Bender & M. Balis-Larsen), pp. 20-21. USFWS, Washington, DC.

Donnelly, H. T. (1980). Survey of the numbers and species of amphibia used in the United Kingdom in 1977. *Laboratory Animals* 14, 65-69.

Duellman, W. E. & Trueb, L. (Eds) (1986). *Biology of Amphibians*. McGraw-Hill, New York.

Ferrell, J. E., Jr (1999). *Xenopus* oocyte maturation: new lessons from a good egg. *Bioessays* 21, 833-842.

Galli-Mainini, C. (1947). Pregnancy test using the male toad. *Journal of Clinical Endocrinology & Metabolism* 7, 653-658.

Hayes, T. B. (1998). Sex determination and primary sex differentiation in amphibians: genetic and developmental mechanisms. *Journal of Experimental Zoology* 281, 373-399.

Heyer, R. (1997). Declining amphibian populations task force. *Species* 29, 66.

Hildebrandt, V. T., Göritz, F., Shaftenaar, W., Spelman, L. & Rosscoe, R. (1997). Sonomorphologische Geschlechtsgestimmung und Einschatzung der reproduktiven Kapazitat bei Riesensalamandern (*Cryptobranchidae*). *Verhandlungsbericht ber Erkrankungen Zootiere* 38, 175-179.

Hyatt, A. D., Parkes, H. & Zupanovic, Z. (1998). Identification, characterisation and assessment of Venezuelan viruses for potential use as biological control agents against the cane toad (*Bufo marinus*) in Australia. *Report to the Australian Federal Government & Environment Australia*.

International Union for the Conservation of Nature (IUCN) (2000). *Red List of Threatened Animals*. IUCN, Gland, Switzerland.

Johnson, B. (1999). Recovery of the Puerto Rican Crested Toad. In *U.S. Fish & Wildlife Service Endangered Species Bulletin*, vol. 24 (Eds. M. Bender & M. Balis-Larsen), pp. 8-9. USFWS, Washington, DC.

Kramer, L., Dresser, B. L., & Maruska, E. J. (1983). Sexing aquatic salamanders by laparoscopy. *Proceedings of the American Association of Zoo Veterinarians*, 192-194.

Maruska, E. J. (1986). Amphibians: review of zoo breeding programmes. *International Zoo Yearbook* **24-25**, 56-65.

Mattoon, A. (2000). Amphibia fading. *World Watch*, July–August, 12-23.

McKinnell, R. G., Picciano, D. J. & Krieg, R. E. (1976). Fertilization and development of frog eggs after repeated spermiation induced by human chorionic gonadotropin. *Laboratory Animal Science* **26**, 932-935.

Miceli, D. C. (1986). Oviducal pars recta as factor in fertilization properties and hormonal regulation in the toad (*Bufo arenarum*). *Advances in Experimental Medical Biology* **207**, 167-183.

Miceli, D. C., Fernandez, S. N. & Del Pino, E. (1978). An oviducal enzyme isolated by chromatography which acts upon the vitelline envelope of *Bufo arenarum* coelomic oocytes. *Biochimica et Biophysica Acta* **526**, 289-292.

Mugnano, J. A., Costanzo, J. P., Beesley, S. G. & Lee, R. E., Jr (1998). Evaluation of glycerol and dimethylsulfoxide for the cryopreservation of spermatozoa from the wood frog (*Rana sylvatica*). *Cryo-Letters* **19**, 249-254.

Nichols, D. K., Pessier, A. P. & Longcore, J. E. (1998). Cutaneous chytridiomycosis: an emerging disease? *Proceedings, American Association of Zoo Veterinarians*, Media, PA. pp. 269-271.

Obringer, A. R., O'Brien, J. K., Saunders, R. L., Yamamoto, K., Kikuyama, S. & Roth, T. L. (2000). Characterization of the spermiation response, luteinizing hormone release and sperm quality in the American toad (*Bufo americanus*) and the endangered Wyoming toad (*Bufo baxteri*). *Reproduction, Fertility and Development* **12**, 51-58.

Pounds, J. A., Fogden, M. P. L. & Campbell, J. H. (1999). Biological response to climate change on a tropical mountain. *Nature* **398**, 611-615.

Propper, L. E. & Moore, F. L. (1991). Effects of courtship on brain gonadotropin hormone-releasing hormone and plasma steroid concentrations in a female amphibian (*Taricha granulosa*). *General and Comparative Endocrinology* **81**, 304-312.

Rabb, G. B. (1999). The amphibian crisis. In *The 7th World Conference on Breeding Endangered Species Proceedings* (Eds. T. L. Roth, W.F. Swanson & L. K. Blattman), pp. 23-30. Cincinnati Zoo & Botanical Garden, Cincinnati, OH.

Rastogi, R. K. & Iela, L. (1999). Female reproductive system, amphibians. In *Encyclopedia of Reproduction*, vol. 2 (Eds. E. Knobil & J. D. Neill), pp. 183-190. Academic Press, London.

Rowson, A. D., Obringer, A. R. & Roth, T. L. (2001). Noninvasive treatments of luteinizing hormone releasing hormone for inducing spermiation in American (*Bufo americanus*) and Gulf Coast (*Bufo valliceps*) toads. *Zoo Biology* **20**, 63-74.

Spencer, B. (1999). The Wyoming Toad SSP. In *U.S. Fish & Wildlife Service Endangered Species Bulletin*, vol. 24 (Eds. M. Bender & M. Balis-Larsen), pp. 18-19. USFWS, Washington, DC.

Sprando, R. L. & Russell, L. D. (1988). Spermiogenesis in the bullfrog (*Rana catesbeiana*): a study of cytoplasmic events including cell volume changes and cytoplasmic elimination. *Journal of Morphology* **198**, 303-319.

Vance, C. K., Kouba, A. J. & Roth, T. L. (2001). Inactivation and reactivation of spermatozoa collected in urine from the common American toad (*Bufo americanus*). *Theriogenology* **55**, 402.

Waggener, W. L. & Carroll, E.J., Jr (1998a). Spermatozoon structure and motility in the anuran *Lepidobatrachus laevis*. *Development, Growth & Differentiation* **40**, 27-34.

Waggener, W. L. & Carroll, E. J., Jr (1998b). A method for hormonal induction of sperm release in anurans (eight species) and *in vitro* fertilization in *Lepidobatrachus* species. *Development, Growth & Differentiation* **40**, 19-25.

Wake, M. H. (1977). The reproductive biology of caecilians: an evolutionary perspective. In *The Reproductive Biology of Amphibians* (Eds. D. H. Taylor & S. I. Guttman), pp. 73-101. Plenum Press, New York.

Wallace, H., Badawy, G. M. & Wallace, B. M. (1999). Amphibian sex determination and sex reversal. *Cellular & Molecular Life Science* **55**, 901-909.

Wells, K. D. (1978). Courtship and parental behavior in a Panamanian poison-arrow frog (*Dendrobates auratus*). *Herpetologica* **34**, 148-155.

Weygoldt, P. (1980). Complex brood care and reproductive behavior in captive poison-arrow frogs, *Dendrobates pumilio*. *Behavioral Ecology & Sociobiology* **7**, 329-332.

Weygoldt, P. (1989). Changes in the composition of mountain stream frog communities in the Atlantic Mountains of Brazil: frogs as indicators of environmental deteriorations? *Studies of Neotropical Fauna & Environments* **24**, 249-255.

Wiese, R. J. & Hutchins, M. (1994). The role of zoos and aquariums in amphibian and reptilian conservation. In *Captive Management & Conservation of Amphibians & Reptiles* (Eds. J. B. Murphy, K. Adler & J. T. Collins), pp. 37-45. Society for the Study of Amphibians & Reptiles, Marceline, MO.

Zug, G.R. (Ed.) (1993). *Herpetology, an Introductory Biology of Amphibians and Reptiles.* Academic Press, London.

24

Reproduction in fishes in relation to conservation

GORDON McGREGOR REID AND HEATHER HALL

INTRODUCTION AND BACKGROUND

Human interest in fishes and their reproduction has long been supremely practical. Archaeological studies from Neolithic 'kitchen middens' of Denmark (c. 9000–6000 BC) provide evidence of a marine capture fishery for herring, cod, flounder and eel (Travis Jenkins, 1927). It is likely that such pre-agricultural 'stone age' humans trapped fishes inshore and on rivers, including populations migrating for spawning. Such practices continue today, including indigenous communities in West Africa using woven fences to trap migrant fishes (Teugels et al., 1992).

Farming freshwater fishes in ponds for food dates from c. 4500 years ago in Sumeria, ancient Egypt, Assyria and China, with evidence that artificial hatching was practised latterly (Hickling, 1971). Basic fish culture existed in the Roman Empire (Higginbotham, 1997), and holding or 'stew' ponds for bream and perch are well known from mediaeval Europe, with proper fish farming established between AD 1400 and 1500 (Hickling, 1971). Carp (Cyprinus carpio) and goldfish (Carrassius auratus) were first bred ornamentally in Korea and China (c. 960 BC) and Japan (c. AD 1500) where artificial selection was used to produce aesthetically pleasing coloured varieties.

The practical benefits of fish reproduction attracted early scholars such as Fan Lai (c. 475 BC) and Aristotle (c. 340 BC). A utilitarian, ethnocentric approach to fish reproduction persists today and dominates scientific studies. The main thrust of modern aquaculture is towards improved utilisation of fish (or their gametes – milt, roe, caviar) for food, products or sport fishing. Similarly, the current sophisticated mathematical models used for managing the world's wild capture fisheries are based on fecundity data or population reproductive success. Peak estimates of cod (Gadus morhua) and herring (Clupea harengus) numbers harvested annually from the Atlantic

Ocean are about 400 million and 3000 million, respectively (Norman & Greenwood, 1963). Sadly, these native populations are in steep decline, and cod has been placed on the IUCN *Red List of Threatened Species*, with 752 mainly freshwater species (IUCN, 2000).

This chapter identifies generalisations in fish reproductive biology and key issues relevant to conservation. This is done with broad reference to comparative studies on systematics, morphology, physiology, genetics, behaviour, ecology, aquaculture and biotechnology, including assisted reproduction.

STATE OF THE SCIENCE

Historical works and the voluminous primary research literature are summarised in *A Bibliography of Fishes* (Dean, 1916–23). In the last two centuries, introductory ichthyology textbooks usually include a chapter on reproduction (e.g. Gunther, 1880; Lagler *et al.*, 1962; Norman & Greenwood, 1963; Moyle & Cech, 1988; Paxton & Eschmeyer, 1998). Other standard specialised works cover reproductive anatomy (Harder, 1975), physiology and embryology (Hoar & Randall, 1969, 1988; Hoar *et al.*, 1983; Scott *et al.*, 1991; Goetz & Thomas, 1995; Jobling, 1995), behaviour (Baerends & Baerends-van Roon, 1950; Lorenz, 1952; Morris, 1970), ecology and environment (Potts & Wooton, 1984) and aquaculture (Hickling, 1971). Such publications are crowned by *Modes of Reproduction in Fishes*, the classic and still highly relevant treatise of Breder & Rosen (1966).

There are numerous journals (e.g. *Copeia, Reviews in Fish Biology and Fisheries, Journal of Fish Biology, Aquarium Sciences and Conservation*) that contain accounts of fish reproduction, and there are specialised piscicultural journals. At least 10 000 research papers have been published on fish reproduction in the last decade. The most recent publications are cited in publicly accessible computerised databases, including the *Zoological Record, Fish & Fisheries Abstracts, FAO Fisheries Database*, and *Fishbase* (http://www.fishbase.org/home.htm). Various specialised databases are being developed within the Fish Taxon Advisory Groups of the European Association of Zoos and Aquaria, the European Union of Aquarium Curators and the American Zoo and Aquarium Association including taxonomic lists, fish breeding records, and husbandry manuals.

Diversity and conservation

Systematics
Aristotle (384–322 BC), the first systematic observer of fish reproduction, recognised about 118 different kinds of fish from the Aegean Sea and was

aware of population migrations for the purpose of reproduction (Gunther, 1880; Norman & Greenwood, 1963). He knew of egg-laying or oviparity in 'scaly fishes' (teleosts) and livebearing or viviparity in sharks and rays (elasmobranchs). Aristotle was aware of, but misinterpreted, the unusual mode in pipefishes (*Syngnathus* spp.), believing that they somehow burst apart to release their eggs, the wound subsequently healing.

Today, the term 'fish' refers to a popular rather than scientific concept of aquatic animals with scales that swim using fins, and breathe with gills. In fact, 'fishes' in the broadest sense are not monophyletic, and comprise an exceedingly diverse group of chordates with and without crania, jaws, bone and scales and with extremely varied reproductive biology. Reproduction in fishes at the whole organism level means producing new individuals similar in form to the parents, to maintain a population and perpetuate a species. This notion is fundamental and profound. Variation among reproductively active individuals, populations and species is central to the theory of evolution through natural selection. Also, the biological species concept (*sensu* Mayr, 1969) relies on the premise that there is reproductive isolation between alpha-level taxa.

Breder & Rosen (1966) have viewed fish reproduction in the context of the biological species concept and the mechanisms that promote reproductive isolation. Alternatively, Kullander (1999) advocates a cladistic, phylogenetic species concept that can focus on specialised reproductive morphology (synapomorphies) or other reproductive features (synapotypies). In this context, minimally diagnosable units (MDUs) may offer the most practical means of selecting alpha-level taxa for conservation. However defined, about 25 000 valid fish species are generally recognised, with *c.* 96% being osteichthyeans or 'bony' fishes (Table 24.1). Many new species are described annually, so 25 000 is likely to be a significant underestimate.

Table 24.1 *Approximate numbers of orders, families, genera and species of fishes (fish-like chordates)*

Higher Category	Orders	Families	Genera	Species
Jawless fish (Agnatha)	2	4	17	72
Cartilaginous fish (Chondrichthyes)	14	50	130	711
Bony fish (Osteichthyes)	45	436	3700	24 374
Total	61	490	3 847	25 157

Data re-calculated from Bannister & Campell (1985), Watson & Heywood (1995), Nelson (1997), Paxton & Eschmeyer (1998), Mittermeier (1990) and BRIM (2000).

Table 24.2 *Approximate numbers of 'fish-like' species compared with other vertebrates*

Major group	Higher category	Total species	Total 'fish' %	Total vertebrates %
'Fish-like' vertebrates	Jawless fish (Agnatha)	72	0.3	0.2
	Cartilaginous fish (Chondrichthyes)	711	3	1.4
	Bony fish (Osteichthyes)	24 374	96	49.2
	Total 'fish'	25 157	–	50.8
'Non-fish-like' vertebrates	Amphibians	4 222	20	8.5
	Reptiles	6 458	30	13.0
	Birds	9 040	42	18.3
	Mammals	4 629	21	9.4
	Total 'non-fish'	24 349	–	49.2
	Total chordates	49 506	–	–

Data re-calculated from Bannister & Campell (1985), Watson & Heywood (1995), Nelson (1997), Paxton & Eschmeyer (1998), Mittermeier (1990) and BRIM (2000).

In terms of species and individuals, fishes far outnumber all other vertebrate classes (amphibians, reptiles, birds, mammals) (Table 24.2). Lancelets (amphioxiforms), lampreys (cyclostomes), sharks and rays (elasmobranchs) and bony fishes (teleosts) represent four major, evolutionarily distinct, chordate divisions whose precise phyletic interrelationships remain to be fully explored. For example, it has been argued cladistically (Rosen *et al.*, 1981) that a lungfish (dipnoan) is more closely related to a cow (tetrapod) than a salmon (teleost), and specialisations in reproductive anatomy and physiology may support that conclusion.

Ichthyogeography

Ichthyogeography is the study of fish distribution and abundance and is partly determined by reproductive modes and capabilities. Fishes are found everywhere, in fresh, brackish and salt water that covers roughly 70% of the planet. Most species live in tropical freshwaters that represent only about 0.01% of available global habitat. There are about 5000 fish species in the Amazon Basin of South America and 1000 in the Congo Basin of Central Africa. In marine systems, the greatest species concentration (> 8000) occurs on the tropical coral reefs of the Indo-Pacific Ocean, Caribbean Sea and Red Sea. There is a corresponding high diversity in reproductive strategies among fishes of tropical freshwaters and coral reefs (Goulding, 1980; Thresher, 1984; Lévêque, 1997). Regional conservation strategies for determining priorities increasingly utilise 'biodiversity hotspots' (Myers et al., 2000) characterised by species richness, high endemicity and major threats (Olson et al., 1998; Abell et al., 2000). However, it should be possible to conserve representative habitats that are not 'hotspots', such as the ocean depths at 1000 metres which contain extraordinary examples of reproductive specialisation, e.g. a 'parasitic' sexual fusion between males and females in the deep sea anglerfish, Ceratias holboelli.

In theory, reproductive isolation and subsequent development of new fish species may arise on 'biogeographical islands'. Such isolated taxa may be especially vulnerable to extinction (e.g. Malagasy freshwater cichlids and Omani blind cave fishes, Garra barreimiae). One of the best examples is the comparatively rapid evolution of cichlid species in the African great lakes of Victoria, Tanganyika and Malawi. Through isolation, ecological niche sepa-ration and mate choice, cichlids in Lake Victoria may have evolved into more than 300 species in under 10 000 years (Greenwood, 1974; Seehausen, 1996; Turner, 1997). Here, the introduction c. 1960 of an alien predator, the Nile perch (Lates niloticus), has resulted in a catastrophic collapse of cichlid populations that reproduce by mouthbrooding (Reid, 1990). Pred-ation on gravid mouthbrooders immediately destroys representatives from two generations.

Species may also be isolated and differentiated by factors other than physical separation. Some African mormyrids (Brienomyrus spp.) are morph-ologically similar, but have species-specific electrical signals to communi-cate, particularly in the breeding season (Sullivan et al., 2000). Distinctive regional variations may prevent different populations from communicating and so mating.

Threatened taxa

Of the 752 threatened fish species on the IUCN Red List (IUCN, 2000, and Table 24.3), 20.7% are considered 'Critical', 19.2% 'Endangered' and 60.1% 'Vulnerable'. Only about 10% of all fish species have been assessed for level of conservation threat. There are 92 recorded extinctions, although only 11 of these are extinct in nature with ex situ populations persisting. Controversy remains over the verification of extinctions (Harrison & Stiassny, 1999). Of the threatened species, 84% are freshwater, 21% are lake endemics, and 16% are restricted to islands. While data suggest that freshwater fishes are especially vulnerable, findings also reflect a geographical bias in surveys and the lack of a thorough global assessment of marine fishes (Vincent & Hall, 1996).

Table 24.3 *Approximate number of threatened fish species compared with other vertebrates*

Major group	Higher category	Threatened species	% taxon	% taxon assessed	% total threatened vertebrates
'Fish-like' vertebrates	Jawless fish (Agnatha)	3	4.2	<10	0.1
	Cartilaginous fish (Chondrichthyes)	39	5.5	<10	1.2
	Bony fish (Osteichthyes)	523	2.1	<10	16.0
	Total chordates	565	2.2	<10	17.3
'Non-fish-like' vertebrates	Amphibians	83	2.0	<15	2.5
	Reptiles	297	4.6	<15	9.1
	Birds	1186	13.1	100	36.3
	Mammals	1134	24.5	100	34.8
	Total threatened 'non-fish'	2700	11.1	–	82.7
	Total chordates	3265	6.6	–	100.0

Data re-calculated from *IUCN Red List* (2000; excluding 'data deficient' categories) and other sources. These data are undoubtedly skewed by a strong research bias in favour of 'higher' vertebrates.

Threats to reproduction can be broadly ascribed to over-exploitation of fisheries or environmental change. Over-exploitation removes breeding adults or immature juveniles from the population or disrupts breeding structure. Environmental change encompasses natural factors (e.g. fluctuations in climate or geology) and anthropogenic factors (e.g. habitat destruction, pollution, alien species introductions and barriers to breeding migrations or spawning such as dams).

Reproductive biology and conservation

Understanding reproductive strategies is essential for determining level of threat and best approaches to conservation management *ex situ* and *in situ*.

Physiology and genetics

Fishes exhibit oviparity, ovo-viviparity and true viviparity and an enormous variation in strategies of egg production (numbers), gestation time and the 'livebearing' or rearing of young. Some livebearers provide nutrition to the developing young through a placental equivalent. In goodeids, ribbon-like extensions from the anal region called trophotaeniae assist with nutrition and respiration in embryos (Hoar & Randall, 1988). Fecundity ranges from single eggs in some sharks to several million in dispersal spawners such as cod and 28 million in the ocean sunfish, *Mola mola*. Fecundity is related to age and size, with fewer numbers generally produced by smaller, young and aged animals. This has conservation implications.

Sharks (Wourms, 1977; Dodd, 1983) – the target of an enormous and overexploited global fishery – are often vulnerable because of slow sexual maturation, long gestation and low fecundity. Even fecund species, such as sturgeon, cod and lumpfish, are at risk from the commercial demand for eggs. Reproductive systems are still being elucidated for most fishes, with fascinating findings. Hormonal and behavioural control varies considerably (Hoar *et al.*, 1983). It has been established that the endangered coelacanth (*Latimeria*) is viviparous, the young developing from eggs the size of tennis balls (Forey, 1998), the largest known.

Some taxa, such as Siamese fighting fish (*Betta splendens*) and seahorses (*Hippocampus* spp.), are sexually dimorphic. There are no well-marked external differences in others (many butterflyfish (*Chaetodon* spp.) and eels, *Anguilla* spp.). There is a genetic basis to sex determination with males producing sperm and females producing eggs, but hermaphrodites are known. Sequential hermaphroditism occurs in some wrasses (labrids), where all fish begin life as females with a single dominant male living within the 'harem'. When a male dies, a female changes sex to become the new dominant male (Chan & Yeung, 1983; Thresher, 1984). Among clown-fish (*Amphiprion* spp.), females are produced from males by sex reversal. There is parthenogenesis in a species of molly, *Poecilia formosa*, which occurs naturally as all-female populations. They breed by gynogenesis, females mating with another sympatric *Poecilia* species, but sperm play no role in fertilisation. Mating stimulates egg development only, with the male not contributing to the genome of the offspring. All-female clones result (Paxton & Eschmeyer, 1998). Most fishes are diploid, but there are natural examples of polyploidy (e.g. hexaploidy in one threatened, unique species group of African *Barbus*; Guegan *et al.*, 1995).

Conserving species entails maintaining representative genetic diversity, with genetic variability an advantage. Reduced variability within a species or population limits adaptation to catastrophic change, such as epizootics and climatic events, and increases overall vulnerability to risks associated with inbreeding (see Taylor, Chapter 5; Koeninger Ryan *et al.*, Chapter 6). Some limited and isolated habitats have naturally low levels of genetic diversity (e.g. pupfish in the deserts of California; Meffe, 1990). Other fishes have developed high levels of genetic variation within a small geographic range, such as the ferox, gillaroo and sonaghen 'forms' of brown trout (*Salmo trutta*) in Lough Melvin, Ireland (Ferguson, 1989). While reproductive mechanisms among these trout forms are similar, distinctive genotypes, biological uniqueness and isolation of the ecological niche perhaps justify a 'specific' (MDU) status for each population.

Hybridisation occurs naturally in fishes and may, by evolution, possibly result in new species. Environmental changes (e.g. adding or removing geographic barriers) can artificially induce hybridisation. Often, such crosses are not viable (e.g. Atlantic salmon with brown trout; Verspoor, 1988). The fish genome has also been manipulated through human interventions involving selective breeding and biotechnology to promote physical traits – such as colour and tail length in guppies for ornamental purposes or enhanced growth rates in trout for food production. Genetic manipulations have been used in aquaculture to produce triploid rainbow trout and tilapia with YY chromosomes, to ensure that physiological energy is channelled into growth rather than reproduction (Thorgaard, 1983; Müller-Belecke & Hörstgen-Schwark, 1995). The potentially deleterious impact of intentional or unintentional release of these cultured and genetically modified fishes is of growing concern (Hindar et al., 1991; Hallerman & Kapuscinski, 1995).

Ecology and behaviour

Reproductive strategies and mechanisms vary considerably among fish species (Table 24.4). Most species reproduce underwater but the spraying characin (*Copella nattereri*) splashes eggs laid out on the underside of overhanging leaves. Many species are triggered to release eggs and sperm by environmental cues, including water flow, temperature, conductivity, salinity, pH and solar or lunar cycles (Thorpe, 1978; Lam, 1983; Munro et al., 1990). Fishes may be migratory for spawning, with discrete spawning grounds or run times that ensure an appropriate encounter with a mate (McKeown, 1984). Mass migrations of salmon (Jones, 1959) and eels (Moriarty, 1978) are well-studied examples, as is the lunar periodicity of tidal spawning in the California grunion (*Leuresthes tenuis*). Some species form behaviourally and ecologically elaborate pair bonds (seahorses; Sadler & Vincent, 1995) or social groupings (some wrasses) to ensure the presence of a mate. At an extreme, the male and female deep sea anglerfish (*Ceratias holboelli*) fuse with each other (Paxton & Eschmeyer, 1998) – perhaps attributable to low population numbers, the infrequency of encounters in their open ocean environment and the risk of losing a potential mate.

Mechanisms for parental care include the production of sticky eggs that remain attached to an appropriate substrate and hidden (e.g. plant spawners; Table 24.4). Some fish secrete kidney glue to retain eggs within a

Table 24.4 *Ecological/behavioural classification of reproductive modes in fishes*

Ecological/ behavioural group	Subgroup	Example of mode	Taxonomic example
Non-guarders	Pelagic spawners	Open water	Cod, *Gadus morhua*
	Substrate spawners	On rock, gravel, plant, or sand	Salmon, *Salmo salar* Gudgeon, *Gobio gobio*
	Brood hiders	Crevice or cave spawning	Rock kribensis, *Pelvicachromis pulchar*
Guarders	Clutch tenders	On rock or plant	Jewel cichlid, *Hemichromis fasciatus* False clownfish, *Amphiprion ocellaris*
	Nesters	Froth nests, hole nests, plant nests, sand nests	Siamese fighting fish, *Betta splendens* Stickleback, *Gasterosteus aculeatus*
Bearers	External brooders	Mouth brooders, pouch brooders	Lake Victoria cichlids, *Haplochromis* spp. Seahorses, *Hippocampus* spp.
	Internal livebearers	Ovo-viviparity, viviparity	Guppy, *Poecilia reticulata* Many elasmobranchs

Much simplified after Balon, 1975 and subsequent versions.

nest (sticklebacks) or on the body (pipefish). An extreme example of egg protection is found in seahorses (*Hippocampus* spp.) where eggs develop within a male pouch (Lourie *et al.*, 1999). Eggs are transferred to the pouch by the female, using an ovipositor. In livebearing fishes, including poeciliids and hemirhamphids (halfbeaks), the male uses a specialised anal fin (a gonopodium) to insert sperm into the female, enabling internal fertilisation. Livebearing is found in sharks, and the young develop internally, sometimes nourished through a placental equivalent. Intrauterine cannibalism occurs in sharks, with young consumed by siblings during parturition (Wourms, 1977). Among cichlids, discus fish nourish fry through a fluid secreted from the skin that is equivalent to mammalian milk (Reihl, 1997). Environmental factors are crucial after mating and spawning. Currents and seasonal water flow variations are primary determinants of larval dispersal. Space, substrate and associated fauna and flora (e.g. refuges, food organisms and predators) are critical to successful breeding, survival, growth and development to maturity.

Although particular informal classifications may be useful in making generalisations in reproductive ecology and behaviour, they cannot be considered absolute. Allocating a species to any one category can be arbitrary, and current ecological and behavioural classifications rarely conform with phylogenies. Substrate spawning, for example, can include representative species from the cichlids, salmonids, percids and cyprinodonts and cover very specialised behaviours. For instance, some 'annual' cyprinodonts (*Aphyosemion* spp.) die at the end of the dry season, while eggs survive in desiccated mud to hatch during the next wet season (Teugels *et al.*, 1992).

The role of reproductive ecology in conserving and managing fishes has been reviewed by Vincent & Sadovy (1998). Adverse impacts on reproduction include changes in environmental conditions (e.g. pollution, Kime, 1995; Rolland, 2000), migration routes (e.g. damming), habitat (e.g. losses due to drought) and fishing practices (e.g. unselective netting). Direct effects of pollution on sex determination of fishes by synthetic feminising oestrogens is of increasing concern (Kime, 1995), and sex ratio imbalances could cause population declines.

Vulnerability to extinction varies with the mode of reproductive behaviour and threat. Behaviours can be adversely affected by introduced exotic species that disrupt natural mating systems, consume eggs and disturb nests of natives (Contreras-MacBeath *et al.*, 1998). No reproductive strategy can be considered 'safe', because of the wide range of threats to fishes and their habitats. Cod, for example, is a pelagic spawner, with females often producing millions of eggs at a time. Fishery overexploitation has decreased fecundity – first by removing the largest and most productive broodstock, followed by the catch of immature individuals. Cod are now considered 'Vulnerable', with the complete collapse of some populations (Voigtlander, 1994; IUCN, 2000). By contrast, some seahorses pair-bond and indulge in a high degree of parental care, incubating a few fry in the male's pouch. Exploitation of 'pregnant' males removes young from the population and disrupts the social structure, causing dramatic declines in populations (Vincent, 1996).

PRIORITIES AND PRACTICAL MANAGEMENT OF REPRODUCTION FOR CONSERVATION

Fish conservation science has been spurred by the global loss of fisheries biomass and rapidly increasing numbers of threatened taxa, with Lake Victoria cichlids of East Africa a prime example (Reid, 1990). The overall aim is to maintain, promote and restore biomass and biodiversity by ensuring that populations and species thrive and reproduce *sustainably* in natural habitats (Reid & Teugels, 2000). Due to the sheer numbers of species and lack of information, conservation will continue to benefit from basic and applied research. The high diversity of reproductive mechanisms has been illustrated repeatedly throughout this chapter. Sound science conducted by public aquaria in collaboration with wildlife agencies, universities and museums should be a high priority, especially integrated in the context of conservation efforts, both *in situ* and *ex situ*. The development of conservation assessment and management plans (CAMPs) in the field is also a high priority. The first zoo-supported (IUCN/CBSG) CAMP exercise was for 329 species of Indian freshwater fishes, with 227 rated as threatened (Molur & Walker, 1998). A CAMP has since been conducted for 20 species of Arabian freshwater fishes (Krupp *et al.*, 2002). Project Seahorse (2001) is a zoo-associated marine conservation initiative combining *in situ* and *ex situ* elements.

In one sense, failed reproduction contributes to failed conservation. This has led to substantially increased reproductive biology research conducted *in situ* and *ex situ*. However, a clear distinction must be made between conservation science applied *in situ* to fish as opposed to fisheries. The true conservationist regards fishes as part of a wildlife heritage in their own right. Fisheries proponents only 'protect' or 'conserve' fishes for human consumption or use, and not always sustainably. Fisheries personnel also intervene to control or modify habitats or biology for immediate human gain rather than for long-term natural or ecological benefit. Similarly, one should not confuse *ex situ* conservation operations (such as fish breeding programmes in zoos, aquaria, universities and wildlife establishments) with commercial pisciculture or the aquarium hobbyist trade (Burgess, 2001).

Conservation breeding programmes

Maintaining a natural, representative genetic diversity, generation-to-generation, is central to conservation breeding. By contrast, commercial pisciculture and the hobbyist industry usually focus on selective breeding or genetic manipulation to increase quantity and improve the perceived quality of the product. The theory, husbandry methods and technologies to achieve fish reproduction are nevertheless closely comparable; and so the separate disciplines can usefully inform each other, while having quite different goals. For example, to facilitate spawning and larval care, standard aquaculture techniques may involve hand stripping (removal of eggs); hormonal treatments; artificial egg incubation; rearing (feeding and culture) and replicating certain environmental parameters (light, temperature, water quality). There may also be restocking; supplementation; enhancement and ranching (Donaldson & Hunter, 1983; Goetz, 1983; Liley & Stacey, 1983). Such methods are equally relevant to conservation breeding programmes.

Reid & Teugels (2000) have advocated using assisted reproduction for conservation when natural reproduction is insufficient to achieve goals. Artificial methods include those cited above and the cryopreservation of germplasm – sperm, ova and embryos (Billard & Zhang, 2001). In each of these areas, a high priority is to characterise species-specific biological norms and overcome obstacles to assisted reproduction. For example, the ability to cryopreserve fish embryos remains elusive. Although fish spermatozoa have been frozen-thawed and routinely used to produce offspring, the large embryonic yolk and complex membranes impermeable to cryoprotectants have prevented successful fish embryo cryopreservation (Hagedorn & Kleinhans, 2000). Such technology has substantial implications for improving aquaculture by allowing year-round fish farming and also for conserving genetic diversity and isolated, rare species.

Fishes raised by commercial establishments via aquaculture may be markedly different from, and genetically unrepresentative of, wild populations from which they originally derive (Vuorinen, 1984). Indeed, their release to natural habitats (accidentally or on purpose) can genetically 'pollute' wild species through cross breeding and even precipitate extinctions. When this occurs in tandem with gross habitat modification and destruction, conservation and fisheries objectives become diametrically opposed. A high priority is continued communication among biologists who focus on conservation issues versus those mostly concerned to improve aquaculture and capture fisheries. While sharing experiences and knowledge, it is essential that fishes developed for commercial production do not inadvertently contaminate wild stocks (Hindar et al., 1991; Hallerman & Kapuscinski, 1995). Conversely, it is important that conservationists recognise the vital role of fisheries and the ornamental fish industry in nutrition, commerce and poverty alleviation (Watson, 2000).

Identifying priorities for ex situ breeding programmes relates, in part, to natural reproductive strategies: r-selection (high number of offspring with little or no parental care) and k-selection (low number of offspring and high parental care). For example, highly fecund species such as cod are inappropriate for ex situ conservation in an aquarium environment, though they can be cultured in larger coastal set-ups. Fecundity is not always the deciding factor for an aquarium-based programme, as the few offspring produced by a whale shark do not overcome the logistical and welfare challenges associated with keeping this species in captivity (as has been done in Japan). Other species that are not currently held or bred in aquaria are of particularly high conservation importance and worthy of review. For instance, the coelacanth (*Latimeria chalumnae*), with perhaps only a few hundred individuals left in a declining population (Forey, 1998), could be viewed as the aquatic

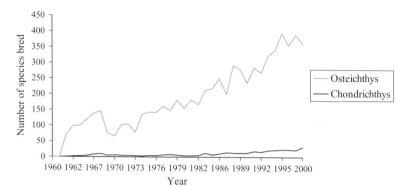

Figure 24.1 Fish species bred in zoos and aquaria (*International Zoo Yearbook*, 1962–1999). The apparent decrease in 1969 represents a change in the recording system.

equivalent of the Californian condor or giant panda. A major challenge is identifying those species deserving the highest priority for *ex situ* breeding. Their survival must be supported by effective, cooperative programmes that balance resources and talents, and are linked whenever possible to nature.

Fish Taxon Advisory Group programmes

The first published paper in the *International Zoo Yearbook* on successful fish breeding in a public aquarium is by de Graaf (1969). Initially ineffective (Maitland & Evans, 1986), aquaria have since developed a substantial role in conservation initiatives, particularly managed breeding programmes. In Europe, this cooperative effort is known as the Fish and Aquatic Invertebrate Taxon Advisory Group (FAITAG; Reid & Hall, 1997). In the USA corresponding conservation efforts are being directed through freshwater and marine fish TAGs (FFTAG/MFTAG), with shark and ray (elasmobranch) breeding and husbandry a current priority. The number of bony fish species bred for multiple generations in zoos and aquaria (per the *International Zoo Yearbook*) has increased from under 50 in 1962 to more than 350 in 1999 (Figure 24.1). This greatly increased success in *ex situ* breeding is attributable, in part, to programmes being more closely related to species-specific needs for adequate space, water quality and diet for adults and growing offspring. Such basic knowledge (e.g. Spotte, 1992; Seehausen, 1996) is required for every unstudied species. The development of coordinated efforts, such as is occurring through the TAGs, will continue to speed progress.

Often, the first essential step is knowing the species, their numbers in captivity and their conservation status. The fish TAGs are compiling a taxonomic database of fish species held in aquaria (Table 24.5) along with a

Table 24.5 *Number of fish species recorded in participating (mainly European) aquaria*

Category	Number ex situ	Number in situ	% in situ
Participating aquaria	30	–	–
Orders	60	61	98
Families	217	490	41
Genera	806	3847	21
Species	1837	25 157	7
Individuals	56 568	–	–

Fish Taxon Advisory Group Database, compiled by Correira & Smith, 2002, ongoing. Records of species subject to husbandry, research and breeding efforts are being compiled within the database.

Table 24.6 *Fish taxa bred within European public aquaria*

Species programme	Families represented ex situ	Species bred ex situ	Species in situ	Threatened species (IUCN, 2000)	% bred ex situ	% bred threatened
Elasmobranchs	more than one	5	711	39	0.7	12
Seahorses	Syngnathidae	13	32	31	40.6	42
Cardinalfishes	Apogonidae	1	200	0	0.5	–
African cichlids	Cichlidae	18	2000	50	0.9	36
Livebearers (Goodeids)	Goodeidae	44	44	10	100	100

Fish and Aquatic Invertebrate Taxon Advisory Group Database compiled by Correira & Smith, 2002 ongoing.

register of specific breeding programmes (Reid & Hall, 1997; Walker, 1994; Table 24.6). Species targeted for collaborative research and breeding have been determined on the basis of threats in nature and suitability for maintenance and breeding *ex situ*. TAG programme management guidelines are also being developed: no small feat for species that vary so widely in life history and reproductive traits. As most fishes are difficult to identify as individuals, issues of managing colonies over generations are now being considered in the context of population demographics and genetics.

The ultimate challenge for fish conservationists is considering the linkage of *ex situ* breeding to sustainability of wild populations. To date, little effort has been directed at understanding the difficulties and feasibility of re-stocking endangered fish species to the wild with individuals or populations produced *ex situ*. A high strategic priority will be to systematically and comprehensively understand these challenges and develop model (test) programmes using guidelines of the IUCN Reintroduction Specialist Group (2001) and in-country protocols.

ACKNOWLEDGEMENTS

Information has been generously provided by Richard Vari (National Museum of Natural History, Smithsonian Institution, Washington), Melanie Stiassny (American Museum of Natural History, New York), Mark Smith and João Correira (Oceánario Ae Lisboa, Portugal); and Fiona Fisken and Helen Stanley (*International Zoo Yearbook*, Regents Park, London). We also gratefully acknowledge the contributions of Frances Jaques (North of England Zoological Society) in manuscript preparation.

REFERENCES

Abell, R. A., Olson, D. M., Dinerstein, E., Hurley, P. T., Diggs, J. T., Eichbaum, W., Walters, S., Wettengell, W., Allnutt, T., Loucks, C. J. & Hedao, P. (Eds.) (2000). *Freshwater Ecoregions of North America: A Conservation Assessment*. World Wildlife Fund, United States, Washington, DC.

Baerends, G. P. & Baerends-van Roon, J. M. (1950). An introduction to the study of the ethology of cichlid fishes. *Behaviour*, Suppl. 1, 1-243. (Note: modified for text citation.)

Balon, E. K. (1975). Reproductive guilds of fishes: a proposal and definitions. *Journal of the Fisheries Research Board, Canada* 32, 821-863.

Bannister, K. & Campell, A. (1985). *The Encyclopedia of Underwater Life*. Andromeda, Oxford.

Billard, R. & Zhang, T. T. (2001). Techniques of genetic resource banking in fish. In *Cryobanking the Genetic Resource: Wildlife Conservation for the Future* (Eds. P. F. Watson & W. V. Holt), pp. 143-170. Taylor & Francis, London.

Breder, C. M. & Rosen, D. E. (1966). *Modes of Reproduction in Fishes*. Natural History Press, Garden City, NY (reprinted by T. F. H. Publications, Jersey City, NJ).

BRIM (2000). http://ice.ucdavis.edu/mab.

Burgess, P. (Ed.) (2001). Marine ornamentals conference, Hawaii. *Aquarium Sciences and Conservation* (Special Issue) 3, 1-240.

Chan, S. T. & Yeung, W. S. (1983). Sex control and sex reversal in fish under natural conditions. In *Fish Physiology* Vol. IX, *Reproduction*, Part B, *Behavior and Fertility Control* (Eds. W. S. Hoar, D. J. Randall & E. M. Donaldson), pp. 171-222. Academic Press, New York.

Contreras-MacBeath, T., Mejia Mojica, H. & Wilson, R. C. (1998). Negative impact on the aquatic ecosystems of the State of Morelos, Mexico, from introduced aquarium and other commercial fish. *Aquarium Sciences & Conservation* 2, 67-78.

de Graaf, F. (1969). Breeding Nyassa cichlids, *Pseudotropheus* spp., at Amsterdam Aquarium. *International Zoo Yearbook* 9, 136-139.

Dean, B. (1916-1923). *A Bibliography of Fishes*, Volume I (1916), II (1917), III (1923). American Museum of Natural History, New York.

Dodd, J. M.(1983). Reproduction in cartilaginous fishes (Chondrichthyes). In *Fish Physiology* Vol. IX, *Reproduction* Part A, *Endocrine Tissues and Hormones* (Eds. W. S. Hoar, D. J. Randall & E. M. Donaldson), pp. 31-95. Academic Press, New York.

Donaldson, E. M. & Hunter, G. A. (1983). Induced final maturation, ovulation and spermiation in cultured fish. In *Fish Physiology* Vol. IX, *Reproduction* Part B, *Behavior and Fertility Control* (Eds. W. S. Hoar, D. J. Randall & E. M. Donaldson), pp. 351-403. Academic Press, New York.

Ferguson, A. (1989). Genetic differences among brown trout, *Salmo trutta*, stocks and their importance for the conservation and management of the species. *Freshwater Biology* 21, 35-46.

Forey, P. L. (1998). *History of Coelacanth Fishes*. Chapman & Hall, London.

Goetz, F. W. (1983). Hormonal control of oocyte final maturation and ovulation. In *Fish Physiology* Vol. IX, *Reproduction* Part B, *Behavior and Fertility Control* (Eds. W. S. Hoar, D. J. Randall & E. M. Donaldson), pp. 117-170. Academic Press, New York.

Goetz, F. W. & Thomas, P. (Eds.) (1995). *Proceedings of the Fifth International Symposium on the Reproductive Physiology of Fish*. University of Texas, Austin, TX.

Goulding, M. (1980) *The Fishes and the Forest. Explorations in Amazonian Natural History*. University of California Press, Los Angeles.

Greenwood, P. H. (1974). The cichlid fishes of Lake Victoria, East Africa: the biology and evolution of a species flock. *Bulletin of the British Museum of Natural History (Zoology Series)*, Suppl. 6, 1-134.

Guegan, J., Rab, P., Machordom, A. & Doadrio, I. (1995). New evidence of hexaploidy in 'large' African *Barbus* with some considerations of the origin of hexaploidy. *Journal of Fish Biology* 47, 192-198.

Gunther, A. C. (1880). Organs of reproduction. In *An Introduction to the Study of Fishes*. Adam & Charles Black, Edinburgh.

Hagedorn, M. & Kleinhans, F. W. (2000). Cryopreservation of fish embryos; is it within the foreseeable future for aquaculture? In *Cryopreservation of Gametes and Embryos of Aquatic Species* (Eds. T. Tiersch & P. Mazik), pp. 161-178. World Aquaculture Society, Seattle, WA.

Hallerman, E. M. & Kapuscinski, A. R. (1995). Incorporating risk assessment and risk management into public policies on genetically modified finfish and shellfish. *Aquaculture* 137, 9-17.

Harder, W. (1975). *Anatomy of Fishes*, Vols. 1 and 2. E. Schweizerbart, Stuttgart.

Harrison, I. J.& Stiassny, M. L. J. (1999) The Quiet Crisis - a preliminary listing of the freshwater fishes of the world that are extinct or 'missing in action'. In *Extinctions in Near Time* (Ed. R. D. E. McPhee), pp. 271-331. Kluwer Academic/Plenum Publishers, New York.

Hickling, C. F. (1971). *Fish Culture* (revised edition). Faber and Faber, London.

Higginbotham, J. (1997). *Piscinae: Artificial Fishponds in Roman Italy*. University of North Carolina Press, Chapel Hill.

Hindar, K., Ryman, N. & Utter, F. W. (1991). Genetic effects of cultured fish on natural fish populations. *Canadian Journal of Fisheries and Aquatic Sciences* 48, 945-957.

Hoar, W. S. & Randall, D. J. (Eds.) (1969). *Fish Physiology* Vol. III, *Reproduction and growth*, pp. 1-252. Academic Press, New York.

Hoar, W. S. & Randall, D. J. (Eds.) (1988). *Fish Physiology* Vol. XII, *The Physiology of the Developing Fish*, Part A, *Eggs and Larvae*. Academic Press, New York.

Hoar, W. S., Randall, D. J. & Donaldson, E. M. (Eds.) (1983). *Fish Physiology* Vol. IX, *Reproduction* Part B, *Behavior and Fertility Control*. Academic Press, New York.

IUCN (2000). *Red List of Threatened Species*. http://redlist.cymbiont.ca/species

IUCN RSG (2001). http://iucn.org/themes/ssc/programs/rsg.htm

Jobling, M. (1995). Reproduction: development of eggs and larvae. In *Environmental Biology of Fishes*, pp. 357-390. Chapman & Hall, London.

Jones, J. W. (1959). *The Salmon*. Collins, London.

Kime, D. E. (1995). The effects of pollution on reproduction in fish. *Reviews in Fish Biology & Fisheries* 5, 52-96.

Krupp, F., Reid, G. McG. & Hamidan, N. A. (Eds.) (2001). Fish of Arabia's Mountain Habitat. Section 7 (136 pp). In Conservation Assessment and Management Plan (CAMP) for *The Threatened Fauna of Arabia's Mountain Habitat*. IUCN Conservation Breeding Specialist Group and Breeding Centre for Endangered Arabian Wildlife, Sharjah, UAE.

Kullander, S. O. (1999). Fish species - how and why. *Reviews in Fish Biology & Fisheries* 9, 325-352.

Lam, T. J. (1983). Environmental influences and gonadal activity in fish. In *Fish Physiology* Vol. IX, *Reproduction* Part B, *Behavior and Fertility Control* (Eds. W. S. Hoar, D. J. Randall & E. M. Donaldson), pp. 65-116. Academic Press, New York.

Lagler, K. F., Bardach, J. E. & Miller, R. R. (1962). Reproductive glands - gonads. In *Ichthyology: The Study of Fishes*, pp. 95-97. John Wiley, New York.

Lévêque, C. (1997). *Biodiversity Dynamics and Conservation. The Freshwater Fish of Tropical Africa*. Cambridge University Press, Cambridge.

Liley, N. R. & Stacey, N. E. (1983). Hormones, pheromones and reproductive behavior in fish. In *Fish Physiology* Vol. IX, *Reproduction* Part B, *Behavior and Fertility Control* (Eds. W. S. Hoar, D. J. Randall & E. M. Donaldson), pp. 1-63. Academic Press, New York.

Lorenz, K. (1952). *King Solomon's Ring*. Methuen, London.

Lourie, S. A., Vincent, A. C. J. & Hall, H. J. (1999). *Seahorses: An Identification Guide to the World's Species and their Conservation*. Project Seahorse, London.

Maitland, P. S. & Evans, D. (1986). The role of captive breeding in the conservation of fish species. *International Zoo Yearbook* 25, 66-74.

Mayr, E. (1969). *Principles of Systematic Zoology*. McGraw-Hill, New York.

McKeown, B. A. (1984). *Fish Migration*. Timber Press, Portland, OR.

Meffe, G. K. (1990). Genetic approaches to conservation of rare fishes: examples from North American desert species. *Journal of Fish Biology* 37A, 105-112.

Mittermeier, R. A. (1990). Wealth of plants and animals unites 'megadiversity' countries. *Tropicus* 4, 4-5.

Molur, S. & Walker, S. (1998). *Conservation Assessment and Management Plan (C.A.M.P.) Workshops: Freshwater Fishes of India*. Zoo Outreach Organisation/CBSG, Coimbatore, Tamil Nadu, India.

Moriarty, C. (1978). *Eels: A Natural History*. David & Charles, Newton Abbot, UK.

Morris, D. (1970). Homosexuality in the ten-spined stickleback. In *Patterns of Reproductive Behaviour*, pp. 13-41, 89-117, 245-398. Jonathan Cape, London.

Moyle, P. B. & Cech, J. J. (1988). Reproduction. In *Fishes. An Introduction to Ichthyology*, pp. 107-131. Prentice Hall, Englewood Cliffs, NJ.

Müller-Belecke, A. & Hörstgen-Schwark, G. (1995). Sex determination in tilapia (*Oreochromis niloticus*): sex ratios in homozygous gynogenetic progeny and their offspring. *Aquaculture* **137**, 57-65.

Munro, A. D., Scott, A. P. & Lam, T. J. (Eds.) (1990). *Reproductive Seasonality in Teleosts: Environmental Influences.* CRC Press, Boca Raton, FL.

Myers, N., Mittermeier, R. A., Mittermeier, C. G., da Fonseca, G. A. & Kent, J. (2000). Biodiversity hotspots for conservation priorities. *Nature* **403**, 853-858.

Norman, J. R. & Greenwood, P. H. (1963). Breeding (Chapter 13), Pairing, courtship and parental care (Chapter 14), Development (Chapter 15). In *A History of Fishes*, pp. 213-226, 227-245, 246-265. Ernest Benn, London.

Nelson (1997) *Fishes of the World*, 3rd edn. John Wiley, New York.

Olson, D., Dinerstein, E., Canevari, P., Davidson, I., Castro, G., Morisset, V., Abell, R. & Toledo, E. (Eds.) (1998) *Freshwater Biodiversity of Latin America and the Caribbean: A Conservation Assessment.* Biodiversity Support Program, World Wildlife Fund, Washington, DC.

Paxton, J. R. & Eschmeyer, W. N. (Eds.) (1998). *Encyclopedia of Fishes*, 2nd edn. Academic Press, San Diego, CA.

Potts, G. W. & Wooton, R. J. (Eds.) (1984). *Fish Reproduction: Strategies and Tactics.* Academic Press, London.

Project Seahorse (2001). www.projectseahorse.org

Reid, G. McG. (1990). Captive breeding for the conservation of cichlid fishes. *Journal of Fish Biology* (Suppl. 37 A), 157-165.

Reid, G. McG. & Hall, H. (1997). The UK Fish and Aquatic Invertebrate Taxon Advisory Group (FAITAG) and the challenges for public aquaria beyond the year 2000. *Proceedings of the 25th Anniversary Meeting of Members of the European Union of Aquarium Curators (EUAC).* Basel, Switzerland.

Reid, G. McG. & Teugels, G. (2000). Progress in the conservation of West African freshwater fishes and aquatic habitats, 1990-2000. In *Wildlife Conservation in West Africa II. Proceedings of a Symposium of the Nigerian Field Society UK Branch*, held at Whipsnade Wild Animal Park, Luton, Bedfordshire, pp. 47-51.

Reihl, R. (1997). *Aquarium Atlas.* Microcosm Ltd, Shelburne, VT.

Rolland, R. M. (2000). Ecoepidemiology of the effects of pollution on reproduction and survival of early life stages in teleosts. *Fish & Fisheries* **1**, 41-73.

Rosen, D. E., Foley, P. L., Gardiner, B. G. & Patterson, C. (1981). Lungfishes, tetrapods, paleontology and plesiomorphy. *Bulletin of the American Museum of Natural History* **167**, 163-264.

Sadler, L. M. & Vincent, A. C. J. (1995). Faithful pair bondings in wild seahorses, *Hippocampus whitei. Animal Behaviour* **50**, 1557-1569.

Scott, A. P., Sumpter, J. P., Kime, D. E. & Rolfe, M. S. (Eds.) (1991). *Reproductive Physiology of Fish.* Sheffield: Fish Symposium 91. (Cyclostyled Proceedings of the 1991 conference.)

Seehausen, O. (1996). *Lake Victoria Rock Cichlids - Taxonomy, Ecology and Distribution.* Verduyn Cichlids, The Netherlands.

Spotte, S. (1992). *Captive Seawater Fishes: Science and Technology.* Wiley-Interscience, New York.

Sullivan, J. P., Lavoué, S. & Hopkins, C. D. (2000). Molecular systematics of the African freshwater fishes (Mormyroidea: Teleostei) and a model for the evolution of their electric organs. *Journal of Experimental Biology* **203**, 665-683.

Teugels, G. G., Reid, G. M. & King, R. P. (1992). Fishes of the Cross River Basin (Cameroon-Nigeria): taxonomy, zoogeography, ecology and conservation. *Annales Musée Royal Afrique Centrale, Tervuren (Série Science Zoologique)* **266**, 1-132.

Thorgaard, G. H. (1983). Chromosome set manipulation and sex control in fish. In *Fish Physiology* Vol. IX, *Reproduction* Part B, *Behavior and Fertility Control* (Eds. W. S. Hoar, D. J. Randall & E. M. Donaldson), pp. 405-434. Academic Press, New York.

Thorpe, J. E. (1978). *Rhythmic Activity of Fishes*. Academic Press, London.

Thresher, R. E. (1984). *Reproduction in Reef Fishes*. T. F. H. Publications, New Jersey.

Travis Jenkins, J. (1927). *The Herring and the Herring Fisheries*. P. S. King & Son, London.

Turner, G. (1997). Small fry go big time: why is one family of fish so diverse. *New Scientist* **155**, 36-40.

Verspoor, E. (1988). Widespread hybridisation between native Atlantic salmon, *Salmo salar*, and introduced brown trout, *Salmo trutta*, in eastern Newfoundland. *Journal of Fish Biology* **32**, 327-334.

Vincent, A. C. J. (1996). *The International Trade in Seahorses*. Traffic International, Cambridge, UK.

Vincent, A. C. J. & Hall, H. J. (1996). The threatened status of marine fishes. *Trends in Ecology and Evolution* **11**, 360-361.

Vincent, A. & Sadovy, Y. (1998). Reproductive ecology in the conservation and management of fishes. In *Behavioural Ecology and Conservation Biology* (Ed. T. Caro), pp. 209-245. Oxford University Press, Oxford.

Voigtlander, C. W. (Ed.) (1994). The state of the world's fisheries resources. *Proceedings of the World Fisheries Congress*. Oxford & IBH Publishing Co. Pvt. Ltd., New Delhi.

Vuorinen, J. (1984). Reduction of genetic variability in a hatchery stock of brown trout, *Salmo trutta*. *Journal of Fish Biology* **24**, 339-348.

Walker, S. (1994). Results of the marine fishes TAG aquarium survey and thoughts on the status of captive marine fish reproduction. *American Zoo & Aquarium Association Annual Conference Proceedings* 1994, 277-281.

Watson, I. (2000). *The Role of the Ornamental Fish Industry in Poverty Alleviation*. Natural Resources Institute Report 2504: Chatham Maritime, Kent, UK.

Watson, R. T. & Heywood, V. H. (Eds.) (1995). *Global Biodiversity Assessment. Summary for Policy Makers*. United Nations Environment Programme, Cambridge University Press, Cambridge.

Wourms, J. P. (1977). Reproduction and development in chondrichthyean fishes. *American Zoologist* **17**, 79-110.

PART VI

Conclusions

25

Postscript – sex, wildlife and vindication

W. V. HOLT, A. R. PICKARD, J. C. RODGER AND D. E. WILDT

Anyone reading the contributions that together make up this book should be impressed by the web of interdisciplinary interactions that springs unbidden from the pages. Chapters about genetic aspects of small populations, whether involving animals in the wild or in zoos, introduce concepts that help us appreciate the need for strong management policies. Accounts of reintroduction programmes, where the genetic principles are applied in practice, succeed in highlighting the complexities of returning animals to nature while, in some cases, requiring other species to be controlled as pests or over-abundant populations. Assessing behaviour or reproductive hormone status without the need for intrusion provides crucial information about the reproductive status of wild populations, as well as helping curators to manage captive animals to high welfare standards. At the heart of this wonderful web of integrative science lies the high priority of always needing to understand the fundamental biology of the species in question.

As discussed by Wildt *et al.* in the first chapter, the discipline of reproduction is often perceived as 'techno-based', with little to offer to real conservation. This, combined with a natural suspicion in the conservation community of 'quick-fixes', has left the field with an image of limited utility (mostly for combating human infertility or accelerating livestock production) or, worse, occasional gee-whiz births published only in newspapers. One of our intentions in compiling this book was to rid the Earth of this impression forever. For this reason the reader sees little mention of 'reproductive technologies', but rather an emphasis on '*the reproductive sciences*', a phrase that much more accurately reflects the value of this science to wildlife conservation and management. In this respect we also were striving to help eliminate a pervasive tendency of disciplinary chauvinism – that is, my field of science is more important than yours. Rather, reproductive science implies no single discipline but an amalgamation of interconnected or networked disciplines. Certainly, if animals do not reproduce, the species will not survive! However, if these same animals fail to eat, they also die out and, as demonstrated by McEvoy & Robinson (Chapter 3), relationships between nutrition and reproduction can be paradoxical and unexpected (as when dietary influences in one generation influence reproductive fitness in the next). The point is that the reproductive sciences represent a diversity in expertise, all interacting simultaneously and all obviously interconnected to ensure that an individual, a population or a species reproduces and perpetuates its genes into future generations.

The common theme that emerges from virtually all chapters is the paucity of reproductive data available on wildlife species. We now know that this inadequacy occurs in 95% of all vertebrates, and is most apparent for the non-mammals, despite these being in the overwhelming majority. Viewers of popular television wildlife programmes are consistently led to believe the opposite. Images of courting and copulatory behaviour in remarkable species from seahorses to cobras, or dramatic scenes of corals releasing sperm and eggs into the sea, give the impression that reproductive mechanisms are widely known and well documented. However, ask a simple question about a reproductive process for most wild species (from sperm shape and numbers to impact of rainfall on timing of gazelle births in the Serengeti) and the answer cannot be found in the literature. Even the most world-renowned reproductive experts recognise both the amazing variation in reproductive mechanisms among animals and the overall dearth of knowledge, especially about birds, reptiles, amphibians and fishes. In fact, to speak in generalities about 'reproduction in fishes' is ludicrous given the vast number of species, the diversity of habitats from which they derive and the many ways in which actual reproduction occurs. For this reason, we solicited chapters on these less well studied taxonomic groups, and we are delighted that these contributions emphasise both a multiplicity and a complexity in means of reproduction. Further, we expect that these chapters (containing knowledge not easily gleaned from other single sources) will stand the test of time as landmark reference information.

The impact of humans on the survival of wild habitats and species has been dramatic. Much of what is understood by 'conservation' represents attempts to prevent human-related impacts from forcing species down the road to extinction. Among the many influences are threats to normal reproduction from man-made chemicals in the environment (see Baillie *et al.*, Chapter 4). Much has been made in the popular press about endocrine disruptors, but in fact there is little hard evidence to prove that such environmental changes actually perturb reproduction. This does not mean that such disturbances are not really there, but the fact is that one cannot measure environmental change without first having control data. Present policies do not provide funding for characterising 'normal', undisturbed species in nature. Unfortunately, the 'sentinel' will be populations or entire species being lost as a result of a toxin, contaminant or major climatic shift. Again, it is essential now to collect normative reproductive and related information on wildlife populations as baseline data for future comparative assessments. Such priorities involving the study of 'new' and rather 'unconventional' species continue to be handcuffed by a severe lack of funding for basic research. Funding agencies look askance if a grant proposal justifies a study on the grounds of intrinsic interest – generally big money follows proposals that have biomedical or industrial applications. Conversely, the other sources of major funding often focus on highly specific, and often considered (at least by the conservation community) as rather arcane phenomena. Hence, traditional reproductive physiology and endocrinology in academe has migrated to the highly molecular. One result is that the same (and common) species are studied time and time again, but generally now at a micromolecular level that seems to have little overt relevance to actual reproductive success and the production of young. Thus, there is little financial motivation to delve into the wildlife research world, and the often-threatened status of species presents obstacles to conducting traditional experimental research. Therefore, we also hope that this text illustrates the ingenuity and perseverance that has allowed state-of-the-art science to be done with often dangerous but always fascinating wildlife species. And we would argue that these challenges, combined with opportunities for integrating disciplines, working with wildlife managers and discovering new knowledge in heretofore-unstudied species, are both exciting and invigorating, especially when the science contributes to the noble cause of species preservation.

We also hope that this book illustrates the practical value of reproductive information for applied wildlife management and conservation. Integrating new data across the life sciences and assisting wildlife authorities or zoo managers in decision-making is one example (e.g. Taylor, Chapter 5; Temple-Smith Chapter 14, and Fletcher & Morris, Chapter 15). The vast power of non-invasive hormone monitoring for predicting reproductive status and events and assessing stress (see Pickard, Chapter 9 and Monfort, Chapter 10) is yet another. We have also illustrated how fundamental studies of basic biology can eventually lead to improved management in zoos (e.g. elephants; Hildebrandt *et al.*, Chapter 11), or help enhance genetic management and reintroduction programmes involving wild populations (Howard *et al.*, Chapter 16). Our goal should, whenever possible and necessary, strive to meet the success of the black-footed ferret programme where the benefits of reproductive technology have become routine – and recognised widely as a useful tool without engendering the fervour associated with, say, cloning.

Therein lies a rather odd paradox in our view – high success/utilitarian artificial insemination in the black-footed ferret receives remarkably little attention whereas the media promote absurd attempts to clone the woolly mammoth as newsworthy. The public indeed have been deceived, leaving an impression that any species can be 'saved' by laboratory miracles before or after extinction. Every such claim about near-reality cloning sends shudders through the community of conservationists, contributing to disciplinary rifts and reinforcing the inaccurate and unfortunate image of reproductive scientists as irresponsible and unrealistic. We believe that two of our distinguished contributors have provided honest, level-headed appraisals of the realistic value of novel technologies in animal conservation (see Loskutoff, Chapter 12 and Critser *et al.*, Chapter 13). None of us would be so bold as to discount entirely the possibility that cloning may some time in the future contribute to genetically managing small populations. At the same time, we look forward to the day when cloning zealots acknowledge the technological, practical and ethical limitations of this approach and simply recognise that this is one more potential wrench in the conservation toolbox, with many challenges yet to be met. One of these certainly is to pay more attention now to the systematic collection and storage of viable genetic material from wildlife populations, that is the establishment of genetic resource banks. The value of these repositories has been espoused for more than a quarter of a century as an insurance policy for the future, for routine genetic management and for innumerable basic research studies by the scientific community at large. Most importantly, we now have a few examples of success (Holt *et al.*, Chapter 17), and as these benefits are realised, we predict that funding sources will see genetic resource banks as yet another brick in building a solid foundation for integrative conservation.

The title of this book was chosen, we admit, with agonising care; we use the phrase '*reproductive science*' and the word '*integrated*' to stress two points: First, to underline our belief that conservation-related reproductive studies generally are not related to applying artificial methods of propagation; secondly, to emphasise that developing broad, fundamental and scholarly knowledge of reproductive systems and phenomena is essential to species conservation and management. There are enormous amounts of research to be done, not solely as reproductive biologists but as science partners in the general community of conservationists. In seeking to make these points we are grateful to every author of every chapter whom, if asked to describe themselves, would claim to be all sorts of specialists, except reproductive biologists! They have vindicated us magnificently.

Index

Page numbers in **bold** indicate illustrations; those in *italic* refer to tables.

LIBRARY, UNIVERSITY COLLEGE CHESTER